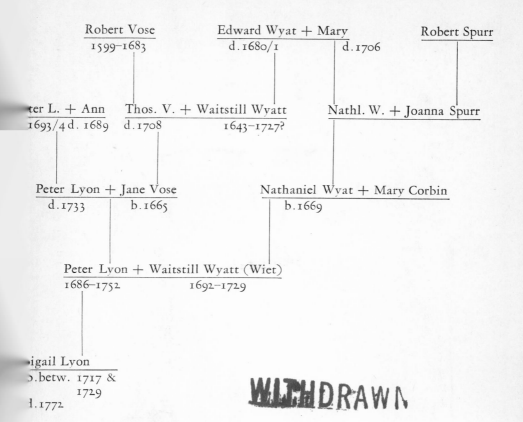

Robert Vose
1599–1683

Edward Wyat + Mary
d. 1680/1   d. 1706

Robert Spurr

·er L. + Ann
1693/4 d. 1689

Thos. V. + Waitstill Wyatt
d. 1708   1643–1727?

Nathl. W. + Joanna Spurr

Peter Lyon + Jane Vose
d. 1733   b. 1665

Nathaniel Wyat + Mary Corbin
b. 1669

Peter Lyon + Waitstill Wyatt (Wiet)
1686–1752   1692–1729

·igail Lyon
b. betw. 1717 &
1729
d. 1772

·zabeth Wisner (Wiser? Wisier?)
d. 1845

·nothy Fuller
778–1835

Ossoli
·50

(*Continued on back end papers*)

THE
LIFE OF MARGARET FULLER

The path that leads from moral standards to political activity is strewn with our dead selves.

—ANDRÉ MALRAUX.

Margaret was a great creature, but we have no full biography of her yet. We want to know what time she got up in the morning, and what sort of shoes and stockings she wore.

—THOMAS CARLYLE.

Margaret had so many aspects to her soul that she might furnish material for a hundred biographers, and all could not be said even then.

—JAMES FREEMAN CLARKE.

Margaret Fuller — from the original painting by Chappel. This is an early
portrait glorifying the young woman who had resigned herself to being
"bright and ugly."

THE LIFE
OF
MARGARET
FULLER

By

MADELEINE B. STERN

NEW YORK
E. P. DUTTON & CO., INC.
1942

PRINTED IN THE UNITED STATES OF AMERICA
BY THE WILLIAM BYRD PRESS, INC.
RICHMOND, VIRGINIA

To

MY MOTHER

ACKNOWLEDGMENTS

I WISH to acknowledge first my gratitude to my friend, Miss Leona Rostenberg. It was she who suggested to me the need for a new biography of Margaret Fuller, who helped me at every stage of the work, from its inception to its completion, by assisting me with the research at Cambridge and Boston, by reading the manuscript, and by offering her truly creative criticism. Without Miss Rostenberg's collaboration this book could not have been written.

I am happy also to thank Mr. Van Wyck Brooks for his interest and encouragement.

It is a pleasant task to make the following specific acknowledgments to those who aided me by granting permission to examine manuscripts, or by providing facts and pictures, photostats and advice: Anselmo M. Alberedo of the Biblioteca Apostolica Vaticana; Mrs. Helen B. Allen, Supervisor of the Treasure Room at Harvard; Mrs. W. L. Ambrose, President of the Ossoli Circle of Knoxville, Tennessee; Mr. F. C. Bentley of Springfield, Missouri; Prof. Arthur E. Bestor, Jr. of Teachers College; Mr. J. B. Black of John Carter Brown Library; Miss Edith R. Blanchard, Reference Librarian of Brown University; Mr. Richards M. Bradley of Boston; Mr. James L. Bruce, Clerk of the Bostonian Society; *Bulletin of the Brooklyn Institute of Arts and Sciences;* Prof. Oscar Cargill of New York University; Mr. Howard Chapin, Librarian of the Rhode Island Historical Society; Mr. James F. Clarke of Boston; Mr. Harry Clemons, Librarian of the Alderman Library of the University of Virginia; Prof. Henry Steele Commager of Columbia University; Mr. T. Franklin Currier,

ACKNOWLEDGMENTS

Associate Librarian of Harvard College; Mrs. John Dole of New York; Mr. Thomas E. Drake, Curator of the Charles Roberts Autograph Collection of Haverford College; Mrs. Margaret F. Eliot of Kingston, Rhode Island; Mr. Raymond Emerson of Boston; Mr. Allyn B. Forbes, Librarian of the Massachusetts Historical Society; Mr. Edward W. Forbes of Cambridge; Mr. Fred F. Fuller of East Milton, Massachusetts; Mr. W. L. R. Gifford, Librarian of the St. Louis Mercantile Library Association; Miss Belle da Costa Greene, Director of the Pierpont Morgan Library; Miss Elinor Gregory of the Boston Athenaeum; Mr. Charles Griffin of London; Mr. Zoltán Haraszti, Keeper of Rare Books at the Boston Public Library; Dr. Edward Southworth Hawes of Boston; the Most Reverend Mr. Ralph L. Hayes of Pittsburgh, Pennsylvania, formerly Rector of the North American College in Rome; Mr. Richard G. Hensley of the Boston Public Library; Mr. David Herman, Secretary of Congregation B'nai Jeshurun; Mr. Granville Hicks; the late Mr. Louis Holman of Boston; Mr. G. F. Hooker, City Engineer of Cambridge, Massachusetts; Miss Mary H. Hutchins of Groton, Massachusetts; Prof. H. Earle Johnson of Clark University; Mr. Theodore F. Jones, Director of the Library of New York University; Mrs. Howard W. Kent of the Concord Antiquarian Society; Mrs. Bella C. Landauer of New York; Mr. Joseph Latorraca; Miss Helen A. Legate, in charge of the Emerson House at Concord; Prof. Orrie W. Long of Williams College; Miss Ruth Lubell of New York; Prof. Thomas O. Mabbott of Hunter College; Prof. Richard C. Manning of Kenyon College; Mr. John P. Marquand of New York; Mr. Lawrence Martin, Chief of the Division of Maps at the Library of Congress; Mr. A. Hyatt Mayor, Associate Curator of the Metropolitan Museum of Art; Mrs. Arthur B. Nichols of Cambridge, Massachusetts; Mr. John A. Parker, Director of the Lowthorpe School of Landscape Architecture in Groton, Massachusetts; Mrs. George F. Patterson, Librarian of the American Unitarian Association in Boston; the Philharmonic Symphony Society of New York; Miss Marion C. Reed, Genealogist, of Boston; Mr. Paul North Rice, Chief of the Reference Department of the New York Public Library; Miss Leona Rostenberg of New York; Miss Marion B. Rowe, Assistant Librarian of the Maine Historical Society; Prof. Ralph L. Rusk of Columbia University; Mr. Henry R. Scott of Boston; Mrs. Franklin Earl Scotty, Associate Librarian of the New England Historic Genealogical Society; Miss Clara Endicott Sears of Boston; Chief of the Stato Civile of Rieti, Italy; Mr. Thomas J. Sullivan of the Cambridge Public Library; Miss Harriet S. Tapley, Librarian of the Essex Institute of Salem; Mgr. Gustavo Tulli of the Città del Vaticano; Mrs. Griswold Tyng of Jamaica Plain; Chief of L'Ufficio dell' Anagrafia of Aquila, Italy; Mr. Alexander J. Wall, Director of the New York Historical Society; Mr. Roger Warner of Boston; Mrs. William F. Wharton of Groton, Massachusetts; Mr. W. G. Wheeler, Assistant Librarian of the Massachusetts Historical Society; Miss Viola C. White, Curator of the Abernethy Library of American Literature at Middlebury, Vermont; Dean James Southall Wilson of the University of Virginia.

Finally, I wish to thank the editors of *Americana, Michigan History Magazine, The New England Quarterly,* and *The South Atlantic Quarterly* for permission to reprint chapters which appeared originally as articles in those periodicals.

CONTENTS

CONTENTS

Book Two: The Old World

Book Three: Between Two Worlds

LIST OF ILLUSTRATIONS

FOREWORD

E VERY READER knows that with each generation comes the need for reinterpreting the past to the present. Today the purpose of biography seems to be to search out the parallels that exist between our day and earlier times, and in order to fulfill that purpose it is necessary to "reanimate the old drawing-rooms, relight the old lamps, retune the old pianos." When the attempt to draw vivid and accurate pictures of the past is successfully accomplished, the biographer actually makes the past, present.

Such was the author's method in writing this biography. Margaret Fuller observed the milieu in which she lived without eclipsing it. She witnessed and analyzed intelligently the trends of her time—the growth of transcendentalism in Concord, the preoccupation with phrenology and animal magnetism in Providence, the search for Universal Unity at Brook Farm, the last stand of the Indians in the West, the awakening of interest in Beethoven and Goethe in Boston, the clash of pigs and poetry in New York, the futile struggle for liberty in Italy. Many a parallel exists between that rich and varied background and our own.

In order to give life to Margaret Fuller and her times, the writer had no need to invent situations or weave fancy into the web of fact. In an age of journal-writing Margaret Fuller was merely one of many who recorded both their thoughts and their conversation. The wealth of factual details found in journals and letters made imaginary ones unnecessary. Margaret Fuller's black mousseline dress, her velvet penwiper, her seal with Franklin's head, are actual; they are not colorful paraphernalia invented

[xv]

for the purpose of writing vivid biography. Indeed all the
details that appear in this book are accurate and may be
found in one or more of the sources listed in the bibliography. Once the details were discovered the writer assembled them in such a way that they would make the past live
again. No lengthy quotations, no impersonal comments
were allowed to intrude upon the picture. Here Margaret
Fuller walks again, her blue chenille cord knotted in her
hair, her carbuncle ring glittering on her finger, speaks
again the words she actually spoke, thinks again the
thoughts that once were hers.

M. B. S.

Sunnybank, June 30, 1941

BOOK ONE:
THE NEW WORLD

CHAPTER I

EAST OF TORY ROW

TIMOTHY FULLER tucked the *Columbian Centinel* under the arm of his greatcoat and glanced at the date to be sure the news was the most recent: May 23, 1810. Suddenly, it seemed to him as if it might be a memorable day. He was glad he had left the Court Street office early. A will could be probated any day—but no man could tarry for a birth. As he walked along the curved side of Cornhill, he tipped his hat in recognition of T. H. Perkins, the merchant prince of Boston, who was trudging along with his market basket full of purple gentians cut from his own garden. Flowers—that would be a fine way to commemorate the day—if, indeed, it were the day. But Margaret was so fond of flowers anyway, that it would be an excellent notion. And so he bought a few blooms from a vendor along the way.

It was a warm, sweet day. The servant girls were beating carpets on the Common; cows were pasturing there. It was pleasant to hear the clatter of stagecoaches upon the cobblestones, to see the sign of the Indian Queen Tavern swing gently in the breeze. The frogs were croaking of spring in the Frog Pond. Still, Boston with its nine blocks of brick buildings was becoming too large a town; Timothy Fuller was satisfied that he had removed to the "Village" during the days of the epidemic. It had been wise—but then the fighting Fullers were, he smiled to himself, always rather wise.

Perhaps the wisest of all had been Great-Grandfather Thomas who came over from England to listen to the "soul-ravishing" Reverend Mr. Shepard—or to gaze into

[3]

the black eyes of a certain Miss Richardson. What was the verse he had written about it?

"He was a pastor, and their sheep
Shepherds upon the mountains keep."

Not a bad play on words for an English blacksmith. The Fullers had done well in America. Let people call them disagreeable and pushing as they would, his grandfather's name was chipped into the corner of Stoughton Hall— for all that the Revolutionists had dismissed him from his Princeton parish back in the days of the redcoats. Now they said that just to be disagreeable a Fuller would be a pacifist during a war and a belligerent during a peace. But Timothy knew that a Fuller followed his conscience and let the world wag. His grandfather had been right. What good was a Constitution that recognized slavery? Back in his college days he had said the same thing—nine years ago, when he wore the black gown hired from Ma'am Hyde on Dunster Street. And he would go on saying it. The world would see the truth of it one day. But you needed a Fuller to recognize the worth of a Fuller. The palefaced conformists of Beacon Hill had not quite approved of his own speech last year at Watertown. But it was still true that they had better destroy the leeks and onions of Great Britain, just as he had said at the time. Brother Abraham probably led to most of the gossip about the pushing ways of the Fullers. But what if he had declared he could darn a stocking better than any woman? He could. . . .

"Good-morrow, Fuller. It's a fine day." Timothy stopped short. He had almost forgotten it was a fine day, and had nearly collided with the Reverend Mr. Abiel Holmes, neat in his black alpaca, hat in hand.

"Good-day, sir. Still propagating orthodoxy among the heathen Port-Chucks?"

"I am indeed, sir. Still spouting heresy among the Court Street barristers?"

"And shall continue, Holmes. As long as James Madison can't ask his own guests to his own dinner party without being dictated to by Clay or Calhoun!"

"Well, we shan't quarrel, Fuller. The day is too lovely. Will you take the stagecoach with me at Daniel Upham's? I'm going back to the 'Village' now."

Timothy had planned to walk back to Cambridgeport; there were so many thoughts turning round in his brain. Somehow it was the day for thinking things out; clearing the past to make way for the future. But perhaps it would be as well to get back quickly. They walked along, two greatcoats and waistcoats, two pairs of pantaloons, along the dirt road near the Hawley Street stable.

"Look at those curls!" remarked Timothy. "One would think the damsels put them on with their hats."

"It must be difficult dressing little girls," returned his companion, "with their muslin pelisses and whalebone hats and fiddle-faddles. That's one reason I'm glad Oliver Wendell is a boy." And he glanced slyly at Timothy.

"Stuff and nonsense! Boy or girl—it makes no difference. I'd like to have a little girl just to show the world she'd be as learned as ten boys!"

And flinging that enormity over his shoulder, Timothy Fuller paid his shilling and boarded the stagecoach for Cambridgeport. The six white horses plunged forward. Abiel Holmes opened his *Independent Chronicle* and hid behind it. Timothy would have liked to talk on this day; but rather than talk to an *Independent Chronicle,* he opened his own *Columbian Centinel* for May 23, 1810.

A farm was for sale. Perhaps one day he would buy one and turn gentleman farmer, and write a life of the great, the misunderstood Thomas Jefferson. . . . What was the news from Washington?

"The Smiths and Gallatin are still at sword points," he shouted. "And listen to this. 'War between France and America is expected!' They've seized, sequestered, and sold our seamen! And all for what—to pay $85,000 for a wedding robe for the Empress of that upstart imperial house of Napoleon! But we're still buying lemons from Lisbon and whatnots from all over Europe. When will America wake up? We offer one cent reward for a runaway servant, and let France take our millions for a parvenu Emperor!"

The Reverend Mr. Holmes was still somewhere behind the *Independent Chronicle*. And Timothy saw an advertisement that set him to thinking along happier veins. "Wanted—a woman with a good breast of milk." Perhaps, when he arrived at his home, there would be. . . .

"Abiel," said he softly, "What is your philosophy about bringing up children?" Abiel slowly lowered the *Independent Chronicle*.

"Timothy, I shall let Oliver Wendell run loose in the library of my gambrel-roofed house—and that is my philosophy."

"Nonsense! A child should be an early riser. He should know his history, his geography. He should step far enough into Euclid to long for a near acquaintance with him. Let him read Aesop maybe, but no other nursery books. Let him read true histories, written in a manly style. I tell you, Holmes, I've been thinking about this for months. They advertise twenty-five volumes of the British essayists at Munroe and Francis'. Now that's a good way to teach a boy to have a round style. And here's Mavor's *Universal History*. Why shouldn't a boy learn the history of the universe?"

"Fuller, the world may be your oyster, but it's a large one; it might catch in a boy's throat."

"I'm a man of business, as you know; and I'm a man

of business even in literature. A boy must be guided
through his Latin, his English grammar."

"Fuller, you said you wanted a girl. Don't forget. And
here's the Davenport tavern. You had better get off."

Timothy Fuller climbed off the stagecoach and walked
to the three-story home at the corner of Cherry and
Eaton. They might talk about Dana House and Opposition House all they liked, but his mansion was the finest
among the pastures of Cambridgeport. Gambrel-roofed
house, indeed.

He straightened his waistcoat and walked under the
pillared doorway, glancing back at the garden and the
salt marsh beyond. John, the servant boy, was at the
door.

"The ladies are upstairs already, sir. They think the
time has nearly come."

Timothy Fuller caught a glimpse of Thomas Dowse's
housekeeper in her flying muslins. The leather dresser of
Cambridgeport was a good sort. He would lend his books,
or at a time like this, his housekeeper. And there was
Mistress Jarvis running about with basins and hot water.
She had left her husband's tavern, even though the
Davenport was giving it strong competition in the concoction of flip. They were good folks all. But Timothy
preferred to sit alone for a moment.

"Let me know when the time comes, John. I'll be sitting down here. And take these flowers to your mistress."

Timothy poured himself a thimbleful of wine from the
decanter on the sideboard, and glanced at the large mirror above it. He looked his full thirty-two years. It was
time to have a child of one's own—to buy proper material
for his suits; to walk with him to Craigie Bridge perhaps;
to teach him digits and the history of the Universe; to
read the Bible to him, the best book in the world. He
smoothed his side whiskers, adjusted his stock, and looked

again at his lean, strong face. Soon the time would come.

Timothy took the wine and placed it on the little table near the open fireplace. He walked to the kitchen to find the tinderbox on the mantelpiece. Lighting his pipe, he returned and sat down on the hair-stuffed chair next to the hearth. The years had been good to him, he thought. He had shown his mettle. He belonged to this little village; indeed, he had helped mark out its very boundaries. There was much yet to be done. Much to learn. Much to teach. The world was out of joint. Every Fuller that had ever been born had been born to set it right. Perhaps if not himself—the one that was about to be—the boy who would cry out in the second-story bedroom—the boy who would study at Harvard—the boy who would not only learn the History of the Universe, but add to it perhaps.

"Master, Master!" John came leaping down the stairs. "Master! The time has come! And it's a girl!"

Mr. Taylor removed his olive green greatcoat and sat down to wait for his pupil. Being somewhat irregular himself in his arrivals for music lessons, he was not a little impatient at having to waste his time in waiting for a ten-year-old girl. It would be much more valuable to rehearse a glee with Augustus Peabody for the next Philharmonic concert in Boston. But then Sarah Margaret was not an uninteresting child despite the fact that she played merely because her father wished her to do so. It was strange, Mr. Taylor thought, how Timothy Fuller's influence could be felt even though at the moment he was probably demanding the floor in the National Congress. That match in the lamp brackets, the wood covered with ashes in the parlor hearth, were undoubtedly evidence that Timothy remembered the cold of Cambridgeport even during his heated polemics against the slaveholding

Crawford. Mr. Taylor turned to glance at the flat-topped bureau with its plum cake and oranges and wine—gifts surely from an ever thoughtful father. The smoking of the kitchen stove was just about to irritate the sensitive music instructor and remind him of his impatience, when Sarah Margaret Fuller made her entrance.

Really, Mr. Taylor considered, the child walks as if she thought herself a queen. Her neck curves so beautifully that one's attention is diverted from the rash on her forehead. But why does she close her eyelids whenever she enters a room? It must be either an affectation or some form of eye strain. After a brief good-morning, Sarah Margaret headed straight for the new pianoforte and seated herself next to Mr. Taylor. The music instructor was reminded that the lesson had begun.

Sarah Margaret plunged immediately into the march that Richard Third's troops had followed to the battle of Bosworth. She seemed to think more of counting the time than of creating any harmony, for those new shoes from Aborn's were tapping the quarters conspicuously.

"Sarah Margaret, you are lowering your wrist and crooking your fingers again. You will never produce any distinctness of tone."

Sarah Margaret glanced at Mr. Taylor without answering. As she did so, her eye caught the mark for height that Mother had made in measuring her.

"Mr. Taylor, are you of the opinion that one's manners increase with years or with growth?"

"Your manners will increase with your diligence, Sarah Margaret. Please raise each finger as soon as a note is struck or you will never play with any exactitude."

"I carried my music into Boston, Mr. Taylor, and the company praised me highly. And at Mrs. Stearns' ball I played *Heartsease* and sang *Blue-Eyed Mary* with great success."

"You will never learn to play in company or among flatterers. Please think of the music. Remember, Richard Third's troops marched into Bosworth to this tune."

Sarah Margaret thought, not of the music, but of Richard Third. *Oberon* was really a better story than Shakespeare's play. She remembered how she had been absorbed in reading it when her father returned home one Christmas. Father did not approve of fiction, but *Oberon* was a very moral tale. So was *The Satirist*—a new work by the promising young authoress, Sarah Margaret Fuller. What would Mr. Taylor say if he knew he was instructing one of the coming writers? Sarah Margaret's thoughts and Mr. Taylor's attention were interrupted by the sound of the sawing and splitting of wood. Mr. Rummarill must be at work.

"Please let us think of the music, Sarah Margaret."

Richard Third. Sarah Margaret recalled *The Chronology of the English Kings* which she had conned under her father's tutelage. It had been far more interesting than the *History of the American Revolution* she had read at Canton. It had been so delightful riding out there to visit Grandmother Crane, sitting on a cricket in the chaise. Grandmother had sat, humming *China,* her blue eyes glancing from Sarah Margaret to her volume of the *Saints' Rest.*

Suddenly, above Mr. Rummarill's sawing, far above the march of Richard Third's soldiers, came the noise of Eugene singing to drown out his sister. Mr. Taylor turned abruptly from the pianoforte, and Sarah Margaret was informed that the lesson had ended.

"Mediocrity is obscurity, Sarah Margaret. Please remember that when you practise."

"That is true, Mr. Taylor. But my ambition cools with success."

Mrs. Fuller entered the parlor to ask about her

daughter's musical progress. Mr. Taylor warded off the
difficulty of replying by inviting Mrs. Fuller to the next
Philharmonic concert.

"I shall accompany Mr. Augustus Peabody, Mr. Win-
ship, and Mr. Richardson in a glee. I am sure you will
find it enjoyable."

Mrs. Fuller accepted graciously, and Mr. Taylor could
not help wondering whether Sarah Margaret would ever
develop her mother's white complexion and blue eyes, as
she had inherited her height. Nor would it do the child
any harm to cultivate her mother's graciousness. But
Sarah Margaret was really herself, not her mother. An
interesting child—but not very skilled in playing Richard
Third's march. With a slight bow, Mr. Taylor picked
up his olive green greatcoat and left.

Uncle Elisha's greatcoat was of a drab brown color,
and he placed it less meticulously on the same chair that
Mr. Taylor had used. The drab greatcoat meant Grusbach's *Greek Testament,* just as the green one had signified *The March to Bosworth.* Sarah Margaret drew the
volume from her father's bookcase and began to recite
the passages she had memorized. A lesson in Greek grammar followed, and then as a reward Sarah Margaret
asked permission to translate a Latin letter she had received from her father.

"I hope you appreciate your father's profound interest
in your studies, Sarah Margaret. When I was a boy, it
was he who first gave me the impetus to read good books
and to study. I shall never forget how he had Watts'
hymns bound for me, and advised me to read the best
Book in the world."

"His Latin letter is really very simple, Uncle Elisha.
I shall translate it without a dictionary.

Mia filia cara . . . Ne hanc epistolam ob linguae Latinae ignoran-
tiam rideas, nosce, puella, pater tuus dictionario caret. . . Siquid
novisti rectius istis, candidus imperti. . .

There are no mistakes,[1] though, are there, Uncle Elisha?
It's too bad. He signs it 'Vale, Sarah Margaretta, Tim-
otheus Fuller.' Margaretta is such a pretty name. There
is no Latin for Sarah is there?—or for Fuller. Margaretta. I wish I had a great Roman name to go with it."

"Come, child, let me note the passages in Grusbach
that you are to memorize for the next recitation."

"Uncle Elisha, I guess I shall soon have a Cicero.
Father wrote to Mother that I was to have one."

"You know your father would not approve of your
saying 'I guess' when you mean 'it is probable.' "

"Well, 'I guess' is better than many expressions I know
of. It's better than 'slaveholder' for instance. And, Uncle
Elisha, father is going to give me one dollar because I
translated *The Deserted Village* into such admirable
Latin. I shall give it to poor Widow Wentworth."

"I hope you will take pains to see that your money is
well spent, and always to save a specific percentage of it,
Sarah Margaret."

"I have more agreeable occupations than counting
money."

"I hope one of them will be to cultivate your memory.
Repeat Grusbach over and over until the next recitation."

Mrs. Fuller stopped knitting her grey woolen hose
long enough to bid Elisha good-bye, and to pin a kerchief
on Sarah Margaret's mantle. For lessons would not be
completed until the child had spent an hour at Mr.
Gould's writing school, and another in her Aunt Abigail's
drawing class.

---

[1]There were, however. "Mia" should be "mea," and "caret" should be
"carere."

Mr. Gould was a most elegant writer, with terms at one dollar a quarter for instructing Sarah Margaret in the art of mending her pens and keeping them in ink, in rounding letters with the very best quills, and ruling her lines with care. But as Sarah Margaret sat writing equidistant letters and watching that her pen shed ink, she could not help feeling that *The Satirist* would never have reached completion if she had taken such pains to rule her lines and finish her letters. But Father was bent on having her write neatly by attending to such precepts, since he was in Washington and could hear from his daughter only through letters, and perhaps also because his eyes were quite weak.

Eugene joined his sister at Aunt Abigail's little drawing class. Mrs. Fuller had heard so many stories about teachers like Ma'am Betty, who chewed tobacco and drank water from the nose of her teakettle while she kept school in a very untidy bedroom, that she was happy because her sister had consented to give the two eldest children lessons in drawing. Sarah Margaret painted a little watch paper to send to her father along with a pretty locket of flowers. Eugene, however, was not very attentive and wished he were a year younger like his brother William Henry so that the necessity of diligence might be somewhat postponed. On the other hand, Sarah Margaret painted with such intent that the blood rushed to her forehead, and she placed the little watch paper carefully on the whatnot until she would send it to her father at letter-writing time in the evening. It was interesting to be the eldest, the most successful, the mistress of all. No. She had no wish to revert to infancy as Eugene had. It was dull to be a baby in a cradle like Ellen, or a toddling lad like William Henry. It was best to be Sarah Margaret—mature—like a queen.

In the evening Mrs. Fuller sat on the chair near the fire in the South parlor, her work in her lap. She was adding the final touches to a pale-hued muslin pelisse, her foot at Ellen's cradle lest the baby should awaken and whimper. Sarah Margaret sat opposite at the table directly under the looking glass. She had just taken a penknife from the drawer of her father's desk, and was sharpening her pen for the letter to Timothy. But her eyes wandered off frequently to the whatnot where lay the shells that the Misses Gray had given her. They were arranged to resemble a Roman castle, and Sarah Margaret's fancy revelled among the lives of the great men of Rome who had swayed their country as Sarah Margaret would one day master her world.

"Sarah Margaret, if you do not wish to write, why not set your hand to needlework? You have been neglecting the needle lately. You know how interesting Eliza Livermore's fancy embroidery is. She has made a figure of a shepherdess with a little child in her arms, holding it out to a man in peasant's clothes."

"Mother, I believe sewing is immoral."

"Sarah Margaret, you say that because you are such a miserable sewer."

"Oh, well, I believe I shall translate the *Lord's Prayer* into Latin and send it to Father."

As Sarah Margaret began to translate, Mrs. Fuller looked contentedly at her family. Eugene was studying his "felix and tenor," having wrapped a sugar plum to send off to his father. Ellen was asleep in her cradle. Sarah Margaret's reddish blond hair was lit by the lamplight as she bent over the table, her eyes close to the paper. The child was vain enough to use paper curlers, but her hair, however lovely its color, remained straight. She inherited that from Grandmother Crane. Mrs. Fuller smiled as she recalled the far-off days at Canton and those "accidental"

walks with Timothy on the bridge near church. She remembered that day—was it more than ten years ago—
when she had ridden to church on a pillion with some
rustic cavalier—and there had seen Mr. Timothy Fuller
for the first time. When Sarah Margaret had been born,
how she had prayed the child would have Timothy's
mind. The prayer would be granted, she was sure. Mrs.
Fuller glanced at her daughter. Certainly it could not be
a Latin version of the *Lord's Prayer* that filled Sarah
Margaret's eyes with tears. Whatever was the child
thinking of?

"May I see what you have written, Sarah Margaret?"
Eugene looked up, walked to the table, and toyed with
the penknife. As he did so he blotted the *Lord's Prayer*
with the point.

"I shall have to tell Father it was your fault, Eugene,
or he will think Mr. Gould has not taught me to write
neatly."

"May I see what you have written, Sarah Margaret?"

"I hope my watch paper will not crack when Father
puts his watch into it, Mother. And may I send my
flower locket in the same package with Eugene's sugar
plum?"

"You may. And now may I see what you have written?" Reluctantly, Sarah Margaret passed a small sheet
of white paper to her mother. Mrs. Fuller read:

When I die this may live.
On the 23d of May 1810 was born one foredoomed to sorrow and
pain and like others to have misfortunes. She had feeling which few
have and which is the source of SORROW as to every one who
possesses it.

"Are you really unhappy, child?" asked Mrs. Fuller,
hiding a brief smile.

"I like to think of such things, Mother, to think of myself as a princess foredoomed. And, Mother, I also do not want to be called Sarah Margaret any longer. I want to be known as Margaret. I shall tell Father so in my letter."

"It would be disrespectful and unkind for you to drop your first name. Sarah is your father's mother's name and given you on that account. Besides, your father, you know, will tell you that that cannot be done without an act of General Court."

"I shall plead with him to let me be called Margaret. Besides, there is no Latin for Sarah. Margaretta is such a pretty name. I will be called Margaret, and not my Grandmother's name!"

The fire was going out in the hearth. Eugene had finished his "felix and tenor." Mrs. Fuller gathered her muslin pelisse and silently walked upstairs with her daughter to the second-story bedroom. Margaret sang sadly and softly, *I know by the smoke that so gracefully curled*. Night had fallen upon Timothy Fuller's home in Cambridgeport.

Latin grammar was undoubtedly of great importance, but the innocent recreation of cotillions also had a place in the life of a young girl. Hence, one afternoon every week, Margaret put on her moccasins to walk to dancing school. As she opened the front gate she turned to look at the elms which her father had planted directly after her birth. "When I die this may live." The elms commemorated her birth. When the garden and the pillared doorway, and the Home House itself were gone, those elms would live on, evidence that Margaret Fuller had been born. Along Windsor Street Margaret could hear Eliphalet Davis lauding his fancy soap, and the tinkling of mugs in Leonard Jarvis' tavern. Soap and flip and the odor from the currier's shop—what had such plebeian things to do with a queen whose family blood needed no ennobling? Besides a queen, she was Duchess of Marlborough, abandoned at birth on Cherry Street in the New World. William Henry united a prince and king in his single person, and Eugene was Prince of Savoy. Margaret looked up to see sprightly Mr. Harrisbury, his plaid cloak hooked across the throat, bowing condescendingly. She granted him a good-afternoon, but thought his smile would not be so patronizing if he knew he was saluting an abandoned princess. I was married at thirteen, she continued to herself. As a child I suffered greatly in my foreign home. My early years were full of presentiments. Huge shapes advanced upon me when I slept, and pressed upon me from the corner of the room. I awoke and screamed. Down fell Margaret, having walked plumb against the old Boston milestone. Her face prickled and she knew that Dr. Shattuck's ugly lotion would have to soothe it, since she would not take rhubarb and calomel as Dr. Holcombe prescribed. Why must a queen have a poor complexion! Perhaps it would disappear as soon as a prince or noble English woman arrived to disenchant her. She rose with as much dignity as she could muster, and walked on, neck erect, head high. She was near the college buildings now, and must watch her step. Francis Sales with his hair powder and pigtail might appear at any moment, or Dr. Popkin in his cocked hat. If she tripped in front of him he would probably try to pick her up with his ever present umbrella. Dr. Abiel Holmes passed by just then and inquired about Margaret's literary pursuits.

"I hope you will visit me and read Rees' *Cyclopedia* with Oliver Wendell. He finds it an actual treasure house." The old gentleman walked on, repeating to himself the words of his next sermon.

As Margaret passed the Harvard buildings she glanced

at a group of men in heated debate. She recognized Professor Edward Everett's rich voice. What an interesting life he must have had in Europe, Margaret thought. His marble eyelids and sculptured lips were truly classical. And there was George Bancroft just back from a foreign journey with Dr. Hedge's son. Margaret remembered that he had told her one must have the qualities of a salamander to pass through Harvard University and remain religious. She did not know the lean, scrawny youth with Everett. He did not look at all like the sensible, well-bred boys who were invited for an occasional dinner at Cherry Street. As Margaret came near the group, she heard Professor Everett say, "Emerson, do you know that Goethe has made friends with a young farmer-artist by the name of Eckermann, who may assist him in his work?" The gentlemen recognized Margaret as she passed, and she bowed, conscious of the dignity of her own demeanor.

She went on, past the shrubberies of Hollis Hall, catching a glimpse of Dr. Kirkland in his shining buckles and full ruffles. On she walked toward Tory Row, not at all like the marshy fields of the Port—Tory Row with its white frame houses glittering in the sun, and its green shutters tapping in the wind. She passed Torrey Hancock's house which Dexter Pratt, the village blacksmith, was negotiating for. Beyond were the Vassall Houses. Perhaps there were secret underground passages in them which none could find—none, except a princess seeking refuge. They were even more beautiful than Elmwood, where baby James Russell Lowell was sprawling on the long green lawn. Margaret turned down a side street, passing a glovemaker's great wooden HAND snapping and creaking in the wind. She was ready to grace the cotillion with her presence.

As she entered the little dancing school, she spied

Lydia Maria Francis and walked across the room to her, neglecting to bid good-day to the irascible French dancing master. He turned impatiently, and called out, "Mees Fullair, how will you enjoy a ball if you have not the proper respect for a dancing master?"

Margaret replied, "Balls, weddings, and cotillions are really nothing to me, for I am not invited to them."

"Leave the room, Mees Fullair. And return with the proper courtesy."

Margaret tossed her head and walked out—her neck erect—she would command the scene despite her humiliation. The whalebone hats of the girls stretched in her direction, and the silly boys were tittering behind their hands.

"Shtop!" the dancing master called out. "You sall not walk so superb. You tink you General Washington!"

Margaret stopped. But the superb air she could not curb. The cotillion commenced. And since Margaret had not mastered all the steps, she took great pains not to fall. A queen might stoop, but fall she must not.

Mr. McTheag ran a school at which the art of dancing received more attention than Latin grammar. And though Mrs. Fuller enjoyed her monthly cotillions in Cambridge, she and her husband considered Dr. Park's school in Boston a more valuable preparation for a cultivated life. It was true that Mr. Fuller had calculated an increase of one thousand dollars in his stocks in the State Bank, as well as in his real estate; yet he saw no reason for sending Margaret to board when a better school was close at hand in Boston. The family was growing. The arrival of baby Arthur Buckminster had created the necessity of a second cradle. William Henry and Eugene needed instruction not merely in Latin, but in latitude and longitude, writing and arithmetic. There was really no doubt that Dr. Park's school was less expensive and far more suitable.

Toward the end of September in 1821, Margaret took the hourly omnibus from Cambridge to Boston, and rumbled into town along with the stagecoaches and chaises from all parts of the country. She had started her quarter at Dr. Park's school. It was quite a challenge to be told that Susan Channing was already the possessor of seventeen medals, but it was not long before Margaret had three to her credit, and boasted that Dr. Park had declared he had never had a pupil with half her attainments at her age. Almost as soon as Margaret arrived at the school she found herself next to the head in the second class in parsing. Indeed, parsing was far less difficult than conversing with frivolous companions who called her awkward and pedantic. To make matters worse, at examination time Margaret suffered from a heavy cold which made her voice very hoarse when she answered Dr. Park's questions; nevertheless she did better than she had expected under the circumstances, and did not care at all when she learned that Susan Channing had told her brother, William Henry, nephew of the great Dr. Channing, that Margaret had extravagant tendencies of thought. She knew that Dr. Park considered her highly talented. Besides, her mother had given her permission to buy chinchilly and velvet for the new bonnet she would wear at Mrs. Farrar's party. Surely that was more important than anything a self-satisfied Channing might say. It was far better to be bright and ugly than pretty and stupid—especially when some knight or lady was sure to arrive to dispel her poor complexion and chubbiness.

She needed older people to converse with, she thought, as she walked past the place where the Exchange Coffee House had burned down, toward John Tappan's fancy muslin store on State Street. It was exciting to be alone in

Boston, buying chinchilly and velvet for one's own new bonnet. Soon she would wear it to Mrs. Farrar's party, and discuss—oh, not parsing at Dr. Park's school with frivolous children poking fun at one's brilliance—but music, and history, and Paley's *Internal Evidences,* and cotillions, and charming young princes, or if necessary, charming young university students. Perhaps she would be the center of the most scintillating group. That was life—and Margaret was avid for it.

Mrs. Fuller's black sarcenet dress contrasted well with her delicate complexion. For three full days before the ball Margaret had been trying on a new coat made by Miss Gookin's nimble fingers. She was not completely satisfied with the plainness of her attire, however, and begged for permission to wear a twisted gold ring, or one made of tortoise shell.

"I should like a complete jewel case, full of precious stones. I should like to wear one in my hair."

But Mrs. Fuller prevailed against her daughter's unorthodox tastes and pinned a handkerchief instead of a jewel on her ruffled gown. The paper curlers had done their duty during the three-day period of preparations, so that Margaret's hair waved prettily over her high arched forehead. She draped the new coat about her and walked back and forth before the looking glass in the south parlor. Eugene objected to his mother's gray worsted hose, but Mrs. Fuller was not one to allow the whims of fashion to take precedence over the cold of a Cambridge winter. And so, in Warner's horse and carriage, mother and daughter drove to the home of Mrs. Eliza Farrar.

When they arrived, Mrs. Coleman's widowed daughter was playing the final chords of *Mary, hist awake* on the pianoforte, while her sister strummed on the pedal harp. Margaret wondered whether she would be asked to entertain. In one corner of the glittering room she saw her hostess' husband, John Farrar, professor of astronomy, and with him Dr. Jackson and "Old Brains," Professor Hedge. She could hear their voices rising in discussion of the younger Harvard group. They were saying something about George Ticknor and his German studies. Margaret hoped she would be invited to a literary discussion with them, for she had decided to borrow some of Thomas Dowse's German works and wished to be advised about the necessary preparation for such studies. But just then young William Stearns, son of the Professor, came across the floor to invite Miss Margaret to a part in the next cotillion. Mrs. Fuller wandered off to speak with Mrs. McTheag and her hostess, and for Margaret the ball had begun.

Harriet Fay was there from the Port in a transparent pelisse; Anna Barker stood with her, the shining center of a group of Harvard boys and gentlemen from the South. One could hardly stop to look at Anna's pale blue muslin frock, for her golden hair glowed in the candle-light and Margaret thought her a daughter of Zeus, a glittering vision. She and young Stearns walked over to the group—without a doubt the most brilliant of the ball. As Margaret drew near, young Miss Davis whispered to her, "Remember to hold out your gown and look as graceful as possible when you dance."

Margaret tossed her head and did not answer. She turned instead to Russell Sturgis and started a discussion of Mozart's *Requiem*—so unlike the music for the country dances and cotillions one hears at Cambridge.

"There are remarkable circumstances about the writing of it which I could acquaint you with."

Mr. Sturgis was polite, but he could not keep his eyes from wandering over Margaret's tight waves to Anna Barker's golden curls. Margaret noticed this, and repeated to herself, "It's better to be bright and ugly." Young Oliver Wendell Holmes and his brother John began—for no reason at all—to compare girls to various beverages, and Margaret thought Wendell's analogy of Harriet Fay to cordial in the kitchen most indecorous. She suspected that if she were not so close to him, he would probably compare her to "black strap" or bitters. Anna Barker would of course be like wine, sparkling and beautiful. Lydia Maria Francis soon joined the group with an excited remark about the arrival of a new dancing instructor, Lorenzo Papanti, who had just come over on the "Constitution." He would probably open a dancing school in Boston before long, and it had been rumored that he might even import some new dances. Everybody listened to Lydia's words with respectful attention. Had she not startled the New World already with her Indian novel, *Hobomok?* Margaret broke in immediately with an account of her last trip to Boston where her Uncle Abraham had taken her to the amphitheatre to see *Blue Beard.*

"Some of the ladies were indecently dressed, for most of them could not be content without showing their bosoms and shoulders completely. It is really *de trop.*"

The arrival of the fashionable Mrs. William Sullivan, who thought it vulgar to arrive at a party before nine, made it possible for the actual entertainment to begin. The pedal harp reverberated, and conversation was confined to whispers behind fans. Magaret wished she might join one of the mature groups to discuss her readings in Alfieri or find out where she might borrow a *Wealth of Nations,* but soon she was mollified by Mrs. Farrar's request that she contribute a song. Elisabeth Ware seated herself at the pianoforte and Margaret walked forth magnificently to sing *Bounding Billows.* She thought less of her voice than of her appearance and hoped that the attention of the audience would be focussed on her curls rather than on her complexion. She planned to play *Bruce's Address to His Army* should she be asked for an encore, but instead Anna Barker sang *Oh, This Is the Spot.*

Directly afterward there was another cotillion and then the party withdrew for an oyster supper. William Stearns sat between Margaret and Anna Barker and the young gentleman commended Miss Barker quite audibly on her singing. To Margaret he simply said,

"Do you plan to teach when you are older, Miss Margaret?"

She sensed the discourtesy of his remark, especially since *Bounding Billows* had been rendered as adequately as *Oh, This Is the Spot.* But she replied,

"It is in my opinion a disagreeable occupation to repeat twenty times to a stupid child A B C, and not have him remember it in all probability. Besides, I shall probably go away to some distant school and study to be a writer."

"Anna," asked young Stearns, "do you plan to be a singer? You could easily do so." Anna smiled and Margaret nibbled thoughtfully at a creamed oyster. Soon the party arose from the long mahogany table with its gleaming candles.

Mrs. Fuller approached Margaret with the suggestion that it was time to leave.

"Oh, mother, let us stay a little longer. I do so want to ask Dr. Hedge about studying German and besides I might be asked to play *Bruce's Address.*

"No, Margaret," Mrs. Fuller said firmly, and she drew her daughter toward Mrs. Farrar to pay her respects before departing.

As Margaret said good-night to her hostess, Mrs. Farrar leaned down and whispered,

"Child, you must let me introduce my sempstress to you, and some day we shall have a long talk about hairdressing, shall we not?"

Margaret moved silently toward Warner's horse and carriage. That night her paper curlers took longer than ever to be properly set and Mrs. Fuller heard her daughter singing carefully La, sol, fa, mi, as she fell off to sleep.

Timothy Fuller returned from Washington in September of 1823 to pay a brief visit to his family. He had a suitable gift for each of his children—(a seal with Franklin's head fell to Margaret so that she might be prompted to write more frequent letters) and at the table near the hearth Timothy's stiff-backed chair was once more occupied. It was natural that he should devote more attention to inquiries about his children's readings than to what he was pleased to dub their "party" views. Perhaps it was because the next day was Sunday and Timothy planned to hold Sabbath services in his home that he chose Grusbach's *Greek Testament* to review with his daughter. The evening passed quietly except that Eugene did not know the latitude and longitude of New Orleans, but this was forgiven him for he had won a medal in geography. Mrs. Fuller took charge of the babies, Ellen and Arthur, and discussed with her husband the advisability of a new railing round the kitchen stove which still persisted in smoking. Soon it was time to snuff out the lamps.

Timothy Fuller had never enjoyed the old yellow meetinghouse near the sloops and schooners at the end of the bridge, where Abiel Holmes still indulged his orthodox belief in original sin. It was better to conduct one's praise of the Lord in one's own way. And Timothy Fuller read from the Bible that always accompanied him to Washington, "Let him who is without sin cast the first stone." He had not progressed very far when Margaret interrupted to remark to Eugene,

"I have no sins to repent."

Timothy heard her words.

"What do you mean, child, by such an irreligious remark?"

"I think prayers and sermons are for sinners. A few years ago when I was small I prayed at the old cemetery to be converted from thoughts of self. Since then I have not been aware that I have any sins to repent."

Even Eugene was silenced by the depravity of his sister's words.

"Do you really mean to say," the father demanded, "that you are Christlike, without sin?"

"If I have any sins I have not found them. When I try to repent, I can think of nothing to atone for."

For once Timothy Fuller could not think of a reply. If his daughter had told him that she had never made a mistake in Latin, it would be simple to point out her error of judgment. But this was a different matter. Surely the child's mother knew of some sin she had committed.

"Is it not a sin," asked Mrs. Fuller gently, "to be disobedient?—to persist in your own belief when your father admonishes you? Even now you are sinning by not heeding his words. And when you beg to remain late at parties and blame your brother for blots on your letter paper, you are also sinning, however mildly. We all have sins, Margaret. But when we admit them, they are half vanquished."

"Let him who is without sin cast the first stone," Timothy Fuller repeated sternly. He went on with the text. Still, he could not help thinking it was time Margaret was sent off to school where she would come under the guidance of trained instructors. She was too much among older people, too much with her family, where she was indulged. It would be wise to ask the Adamses to recommend a school. They knew the best academies, as they knew the best wine and the best political tracts. Besides, it was expected that a returned Congressman should visit the family of the Secretary of State since they lived as near as Quincy. Timothy Fuller blessed his wife and children and the family sang one of Watts' hymns. Then he turned to his wife, saying,

"Tomorrow morning we shall take Margaret with us to the Adams' home at Quincy."

It was at ten in the morning on the last day of September that Mr. and Mrs. Fuller with their daughter Margaret rode forth to Quincy to call on the venerable John Adams and his family. He was sitting to Gilbert Stuart, but attempted to converse nevertheless.

"Not much can be expected from an old man of eighty-eight," he smiled. But Timothy Fuller knew that dimmed eyesight and poor hearing had not impaired the ex-President's mind. John Quincy Adams' wife was present and his son Joseph as well as the widow of the late Judge William Cushing, but Timothy was careful to address his remarks to ex-President Adams as he sat before Gilbert Stuart's easel. Naturally, the talk turned at first around the possible nomination of Adams' son for the presidency. The excitement, Mr. Fuller remarked, sipping the cordial that Joseph Adams had offered him, was already intense and there were rumors of corrupt bargains between Clay and Jackson.

"Most of the Republicans are opposed in theory to the policies they themselves advocate. I myself, you know, lost my place as first honor man by my Jeffersonian beliefs. The slave question might lead, as your son has said, to the dissolution of the Union."

But John Adams in his eighty-ninth year was more interested in recalling the brilliance of his son's youth than the astuteness of his maturity. He preferred to remember how at seventeen the boy had surpassed all in Roman and English history.

"Indeed," he murmured, "if you had examined him in English and French poetry, I know not where you would have found his superior."

"As a matter of fact," returned Timothy, "my daughter here is better skilled in Greek and Latin than half the professors at Cambridge."

John Adams smiled, remembering that his son had told him Timothy was not one to neglect an opportunity for getting the floor. As long as he did not raise a dissenting voice it would be well. Diplomatically he turned the talk to conditions at Cambridge.

"There are rumors of great innovations under President Kirkland. Indeed, the youngsters are entering upon vague cosmic theories that can do them no good. There is a young gentleman by the name of Emerson who keeps a school where, they say, Greek and Latin are subordinate to doggerel about flowers."

Margaret wondered whether she would enjoy being taught by the lean and angular youth she had seen on Harvard Street. But her father quickly decided.

"Then we shall by no means send Margaret to Emerson's school. I wonder if you can recommend another?"

Mrs. Adams remarked that she had heard of a young ladies' school at Groton where music and art went hand in hand with the classics. It was run, she said, by two sisters named Prescott and had a fine reputation. Margaret weighed the young ladies' school against Mr. Emerson and his cosmic theories and decided definitely that she would hate the Misses Prescott.

"One must be so careful during times like these," Mrs. Cushing observed. "Think of that Frances Wright, for instance, coming here with her peculiar theology and her radical theories about the social degradation of woman."

"Theology is becoming rather peculiar at home, also," the venerable Adams returned. "First Henry Ware started the furor and now William Ellery Channing is out-Heroding Herod with his sentimental belief in human divinity."

"Well," replied Timothy, "you must admit that is far better than believing we are totally depraved. But there is a happy medium between Calvinism and Channing's wishy-washy sentimentalism about goodness. My daughter thinks she has no sins to repent and so I presume she would make a fine disciple of Dr. Channing."

Margaret blushed and turned to look at Gilbert Stuart, who, though he had not said a word, was listening attentively to every remark and no doubt jotting down every gesture in his mind's accurate eye.

"Yes," said Joseph Adams, "these are troublous times indeed. One must watch out for an alert young miss surrounded by the radicals of Cambridge."

Mrs. Fuller disclosed the fact that Margaret had been reading Smith's *Wealth of Nations* and finding it most absorbing.

"Then," declared the venerable John Adams, flushing with excitement, "she is no different from Daniel Webster, who is shouting from the housetops that mercantilism is exploded." He trembled a bit and his voice quavered. He sipped his cordial and turned toward Gilbert Stuart.

"*Laissez faire* is a good enough theory," remarked Timothy, "but how are we to reconcile it with the cotton mills in New England—there is one in Lowell already— and the Irish streaming into Boston?"

There was no answer, for dinner was at that moment announced in the Adams' home. Gilbert Stuart wiped his brushes. Old John Adams nodded good-bye. The Fullers paid their respects to their host and departed. Timothy was pleased that he had impressed the aged man with his knowledge of affairs and that he had also learned of a school for his daughter Margaret. The child's ailments and curious talk of dreams and her failure to find any sins in her inner being were not healthful. Groton it would be. And the sooner the better.

CHAPTER II

MISS PRESCOTT'S SCHOOL

WELL PROVIDED with clothes, a new bonnet, and books, Margaret boarded the stagecoach with her Uncle Elisha on the morning of May 12, 1824, and the four horses trotted toward Groton. Margaret's feelings were somewhat at sixes and sevens. She carried with her the huge sum of $6.50 and hence felt financially independent. One dollar was for her passage, five dollars was a gift from her father, and the fifty cents had been added for contingencies. On the other hand, she was determined to hate Miss Prescott and her sister, as well as the ornamental branches of female education which they taught. It was difficult to leave Cambridge and go among strangers, especially when she could have partaken of the life of the University gentlemen instead. Margaret hardly listened when Uncle Elisha told her the amusing story that was circulating about their driver, Phin Harrington. He was a man of very small size and Uncle Elisha whispered to Margaret that on cold and stormy nights he would get inside of one of the lamps fixed to his box in order to warm his feet by the lighted wick!

Elisha quickly perceived that his niece was not of a mind to enjoy his wit, and in order to divert her, asked what subjects she planned to study at her new school.

"Father wishes me to give my principal attention to arithmetic and mathematics, and to devote about four hours a week to Horace and Virgil, and two to Italian. But I am sure I shall not enjoy arithmetic. And I know I shall not like Miss Prescott."

"Nevertheless, I expect you will resolve to earn her

good opinion; all your enjoyment at Groton will depend upon this, Margaret, as well as upon your making a favorable first impression upon all. You can do this only by modest and unassuming deportment."

"Why should I be modest if the other girls are not?"

"You must not put an unfavorable construction on anything said or done by them, Margaret. You should develop charitable feelings toward those of your own sex, and never speak of them with ridicule or contempt, as you may be inclined to do. Miss Prescott wants to cultivate not only your mind, but your health, your manners, and your morals. That, after all, is female education."

Margaret looked dismally at the road, at thirty miles of it. The name Groton, she had heard, came from an Algonkian one signifying "swamp" and as the stagecoach rolled over the boggy meadows near the town, she felt the name was apt—unfortunately apt. Uncle Elisha had dozed off. But soon Margaret was aroused from her unhappy thoughts and her uncle bestirred himself, for Phin Harrington was blowing his bugle to give notice of their arrival. At this blast the taverns would put food on the tables and the dogs would bark after the four horses as they galloped into the village of Groton.

The Prescott School was on the east side of Main Street, not far from Joseph Hoar's stable where the horses would be changed. Margaret and her uncle climbed down from the stagecoach and approached the white frame house next to which Miss Prescott resided. There were three high chimneys, Margaret noticed, and moss-green shutters shaded by gnarled sycamores. It was brighter than she had expected. Miss Susan Prescott herself came forth to greet them. Margaret had not anticipated seeing a principal so young and pretty. Uncle Elisha glanced at his niece and noted the change in her expression.

"That story about Phin Harrington *was* amusing, wasn't it?" he chuckled.

"It was indeed, Uncle Elisha," Margaret smiled—for the first time since she had boarded the stagecoach.

It was not long after Uncle Elisha's departure that Margaret began to follow the routine of instruction as if she had boarded at the Prescott School all her life. The most difficult part of the day was rising for prayers at 6:30 in the morning, but then all the girls did it—and what they could do surely Margaret could do. She stood behind Caroline James and it was fun to pull her long pigtails during morning prayers. After all, Margaret felt she still had no sins, and therefore no need of praying—especially so early in the day. After breakfast came studies from 8:30 to 12 and then again from 2 to 4:30. The hours were not nearly long enough to study all the possible exercises offered at the Prescott School. Miss Mary Prescott, the principal's sister, had given her the list:

Reading, writing, orthography; arithmetic, mental and written; English grammar; Geography, Ancient and Modern; Rhetoric; Perspicuity; Logic; History; Chronology; Mythology; Composition; Geometry; Astronomy; Natural, Moral, and Intellectual Philosophy; Elements of Criticism; Chemistry; Botany; French Language; Projection of Maps; Drawing and Painting in Water Colours; Painting on Silk, Wood, and Velvet, by Theorems; Plain and Ornamental Needlework of various kinds; Music on the Pianoforte.

Margaret observed, however, that in spite of the variety of subjects available, all offered for $15 the quarter, there were only four teachers. Miss Susan Prescott instructed the pupils in French and, with her sister, in English; Miss Ann Reed taught drawing, painting, and needlework, and Miss Eliza Hewitt, music. She often wondered just who would give instruction in Perspicuity or Astronomy should a scholar actually ask for tutelage in such a subject.

Margaret herself spent her mornings conning Blair's *Rhetorick* under Miss Mary Prescott's teaching. Miss Holmes, daughter of the carpenter to the University, Virginia Shaw, daughter of the late Commodore, and a ward of Amos Lawrence's studied rhetoric with her. They were amazed by her proficiency, but, as Margaret informed them, she had been studying Blair almost since she could prattle. There was nothing new in it for her.

Hedge's *Logic* followed Blair's *Rhetorick,* and here too Margaret was at home. She observed to wide-eyed Susan Butler, the belle of Groton, that she knew "Old Brains" personally, and had often seen him crossing Harvard Yard. Hence there was nothing remarkable in her ability to soar over his syllogisms.

At two o'clock Margaret sat at the pianoforte while Miss Eliza H. Hewitt marked the time. Miss Clarke of Princeton and the two daughters of Mr. Train, official of the State Prison, usually popped noisily into the music room to interrupt the lesson and then Margaret went on to Greek grammar, reciting from pages already well thumbed by her Uncle Elisha.

The last lesson in the day was for Margaret the most difficult. She sat between Sarah Brazer and Margaret Walsh with Virginia Shaw and Susan Butler opposite. On they plodded through Colburn's *Arithmetic.* One afternoon as Margaret looked about her, her thoughts wandered off to Susan Butler. She reminded her somewhat of the beautiful Anna Barker. Susan was the daughter of the town clerk and everyone called her the pride of the village. It would be lovely to have curls like Susan's and twinkling eyes instead of eyes that watered after a morning of Hedge's *Logic* and Blair's *Rhetorick.* Susan looked like a princess. Perhaps she too had been abandoned, like Margaret, in the New World—abandoned by a pirate or an evil demon.

"Miss Fuller, what is your answer to the last problem in mental arithmetic?"

Margaret had not even listened to the problem. But it would not do to let Susan Butler, a sister princess, witness her downfall. She did not reply.

"Miss Fuller, what is your answer to the mental arithmetic problem?"

Better to be defeated in the fight than surrender!

"Miss Reed," she said in a determined voice, "I am not interested in Colburn's *Arithmetic*. Frankly, I feel myself rather degraded from Cicero's oratory, which I studied at home, to 'one and two how many?' "

Sarah Brazer tittered. Margaret Walsh paled. Susan Butler exclaimed,

"Margaret—you must apologize to Miss Reed!" Margaret was silent and Miss Reed remarked,

"We shall discuss this incident with Miss Prescott this afternoon, Miss Fuller. Let us proceed to the next problem, young ladies."

Miss Susan Prescott, daughter of Judge James Prescott, was not one to forget she was a lady, even though her young scholar seemed to have lost her self-control. She realized also that Margaret would not be affected by a discussion of the ornamental branches of a young lady's education and so she directed her admonitions into mathematical rather than moral channels.

"You understand, Miss Fuller, that you must study arithmetic before you can enter the loftier regions of algebra and geometry, just as instruction in Latin grammar must prepare the way for a reading of Virgil. With diligence you should soon be able to pass the confines of arithmetic, and proceed to more agreeable studies in advanced mathematics."

Margaret, having expected a harangue about ladylike deportment, was overcome by this scholarly appeal.

"You know best, Miss Prescott," she murmured. "I am sorry for my discourtesy to Miss Reed."

"I knew you would understand, Margaret."

Margaret looked up gratefully for the honor of being addressed by her first name.

"Is there anything else you wish to discuss with me?" Miss Prescott asked.

"Would it be too presumptuous for me to call myself your adopted daughter, Miss Prescott? I should appreciate that honor greatly, since I am alone here boarding with you."

"Very well, Margaret, you may have that privilege. And now it is teatime. Hurry, or you will be late."

By the time Timothy Fuller arrived in Groton for a brief visit to his daughter, Margaret was eager to impart to him not merely her readings in Hedge, Blair, and Colburn, but also her knowledge of the town through which she had walked so often with her schoolmates. As Miss Prescott's adopted daughter she was, if not the pride of the village like Susan Butler, at least a familiar of its roads and hills. Timothy Fuller, ready to pay his respects to his friends, William Lawrence and Judge Dana, walked with his daughter down the main street of the village on a day nearly as cold as November, though it fell in late spring.

Margaret eagerly pointed out the inn kept by Isaiah and Joseph Hall and told her father that it had been occupied by the Reverend Mr. Samuel Dana before the Revolution.

"Before you continue with your interesting observations about Groton, Margaret, I wish to inform you that you have another baby brother. His name is Richard Fred-

erick, and I hope that when you return home you will see
fit to help your mother a little more than you ordinarily do."

Margaret's feelings were somewhat confused by this
strange subject of birth. Perhaps it was to hide them that
she turned the conversation to Alpheus Richardson's
bookstore, which they were just passing on the south corner of Main and Elm Streets.

"He owns a bookbindery also, father. It is possible to
buy ever so many interesting works from him. Margaret
Walsh and I once sat in his store reading *Paradise Lost*
aloud to one another a whole afternoon."

"If you wish to read *Paradise Lost,* Margaret, I shall
send you my own copy. You need not filch the time from
your studies then. You may read it between teatime and
evening prayers."

As Timothy Fuller and his daughter turned down toward the center of the village, near the barns and stable
of Joseph Hoar's tavern, they heard the cracking of whips
and the rumbling of carrier-wagons, carts, and stagecoaches.

"There must be twenty carriages on the road at this
moment," Timothy observed. "I presume those drawn
by six horses are carrying grain and pork into Boston or
returning with molasses and sugar."

"That's Aaron Corey, cracking his whip over those six
rearing bays. Father, he goes far out of his way to deliver
a message or leave a newspaper and many of the girls at
school are permitted to travel alone with him, for he is
so careful about looking after ladies and children. Horace
George is driving the next accommodation stage over
there. He lets the boys ride on the rack behind in sleigh-
ing time."

Past Aaron Lewis' tavern they walked, weaving their way
across the crowded road where horses trotted and car-

riage wheels creaked and wagons rumbled. The air was becoming chill. Groton seemed to stay cold even longer than Cambridgeport. Timothy cautioned his daughter always to wear the flannel shirt her mother had sent her. Margaret was somewhat annoyed and drew her father's attention to "Torrent Number One."

As Timothy Fuller examined the gooseneck and reel of the town's first fire engine, Mr. and Mrs. William L. Lawrence passed along the road toward Main Street. The group paused for conversation, Mr. Fuller informing Mr. Lawrence that he was at the moment on his way to pay his respects to him. Margaret thanked him for having made the necessary arrangements for her to board with Miss Prescott; there was some little talk about the coming elections, but the rumbling of carriages and the cries of the drivers were too loud for polite conversation. Respects, Timothy thought, could not be paid amidst such tumult, and so they bade the Lawrences good-day and walked on toward Judge Dana's home.

Out toward Farmers' Row they proceeded, where Judge Dana had built his summer house. Margaret was impatient at a second paying of respects, and longed to return to school where she was rehearsing a part in a dramatic performance of *The Rivals*. But she sat quietly while her father discussed the business developments of Groton with the Judge and his family. Skirts and muslins rustled, a decanter of wine was lifted from the flat-topped bureau, pantaloons were crossed comfortably, and respects were paid. Timothy Fuller looked at the summer farmhouse, and could not help mentioning the fact that one day he would enjoy living in such a place.

"Here you have time to think—with acres around you, and the complexities of the city far away. I should like to retire in just such a place, and read, and study, and think."

"Perhaps you will one day," murmured Mrs. Dana politely. But as they left the farm Margaret hoped inwardly that her father's wish would never be granted. Groton was not so uninteresting when one was at school outshining one's fellows in Hedge's *Logic* and Blair's *Rhetorick*—but shut up in a dismal farmhouse—Oh, Jupiter—let it never happen!

The performance of *The Rivals* was pronounced a success, and Margaret, with a dab of rouge on her cheeks and a vivid red sash on her frock, was able to forget the flannel shirt underneath. The months passed, marked mainly by the books that were sent her from home. June had brought *The Provoked Husband,* a play about a gentleman whom Margaret found quite harmless though provoked. *Paradise Lost* followed, and December brought Stearns' *Elements of Philosophy*. They came along with advice from home and though Margaret longed for news she satisfied herself with the advice, since it was accompanied by so many charming books. As the months passed Margaret became more and more a part of the books she read. In between the leaves she slipped her own poems, for the author of *The Satirist* found herself turning to verse as winter melted slowly into spring.

One evening directly after tea, Margaret, with her friends, Virginia Shaw, Susan Butler, and Margaret Walsh, walked over the hills toward Baddacook Pond. Over Brown Loaf Hill they scrambled, Margaret in the lead, leaping over the craggy rocks with a high courage— with a joy in the approach of spring. The air was chill and the girls walked briskly along Reedy Meadow Road, to the hillock near Aaron Corey's home. Close to Baddacook Pond they rested, Margaret exulting in the cool air of evening redolent of peach, wild cherry and apple. The scent of heliotrope was borne from Aaron Corey's little garden. "So hand in hand they walked," Margaret intoned, "the loveliest pair that ever yet in love's embraces met—Adam, the goodliest man of men since born his sons; the fairest of her daughters, Eve." Margaret Walsh sat, chewing noisily at a blade of tall grass. Virginia Shaw listened more to the drone of the wild pigeons than to Margaret's monologue from *Paradise Lost,* and Susan Butler gave her exclusive attention to waving a curl with her forefinger.

Margaret looked about her. Suddenly, she felt as if a flower were blossoming within her. She glowed—conscious of being alive—wildly alive, she thought—in the cool of an early spring evening. The sun was setting over the bogs of Groton, fiery, magnificent. It was as though the sun were melting a hard core within her, and she opened herself to the beauty, glowing and vibrant. She picked up her little red-backed journal and started to write. Susan Butler glanced at Virginia Shaw, murmuring,

"I think it's very impolite to write a poem when there are other people present."

Margaret did not answer—the lines were flowing—lines about sunset and wild pigeons, apple blossoms and heliotrope—most of all about the heliotrope—the tiny purple flower of fidelity.

"Margaret," Susan Butler interrupted, "we shall be late for eight o'clock prayers. Do hurry! or finish when you get back." Margaret looked up.

"Prayers—who wants to hear a prayer in a drawing room. I am praying—here—right now. This is my prayer —to the heliotrope—flower of faith—created by Zeus, the master of the gods."

"There are more important things for you to think of, Margaret Fuller," admonished Margaret Walsh. "I think you're just trying to be the center of attention with your heliotropes and Jupiters. You had far better smooth your hair properly and return for prayers or we shall be in trouble."

"Oh, Margaret, do stop," Virginia Shaw pleaded. "We shall leave you if you don't stop this instant."

"Leave me then. I cannot go until I have finished my poem."

The girls looked at one another, and slowly—one after the other—they trooped away, leaving Margaret on the hillock near Baddacook Pond, leaving her with her heliotrope and her prayer under the sunset. She sat waiting, but the poem would not complete itself. The lines would not flow forth. The girls had broken the spell with their stupid determination to be punctual for prayers. She longed for vengeance—for retribution. They had exiled her from her Garden of Eden and the poem had been chilled before it bloomed. She would love to tell subtle tales about them and sting them with innuendoes. She would love to make their perfidy known and resented as she resented it. Miss Prescott would probably call her into the parlor for a judgment scene, and in revenge she would dash her head against the fender of the hearth. Perhaps she would die, and they would think of her as a queen, wounded beyond forgiveness. But then there would be no more sunsets, no more wild pigeons, and the heliotrope would die, too. No, it would be better to be mortally ill, sick with convulsions. Then Miss Susan Prescott, her adopted mother, would come to her room with a soothing draught of tea and the heart of stone within her would melt as she emptied her heart to her teacher. Or she would dance before the girls, brilliant in her red sash, long gold earrings tinkling, the lovely rouge burning on her cheeks. The girls would try to seek vengeance. They would resort to low tricks in retaliation. They might even smear huge dabs of rouge on their own cheeks before they came to the dining-room table. But she would not care. On she would dance—reciting her poems loudly—dancing the mad whirls of the dervish until she fell in convulsions on the floor. She would be carried to her room, ill, swooning, and after many days of semi-consciousness and delirium, she would awaken to life, surrounded by girls who regretted their lack of understanding, who would welcome her again into their midst, who would realize that among them walked one different from themselves.

Margaret looked up. The sun had set, but the heliotrope still sent its sweetness into the air. Poetry was more comforting than people. The heliotrope was more faithful than Margaret Walsh. Slowly she walked back, a maiden bard over the hills, alone with the scent of the night about her, and a poem in her red-backed journal. She would no longer open her mind to people; betrothed to the heliotrope and to the beauty of night she walked, a queen no longer, a young girl in whom a flower had blossomed, a poem unfolded.

She returned quietly and took her place again, but though she had come back too late for evening prayers Margaret knew that the prayer had been prayed and that she was the older for it. Miss Prescott and Margaret Walsh, Susan Butler and her golden curls mattered no longer. For Margaret Fuller had prayed in the night and she knew her prayer would be answered. It was time to leave Groton, time to return to a broader life at home. There was no life for her any longer in the little frame house with its sycamores shading the green shutters. But there was life in the world outside. Lafayette had gone in procession from Boston to Charlestown and as the stories of the fanfare and glittering parade reverberated in her ears, she felt it was appropriate for her also to return. Lafayette had conquered the hearts of the men of the New World. She would conquer their minds from her dwelling place in Cambridge.

CHAPTER III

THE CLASS OF '29

TIME FLOWS. July will revolve into August; autumn will freeze into winter, and then the year 1825 will move like a ghost into the past. Each year will slip by and I shall remember a word spoken, a party perhaps, a poem written, a muslin dress, a new friend, one day that will stand out as the years flow by. So Margaret thought. But if I grow, then the years will not flow futilely. If I pour the hours into a mould of my own shaping they will be fixed. She sat in the second-story bedroom at Cherry Street and fashioned a mould to trap time. Each hour was neatly charted into its own channel. "Stand still, ye ever moving spheres of heaven!" Over her dressing table she pinned the program that would arrest the futile flow of time.

Walking 5-6

(Surely, she thought, if she had been able to rise at 6:30 for prayers at Miss Prescott's school, she could bestir herself at five for a walk through the green meadows of Tory Row, where prayers were voluntary, and God, or Jupiter, more beneficent.)

Pianoforte Practice 6-7

(Margaret found it far more satisfying to practise without Mr. Taylor or Miss Hewitt to mark the time. She herself could enjoy the harmony and overlook the crooked wrist.)

Breakfast 7-7:30

(This was a little too much time, Margaret considered, for sitting round a table where Arthur prattled about the

[42]

Soap Works and Eugene discussed the birds that nested in the back of the house. But if the body lodged the spirit, it must be fed.)

Readings in Sismondi's *Literature of the South of Europe* 7:30-8

(A book so much more to her taste and so much more important than Colburn's *Arithmetic,* which had consumed her precious hours.)

Readings in Brown's *Philosophy* 8-9

(Most suitable, she thought, for one who had determined to transpose time into eternity here on earth.)

And at nine, when Ellen stood gazing at her curls before the mirror, Margaret donned her crinolines and gloves and well-cleaned boots to walk to the Cambridgeport Private Grammar School, where she would dazzle both Cambridge and Port-Chucks with her learning.

The "Port School," a mile away from the Harvard buildings, was kept in a long, low, dark room. Margaret squinted as she entered from the sunlit street. The walls were nearly black. Was there a bench that had not been cut up by Oliver Wendell Holmes? But then, Margaret thought, after five years of listening to the dronings of the dark-eyed and austere Master Biglow, how else could he amuse himself? The air was hot and close. It was not remarkable that young Richard Henry Dana had rebelled and been dragged by his ears across the room and over the benches and then beaten by Master Barrett with his long pine ferule. How different it was from the bright rooms in Groton where no chest could be unlocked for the long and evil flogging stick. As Margaret took her place on the girls' bench, she arched her neck in the direction of young Dana, who sat next to his little brother Edmund whom he piloted to and from school every day. Wendell

Holmes looked at her and whispered to his brother John,
"She has a neck like a swan's—but from certain angles it might be said to resemble a snake's."

John chuckled, Mr. Perkins entered, and the Greek lesson began. For nearly two and a half hours it continued, the scholars reciting in turn the passages they had memorized and parsed. At length theme-reading began and Margaret was called upon to read her essay. She arose, her face kindling and reddening, every feature dilating, as she glanced in magisterial manner about the low room. Her neck seemed to undulate with excitement and her eyes had a watery, aquamarine lustre as she looked down at her paper.

"It is a trite remark," she began in a loud, almost supercilious tone.

Wendell nudged his brother John.

"What does 'trite' mean?" he whispered. John shook his head, bewildered. Just then the bells of the Cambridgeport Parish Church tolled twelve. Mr. Perkins interrupted Margaret's oratory to call over the names of the day's delinquents. Richard Henry Dana was doomed again for the pine ferule and vowed to himself to run away to sea if he could not change to Mr. Emerson's school.

Margaret gathered her gloves and her theme, and started out with Wendell Holmes. Deprived of the opportunity to read her essay, she pounced upon young Holmes and immediately delivered to him an account of the latest "naw-vel" she had read. As they went their ways, John said to his brother,

"She may be a Port-Chuck, but she's smart."

"I wish I knew what 'trite' meant," murmured Wendell. Margaret walked ahead, conscious of the fact that the morning had marked another conquest.

She returned to follow the afternoon schedule above her dressing table.

Pianoforte 1-2

(It had been very well to discuss Mozart's *Requiem* when she was a child, but now Margaret felt she had matured sufficiently to interpret his music herself. How lovely it was to play, as she called to mind Wendell Holmes' perplexed grimace when she had used the word, "trite.")

Dinner 2-3

(It was amusing to discuss Sismondi with her mother over the blancmange. It was true that Mrs. Fuller seemed to give more attention to the needs of baby Richard than to the literature of the South of Europe, but then it was not essential for two to take part in a conversation. One could really suffice.)

Italian 3-5

(How delightful it was to round out the vowel sounds and let them slip from her tongue. It was like being a great lady in the South, where sunshine glowed upon the Mediterranean and charming noblemen bowed before her. Dulcet, its tones—oh, that she had been born in Italy—Italia.)

At six Margaret relaxed her program for a walk or a drive—or occasionally a party. She felt herself no longer the little girl who had twisted her hair into paper curlers and been relegated to the younger group at a cotillion. One who was learning Italian, who had astonished Oliver Wendell Holmes with her learning, might well expect to be the leader of a gay soiree. It might be an oyster supper at the Holmes', or a garden party at the Farrars', or more rarely an affair at the Fullers' new home on Dana Hill like that spectacular gathering her father had arranged in honor of President John Quincy Adams. Usually it was less ostentatious, but seldom less exciting.

It was on a pleasant evening that Margaret donned her jaconet muslin gown and her citrine kid gloves for a little party at the home of Anna Parsons. She carried a large, crisp handkerchief and swayed into the room. Elizabeth Randall was there from Boston and Anna Barker again on a visit to the Farrars from New Orleans. Harriet Fay was there, too, her leg-of-mutton sleeves much in evidence. Margaret walked around, nodding at a group of younger sisters and brothers from Miss Jennison's Dame School, waving her handkerchief, conscious of the dignity with which her recent sojourn in Groton invested her. Thacher and Waldo Higginson kept to themselves, discussing the latest caprices of their English schoolmaster, William Wells.

Margaret thought the party too immature for her years of wisdom and soon set about to lead the entertainment herself. She held her handkerchief by the corner and waved it about as if she were conducting one of Mr. Taylor's glees with a baton instead of directing children in a game of charades. She swayed from one to the other, conscious that Thacher was admiring her grace. Later on, jelly, sweets, and lemonade were served. Margaret took a share of the cake. But still aware of her role as leader, she examined the cake plate carefully, quickly counted the pieces, and glanced around the room to ascertain the number in the company. There would not be enough portions to go round. She would be the magnificent lady bountiful and see that nothing went amiss. Ostentatiously, she replaced her slice of cake, remarking loudly,

"I fear there will not be enough to go round." Anna Barker glanced at Elizabeth Randall and murmured,

"How tactless of Margaret."

But Margaret waved her handkerchief grandly, offering

the cake to young Waldo Higginson. She was sure she had saved the day.

A little later she and Anna Parsons, Elizabeth Randall and Anna Barker retired to the dimly lighted stairs for a chat. Anna Parsons confided to Margaret that very often, just before going to sleep, she had visions and seemed to be able to foretell the future. Sometimes when she simply touched an article worn by a person she seemed to be able to feel his character.

"My dear," replied Margaret, suddenly opening her luminous eyes, "cherish your gift. Perhaps you have second sight like St. Francis. You will be able to have glimpses of the inner light one day."

"Do you really believe so, Margaret?" asked Anna, looking up wide-eyed.

"I myself sometimes have visions when I turn my head to one side, but I cannot perceive character so well."

Elizabeth Randall was not particularly interested in second sight, and so she turned the conversation to the parties she had attended during the year in Boston. Margaret immediately interrupted with a detailed account of the affair the Fullers had arranged in honor of the President. There had been music and dancing, John Quincy Adams had driven up in a magnificent chaise, and, she went on,

"I myself wore a beautiful pink gown covered over with white muslin and we all danced quadrilles. I'm sure you must have heard about it."
Margaret turned to Anna Barker, who nodded indifferently and began to discuss a cotillion at the Farrars.

After the girls left the stairs before withdrawing for the evening, Anna Barker remarked to Elizabeth Randall,

"I heard that Margaret was laced so tightly at the Adams Ball that she had to hold her arms back as if they

were pinned. They say she seemed unable to see her partner, she danced so awkwardly."
Elizabeth Randall smiled.

"With all her plainness she does seem magnificent, I
think. When she described the party her eyes were
lustrous. And when she talked about second sight she
made me feel for a moment as if she were St. Francis
himself."
Margaret walked ahead, waving her handkerchief in farewell. She wondered if Anna Parsons might one day be
able to discern her character from the ring she wore or
a poem she had written, or perhaps from the very handkerchief she was now holding. She waved it once more in
Anna's direction and raised her left hand in a final *vale*
to all. Then grandly she swept out of the room.

It had not been long after the birth of baby James
Lloyd in 1826 that the Fuller family removed from the
Home House on Cherry Street to Dana Hill on the bend
of the road from Boston. Arthur sobbed vociferously,
"Oh, I shall not see the Soap Works any more," but
Margaret was glad to be near the greensward and white
palings and gravel walks of the Harvard buildings. In the
autumn days Mrs. Fuller liked to rest underneath her
pear trees, while Richard and Arthur mashed apples for
cider, and Margaret sat in the garden reading Russell's
Tour in Germany.

Now that she no longer attended the "Port School" she
had more time for her walks in the village. Very often
Henry Hedge, son of "Old Brains," would escort her
through Tory Row. It was delightful to stroll with a
twenty-one-year-old divinity student who had spent five
years in Germany with George Bancroft, and who, for all
his learning, could still appreciate her own powers of
discernment.

"You must study German so that you can read Goethe," Hedge remarked as they walked past Dexter Pratt's smithy. "You will be completely won over by him, if for no other reason than that he venerates women. The highest principle with him is represented by the feminine form. *Das ewig weibliche zieht uns hinan.*"

"I have been reading Russell's *Tour in Germany,*" Margaret replied, "and for a long time I have wanted to borrow a copy of *Faust* from Thomas Dowse."

"We are fortunate to have Mr. Dowse's library in our town. It is almost impossible to get any German texts in Boston. He owns the Moses translation and Lord Gower's as well as Dr. Pratt's *Werther*. It would be well to start with a translation since you have not yet mastered the German tongue."

"I shall set about it soon. Just now, however, Lydia Maria Francis and I have planned to read Locke together before embarking on a course in English metaphysics. We propose to continue with de Staël's analysis of Locke's system. Everything is so simple after one has mastered your father's *Logic.*"

"A new book has just come out," Henry replied, "that should be of interest to you if you are engaged in metaphysical studies. It is called the *Growth of the Mind* by Sampson Reed. The author is a druggist, but most of his pills are compounded of Swedenborgianism. He believes that the human mind is the soul and the world around us the body—that everything is an effluence of God—music, His voice and poetry, His language. It's all very much like the utterances of Ralph Waldo Emerson. He left Harvard as I entered, but he left a trail of cosmic oratory behind him."

"It sounds very interesting indeed. But I can't help feeling that I should like to shape my philosophy as the birds build their nests—make one method and then desert it and make a new one. I seem to outgrow a philosophy as soon as I have mastered it."

"Well, you are still very young, Margaret, for all your wisdom."

Margaret lost the opportunity of replying to this thrust, for Henry Hedge was raising his hat in salutation of William Henry Channing, whom Margaret recalled only as the brother of a girl who had won seventeen medals at Dr. Park's school.

"He will be graduated," Hedge remarked afterward, "with the class of '29. It is a promising group—Oliver Wendell Holmes is among them. But to return to Goethe. Do you know that for all his profundity he is curiously superstitious? He once tossed a valuable pocketknife into the River Lahn to ascertain whether he would succeed as a painter."

"How interesting!" Margaret exclaimed. "I have often been tempted to do the very same thing. I should like to study Goethe's life one day. What was that German phrase you used a while ago? It sounded enticing."

"*Das ewig weibliche zieht uns hinan*—the ever womanly draws us above."

"How beautiful. And how true."

"Yes. I wish that I had more time for my German studies," Henry continued, "but divinity instruction comes first just now. I know I shall never be a distinguished preacher, but I do hope to become a good pastor."

"There are few persons, Mr. Hedge," Margaret returned, mindful of his remark about her vulnerable sixteen years, "who can form so just an estimate of their own powers as you have done."

"Thank you," he replied graciously, "for your candor."

"And thank you," said Margaret, "for your interesting discussion of German literature. Once I can forego my Italian for a while I shall be sure to study German.

Goethe must be an extremely fascinating personality."
They were near the Washington elm under which the
General first drew his sword. The professors' houses were
white in the sunshine. Henry Hedge doffed his hat and
Margaret walked home, quietly pondering Goethe's
phrase—*Das ewig weibliche zieht uns hinan.*

Rising at five was a little more difficult in the winter
than in the summer, and Margaret often indulged herself
by lying in bed for a while, reading Locke or framing
imaginary dialogues between Goethe and Eckermann,
Mme. de Staël and Mme. Récamier—scraps of talk about
love and poetry, music and philosophy—dialogues sometimes between Henry Hedge and Margaret Fuller. Poised
on the crest of life she was, as she lay dreaming of herself as the grand lady of a salon, the cynosure of a great
university, whose wisdom the sagest professors vaunted,
at whose feet the young men prostrated themselves. Sorrow was her lot too, she thought, for none could mature
without sorrow—the sorrows of the night that banish
life's primal freshness. How far away they seemed, those
days when she had dreamed of being a princess abandoned on a lonely shore, even that time when she had
prayed to the heliotrope and longed to die, when plumed
with glittering thoughts her soul had soared far beyond
the level of those about her. How swiftly time had passed
since she had returned to Cambridge. No program could
ever arrest its flow. What did the years leave in their
traces—what marks were left of their passing?

She sprang out of bed and stood before the window.
There was a twine factory in sight, but Margaret saw it
not. It was transmuted into a land of dream, the window
became a casement, and Margaret Fuller, aged seventeen,
was changed into a great lady whose conversation reverberated round the world. She turned to her red-backed
journal and scribbled hastily. The breath of dawn was a

draught of life to her—youth's portion to be drunk in the glorious morn. A tear blotted the page; the dream was vanished. The last stanza turned all into night. How mature she had become, she thought, as she inscribed a title for her poem.

STANZAS WRITTEN AT THE AGE OF SEVENTEEN

She intoned what she had written, as she stood before the window.

Come breath of dawn, and o'er my temples play;
　　Rouse to the draught of life the wearied sense;
Fly, sleep! with thy sad phantoms, far away
　　Let the glad light scare those pale troublous
　　　　shadows hence!

I rise and leaning from my casement high,
　　Feel from the morning twilight a delight;
Once more youth's portion, hope, lights up my eye
　　And for a moment I forget the sorrows of the
　　　　night.

O glorious morn! how great is yet thy power!
　　Yet how unlike to that which once I knew,
When, plumed with glittering thoughts my soul would
　　　　soar,
　　And pleasures visited my heart like daily dew!

Gone is life's primal freshness all too soon
　　For me the dream is vanished ere my time;
I feel the heat and weariness of noon,
　　And long in night's cool shadows to recline.

Slowly Margaret fastened her blue watered-silk dress. A morning begun with a prayer might be sweet, but a morning begun with a poem—that was true divinity. She wondered if the feelings surged through Goethe as they surged through her. Suddenly, she tore the leaf out of the journal and hurried downstairs. If Mother were busy with Lloyd she would read it to Mrs. Higginson. Mrs. Higginson always knew greatness when she saw it.

It was customary for Mrs. Fuller to run over to her neighbor's home at the head of Professors' Row for a chat about the qualities of the Higginsons' brass-handled tub concealed in a mahogany washstand or for an exchange of opinion about the most recent Philharmonic concert. And Mrs. Higginson frequently came calling at Dana Hill to discourse on puddings or poetry. In the evening she found the family seated together in the large parlor, Timothy at one corner of the open fire, his stand, with its papers and lamp, next to his chair. He was preparing a legal document regarding the ownership of his client's cow and lifted his eyes from his papers only long enough to assure himself that Arthur was studying his latitude and longitude, and Ellen her *Chronology*. Richard was cautiously sucking his portion of licorice— just up to a point which he had marked on the sweet. Mrs. Higginson seated herself next to Mrs. Fuller to examine the fancy work she was embroidering. The ladies then discussed the state of Mrs. Fuller's pear trees and were just ready to embark on an analysis of the mince pie the Fullers had enjoyed for dinner, when Margaret decided she could hear the plebeian talk no longer.

She arose, picked up a footstool, and carried it to Mrs. Higginson's feet. She sat on it, and opening her eyes widely, gazed up at the visitor.

"How is Wentworth progressing at Miss Jennison's Dame School?" she inquired. Before Mrs. Higginson could reply she went on. "Arthur tells us that Miss Ellis commands all her boys to cut long rods for her so that she can punish them. I think that method of teaching is needlessly cruel, do you not, Mrs. Higginson?"

"Perhaps when children are more amenable, it may be

outmoded. Let us hope that when you are ready to teach such penalties will no longer be necessary."

Mr. Fuller looked up from his client's cow to hear his daughter's response.

"I hope I shall never teach, Mrs. Higginson. The gift I covet is the gift of eloquence." Margaret looked, rapt, into Mrs. Higginson's eyes. "I long to be a Pericles rather than an Anaxagoras. I may tell you in confidence that I am planning six historical tragedies, and perhaps also some tales of Hebrew history."

"Well, women are doing remarkable things these days," Mrs. Higginson replied. "I hear that Frances Wright has organized labor with some Negroes on the Bluffs in Tennessee."

"And," Mrs. Fuller remarked, "there are two sisters by the name of Grimke, I believe, who have just come North to acquaint us more thoroughly with the evils of slavery."

"Das ewig weibliche zieht uns hinan," Margaret quoted. "It is the time for women to march in the vanguard of civilization."

Ellen looked up at her sister, and Mrs. Higginson thought, how beautiful the child is—that broad brow and exquisite coloring. She looked at Margaret's flushed forehead and watery eyes. With Ellen's beauty, Margaret might . . . but then, such thoughts were unworthy.

"It would be excellent if Margaret had a companion in learning," remarked Mrs. Higginson. "Dr. Freeman's grandson, James Clarke, is a remote cousin of yours, is he not? I hear he is one of the leaders in the brilliant class that will be graduated next year."

"I am not well acquainted with him," Margaret replied. But to herself she vowed that she would soon acquaint him with the history of her mind, if indeed he were as worthy as Mrs. Higginson believed.

"Old Charley" began to neigh in the stable. Richard yawned and pocketed his licorice. Arthur's head nodded over his latitude and longitude. Mrs. Higginson arose and Margaret removed the footstool. It was time for Mr. Fuller to escort the visitor to Professors' Row.

Cambridge, Margaret thought, as she walked to the meetinghouse for the Commencement of 1829, had changed almost as much as she had. Surely there were three times as many people as when she walked along this very path to dancing school. And President Quincy was making as many innovations in the College as President Kirkland had before him. Edward Everett, whom Margaret recalled as the Adonis of her childhood, was now Greek professor; George Bancroft, who had gone to Germany with Henry Hedge, was a tutor; and under Ticknor's management the whole department of modern languages was being reorganized. If only a woman could attend Edward Channing's lectures on English literature or Pietro Bachi's Italian conversations. And, Margaret thought, for a few lessons in German from Charles Follen, she would give up all her eloquence. It was fortunate that the revolutions abroad had exiled so many of the greatest intellects—fortunate for Harvard. As Margaret skirted her way along the Botanic Gardens she recalled that Thomas Nuttall had come over from England to arrange them.

She felt herself a part of all this change. The girl who had pinned a program over her dressing table and bidden time to cease, had become—what?—a friend of Henry Hedge—a poet—an admirer of Mrs. Higginson? Which of the marks that time was impressing upon her would remain? The years were not important, Margaret reflected. It was the days that would be remembered. On such a day as this it was good to be alive in an expanding world. She looked down approvingly at her white gauze dress with its satin stripes. How neatly it clung to the waist! Judge Story smiled affably as he raised his silk hat and walked along with his son William and his son-in-law, George Curtis. The air was cool and pleasant after Monday's showers. This twenty-sixth of August, Margaret was sure, would be óne of the memorable days.

The college lawns were radiant. Satins and cerise gauze, muslins and crinolines swished along the paths and beavers vied with silk hats, while the ladies wore huge bonnets bedecked with flowers and ribbons. By half-past ten they had all assembled in the meetinghouse. Dr. Follen was on the platform, looking very serious and very Teutonic. Thomas Nuttall was wearing one of his own flowers in his lapel. The hall was packed with ministers for whom no seats had been reserved and Henry Hedge walked over to Margaret as the Reverend Dr. Porter began his ten-minute prayer. While William Henry Channing pursued his colloquy on "An Active Profession as Injuring or Assisting the Efforts of Literary Men," Henry pointed out to Margaret the mild face of Waldo Emerson's brother Charles, who had been graduated the year before.

Margaret became interested in George Phillips' essay on "Incorporaing Historical Truth with Fiction" and thought it might be fruitful to try that sort of amalgamation in an autobiographical romance. Soon sprightly Oliver Wendell Holmes delighted his audience with a poem without a subject. As he stood before the meetinghouse, not more than five feet tall in boots made no doubt by Mr. Russell of Cambridge, Margaret and Henry Hedge were reminded of his description of himself as "a plumeless biped." They chuckled as much at his lively little figure as at the jewels of wit he sent coruscating in the air. The forensic between Joel Giles and Chandler

Robbins was dull by contrast and Margaret noticed that
Pietro Bachi and Charles Follen were becoming a little
impatient at the discussion of "The Inequalities of Genius
in Different Countries." Of course, they would try to determine whether such inequalities arose from moral
causes. Margaret thought the issue too characteristically
Cambridge for her taste. At last, as Thomas Nuttall's
flower was wilting perceptibly, Charles Storrow delivered
the concluding oration. On and on he wandered through
all conceivable "Diversities of Character," while Judge
Story's head nodded and even President Quincy began
to twirl his thumbs. Finally, the valedictory was delivered.
Dr. Porter allowed himself only five minutes for the closing prayer. The graduates of 1829 listened politely while
Judge Cranch received an honorary degree.

"There," Hedge remarked, "is James Clarke, chatting
behind his hand to Sam Smith. It is indeed quite an
eminent group."

The Reverend Mr. John Pierce set the tune to the
seventy-eighth psalm and at the suggestion of Judge Story
sang every stanza. The seats were let down, as John
Holmes always said, like the discharge of boards from
a cart. Scarfs and silks rustled; silk hats reappeared. The
class of '29, fifty-nine strong, had been graduated from
Harvard College.

After having plodded through Commencement no
graduate was loath to revel, no visitor unwilling to offer
a toast. Nodding at Dr. Follen, Henry Hedge piloted
Margaret through the muslins and satins on the Yard to
Porter's Tavern, where James Freeman Clarke and his
sister Sarah had already taken a table with William
Henry Channing, Oliver Wendell Holmes, and his
brother John. Anna Barker was there also, charming in
her chintz morning dress. Margaret entered, squinting
from the brilliant sunshine, and took her place at the

table. After congratulations were exchanged John Holmes gayly declared,

"Now I know I am destined to be *frère de mon frère* and nothing more."

"Wendell," William Channing decided, "should really be a poet and not a lawyer or a doctor."

"Why not all three?" Margaret asked.

"You may be able to rock a cradle, read a book, eat an apple, and knit a stocking all at the same time," John Holmes returned, "but Wendell is such a little man. . . ."

"Just a plumeless biped, as you know," Wendell put in, in mock, self-deprecating fashion.

"Ah, but the plumes began to sprout today," returned Hedge.

Cakes were served and John Holmes began to tell one of his anecdotes about the boy who kicked and screamed for more sweets or vowed that he would tell that his breeches were made of his mother's old window curtains. Sarah Clarke clapped her hands at John's wit. The Reverend Mr. Pierce turned from the table where he sat with Chandler Robbins to silence the group with an austere glance. Aping the minister's solemn demeanor, James Clarke sedately asked Oliver Wendell Holmes how clerical affairs were proceeding with his father.

"As a matter of fact," Wendell replied, "my father has just lost his post for his conservatism and will have to establish a new congregation. It serves him right for refusing to see the light of the new Unitarian liberalism. These whey-faced brethren with their weedy flux of ill-conditioned hair," and he glanced toward Mr. Pierce, "have ruined my father's discernment."

"My father," Margaret remarked, "thought that would happen years ago. After all, you can't sit anchored to your moorings when the tide changes, can you?"

Jellies and blancmange interrupted the clerical discussion and Anna Barker remarked that excellent ices were served at a small tavern near Papanti's new dancing school on Washington Street.

"It would be jolly," suggested Sarah Clarke, "for us all to go to Boston one day and watch Lorenzo Papanti put the youngsters through their steps. We might see the art exhibition at the Athenaeum Gallery, too."

"Sarah thinks if she visits the Athenaeum often enough some of her own paintings will grow on its walls."

"Are you going to be a painter?" asked Margaret. "Even though we're cousins our kinship must be thirty-seven times removed. I'm sorry I know so little about your interests."

"I'm going to paint, I hope, though I doubt whether I shall ever be a painter."

"Hear, hear!" John Holmes cried out, banging his spoon for attention. "On this day of your commencement you must all declare your future intentions. We know Wendell is going to be a lawyer, unless he becomes a surgeon, or unless he sits comfortably on Pegasus." (Margaret thought he would surely never allow Pegasus to gallop, but would hold the reins for a very tame trot.) "But what are you going to become, James?"

"A minister, of course, in strict antagonism to your father."

"Good for you!" cried John. "Now what lies in store for you, William?"

"The ministry, of course. Again in strict antagonism to your father."

"Hurrah again! And now for the ladies. Margaret, what will you become?" Wendell Holmes suggested that she become a siren, a supercilious, satirical, sprightly siren.

"The *olla podrida* of human nature," Margaret returned, "can never represent a compound of more varied ingredients, of higher gusto—or more to my taste."

Lemonade glasses were raised. "To the future!" The

glasses clinked and for a moment the table at Porter's Tavern was solemnly quiet. James Clarke and the others rose to leave with Margaret, but above all other sounds the words rang in her ears, the phrase danced through her veins—to the future!

It seemed somehow fitting to Margaret that at a time when she was launching upon new currents of thought with new companions, the family should also pluck up its roots and remove from the old house on Dana Hill. There was something suitable in living on Tory Row near the University buildings now that the passing days had brought her closer to Harvard life. Brattle House was not far from the gambrel-roofed dwelling where the Holmes children had been born. A moment's walk would take Margaret to the massive door of Craigie House, whose broad piazzas were set back from the road. If she had no wish to raise the ponderous knocker, she might walk a little farther up the path to Lechmere House, laden, as everyone said, with books and wine, rich plate and ancient furniture. But she had no need to stroll beyond the grounds of her own new home for a delightful ramble. Brattle House itself still reflected more the taste of the genial old bachelor, Thomas Brattle, than that of its present owner, Margaret's crotchety Uncle Abraham. The square building had few pretensions, but its gardens and fish ponds and stone spring house extended their beauty to the River Charles. As Margaret wandered along the spacious lawns she could hear the chimes of the old clock on the stairs of Craigie House, or the tolling of bells in the steeple of St. John's Chapel, or even the pounding on Mr. Pratt's anvil in the smithy, but, looking at the fish ponds and the river, she could dispel these sounds of Cambridge and feel herself verily in an Italian garden with a brilliant foreign gentleman at her side.

James Freeman Clarke might not be foreign, but brilliant he was as he walked with Margaret beneath the lindens or in the garden, discussing the history of her mind or sympathizing with her inner struggles. One summer afternoon as they wandered along Tory toward Church Row, the talk wove in and out of Coleridge and Combe, tugged back to Harvard for a remark about Hedge's pulpit in West Cambridge, and careered to Europe for a discussion of German philosophy. But as the conversation veered in and out of these channels, Margaret felt her own eloquence give way to the unbounded sway of sentiment in the palace of her heart. Dear James—how mild and gentle was his face as he told Margaret about his family and his mother's boarding house at Ashburton Place, about his sister's painting and his brother William.

"My brother plans to go West some time. The West must be a fascinating place, especially now when there is so much controversy about the rights of the Indians."

"Shall we civilize them to Christianize them or Christianize to civilize? That, I suppose, is the crux of the question," Margaret returned. "But I should still prefer a journey to Europe rather than to the West."

James could hardly hear her remark, for young Jimmy Lowell was thundering by on his little white pony.

"I remember," said Margaret, "when he was a baby toddling over Elmwood lawn. It's just like a Lowell, isn't it, to gallop to Mr. Wells' school, although he lives only a few rods away. Yet I doubt whether he has changed as much as I in these years."

She recalled her longings to be a queen as she walked so many hundreds of years ago down Tory Row to dancing school.

"How have you changed, Margaret?"

"Inwardly. The changes that have taken place within me I have confided to no one. Nothing has happened, and yet everything has happened. I have changed more in a day sometimes than in a year. There are fateful days in my life that the tide will not wash out. They have changed me from a precocious child to a groping woman. You with your interests in Channing's philosophy and social-istic concepts are still enough of a sentimentalist to under-stand, are you not, James?"

"Yes," he replied, almost reverently. "But I think my brother William might understand even more. He is a little like you, Margaret. He too, at the moment, is less interested in the changes of the world around him than in those within himself. That is one reason he is determined to go West—to live simply in a place where no city com-plexities can disturb his thoughts."

Margaret was not particularly interested in William Hull Clarke. She did not reply.

"Do you see that young man over there?" James re-marked—"the one with a folio under his arm and an-other under his nose? That's Theodore Parker. He is an omnivorous reader. They say he could easily collide with a tree because his head is always buried in a book, whether he's talking, walking, or eating. He has just en-tered Harvard; mark my words, we shall hear from him one day."

"And not from you, James? You are too self-effacing."

They were under the lindens of the Brattle House gardens again. James Clarke did not seem inclined to pur-sue the subject of himself. He looked out toward the Charles and then doffed his hat to Margaret. She turned slowly toward the house. She was thinking no longer of Combe and Coleridge. There was something within her that could not be found in their pages. If only James were a little more unusual, a little less the product of Cam-bridge. He said his brother was like her. Margaret began to wonder about the strange young man who was bent on going West.

It was not long after her walks with young Clarke that
Margaret determined to use as much zeal in clearing her
complexion as she had in studying Italian. Since Oliver
Wendell Holmes had already stopped his studies at the
Dane Law School and was seriously considering medicine as a profession, Margaret approached him for information about doctors who might be of use to her. She
should have remembered, she thought, that Wendell
would never give a straight answer to a simple question,
but she listened politely while he capered about and shot
his darts of wit at the entire medical profession of Cambridge.

"There's Dr. Waterhouse, for instance. His hair is tied
up in a ribbon behind and I am certain he uses powder.
He marches about, brisk and dapper, with his gold-headed
cane. The good people of Cambridge listen to his learned
talk when they are well and send for another doctor when
they are sick."

At least, Margaret thought, I know enough not to call on
Dr. Waterhouse.

"Then," Holmes pursued, "there is Dr. Gamage. You
have seen him riding on his rhubarb-colored horse with
his saddlebags behind him. He will look at your tongue,
feel your pulse and shake a horrible mound of ipecac from
one of his phials—no matter what your ailment happens
to be."

"Well," considered Margaret, "I shall not call upon
Dr. Gamage."

"Your last possibility here at Cambridge," Holmes
continued, "is Dr. Jennison, who drives about in an
ancient chaise drawn by a venerable nag. But I may tell
you in confidence that he is employed by only one family."
Margaret determined privately to call upon Dr. Shattuck
in Boston or Dr. Robbins. But she could not refrain from
remarking to Holmes,

"You do not seem to take the body very seriously.

After all, since the body is the temple of the spirit, I have always thought it must be regarded not as an evil, but certainly not as something trivial or jocose. A man of science must have a definite view about his relation to external interests and temporal pursuits."

"I see no reason, Margaret, for bothering myself about such things. The main thing for a doctor is to keep on with his job."

Oliver Wendell Holmes capered about a bit more, hoped with a very evident twinkle of his eye that his information would be of some value, and departed.

Margaret felt that her own mind must be superior to young Holmes', just as it was inferior to Goethe's, and she arranged to consult Dr. Robbins directly. Thanks to his medicine, the flush on her forehead disappeared and she felt less conscious of her complexion when she walked with James Clarke or Henry Hedge. The headaches that had been annoying her recently were less violent; she could lie down in the middle of the day and sleep for hours, if she were so lavish of the time.

As Margaret had set about renovating her outer being, she determined, not long after Dr. Robbins had effected his cure, to restore her inner being to its pristine freshness. She felt that for this she would give up all her knowledge and her talents, which, in the light of the experience of religion, somehow seemed to lose their importance. James Clarke surely must have had such an experience or how could his face reflect that mild assurance, that calm persuasion that man in his goodness was but a part of the cosmic beneficence that permeated everything.

On Thanksgiving Day, after having attended church merely to please her father, Margaret walked along the Charles, and as she watched the chill sky of autumn over the flowing waters, she felt herself become a part of the

river and sky, a part therefore of God. Her experience
was similar, she reflected, to that of the old mystics or
the Neo-Platonists about whom Henry Hedge so often
spoke. The fields were so different from church. Here
God was manifest—there, hidden behind the trappings
of ritual. It seemed suddenly unimportant whether or not
the world ever recognized her worth. Indeed what was
her worth before the power suffused through sky and air
and field? Winter might cut through the river with its
piercing blade, but in her heart there would be spring.
For she was a part of all that lay around her, part of its
unity, part of God's essence. Her destiny was but a flower
of that ever-generating root, and if the flower perished,
there would be other blossoms, other fruits. Margaret
felt something she had never felt before—humility. She
bowed her head and walked away. This knowledge she
must cherish in her heart; never must she forget this
veritable Thanksgiving day of 1831, in which she had
culled a new truth from the fields of Cambridge, a new
life from the skies of the New World. This, she believed,
was another of those memorable days that would with-
stand the flow of time. As she walked back toward Brattle
House she determined to study Fichte, Kant, and Goethe,
and borrow *Werther* from Mr. Dowse's library. The
new belief that grew within her she would enrich with
knowledge and thought. The mind would water the seeds
of the soul and bring them to a new flowering.

It was not until 1832, when Goethe lay dying in
Weimar that Margaret actually began the study of German. As she sat copying out a scene from Schiller's
Robbers in her strongly bound album, she murmured to
herself those words of Goethe, "Extraordinary, generous-
seeking," words that seemed to typify James Clarke. It

would be fine, she thought, to translate Schiller's poem to his friends, for his friends were so much like hers—all, extraordinary, generous-seeking. Just then James Clarke tapped the knocker and asked Margaret to join his sister and himself, Henry Hedge and William Channing in a drive to Boston.

"You remember we planned it at Porter's Tavern on Commencement Day. Anna Barker is with us also."

Margaret quickly smoothed her muslin gown, shook out the leg-of-mutton sleeves and placed her new gros de Naples bonnet at a careful angle. They were off to Morse's hourly stage. The burly, red-faced driver collected the twenty-five-cent fares and cracked his whip as the stagecoach lumbered through the open meadows, past Dana Hill, on toward the "Port." The toll keeper's snappish dog barked; some youngsters called out open irreverences at the gay party, recalling to Margaret the Port-Chucks of her childhood. She could not quite throw off the thought of Goethe and Schiller, however, and when Anna Barker admired the amulet she was wearing, Margaret mentioned the fact that Goethe also seemed to believe in talismans.

"Caroline Sturgis, a little girl in Cohasset, whom I met recently, sent me an amulet case. I should like so much to have figures of camels and antelopes and lizards, and of course, a unicorn. I think the combination of all would signify my name."

"You know that the twenty-second of March was considered by Goethe as his fatal day," Hedge remarked.

"Oh," Margaret replied, "Goethe's demonology and mine go hand in hand."

"But you cannot say he ever fancied his name in the form of unicorns and lizards," objected Sarah.

"No," James murmured, "that's the woman's contribution to demonology—amulets."

"Woman's contribution!" exclaimed Margaret. "There's a very fine woman's contribution in the last issue of *The Token*. It's called 'The Gentle Boy.'[1] I'm sure it's by a woman, although there's no signature. And even though there are no amulets, there is a very decided and charming symbolism."

"And," added Anna Barker, "if it were not for women half the wonderful devices of our day would never have been thought of. Look at the marvelous sewing machines they've just invented—all for us—the women!"

"Really," William Channing contributed, "we meant nothing against the women, did we, James? And how we've wandered—all the way from amulets to sewing machines. But that's the woman of it."

They all laughed gaily as Morse's hourly stage clattered over the cobblestones of Washington Street. The party descended and Anna Barker bought some candy and Margaret a bandbox at one of the shops, while the gentlemen idled on the brick walk outside. After the purchases had been made, they all sauntered down Washington Street to Papanti's Hall. There they looked on while the bewigged and peppery dancing master glided around the room, accompanying himself on the violin. There was a six-foot girl in mortification as she was put through the steps with a four-foot boy.

"They say," Anna Barker whispered, "that Papanti's wigs cost as much as one hundred dollars a year." Lorenzo Papanti's tall, lithe figure was skimming the floor of the hall with such ease that he seemed deaf to the noise from the second story, where his actress wife was teaching the first steps to the younger children. His attention was turned to one lad who refused to dance, and he glided over to tickle the boy's legs with his fiddle bow. Then the younger children appeared from the dress-

[1] Margaret was wrong. "The Gentle Boy" was by Nathaniel Hawthorne.

ing room, each making a bow or sweeping curtsy before entering the hall.

Mr. Papanti approached the party of onlookers, assuring them that one day he would own a fine establishment—perhaps on Tremont Street.

"You must send all your children to my dancing hall then."

It had been amusing and yet so reminiscent of their own childhood. Papanti turned to Margaret and remarked, "You have a magneeficent air, Miss Fullair. I am sure you must dance well—although if you dance with Papanti you sall not be so magneeficent. Papanti sall be magneeficent." He laughed delightedly at his own wit. Was it yesterday or an epoch ago when a dancing master had said, "Miss Fullair—You tink you General Washington!" That too had been a day that would not be forgotten.

They waved good-bye to the children and shut the door on this glimpse into their past. Cutting through West Street they walked toward the Common, where the uniforms of the militia shone in the sunlight and children were playing at Blindman's Buff. It was but a short stroll from there to Pearl Street with its shade trees and stately houses, and the four-columned Athenaeum that generous Mr. Perkins had donated to the cause of art and literature. Mr. Bass, the kindly librarian, ushered them in. As they turned to the Portrait and Sculpture Galleries, they spied Elizabeth Peabody and Lydia Maria Francis, now Mrs. David Child, exercising their newly acquired privilege of reading books in the Athenaeum sanctum. Margaret paid her respects to Lydia, who was examining an English edition of her own recently published *Mother's Book,* and, on tiptoe, walked back to her party who were at the moment peering at Stuart's portraits of George and Martha Washington.

"Typically Saxon," James remarked.

"The Athenaeum should be more representative of foreign nations," Margaret commented. "Greek and Jew, Italian and Saxon are surely but leaves on one stem at last—though Italy is ever dearest to me."

As they walked along the gallery, gazing intently at the casts by Crawford and Clevenger, a young gentleman approached to pay his respects to James Clarke.

"May I present Mr. Samuel Ward, who is undoubtedly filching time from the banking firm of Baring Brothers to indulge his artistic propensities."

Margaret looked at Mr. Ward. He was standing near a Clevenger cast under a shaft of sunlight that burnished his blond hair and made his fair face radiant. Mr. Ward looked at Anna Barker for quite a while before he turned to Margaret. Anna did look beautiful with her golden curls and her shining face not less pure than the wind. They exchanged their views about the paintings and the marbles, all agreeing that Gilbert Stuart had made old Mr. Perkins come alive in his portrait of the merchant prince. Margaret mentioned the fact that she had met Mr. Stuart while he was painting a portrait of old President Adams, "But," she added, "I was a mere child then and could hardly make the most of such an opportunity." Suddenly, a noise from above interrupted the conversation. Mr. Bass came downstairs leading two young culprits by their ears.

"The Athenaeum," he was saying, "is not a playground. Please refrain from playing marbles on the floor of the alcove."

"We Bostonians," Mr. Ward remarked, "must enjoy even our marbles under the shade of books. Well, I must be off. I have indulged my artistic propensities, as James would say, long enough."

He spent a full moment shaking Anna Barker's hand,

nodding pleasantly to Margaret and the others, and the fair young man had gone.

To Margaret the room seemed suddenly empty; the shaft of light had disappeared. After Sarah Clarke had made a second examination of Gilbert Stuart's brush stroke, Margaret and her friends also left. Lydia Child and Elizabeth Peabody, who had the reputation of being avid scholars, were still intent on their books. Margaret turned as if to bid the room farewell. She felt as though something important had happened there.

Sarah Clarke was bubbling over with delight in the paintings she had just seen and entertained the party with an account of Washington Allston's Cambridgeport Studio.

"I visited him, although he hates visitors. I hope to be able to study with him soon. Now that he is the husband of Richard Dana's sister, I may be able to convince him that as a representative of the Cambridge arts, I must be given the proper instruction."

On she sallied, as the company strode toward Mrs. Mayer's confectionary shop, with a remark about Thomas Crawford or an anecdote about Gilbert Stuart's nephew, Stuart Newton. Sarah Clarke was never silent when painting was the subject of a conversation. Margaret and Anna Barker, however, were strangely solemn. When they thought of art they usually thought of Raphael; today Raphael seemed to be embodied in a fair young gentleman who had stood under a shaft of light in the Boston Athenaeum.

After an ice at Mrs. Mayer's confectionary shop they boarded Morse's hourly stage again for the journey home. It had been a lark indeed. Margaret's feelings surged as she revolved in her mind those recollections of her childhood, fleeting glimpses into the past evoked by the children at Papanti's Dancing Hall, and those evanescent images—almost of the future—that beckoned her on, when she had stood near the Clevenger cast in the Athenaeum. This day, like the day she had spoken with Anna Parsons, the afternoon she had heard Henry Hedge quote from Goethe, the morning she had written a poem, Commencement Day, and the walk with James Clarke, Thanksgiving Day when she had renewed her being—yes, this day, like those others, would stand high against the flying years.

In the evening Margaret sat alone on the piazza of Brattle House, hearing the west wind rustle the vines, watching the moon's face. The wind was set to music in her soul. This day, she felt, had been an era, a time of sweet and strong composure. She opened the nosegay she was wearing and took from it a geranium leaf. She would send it to James Clarke.

"You may put it," she wrote, "in a locket and wear it as a memento that the most striving souls have their halcyon hours. It would be Elysium to have just performed some great and glorious deed or to have just finished some beautiful work—the Apollo Belvedere for instance or Shakespeare's *Tempest* and to pause this day and feel creation and one's self a worthy part thereof."

To pause—for after such a day there must be pause— and feel creation *in* one's self—to transcend the stunted life around, and rise to heights undreamed by women. What women can do, Margaret thought, now and here, as authors perhaps, with Harvard close at hand and the Athenaeum hardly more than a walk away! To pause— and feel creation in one's self. . . .

"Margaret!" Timothy Fuller walked up the steps of Brattle House. His voice was almost excited. "Come in! I have news for you."

Margaret stirred reluctantly, hating to leave the moonlight over the piazza, hating to break the spell.

"Margaret," her father announced, "I have just arranged to purchase Judge Dana's house on Farmers' Row in Groton. You remember we visited there when you were at the Prescott School."

Margaret remembered. She remembered the isolated country village, the untutored rustics, the trivial talk. There would be pause enough, she thought bitterly. At Groton time would be all pause with no high days raised from the succession of the dull and fleeting years—no days like those she had known at Cambridge. There would be pause—but creation would not follow. It was as if she had been borne on the crest of a wave and the wave had broken beneath her, as if a tide had ebbed before its time. To pause indeed—But how to feel creation in one's self?

CHAPTER IV

FARMERS' ROW

A S THE FULLER family approached the white
house that Judge Dana had built near the northerly
end of Farmers' Row, Margaret felt that destiny was
tricking her back into the past at a time when she longed
to plunge into the future. Once again she was the little girl
who had listened to the rustling of muslins and the tinkling of glasses, the little girl who had prayed to Jupiter
that her father would never live in a farmhouse. The
gradual eminence on which the house was erected to overlook the blue Wachusett, Monadnock, and Peterborough
Hills brought no delight. Even the robins and the pines
in the semicircle before the dwelling could not soothe her.
Judge Dana's home was still a farmhouse, for all its white
columns and balconies, and fifty acres of land. From the
back the hills could be seen—blue in the distance, but
Margaret saw only sorrow before her.

Life became more difficult after the family was settled.
Every morning Margaret was awakened by the rumbling
of the butcher's cart driving into the yard or by Timothy's
call to the children. It was his command that the boys
respond to his signal by striking their feet upon the floor.
Then came the sound of the cold baths which Timothy
Fuller insisted upon, the sound of Mrs. Fuller closing the
windows that her husband had opened at bedtime, sometimes the softer sound of Mr. Fuller running barefoot
through the snow. Very occasionally there was a more
terrifying noise—the crack of the old black riding stick,
not on "Old Charley's" back, but on Richard's or William
Henry's. The old steed began to neigh; the roosters

called the sun from over the hills. Richard, William
Henry, and even little Lloyd dashed down to the poultry
coop, for each had been given a chicken as pet. Arthur,
ill already from his exposure to the cold of Groton,
called for Divie, his tame blue dove. Mrs. Fuller walked
down from the piazza to her border of rare blooms and
Ellen went to minister to her own crab apple tree. For
the family the day had begun. But Margaret, looking
down into the orchard of apple and pear and cherry
trees, felt that it had ended in its very beginning. What
would the day hold for her? She would sew and wait on
Arthur. The day would die in dullness as time moved
slowly, relentlessly, on.

Margaret watched her father, the lawyer who had represented his state in Washington, loading grain with John,
the drunken hired man. She watched her mother, who had
danced cotillions in Cambridge and sung psalms in the
chaise during the journeys to Canton, superintending the
dairy, making butter and cheese for the family. She
watched the hired man draining the lowlands; her mother
stooping over the flower bed, her simple gold wedding
ring bright among the brambles. She saw the boys devouring huge chunks of brown bread after a day in the fields,
and she felt that their life was ill-starred. Even the view
from Arthur's chamber, with its low-lying hills and blue
mists, seemed tamely smiling and sleepy. She longed for
torrents and cataracts. But there were no torrents or
cataracts in a Groton farm.

In the midst of life Margaret felt herself dying. James
Clarke was already out West with his brother William.
She thought of the richly bound album she had given him
before his departure, having written on the first page the
words, "Extraordinary, generous-seeking—Be revered—
In thee the faithful hope that still looks forward and
keeps the life-spark warm and future action beneath the

cloak of patient sufferance." James was alive out there, grafting his own ideas onto the system of Unitarianism, thinking new thoughts, accomplishing new deeds. Eugene was at Harvard, wandering over the gravel paths, holding a book perhaps that would open a broader life to him. But how could she mould her turbulent thoughts into shape?

Her lot was to teach her sister and her little brothers. She watched them drowning in the deep places of Virgil, incessantly moving about as if catching at reeds of safety in their recitations. Their awkward ways irritated her inexpressibly. Sometimes she laughed outright at their responses. One day in the winter parlor after the boys had plodded through a passage in Virgil, she turned to the geography lesson.

"Richard, where is Turkey in Asia?" Richard bobbed up and down in his seat, looked out of the window, waved his arms about, and replied,

"Turkey in Asia is in Europe."
Margaret looked very weary for a moment and then laughed.

"Your answer is so inane that it deserves to be recorded."
She turned to the end of the geography book and while her brother looked on, bewildered, wrote, "Richard, being asked where Turkey in Asia was, replied that it was in Europe!"

It was true that with the establishment of a miniature Athenaeum in Groton, Margaret was able to read the foreign and quarterly reviews. Then she had her copy of Jean Paul and a volume of Goethe's *Werke,* just published in Stuttgart and Tübingen. While her mother sat sewing of an evening and Arthur was in bed convalescing and the lessons were over, she often sat reading Jahn's *History of the Hebrew Commonwealth* or dipping in and out of the *Old Testament*. There was *The Hunchback of Notre Dame* also that fascinated her while the hogs outside grunted themselves to sleep and night spread itself over Monadnock. But Margaret realized that her own plans and works, her own inventions no longer interposed themselves between herself and Heaven.

It was with a mild surrender that she acquiesced in her father's suggestion that they read together in the history of the United States. After writing letters to Henry Hedge about Uhland and Novalis (letters were all that remained after their exciting conversations), after submerging herself in the Poetry of Being, she felt that it would be unprofitable to analyze the petty feelings of half-bred men who had given themselves to the paltry game of politics. But as Timothy Fuller read aloud passages from the letters of Thomas Jefferson, Margaret began to perceive the true stamina of the man, the wisdom of a philosophy which had led him to find the just principles of a sound government amid fragments of republics and monarchies.

"I am beginning to appreciate the United States and its great men," she confided to her father. "Perhaps my violent antipathies were the result of an exaggerated love of the Poetry of Being. There is something great about good government, just as there is about good poetry."

"If your life at Groton has given you nothing more than this," Timothy Fuller replied, "you may be grateful."

Yet Margaret could not abandon the philosophy of the poets for the philosophy of the statesmen. She was glad that her mind was regenerating in regard to her country, but she did not feel ready just yet to renounce her Germans for Jefferson. Perhaps some time in the future, when there was a cause to fight for, she might delve more deeply into the history of government, but now Goethe tugged her back to poetry and Novalis to mysticism. She believed she would like to compose a piece about German philosophy and send it to Henry Hedge. At any rate, she would not stop studying, let the hogs grunt and the chickens scratch as they would.

Again it was to please her father that Margaret attended the First Church in Groton. The walk through the village with Arthur was usually more entertaining than the Unitarian service. On Farmers' Row the boy turned to look at a wheeling partridge or a wild rabbit, but as they passed into Main Street they had to nod perpetually in salutation of the good folk of Groton—all like them on their way to church. The Reverend Mr. Sanderson patted Arthur's head as he scurried along. Arthur was irrepressible when he mimicked the ministers, calling them members of the "Universal Band." Dr. Mansfield on horseback with his saddlebag fell prey to the lad's wit. And Dr. Bancroft, erect in his sulky, was almost as amusing, Arthur was saying, as "that eccentric man who wore a brass hat to protect his head in thunderstorms." Mr. Park hailed them. He was town clerk after Susan Butler's father had been promoted to the office of postmaster. Very little had changed, Margaret considered, as she walked on, holding Arthur's hand.

Just as they passed the office of the Farley Brothers, lawyers of whom Timothy Fuller had often expressed approval, they were stopped by Naomi Farwell, the hermitess of Groton. Groton, Margaret decided, could never allow itself a village imbecile, and so made up for the lack in a hermitess.

"Miss Fuller," mumbled the old lady, "remember the

falling stars of the winter. Thousands and thousands of them there were, that fell before the dawn on November 13, 1833. The world will end soon!"

Naomi Farwell shook her head and walked away.

"Whatever did she mean, Margaret?" asked Arthur.

"Some nonsense preached by William Miller, I suppose. He says the world will end soon and I infer falling stars are a sign of the finale."

Arthur looked thoughtful, but there was no time to ponder the point, for they had arrived at the First Church of Groton. The pews were so high that Arthur had to peep through the rounds that ornamented their tops to discern the faces of the congregation. The Reverend Dr. Charles Robinson was ascending the winding stair to the high pulpit. He placed his hands lightly on the damask cushion. His voice thundered from the sounding board above his head. Someone whispered jocosely to Margaret,

"It's like a hogshead with the minister speaking out of a bunghole."

She listened for a while to the preachings of the Reverend Dr. Robinson, but at last felt she could listen no more. She looked about her at the congregation. There was Colonel Tarbell deep in sleep. And in the middle of the minister's roundest phrase, Mr. Jacobs came rushing in with his heavy boots and a stout whip in his hand. The Reverend Dr. Robinson droned on. How wrong his composed belief was, Margaret thought. It was a time to struggle. There was Garrison, for instance, with his New England Anti-Slavery Society, fighting a great battle. Had not her own friend, Lydia Child, with whom she had read Locke so many years ago, published a remarkable tract? What was the title? *An Appeal in Behalf of That Class of Americans Called Africans.* The title alone sounded the battle cry. Margaret had heard that the work had disbarred Lydia from the Athenaeum. She was accomplishing something. But where was Margaret? Sitting quietly in the First Church of Groton, watching Mrs. Tarbell awaken her husband with peppermints and cloves, watching Mr. Richardson and his family enter, always a trifle behind time.

It was a time of action, everywhere but here. Sylvester Graham had been mobbed by the bakers because of the popularity of Graham Bread. Jimmy Lowell and Richard Dana had just entered Harvard, and Eugene had told her that William Channing's erratic cousin Ellery was a freshman. He had said too that there was a curious young student there who had strange notions and a strange name— Thoreau. Here there were no notions at all. Mrs. Loring's tall calash was bobbing up and down, as the lady nodded off. The venerable heads of Judge Dana and Squire Park were peering up out of the square pews. Margaret wished suddenly that she had been born a little later. Oberlin College for women had opened, and perhaps she might have attended. Yet it was not so much the time, really, as the place. She had heard that Elizabeth Peabody was studying Basque. How could one study Basque in Groton? Miss Peabody was in Boston, assisting Bronson Alcott in a school he had just opened. The Temple School it was called. Elizabeth Peabody was fortunate indeed. Things were happening in the world, books written, deeds accomplished, life lived. Harriet Martineau was sailing for America, it had been rumored. Her article about political economy in *The Select Journal of Foreign Periodical Literature* had been interesting. How Margaret would have liked to reply to Andrews Norton's attack on Goethe in the same issue. She had heard that Ralph Waldo Emerson, that scrawny youth she had seen on Harvard Yard, was amassing a huge collection of German books. If only he were addressing the congregation now instead of Charles Robinson. Mrs. Farrar had heard he was the only clergyman of all possible clergymen. Perhaps she would meet him one day.

The world outside was bristling with action. Here Squire Butler, the paragon of integrity, was calling out an intention of marriage. Here in Groton, in the First Church, Mrs. Loring in her calash, Mr. Jacobs in his riding boots, Colonel Tarbell sucking cloves, Margaret Fuller, her brain teeming with thoughts, were rising for the benediction. "Amen." The pew seats slammed down heartily.

As Margaret wrote out her course of study and pinned it above the dresser, she smiled, recollecting that other program she had set herself after leaving the Prescott School. Instead of learning Italian she would be able to meditate upon the works and opinions of Alfieri; in place of Sismondi's *Literature of the South of Europe,* there were the historical and critical works of Goethe and Schiller; instead of spending a morning listening to Greek recitations, she would study with her father the government of the United States as well as the history and geography of modern Europe. The elements of architecture would find a place in her schedule, for the great German master had been interested in architecture and perhaps one day Margaret Fuller would be the biographer of Johann Wolfgang von Goethe. At any rate, it was necessary to study with some purpose in mind. If Lydia Child could struggle for that class of Americans called Africans, surely Margaret Fuller could reap a tangible harvest from the years at Groton in those three evenings of the week when she was free to pursue her thoughts and read her books.

Pursue her thoughts she did, as she sat in the winter

The "Home House" on Cherry Street in Cambridgeport, Mass. In the second story bedroom Margaret Fuller was born on May 23, 1810. The elms that Timothy Fuller planted appear in the foreground.

The Young Ladies' Seminary at Groton, Mass., conducted by the Misses Prescott; now the Lowthorpe School of Landscape Architecture. Here Margaret Fuller studied in 1824.

Fuller Residence at Groton, Mass., now the home of Mrs. William F. Wharton. The Fuller wing is at the extreme right. Here Margaret Fuller lived with her family from 1833 to 1836.

parlor, turning the pages of Novalis or Jouffroy. Mysticism, she reasoned, is not fanaticism, nor is it Swedenborgianism, nor any ism, unless perhaps spiritualism. In its final essence it probably implies listening to the voice of the soul within in preference to the trumpet calls of the outward world. But Margaret was not quite ready to close her ears to those trumpet calls. When she read Jouffroy she longed to be a thinker, and felt that struggling in a revolutionary movement was naught unless there was something positive to be accomplished. Lydia Child and Garrison were striving merely to get rid of obstructions. In the end, even liberty, *toute seule,* was nothing but an absence of evil. If she could not be a complete *Natur,* surely she could be a thinker, one who might scrutinize the flaws in Spinoza's method and in all other existent systems of thought. But when she turned to Vasari and considered the sensuous, loving undulations of Raphael or the straight upward graspings toward heaven of Michelangelo, she longed to be an artist and shape creation from moss or cloud or wave. Yet, the Stuttgart edition of Goethe was never long out of her hands. As she pondered her master's phrases, she felt that she, like Goethe, would never completely give way to her feelings, but would live a life active and thoughtful at once. Her thoughts rounded the circle again, returning to the debate between the inner voice of the soul and the trumpets of the outward world. To combine thought with action—that was the end-all of her being; not to bask, content, in any ism—whether it be mysticism or Pantheism or Swedenborgianism, but to live actively, seeking wisdom always. Action married to thought—surely that meant writing. Eugene was teaching after his graduation, in an academy near by at Stow, and Richard was attending his school, boarding with the kindly Miss Brooks. There was less to do on the farm now. Margaret was ready to write.

One day at the Groton Athenaeum Margaret had sat reading *The North American Review*. The issue for October, 1834, contained a reprint of a lecture which her acquaintance, George Bancroft, had delivered before a society of young men in Massachusetts. Bancroft might know his Germany, Margaret thought, but surely he was wrong in considering that Roman slavery had ruined Rome and that in the plot against Caesar, Brutus was merely the dupe of more sagacious men. Her knowledge of Plutarch's Brutus and Shakespeare's roused her indignation at Bancroft's fallacious interpretation of the character.

She returned home to discuss Brutus with her father. Somehow it was easier now to talk with him than it had ever been before. Perhaps it was because of her interest in his beloved Jefferson; perhaps it was simply that she was growing older; but there it was. The two sat together, reconstructing the Brutus of old, who had thought independently and been far more sagacious than those by whom Bancroft said he had been duped.

"Why not reply to the attack?" suggested Timothy. Suddenly, Margaret realized she had found her opportunity to weld thought with action. She would write a letter to Nathan Hale, editor of the *Boston Daily Advertiser*.

Margaret began mildly enough, alluding to Plutarch's defense of the character of Brutus, mentioning the painful surprise with which she had read of the Roman's sycophancy and cruelty in certain paragraphs of *The North American* article. But as she proceeded she could not refrain from one dart at Bancroft's temerity. "As the avenues to the temple of fame become more and more thronged with eager devotees," she wrote, "there has arisen a class, who seek to win notoriety by broaching new opinions on characters as well settled as the relation the earth bears to the sun." She signed the article "J" and dispatched it to Mr. Hale. On November twenty-seventh her reward was manifest. The article was published in its entirety. Margaret Fuller had appeared in print.

Three days later, when Timothy Fuller fetched his copy of the *Daily Advertiser* from Postmaster Butler, he found a reply to his daughter's essay. It was signed "H" and substantiated Bancroft's interpretation of Brutus by citations from Gibbon and Middleton's *Cicero*. Margaret and her father tried to uncover the man beneath the letter "H" and came to the conclusion that it was probably some bigwig from Salem who had allied himself with the Harvard professor.

"Perhaps," she remarked, "it may be that young writer by the name of Hawthorne[1] whom Elizabeth Peabody mentioned to Lydia Child. He lives in Salem. He must be a timeserver—truckling to George Bancroft so indiscriminately."

The start had been made. Margaret Fuller had leaped from the springboard. Her father filled the wine glasses in honor of the occasion and Arthur was extremely careful to study his European geography for his renowned sister. Mrs. Fuller clipped both article and reply from the *Boston Daily Advertiser* and treasured them. But this was merely the beginning. Margaret would go on now, evolving thought into action—on the written page.

Margaret had found herself in Goethe. She would open her career, therefore, by mingling her own thoughts with those of the great German in a translation of his *Tasso*. She would paraphrase rather than translate—as Coleridge had done with *Wallenstein*. Broken lines or faults in meter were permissible; she would adhere to the spirit rather than the letter of the play. The spirit she

[1] It was. This was the first occasion when Hawthorne and Margaret Fuller clashed in opinion.

understood—that kindred feeling with which the poet Goethe had analyzed the poet Tasso. She would paint in vivid English the generosity and worldliness of the realist Antonio, the taste and unconscious selfishness of Alphonso, Duke of Ferrara, the delicacy of Countess Leonora, and of Princess Leonora. In *Tasso,* she felt, Goethe had found himself, after he had exhaled his mental boyhood in *Werther.* And in Goethe she had found herself.

Winter slipped into spring; she moved from the parlor to the garden, her copybook before her next to a volume of the *Werke.* The robins laid their blue eggs in the semicircle before the house as she paraphrased the scene in Alphonso's garden and saw Tasso as one in whom "the dead and mute find life and voice and daily glow with colors not their own." Antonio and Tasso must be enemies. Yet could their natures have but met and formed a whole, "the whole thus made might lead a world in chains." Such a union had been effected in Goethe. Perhaps Margaret Fuller might one day weld within herself the realism of Antonio, the mystic poetry of Tasso—the trumpets of the outer world and the voice of the soul within. Then she too might lead a world in chains and sail "unto the sea of future times." With Tasso, as she translated, night and day alternated in her being, while without spring had tripped into summer, and summer had melted into the fall of the year.

From Goethe she turned to Körner, ever seeking her own image reflected in their pools of thought. She went on to translate those lines which Körner had composed as he stood sentinel on the banks of the Elbe. His Fatherland became her own country, the country she had come to know with her father. Her own seal ring, the wild freedom of the horse Konick, even Crabbe's verse became her subjects. The pen had been loosed on the page and could not stop.

For all the wild activity within her that gradually was
taking shape in the notebook, Margaret sometimes
longed for an intellectual guide—for one who would comprehend her wholly and enable her better to comprehend
herself. To drink a cup of the strongest coffee and then sit
down to pass an afternoon with a friend, with one who
would refrain from trivial gossip about the coldest day of
the year, or the upsetting of the Groton coach, with one
who would discuss Goethe, and Tasso, and Margaret.
Once again she felt the old discontent, the loneliness of
the village after her winter contemplations. Even Dr.
Channing, she had heard, had been aroused to protest
against the anti-Garrison meeting, and had published his
Slavery; out West, Ephraim Peabody had started *The
Western Messenger* and in the spring of 1835 Margaret's
article on Crabbe was accepted for publication in the new
journal. It was time to leave the study and walk forth into
the outer world.

At length it came—the opportunity for release. Though
it would be a trip of little more than a week, it would
bring change and new thoughts. Mr. and Mrs. Farrar
were going to Trenton Falls and had invited Margaret to
join their party. The plan, she had told her father, was to
set out about July twentieth and go on to New York, up
the North River to West Point, through Catskill, and on
to Trenton Falls, where they would spend a week.

"I shall need fifty-seven dollars, but you will not think
of the money, will you? I would rather you took two
hundred dollars from my portion than felt even the least
unwilling."
Timothy Fuller was willing. Even if Margaret had told
him that a certain Mr. Samuel Ward was to be in the
company, he probably would have acquiesced.

The journey was gay and Margaret chatted cheerily
about a stately matron and a foreign gentleman on the

steam car. How delightful it was to go so fast! There was no time to think. She was glad, for she had thought so much during the long winter alone. Then there was the trip by water, and though the morning was damp, West Point lay fair before the eye. With Mr. Ward she rambled along the wooded paths, looking beyond to the cloud-capped mountains. Then on they sailed, leisurely, past the Highlands and Hyde Park to fairy Catskill. How much more Titan-like were its blue mountains than the tame Peterborough Hills she had seen from Farmers' Row. Through the valley of the Mohawk they passed on to Trenton Falls. There they paused, the gladness leaping within her.

How short a week it was to talk and look upon his fair young face, to sit beneath the mill where the stream moved gently on, to watch the Falls by moonlight. One evening of the tiny week was ruined, for Mrs. Farrar was ill and Margaret felt she must bring her tea and wait upon her, and say no when Mr. Ward invited her to see the Falls again by moonlight. One perfect evening yet was left; the moon still gleamed upon the dashing spume, lighting the mill, glimmering over the stream, over his fair hair. She felt as she had felt when the shaft of light had glistened on that head—the shaft of light in the Boston Athenaeum—the glimmer of moonlight now at Trenton Falls. Was it Raphael, or a merchant and lover of Raphael? As she spoke of her bright angel whose paintings floated to meet her soul's horizon, she thought indeed not of Raphael, but of him who stood before her. What did he think as he looked so pensively upon the robe of lilac gros de Naples and her muslin mantelet?

"I think you should know, Margaret, that I plan to sail for Europe next year and stay quite a long time."

The moon still shone upon Trenton Falls, but the waters looked harsh and frightening. Margaret did not

answer. She held her head high and walked back with
him. The wave had crashed again beneath her, but a week
of rapture was behind it, and would always be behind it
to cast its glow whenever she looked backward.

But Margaret, during the late summer of 1835, somehow had no wish to look backward. She forced herself to
look forward and think instead of feel. She wrote a review of Bulwer-Lytton's novels with special attention to
The Last Days of Pompeii and decided that though the
author assailed the fabric of society too violently, he was
on the right track; indeed his very errors savored of progress. Somehow Pompeii seemed far removed from Trenton Falls, as good a place of refuge for her as any other.
In August her article appeared in *The Western Messenger* and Margaret was content that she had turned the
summer to some account.

In September, just as July was beginning to sink into
the past, there came another invitation from the Farrars,
but this time it was Margaret's mind and not her heart
that was stirred in anticipation of a meeting with Harriet
Martineau. It would be exciting to see the English writer
who was known as such an ardent abolitionist. Besides,
Margaret thought, Harriet Martineau would return to
England one day—and perhaps she might accompany
her. Perhaps this meeting would be a fateful one. Europe
might be its outcome.

When she finally stood on the piazza of Mrs. Farrar's
house, holding her rice-straw bonnet and looking toward
the road, she heard the rumbling of carriage wheels and
her heart beat wildly when Miss Martineau drove up. It
was a slight, unpretending woman who advanced to meet
her. Miss Martineau's rich, brown hair, folded away
from the middle of her forehead, lay low over her gray-
green eyes. But it was the ear trumpet rather than the
woman that attracted Margaret's attention at first. Miss

Martineau handed her one end of the long black trumpet, saying,

"I have heard much about you, Miss Fuller. We shall have many subjects to discuss."

She listened carefully for the courteous reply and then, having greeted the Farrars in the drawing room, led Margaret back to a chair on the piazza.

"You must not mind my trumpet," she said. "Dr. Flint has done me the honor of writing a sonnet to it and Mr. Emerson, whom I visited last month, says it acts as a chain, making Siameses of two interlocutors."

Margaret gingerly picked up her end of the trumpet and called through it,

"I should enjoy so much an account of your travels, Miss Martineau."

Harriet Martineau smoothed her brown hair, blinked a little in the sunshine, and spoke.

"We landed just about a year ago, and visited—oh! so many places—but frankly, the events of the past few months in Boston have given me more food for thought than Mammoth Cave and Niagara Falls together."

Margaret was just about to pick up the trumpet to inquire about those last few months, when Miss Martineau waved her aside and continued, "I was nearly mobbed in Boston, Miss Fuller! Had it not been for Mr. Emerson I should have had no shelter anywhere. You have heard that he has just removed to a new home in Concord and taken his bride, Lidian Jackson, with him. He has a delightful, plain, square, wooden house standing in a grove of pines. You must visit there some day. But I am digressing from Boston. Of course you have heard of the meeting last month at Faneuil Hall, at which the merchants and lawyers tried to denounce the abolitionists. The less that is said of that meeting the better. Next month there will be a ladies' gathering in protest against the anti-abolitionists. I trust you will attend, Miss Fuller."

This time Margaret grasped her end of the trumpet
firmly and stated distinctly,

"Liberty alone is merely the absence of evil, Miss Martineau. Surely you remember your Jouffroy. I am more
interested in positive results. Abolition in itself is but one
of many causes. I prefer to participate in none as yet,
but rather to scrutinize all."

"Well, we shall expect great things of you, Miss Fuller.
But you must bury your pedantic interest in Jouffroy if
you are ever to contribute anything yourself."

"If I am pedantic," Margaret called through the
mouthpiece, "you must attribute it to my early years. At
nineteen, I dare say, I was the most intolerable girl that
ever took seat in a drawing room."
She thought for a moment of Porter's Tavern and the
class of '29, of the days when she had tried to shine as
the grand lady of Cambridge. But Miss Martineau was
tugging the conversation back to abolition.

"This movement is without a doubt the most significant thing that has happened to America."

Margaret had no time to reply, for Mrs. Farrar had
come forth to call her friends to church. During prayers
Margaret knelt beside Miss Martineau and prayed that
Harriet's mind might be kept firmly poised in its native
truth, unsullied by prejudice or error. After church she
broached the subject that had been seething in her mind
all through the day.

"Miss Martineau," she said, forgetting at first to use
the ear trumpet, "when do you plan to return to Europe?"

"Not for another year, I expect. It would be spendid
if you could go with me. Europe is really what you need
now."
Samuel Ward would be going to Europe about that time.
She would see the Raphaels and Leonardos, the villas of
Rome, the great men of England.

"Oh, Miss Martineau!" Margaret grasped the trumpet. "I am sure it can be arranged."

For the rest of the day, let Miss Martineau talk of Garrison's bald head and burning hazel eyes, let her voice her mistaken notions about Hannah More and Miss Edgeworth, let Mrs. Farrar discuss Henry Hedge's new post in Bangor, Margaret heard and thought nothing but Europe. And on the coach going back to Groton, it was Europe that the wheels were rumbling, Europe that the driver was cracking from the whip. Even the last stray robins on the semicircle before the farm were chirping Europe.

Throughout the fall, sewing, or teaching Ellen her Virgil, watching Arthur and William Henry load the grain and her father work on the lowlands, Margaret walked and moved in a dream, the dream of Europe. Even in that strange illness to which she succumbed shortly after she had returned from Cambridge, she did not complain, but lay in bed, looking at the bare walls, on which the word "Europe" seemed to flash in lightning strokes. Her mother called it brain fever, but Margaret was happy. If her eyes were clouded at times, they would soon awaken to bright visions of the Colosseum, of the ruined Forum, of Raphael's angels.

On the forenoon of September 30, 1835, Margaret came downstairs to join her father at dinner. Her feverish fits had gone.

"Perhaps," Timothy remarked over his rice and milk, "it was a touch of cholera, which I hear may become epidemic in Groton."

"Whatever it was, it has gone."

"You were brave throughout it, Margaret. I realized then that though you have defects, there is no fault within you."

She looked at her father gratefully. This was high praise

from him. He stood up and walked to the window, where the distant Wachusett lay blue under the autumn sky.

"Life has been fairly good to us here, Margaret," he said. "Eugene is prospering with his pupils, and William Henry enjoys his work at Avon Place. Ellen may have her fits of temper, but she is a sweet child. It will not be long before Arthur and Richard are at Harvard. Richard is always his mother's dear lamb. Lloyd does seem rather backward, but perhaps he will develop in time. I think the years here at Groton have done us all good."

It was strange, Margaret thought, for her father to be in a mood for reminiscing.

"Our worldly prosperity," he went on, "may have dwindled somewhat, but we have increased the store of our inner riches. That, after all, is the important thing."

Timothy Fuller turned from the window. As he did so, he seemed to lose his footing and slipped to the floor. Margaret turned toward him to find that he had been taken violently ill. A spasm overwhelmed him; he trembled with chills. Margaret called the boys and together they carried him upstairs to bed. Arthur summoned the physician, while Richard stood, frightened, outside the door.

Timothy Fuller took his wife's hand and looked at the plain gold wedding band upon her finger. He spoke calmly.

"I feel that this illness will be mortal."

He said no more. The doctor came and called it cholera. The minister came and prayed solemnly. Quietly, imperceptibly almost, night stepped into the room. Then slowly the first dawn of October crept pale over Farmers' Row. Timothy Fuller was no longer among them.

Margaret called Lloyd and Richard, Arthur and Ellen into the room. In the dimmest corner sat Mrs. Fuller,

numbed and silent. The children wept aloud and knelt
with Margaret.

"If ever," she cried, "I have been ungrateful to my
father, I will atone for it by fidelity to his children. I
pledge myself to this, oh, God!"

Like the Indians at their council fires, the Fuller family
gathered round the table to discuss their future prospects.
Dark and portentous they seemed. Abraham Fuller had
come to straighten out the complexities of property left
by a man who had died intestate. There was the Cambridgeport house, he had told them; there were two farms,
one in Easton and one in Salem; there was a mortgage
for the purchase-money of the estate on Dana Hill; there
were a few bank shares. Margaret had paid no heed to
this inventory. Mrs. Fuller had looked weary and perplexed.

"Finally," he had said, "I should say the estate may be
appraised at about $20,000. But recollect, this must be
divided among a wife and seven children. There will be
very little income for each, not more than $500 a year.
Life will be difficult for you."

During the winter the boys worked the farm with an
inexperienced hired man whom Arthur dubbed "The
Haughty." Margaret smiled as she watched them assault
him with cornstalks. They were so young. They did not
understand. Even Mrs. Fuller, as she tended the dairy,
making butter and cheese, did not seem to understand.
In November the cow and the two large hogs were killed
for the family table. Though the boys thought the experiences of the winter great fun, Ellen, less easily amused,
often gave way to fits of temper for which her sister admonished her. On one such occasion the child had remarked,

"Christ said the Kingdom of Heaven was like a little child. How can any Christians think that children are born *wicket*?"

Like all the others Ellen was preoccupied with her own thoughts. None of them understood what had happened —none but Margaret, who realized too well what her father's death had signified.

For her there would be, first of all, no Europe. If she had been able to write like a man, she must earn bread like a man. There was no ism to help her out of this necessity. Not St. Simonianism, not Unitarianism, nor any other yet discovered ism. In December Margaret was able to write a piece in praise of Henry Taylor's *Philip van Artevelde,* to hail with joy a new poet after so many stars had withdrawn from the firmament. The article appeared in *The Western Messenger,* but her success brought no comfort. Even her reading was capricious. She dipped in and out of her books, submitting them to the test of sortilege, too impatient to finish them. Her father had died at the time when she had loved him most, and in his death he had forced upon her the cares of a family. She would not break her pledge, but confidence and hope were gone. The conflicts of the last two years through which she had wavered from thought to action and back again to thought had left her weak and weary when more than ever she must be filled with power. She felt that she was like the hero of Balzac's *Mystical Book,* who exercised alternately a masculine and feminine influence. If only the masculine influence were potent in her now!

Her walks were erratic, too. She wandered restlessly along the dull-brown fields of April, over paths on which last year's leaves still lingered. One day she came upon a pool, and watched, bespelled by its undulations. The force of water was magic. How well she understood the feelings of those who had been tempted to drown themselves. She longed for an arm of flesh and blood to cling to. But there was none. There was no father. Samuel Ward would be preparing for his journey to Europe—a journey that should have been hers. She would write to him and tell him how she felt about the magic of water. But he would not reply. . . .

It was a sad birthday, that of May 23, 1836. No mark remained of all the time that had gone; she had won no trophy; Samuel Ward had been cold. She wrote a poem, drew it out of her sorrow, to cry aloud, "Before the fierce glare of Reality the beauteous visions of my morning fly." Reality. In the newspapers reality meant talk of the annexation of Texas and the greatest speech of John Quincy Adams' career. If she could but turn back to that morning at Quincy, when her father had led her into the room where Gilbert Stuart stood painting, back to the time when she had found no sin within her soul. But there was no turning back. There was only the compulsion for driving onward.

When she felt most futile, most incapable of driving onward, Margaret heard that Harriet Martineau had discussed her with Ralph Waldo Emerson. She had told the gentleman of Concord of Margaret's severe disappointment in being denied her journey to Europe and he had replied, "Does Margaret Fuller—supposing her to be what you say—believe her progress to be dependent on whether she is here or there?" The spark kindled again in Margaret's mind. She would show Emerson that she was even more than what Miss Martineau supposed her to be. Surely Harriet could arrange a meeting.

After the lonely winter in that bitter house on Farmers' Row, Margaret stepped forth renewed. The winter of her discontent had passed. In the summer Lidian Emerson sent the invitation. She was to visit Emerson at his home in Concord.

On July 21, 1836, Margaret Fuller boarded the Groton stage for Boston. There she changed at Earl's Tavern on Hanover Street for the Concord coach driven by Obadiah Kendall. She was on her way to meet Ralph Waldo Emerson! Through the North End of Boston the coach rumbled on, through Prince Street and Charter Street and Ann Street. Margaret glanced out at the ragged urchins and poorly dressed women who contrasted with the silken parades of Washington Street. Within the coach there were lawyers returning from court, ministers exchanging with their country brethren, traders going to supply the country stores, ladies returning from a visit to the city. Margaret might have formed acquaintances or joined conversations on the crowded carriage, but she had no desire to talk.

She was turning over in her mind everything she had heard about Emerson, considering the best way to win him over. Mr. Fullerton had said, she recalled, that he had dined in boots at Timothy Wiggin's. Surely then he was above the trivial conventions of the day. Everybody knew by now that he had left the ministry because he refused to partake of the communion service. He must be following his own light, there in the village of Concord. Margaret remembered what old President Adams had said of his doggerel about flowers and his vague cosmic theories. At last she would be able to discuss those theories with him. He had been to Europe and made friends with Thomas Carlyle. How much there would be to talk about. Carlyle loved Goethe as ardently as she did. And Emerson, it was said, was collecting fifty volumes of the German's works. Margaret longed to be in his library, taking the books down from the shelves, glancing through them, turning aside for a brilliant bon mot to her host. But he was a man as well as a philosopher. Lidian was his second wife. How could she appeal to the man in Emerson? They said he was retiring, turned into himself. She would capture him unawares. She would amuse him with her stories, amaze him with her learning. She would attract him by her charms. But why had he buried himself in that square, wooden house Miss Martineau had described? Why would he not come forth and live in the world? Through the dust and mud the coach lumbered on. At last Obadiah Kendall halted his horses before Mr. Emerson's house. There it was—the square, white, wooden dwelling, standing in a grove of pines. What would it hold for her?

Margaret walked through the open gate, over the marble flagstones to the broad, low step before the door. The door opened. Ralph Waldo Emerson was standing behind it. Margaret Fuller looked at the tall, slender, palefaced man, at his long and narrow but lofty head, at his sloping shoulders and thick brown hair. She looked into his strong blue eyes; she glanced at his prominent nose casting a broad shadow over his firm chin. Surely his face had been carved out of rock, rock that no force of wind or water could ever change. He looked at Margaret Fuller. She was plain, he thought, though becomingly dressed. That trick of opening and shutting her eyelids was very disconcerting. Her neck arched magnificently; she seemed too full of fire. We shall not get very far, he thought. But he roused himself and welcomed her courteously to Concord.

She followed the slender figure in the quiet gray suit. Her eye was caught by a picture of Diana above a solid table. Emerson opened the first door on the right of the hall and led his guest into a plain, square room.

"This is my study," he said.

He paused till Margaret had had time to look at the simple wooden shelves lining two walls, shelves packed with books. She looked down at the round pedestal table, grained with gold, in the middle of the room. The table was piled with books also, and the pen next to the morocco writing pad was still wet. The painted china pen wiper lay near it ready for use. She stepped onto the red hearth rug, walked toward the fireplace with its bell metal shovel and tongs at the lower end of the room, and looked up at the copy of Michelangelo's "Parcae." On the mantel shelf she noticed a marble match holder and paper container for lighters.

"That is my bronze Homer next to the match holder." Margaret examined it. Then she turned to look out of the windows at the pine trees that brushed against them. She was in the inner sanctum at last!

Emerson seated himself on the rocker close by the table. There were half sheets of paper on the floor, covered with illegible writing. Margaret sat down on the black round-about chair near the fireplace. She heard a thrush sing its throaty song. How silent the room was. She must begin.

"I see, from your volumes of Goethe, Mr. Emerson," she said in what seemed to him a high-pitched, rather nasal voice, "that you are interested in the master."

"It was Thomas Carlyle," he replied, "who first brought Goethe to my attention. But my own German is very poor indeed."

"I should enjoy giving you lessons in German," Margaret said impulsively, moving restlessly in her chair. Emerson did not answer for a moment. We shall not get very far, he thought again. Then he took up the thread by mentioning the fact that Henry Hedge had spoken to him about Margaret Fuller's translation of *Tasso*.

"Henry is an excellent German scholar, but I fear only a good pastor."

The sketch of Hedge was perfect. Emerson did not want to smile, but he did smile a little, with his mouth shut. He hoped Miss Fuller would not insist on making him laugh.

"Since Henry Hedge has gone to Bangor and James Clarke is out West, I have become very friendly with James' sister Sarah. She is studying now with Washington Allston—his only pupil."

"You are interested in art, Miss Fuller?"

"Exceedingly. My friend, Mr. Ward, has gone to Europe to obtain copies of the masters. When he returns home with his portfolio we shall look at the reproductions together."

"You will be interested then in my Flaxman statuette of Psyche."

Emerson rose to hand the little figure to his guest.

"Flaxman," she remarked, holding the statuette, "has restored to us Greek simplicity of thought. 'Eternal beauty from the sculptured stone'—that is a line from one of my own poems to him."

"You love your Greeks then," Emerson murmured.

"I love the Romans better. There is something of the pagan in me, Mr. Emerson."

Emerson was afraid there was.

"Like Goethe, I believe in fate. This carbuncle I wear in my ring is the only possible stone for me though my name, Margaretta, signifies the pearl. My carbuncle casts the male light and I always wear it on extraordinary occasions." She smiled winningly at Emerson.

There is a charm about her, he was beginning to think, underneath all this chatter about demonology.

"My demon has not been kind to me this last year," she was saying. "My father, you know, has died. And I have been ill. Perhaps it is my proneness to headaches that gives me a kind of second sight like that of St. Francis, when I turn my head to one side. But I must not trouble you with second sight when you have hardly had a first sight of me."

Again Emerson felt that annoying impulse to laugh. He would not open his mouth to emit the sound and so his eyebrows lifted a bit and his nostrils quivered betraying the ground swell.

"I prefer the daylight to limbo. The whole world is an omen and a sign. Why look so wistfully in a corner?"

He glanced down as if for refuge at the books on his table. Margaret followed his eyes.

"You have the Athenaeum copy of Grimm, I see."

"Yes. That is one of my indulgences in the city. Last year I borrowed much of Goethe, Schlegel, and Wieland. I hope to take Novalis from the Athenaeum when I go to town next."

His voice is so rich, Margaret thought, even that hesitancy between words, as if he were sorting his keys to open the cabinets of his thoughts. Yet how he struggles away to the impersonal as if he feared the least intrusion of himself was an offense.

"I have plodded through Novalis. But I see I shall have to borrow your Goethe letters to Merck and to Zelter one day. I have been thinking of writing a biography of Goethe, you know."

"You would be making a fine contribution to scholarship and I should be happy to let you borrow whatever I possess that might throw light upon your work. For myself, I never plod through books, I am afraid. I rather skim or dip, and pause to let my own thoughts simmer. When I read Plotinus, I am interrupted by a bobolink or a bluebird and I realize that nature is the circumstance which dwarfs every other circumstance."

"You have been writing on the subject of nature?" Margaret inquired, craning her neck forward.

"A little essay that will be published shortly. I believe, you see, that things are so strictly related that identity makes us all one. A man tying his shoe is one with moon and plant, with gas and crystal. Plotinus and the bobo-link are unified, for that famous aboriginal push still propagates itself through every atom.

"You would transcend even Pantheism then, Mr. Emerson?"

"Your Goethe strove to find the Arch-plant, you recollect. He understood that a leaf is a compend of nature, and nature a colossal leaf. The drop is a small ocean, the ocean a large drop."

"And man, Mr. Emerson, what is man?"

"Man," he said, deliberating, "is the point wherein matter and spirit meet and marry. The Universal Central Soul comes to the surface in my body."

"You judge the world then from yourself, Mr. Emerson?"

"From myself—from yourself—for we are parts of one identity."

"But I know not what you think of me," Margaret remarked, looking into his bright blue musical eyes.

"Are you sure? You know all I think of you by those things I say to you. You know all which can be of any use to you."

But you have not mined me yet, she thought. I shall be of more use to you than you anticipate.

There was a knock on the door and Mrs. Emerson walked in—tall, slender, somewhat angular, carrying in her arms a beautiful baby. Emerson rose to introduce Miss Fuller to his wife, Lidian.

"I call Mrs. Emerson, 'Queenie.' Since you will be our guest for a few weeks you may as well hear the epithet now as later. And this is Waldo, my son."

Margaret followed them into the dining room. So she followed them every day during those extraordinary weeks at Concord. She saw Mr. Emerson seated at the table, eating his favorite dish, apple pie with coffee for

breakfast. She drank tea with him in the evenings while
Mrs. Emerson sat in her red plush sewing chair withdrawn into a corner—for she loved nooks and corners.
She partook of meat with him once every day. At six
every morning she heard him rise and at ten every evening
she bade him good-night. She saw him in his gray suit
often and occasionally in his black coat and silk hat. On
Sundays she saw him take his hat and gloves from the
drawer that had been built into his Sunday chair. Once
when it rained she saw him in the blue cloak that fell in
large straight folds and made him look as though he had
come to his immortality as a statue. She heard him discuss
the most intimate details of his life as though they were
impersonal attributes of a divine consciousness. The bath,
he said one day, was, "the cutaneous sublime, the point
where the extremes meet, the bitter-sweet, the pail of
pleasure and pain." Once when she had asked Mrs. Emerson about the ingredients of that ever favorite apple pie,
he had interrupted, "No! No! it is made of violets; it has
no common history." In the garden with its orchard of
Flemish Beauties and Pumpkin-sweetings, she watched
him playing with his beautiful boy—nature after Dante—
the bobolink after Plotinus. Often she walked with him
from four in the afternoon till teatime.

"One of my favorite walks," he said, leading her
through the ever open gate, "is toward the Old Manse,
where I wrote my little Nature essay, and from there
down the river to Peter's Field and Caesar's Woods,
then across the meadows and hills to the Virginia Road,
near Bedford, where the Thoreau family lives. I think
it is the day for such a walk."

Emerson, walking so quickly that she had difficulty
keeping pace, told her of the beauty of the Musketaquid
with its sluggish, barely perceptible current. As they
passed the old Hosmer House, set back from the road

and guarded by its rambling stone wall, Emerson told his companion that Edmund Hosmer often ploughed and harrowed for him, and sometimes, in his old shabby cap and blue frock he would attend an evening gathering in the parlor. "Hosmer needs to be watched lest he should cheat himself." Margaret smiled and Emerson continued. "There," he said, pointing to a near-by house, "is a typical Concord home—the front door painted green, with a knocker. But it is always bolted, and you might as well beat on the wall as tap there; the farmer slides round the house into the quiet back door that admits him at once to his fireside and loaded table."

"There is no village, though, quite like Concord, is there?" Margaret commented.

"We have no seaport, no cotton, no shoe-trade, no water power, no marble—nothing but wood and grass; even our ice has bubbles in it. And so instead of supplying the world with granite or coal, we are reduced to manufacturing schoolteachers. I think if the town sticks to that staple, it will become the best in the world."

"I believe that I shall plan to teach soon, Mr. Emerson. My brothers rely on me to see them through college. It is still fortunate, you see, that my carbuncle sheds the male light."

"Have you considered Bronson Alcott's Temple School? I hear that Elizabeth Peabody is leaving him and he may be interested in asking you to assist him. I shall invite him to Concord while you are here, if you wish to discuss the matter. You will find him a most radiant effluence of that divinity of which we are all a part."

They walked silently on, Emerson occasionally pointing out a cardinal flower or some swamp hornbeam. Margaret thought the Thoreau home an ugly, square, flat-faced house, but she longed to ramble through the Old Manse, dull red in the summer afternoon. As they passed the dwelling, Emerson began to tell her little stories about his Aunt Mary, who had been born there. For years she had had her bed made in the form of a coffin. "Her friends used to say, 'I wish you joy of the worm.' Once when Mrs. Thoreau visited her she shut her eyes throughout that lady's stay because Mrs. Thoreau had appeared in pink ribbons. Her wit was fertile, but she never used it for display any more than a wasp would parade his sting."

On the way back Emerson was silent, murmuring a brief reply to Margaret's sallies into Plato and Pythagoras, Richter and Swedenborg. He walked, a gaunt and granite figure, as impersonal as the air in which he moved. And cold he was, like granite too, that stands against wind and water. It would be long before she could break upon that stone.

In the evening Margaret suffered from a nervous headache.

"I was too jubilant this morning," she explained. "You see my demon is failing me again."

She waited for a moment while Emerson stepped out to look at the stars before retiring.

"It is his habit," Mrs. Emerson remarked, "always to step out on a clear night and observe the stars before he goes to bed."

Surely, Margaret thought, he is himself strayed from the skies and trails the star dust behind him. Had I but his calm assurance and he my own fire. The spasms of pain shot through her head. She could not stop to look at the stars.

It was on August second that Emerson donned his black suit and silk hat to fetch Bronson Alcott to Concord. Margaret was in the study when they returned, ready to greet the radiant effluence Emerson had promised her. It was the body rather than the spirit of Bronson Alcott that impressed her first as his long lean figure strode across the doorway, but in those serene eyes that glanced about the room the radiant effluence was manifest. Since Emerson had missed his walk he inquired whether Mr. Alcott would enjoy a ramble with them.

"I prefer the talk to the walk," he declared.

So they seated themselves round the table in the study, Alcott on the black Boston chair with its green velvet cushion, Emerson, of course, on his rocker. Alcott looked about him from Margaret Fuller to his host, as if searching for gleams of insight before he began. Then he plunged into a discussion of the Golden Age and man's lapse from virtue. "He is a lovable but tedious archangel," Emerson reflected. "Surely, he is a man of one idea," Margaret decided. On he wandered from the virtue of apples to the philosophy of the spinal cord and back again to the Golden Age. His temples were gray and worn, but his eyes never lost their radiance.

At last he mentioned his school. His pupils, he said, were learning to live as if in the Golden Age. They were beginning to talk like philosophers when they conversed about the gospels. But Elizabeth Peabody was eager to leave for Salem. There were other difficulties also. Many people, including Harriet Martineau, had accused him of pampering the bodies and overstimulating the imaginations of his children.

"They do not understand," Alcott pursued, "that the contemplation of spirit in the inner being is ever the ground of true religion. Surely spirit is more completely unveiled in children than in those who have grown wise in the ways of the world."

Certainly Mr. Alcott knew more of children than of those who are worldly wise, Margaret thought. His philosophy of education sounded as if it might stimulate her. Elizabeth Peabody's *Record,* she had heard, was a most interesting account of the Temple School. At least she would not have to teach the A B C to pupils who were contemplating their inner spirit.

"Will you consider the possibility of coming to assist me in the winter, Miss Fuller?"

"Indeed I shall, Mr. Alcott."

Emerson looked at his friends. It would be illuminating to observe what would happen when the carbuncle gleamed on the archangel and the fire of Margaret Fuller leaped into the mild and gentle corners of Bronson Alcott's mind.

On the eleventh of August, just before Margaret Fuller boarded Obadiah Kendall's stagecoach for her return to Groton, Emerson offered her the autograph of Jeremy Bentham as a departing token.

"I shall lay it in lavender, Mr. Emerson. It is a most appropriate gift to a lady of enthusiasm."

Mr. and Mrs. Emerson with baby Waldo stood before the doorway to wave good-bye. As he turned back to his study Emerson reflected that Miss Fuller was a very accomplished and a very intelligent person; yet by no means free from the egotism of time and place and blood; rarely impersonal, yet—because of that, perhaps—a personality. He picked up his pen and sat down in his rocking chair, the paper on his knee. He was looking at the stars once more.

Margaret on the coach and back at Groton was looking at the stars also—stars that she carried in her mind, stars fallen from Mr. Emerson's own eyes. If he could cast his glittering rays upon her, she would warm him with her fires. They were still at the beginning of things.

When the news finally reached her that Elizabeth Peabody had decided to open classes for women in literature and history at Salem, Margaret wrote to Bronson Alcott.

"My acquaintance with your views and character is not sufficiently thorough," she informed him, "to give me a confidence that I could satisfy you. But I think, as far as I understand your plan, I might carry it into execution as successfully as most persons; and I would like to become more conversant with your method of teaching." Perhaps that was a little too self-deprecating, she considered. She continued, "It would be but an experiment on both sides, for, as I have never yet been subordinate to anyone I cannot tell how I should please or be pleased." The proposal was definitely attractive. It would mean Boston, and eventually it would aid toward sending Arthur and Richard to Harvard. It might also mean more frequent encounters with Mr. Emerson. Yes, the proposal was decidedly attractive.

Not long after Margaret had written the letter, she read an announcement of the publication of Emerson's *Nature*. She and Anna Barker bought copies and exchanged them. Margaret still hoped that Emerson would honor her with a copy, however, and at length he did. She placed the essay near her Goethe on the book shelf. But it would not stay there long. Groton with its pain and waves of despair would soon be part of the past. The world was still before her.

The gift of Emerson's *Nature* was soon followed by an invitation to Margaret to visit Concord again, this time for the purpose of participating in a meeting. Margaret was not quite clear about the nature of the society to which Emerson referred. She simply knew that at the bicentennial celebration of Harvard College he had met George Ripley, Henry Hedge, who had come down from Bangor, and George Putnam; that they had entered into conversation about the growing narrowness of Unitarian doctrine, and then had talked further at Willard's Hotel. The result had been a small meeting at George Ripley's home in Boston on the nineteenth of September, at which Mr. Alcott, James Clarke, back from Kentucky, and Lydia Child's brother, Convers Francis, had joined the ranks. The club had no name and Margaret was not certain about what the members intended to discuss, but the meeting would be stimulating, she was sure.

As she walked through the ever open gate of Emerson's home in Concord, Margaret heard voices in the study and turned into the room immediately. A fire burned behind the cast-iron grate. Alcott was there with Elizabeth Peabody. Margaret had not noticed those two deep wrinkles spreading down from his mouth, or the lankness of his long hair. Elizabeth Peabody had not been very courageous in abandoning him when he probably needed her more than ever. But then, for all her learning, she was a timorous creature. Margaret observed that she was becoming quite stout and almost untidy. She looked half asleep though Margaret knew well enough she could hear the most hushed whisper especially if it concerned herself. She had no doubt heard the whispers in the parlors of Back Bay after Alcott had invited Sylvester Graham to address the Temple School. That was why Salem seemed to her more attractive than Boston at the moment. She might be learned, but she lacked a man's courage. It was surely the time for Margaret to take her place.

James Clarke rose to greet her. He looked firmer, more resolute after his western sojourn. He had taken over *The Western Messenger* from Ephraim Peabody, and as he introduced Mr. Peabody to Margaret, assured her that he expected as many articles from her as his predecessor had received. Standing near-by was the Reverend Mr. George Ripley, who, Mr. Emerson was saying, knew "everything about Herder and something of Kant. And here," he continued, "is Mr. Theodore Parker, of whom you may have heard." Margaret recalled the young lad who had carried a folio under his nose as he walked through Cambridge. "He is pulling up the weeds in the old social order, while Mr. Ripley, I suspect, is occupied in planting the seeds of a new one." In his black broadcloth Theodore Parker seemed stocky and ungainly with hands that still bore traces of having managed the plow. He was strong to pull up weeds—and there were enough rank ones to be uprooted.

John Sullivan Dwight next approached Margaret and actually blushed when he was introduced as "one who would sing his way to heaven rather than preach himself there." He was quite small, Margaret thought, short and slender, but he had a genial face. "Now," Emerson said, "let me present Mr. Brownson. At the moment he is organizing a society in Boston for Christian Union and Progress. But if you wish to hear about it, ask him immediately, for in the next hour he may have turned his interests elsewhere." Orestes Brownson, having decided some time ago that woman was the weaker canoe, paid little attention to Margaret and turned to Cyrus Bartol, who was discussing the flaws in Emerson's religious views. Margaret glanced at Cyrus Bartol and was charmed by his elfish attitude, suggested, no doubt, by those searching eyes of his. Though she knew he lived on Chestnut Street, among the patricians of Boston, she had heard that his mind was like a mint, continually sticking at bright coins of thought.

She looked about the study; it was actually crowded. The black haircloth sofa and the red plush easy chair were both occupied. Caleb Stetson was sitting in a corner near the green plush wood box, gravely discoursing with Convers Francis. How many bright and eager faces there were. Just as Convers Francis was about to rise and open the meeting Mrs. Sarah Ripley entered—Sarah Alden Bradford Ripley, who reflected her pedigree, as everyone knew, in her great learning. She was rather tall and moved quickly, angularly, as she went about from one to another. Her eyes were charged with intelligence. Margaret had heard that years ago Mrs. Ripley had in some strange manner learned German by means of a French and Russian dictionary. She could shell peas, it was said, rock a cradle, teach a rusticated youth his Latin grammar, and read the Greek Testament at once. Margaret knew she was the half-sister of Emerson's Aunt Mary; the Fullers would find it difficult to surpass such a family. In her plain black robe and simple lace cap one would never have guessed that she was "up to her mind's elbows" in a study of carbon. But so she was saying. And so she was.

The room suddenly became silent as Convers Francis, the senior member, arose and called the meeting to order.

"We have no name as yet and so I hardly know how to address you. Perhaps it might be wise to consider a name for ourselves."

"The Symposium Club would be appropriate," said Alcott, his azure eyes gazing serenely at the ceiling.

"Why not call ourselves the Hedge Club?" suggested James Clarke. "We shall probably meet whenever Henry Hedge can run down from Bangor."

"The philosophy which we are meeting to discuss will probably be derided by the Boston merchants as transcendental," Emerson deliberated, "since we seek to transcend the categories of the real for the ideal. I should like to propose as our seal two porcupines meeting with all spines erect and the motto, 'We converse at the quill's end.' For so we did converse at our last two more informal meetings, and so I hope we shall continue."

"I am still not quite clear," interrupted Margaret, "as to the nature of this transcendental doctrine."

"We have no doctrine. Behold, we make all things new." Alcott smiled benignly.

"We have some doctrine," returned Theodore Parker, closing his brown hand into a fist. "I am sure none of us would carp at Kant's principle of the fidelity of the mind to itself or at Frederick Jacobi's insistence on faith."

"I prefer the word 'Intuition' to the word 'Faith,'" interrupted Alcott. "By intuition we know that God is a creation of the soul. We need no Schleiermacher to understand that religion is not a system of dogmas, but a feeling, an inward experience—intuition."

He spoke the word as though he were caressing all its syllables.

"O for the safe and natural way of intuition!" Margaret whispered sarcastically to James Clarke. "Alcott is afraid to grope like a mole in the gloomy passages of experience."

Elizabeth Peabody opened her eyes.

"In this respect," she summed up tersely—"we differ from the Unitarians, who look without for knowledge rather than within for inspiration."

She cannot forget, Margaret thought, that she once assisted Dr. Channing.

"Precisely," murmured Dr. Francis. "The seeds of truth are contained within the soul."

"Within everyone's soul," Emerson reminded. "For mind is immanent in all things and the individual intellect is indissolubly linked with the primal mind."

"Then," decided Margaret, "we must work in behalf of the slave, in behalf of all souls that are degraded by others—since all are divine."

"We must indeed," agreed Alcott. "But before we allow ourselves any activity we must round out our contemplations."

"We must watch the stars before we pull the wagon," observed Emerson in his penetrating voice.

"Emerson," Margaret murmured to James Clarke,

"may be an authority on stars, but surely not on wagons." As she listened to the group weaving their way in and out of Kant and Fichte, Novalis and Richter, Cousin and Coleridge, she felt that though it was all very exciting, somehow it did not lead very far. Alcott was off on a tangent about the spinal column, James Clarke had introduced the necessity of self-culture, and Orestes Brownson was dilating upon the body as the dwelling place of the soul. Emerson expanded magnificently on the spiritual nature of man and at last the meeting broke up. Beyond the mere loosening of tongues, Margaret felt they had accomplished very little. Go help the man in the street, she wanted to cry, instead of calling him a spiritual soul. Emerson must have noticed her look of annoyance, for he turned to her and said,

"It is true that with a wave of her hand, Mrs. Barlow told me that transcendentalism means 'a little beyond.' But if we open our minds to the new influx of light from the Divine Mind, we shall be able to trail some of the cloud-glory back to earth in good time. Be patient."

"But, Mr. Emerson, I lack your rather provoking equilibrium. You forget that one cannot learn the universe by thought alone."

With that she strode out of the room, waving good-bye to the "transcendentalists," the microcosms who sometimes, she decided, thought they were whole planets.

Back at Groton Margaret reconsidered the new thought and longed more than ever to leave the clouds for the earth. In October she opened a letter from Emerson and learned that Francis Sales and Pietro Bachi would be willing to teach the pronunciation of German, French, and Italian to any ladies who might read those languages with Margaret Fuller during the winter. She immediately sat down to indite a circular announcing instruction in German, Italian, and French literature for classes of ladies. She would thus "appropriate to them," she wrote, "some part of the treasures of thought which are contained in the classical works of foreign living languages." Her Uncle Henry, she knew, would be glad to allow her the use of his rooms at 2 Avon Place. She would be ready to start in November. Then Margaret added three regulations governing the hours and the price. There would be twenty-four lessons, two each week; $15 would be the price of the entire course.

With her work at Alcott's school, these classes would give her independence. She was not one who could be contented with exploring the skies. The last three years had been full ones, for all her despair. She had suffered in the white frame house during Arthur's illness, during the loading of grain, during the draining of the lowlands. Trenton Falls had been rapture, but that too had ended in despair. Then Father had died, died before his time. But she had studied much and written well. She had met the new thinkers of the day. All of them, even the gentle, impersonal Emerson, were overwhelmed, she considered, by the very thoughts through which they sought freedom. She was a little weary of thinking, weary of feeling. It was time to carry the thoughts downward into the earth, to root them in action. It was time to forget the inner struggles she had experienced in Groton, to slough off the airy meditations that enfolded the gentlemen of Concord; it was time to rise up, and go forth into the world, to work—to act. She had had her fill of thinking. She knew that from the meeting at Emerson's home. The wave was at the crest again. She would take it at the full.

CHAPTER V

MR. ALCOTT'S TEMPLE

I T WAS fortunate for Margaret that her Uncle Henry
lived at number 2 Avon Place and was willing to rent
rooms to his niece. The day began with a brief good-
morning to Uncle Henry as he lingered over his hot biscuit and coffee before leaving for his law office at 6 State
Street. Before the month of January was over the walk
from her rooms to Alcott's Temple School became as
familiar to Margaret as Tory Row or Main Street in
Groton. As she crossed Washington Street she passed the
imposing houses of Handasyd Perkins and James Savage,
banker and antiquarian. She was sure to see a few fashionable ladies in their French furs, ready for an early
morning shopping excursion. The Boston winter was cold
enough for the men to wear their beaver caps and coats
of buffalo skin. Occasionally the scene would be varied by
the passing of Maria Chapman, bent, no doubt, upon
some abolitionist mission, while the ladies would wrap
their French furs closer about them and murmur to one
another, "There goes Captain Chapman." Washington
Street was no sooner crossed than Margaret found herself on Temple Place and once there she saw the two
lofty Gothic towers of the Masonic Temple rising clearly
above the Great Mall, flanking the entrance of the granite
building on the upper story of which Mr. Bronson Alcott
held his school.

Margaret arrived a little after nine in the morning and
entered the high square room with its Gothic window
overlooking the Common. She never wearied of wandering about the room as the children sat writing in their

journals. Alcott greeted her always with a remark about his educational philosophy. One day he would be sure to murmur, "Today we shall learn humility from these enlightened children." On another occasion he would whisper, "Soon we shall help young George to harmonize his outward life with his inner light." Or again he might remark, turning his sky-blue eyes to his assistant, "Soon Lemuel Shaw will learn to discriminate spiritual happiness from bodily ease." Then he would hand Miss Fuller a few pens to mend while he prepared pencils and both would wander noiselessly about the room.

Margaret liked to walk on tiptoe to the bust of Plato that surmounted the bookcase opposite the window. Fixed into the center of the case was a cast of Jesus in *alto relievo*. Plato and Christ—in Bronson Alcott's Temple! Then she glanced around at the children, each seated on a chair at a little distance from his neighbor. There were children of Unitarians, of Calvinists, of Baptists, of Swedenborgians, Episcopalians, Methodists, Universalists, and Free Inquirers. One day Mr. Alcott had confided wistfully that he longed to have a Catholic and a Quaker. Plato and Christ looked benignly on. From another corner Margaret saw that Socrates also watched the scene approvingly while Shakespeare and Milton stared enigmatically from their pedestals. Little Susan Perkins, she noticed, had just been ready to whisper when her eye was caught by the figure of Silence with finger on its lip, and the child had turned quietly back to her journal. The Italian sculptor in School Street would have been gratified. Margaret wondered if the pupils would be induced to aspire, also, when they glanced at the statue of the Child Aspiring, his arms stretched out and up toward heaven, his mantle curving downward. The clock ticked on. Harding's portrait of Dr. Channing looked down sweetly. The stove brought warmth into the room. Mar-

garet walked over the bright carpet to the black tablet
that had been adorned with a diagram of the human
brain. Then she seated herself at the assistant's table, on
which a small figure of Atlas bent under the weight of the
heavens.

As Alcott took his seat Margaret noticed for the first
time that the head of Christ had been placed as if to sur-
mount his own. He leaned over the arc of his desk and in
a low voice asked the children to carry their chairs and
form a semicircle around him. Little Samuel Tuckerman
scraped his chair as he dragged it along. Alcott mildly
bade them all move their chairs back and forward again.
The lesson had begun. In his prospectus of the month
Alcott had described the ten o'clock period as one devoted to spelling. But by this time Margaret as well as the
children knew that there would be more conversation on
the meanings of words than recitations of spelling. Before long the word "conscience" led to Mary Ellen
Bridge's remark that heaven was located in her best part,
while Susan Perkins swung her slate before her to record
her belief that Dr. Channing was like Jesus. Even George,
who said he could see no benefit in temperance and would
eat "a lot, if things tasted good," had opened Mr. Alcott's copy of *Pilgrim's Progress* for fuller illustrations
of the meaning of "conscience." The sand in the hour-
glass had run through the aperture. The tiny alarm clock
pealed sweetly the end of the hour. Alcott, tossing his
long hair back, asked,

"How many of you have been interested in this lesson?" All hands shot up. Rising from his desk, Alcott
whispered to his assistant, "You see that spelling does develop the imaginative faculty."

Having contemplated spirit in the conscience of the
Infinite Being, the children trooped out toward the Common to contemplate spirit in external nature. Margaret

and Alcott walked with them during their period of recreation. Sometimes five-year-old Louisa May Alcott could be seen dashing around the Frog Pond, while her sister Anna shouted warnings that she would one day fall in. Though Louisa had once announced that she loved everybody in the whole world she was more interested in fun than in her father's explanations of Eastern philosophy which he intoned as he stood with little Emma Savage before the ginkgo tree. Lemuel and Samuel preferred racing after the boys who were coasting down the snowy slopes, their arms akimbo and their legs stuck out. Martha and Abba discussed one of Krummacher's parables as they wandered about the white paths, and John Ware was delightedly narrating a story without an end to his friends, Edward and Nathan.

After recess Margaret retired to the anteroom with a group of older pupils to give her Latin lesson while Alcott taught arithmetic to cultivate the rational faculty of the younger division. Today Margaret knew that she would have to teach Latin from the point of view of the English definition of "conscience," for Alcott insisted on the interrelation of subjects. She needed all her ingenuity to unearth illustrations of "conscience" in Leverett's *Latin Tutor* or the *Historia Sacra,* but it was simple enough to find correspondences in Virgil. Abba was ardently voicing her opinion of the conscience of Aeneas when he turned from Dido. It was far more interesting certainly than teaching Richard the location of Turkey-in-Asia. Margaret sat alert at her desk while Martha waved her hand to dispute the case in behalf of the abandoned Dido. There were low murmurs from the adjacent room—murmurs that had begun in recitations from Fowle's *Child's Book of Arithmetic,* but which now turned to a debate on the aesthetic properties of arcs and circles.

It was an unusual school, let Harriet Martineau write all she would about Alcott's engendering hypocrisy in his children, relaxing their bodies and pampering their imaginations. He had his ideals, rather, his one ideal. His very mistakes arose from his great simplicity. He was, perhaps, too impatient of the complex. He loved the mind with greater zeal than the body and did not quite understand the reaction of matter to spirit. But, as she listened to Abba heatedly siding with Aeneas in the matter of conscience, Margaret felt that without Alcott's teachings the girl would never have been able thus to fortify her own soul. Surely, Ellen, for all her sister's efforts, would be incapable of such high morality. It was stimulating. Margaret began to feel that perhaps it had been too stimulating. Her head ached; she knew she would have to rest in order to be ready to receive her private pupils the next morning.

The Temple School was perhaps a little one-sided. It was the temple of the spirit. There was the world, too, Margaret reflected, as she walked out of the anteroom, past the figure of Atlas; and there was the body that cried aloud for its own temple. Variety in unity. Alcott knew only the unity. Margaret realized that she was destined for a bitter knowledge of the complex, that she would never find the simple refuge to which he had dedicated his Temple.

On her way back to Avon Place, Margaret occasionally bought a bit of bombazine and velvet from Mr. Daniel's store on Washington Street, with which to primp the skirts she wore fulled on to the waist. She liked to look her best for the private pupils who visited her a few mornings in the week. The scholars who had come for tuition in German would not be very interesting and she

felt it good success when they could translate a few pages
into halting English. Mary Channing, however, Dr.
Channing's only daughter, was able to advance to Schiller's *Don Carlos* and Goethe's *Hermann und Dorothea*.

With the Italian class lessons proceeded more smoothly.
Margaret had ceased to regret the fact that Pietro Bachi
and Francis Sales had, after all, been unable to give her
pupils instruction in pronunciation. It was not unpleasant
to be the sole recipient of the young ladies' plaudits. As
she lay back luxuriously on her sofa, reading aloud parts
of Tasso and Petrarch, and the whole hundred cantos of
the *Divina Commedia,* she basked in the admiring glances
of Jane Tuckerman, daughter of Gustavus Tuckerman,
the Boston merchant. Margaret would pause to show
Jane the Athenaeum copy of Dante she had obtained
through the kindness of her uncle's friend, Thomas Davis,
a shareholder in the Society. The Flaxman designs were
so lovely, and Jane occasionally would conclude the lesson
with a little song. The child had a beautiful voice; soon
she would be able to roll her tongue about the luscious
Italian syllables. Then there was young Mary Ward,
whose name conjured up that other friend named Ward.
Samuel was in Europe now, Margaret thought, looking at
the Raphaels or Leonardos. Her head ached a little and
her spine seemed to send spasms of pain into her brain.
But on she read, canto after canto. Perhaps he would return soon. . . . Susan Burley, the grand lady of Salem, had
sent her niece to Margaret as a private pupil. Her name,
appropriately enough, was Flower; her petals opened as
Margaret read on. When Marianne Jackson was not ill
she also came to sit at her teacher's feet, and later in the
morning appeared a little boy who could not use his eyes.
To him Margaret read the *History of England* along
with Shakespeare's historical plays and even taught him a
little Latin orally, much in the manner she followed at

Alcott's school. Sometimes, when her headaches had disappeared, she would serve rice tea to her pupils from the little tin kettle that Mrs. Farrar had sent to her.

They were pleasant enough, these private lessons in the comfortable room on Avon Place, but somehow Margaret did not feel herself so much in and of the world as she had anticipated. The admiration of these young girls left her unsatisfied, even when they coupled it with a knowledge of *Goetz von Berlichingen* and Ariosto. Perhaps the room was too small or the audience too limited. Perhaps, as Dr. Randall had suggested, she was overtaxing her eyes. There was something amiss, despite the rice tea and the bombazine, despite the rolling cantos of the *Divina Commedia*.

The girls were not loath to confide in Margaret after the morning lessons were over. Many were the tales that Mary Channing had told her of her earlier teacher, Elizabeth Peabody, who used to come to read to her father in the evenings. He was looking for another reader, now that Miss Peabody was in Salem. Perhaps Miss Fuller might consent to fill her place? On and on the girl prattled and though Margaret had met Dr. Channing at Newport, she became more familiar with his habits now than she ever had been when she saw him face to face. She heard about the little hand bell with which he called the family to worship at their summer home; she even heard that Dr. Channing could stomach nothing more than black tea and one slice of brown toast for breakfast.

The girls were ready enough with their confidences, but Margaret longed for more significant ones. If only, she mused, Ralph Waldo Emerson or Samuel Ward were so quick to impart his personal self to her. The mornings proceeded. Sometimes the headache was less violent, sometimes more. Sometimes the bombazine trimmed the skirt, sometimes the velvet. But nearly every lesson was punctuated by the *Divina Commedia,* and Flaxman's drawings, and Jane Tuckerman's charming voice, and the tin kettle of rice tea. It was not unpleasant. But where was the crest of the wave in time's smooth waters?

On Sunday morning Margaret walked to the Temple School to record Alcott's Conversations on the Gospels. The mild and blue-eyed teacher had announced as his text for January eighth the "Sermon on the Mount." Two volumes of these Conversations, Margaret knew, had already been published and a storm of disapproval was lowering on the promontory of Beacon Hill. It was in the character of a courageous and tolerant spirit, therefore, that she proceeded to report Conversations for a third volume. Moreover, these talks were so interesting, that, seated at the assistant's table, Margaret sometimes held her pen aloft, unable to write and listen at once.

Alcott, reaching over the arc of his desk for the tumbler of water near-by, began by saying, "Nothing, I hope, is to be said here without thought. Nothing is to be expressed, no hand is to go up without thought." Samuel Tuckerman and John Ware, Susan Perkins and Mary Ellen Bridge looked gravely at the face that shone forth below the head of Jesus. Alcott was gratified. He opened his Bible and began to read the "Sermon on the Mount." The winter sun cast warm lights upon the carpet. Alcott looked up from the book and paused.

"In which of the verses have you been most interested so far?"

Abba repeated the sixth verse and Alcott spoke quietly,

"All of you who take more pleasure in indulging your appetites than in doing right may say so."

Edward, Lemuel, and John raised their hands. Then Alcott began to think aloud; at least so Margaret concluded, for he was wandering far afield, losing himself in abstractions about spiritual desire. Edward, Lemuel, and John looked for succor toward Miss Fuller, whose pen was suspended above Atlas' burden. Alcott, who satisfied himself with apples and expected to restore the world by a return to acorns, did not understand the importance of matter. But John and Edward and Lemuel did. So did Miss Fuller.

Quickly she started up and down the page, racing her pen to make up for the time lost in speculation. They had turned to verse three and with it to a conversation on persecution. Charles was remarking,

"Mr. Kneeland is persecuted. I don't think he ought to have been if he thought he was right. He may take a wrong view and think the Bible is a dream and yet be a good man. I don't think he ought to be persecuted for what he thinks."

Margaret thought of Abner Kneeland, who had been imprisoned for atheism and for whose release Dr. Channing had signed a petition. She wondered how many good Boston churchgoers were atheists in heart as they were in action. But Samuel was speaking now. She must race the pen.

"He ought to be punished if he tries to make other people think as he does."

George was quick as a flash in reply.

"He only does as we do. We try to make people believe in God."

Now Charles was bubbling over with eagerness to list the names of other men who had been persecuted. There were Mr. Graham and Mr. Brownson, and also, he was saying, Mr. Emerson.

"How has he been persecuted?" Alcott asked, smiling the shadow of a smile.

"Why," returned Charles, "people seem to misapprehend his opinions."

Alcott quickly turned to his tumbler of water and

Margaret bent her head close to the paper. Verse five led them on to a discussion of meekness, and when Alcott asked—surely with patent self-consciousness, Margaret thought, and with no meekness at all—

"Is there any one in this schoolroom who is meek?" several answered in unison, "Mr. Alcott." Later, John Ware confessed that one Sunday, after a Conversation on the Gospel, he had stuck a pin into his cat. At the end Mr. Alcott looked thoughtfully over his arc and murmured,

"You must attend if you wish to have thoughts rise in your minds. The thoughts cannot be *put* into your mind; they must spring up themselves. The mind is not like a tumbler into which anyone can pour what he pleases, but like a place where seed is sown."

Looking toward the portrait of Dr. Channing, he continued, "I am glad you believe in the Soul for a great part of the world do not. They believe in the body, but not in the Soul."

Now, thought Margaret, who is filling the tumbler with Spirit?

"How many of you have been interested in our Conversation today?" All raised hands, though John Ware, mindful of his confession, held back some time, and Lemuel, still insistent on the right to indulge his appetite, was last.

Alcott, looking over his assistant's report for the day, reminded her of the necessity of seizing the spirit rather than the form of the conversation. Margaret felt again that he was decidedly one-sided, that there was something in his view of life that revolted either her common sense or her prejudices. But he was satisfied with her ability to adopt his spiritual philosophy.

"You are," he said gravely, "a person given to the boldest speculations, and of liberal and varied acquirements. Yet, you are not wanting in imaginative power. That is all-important."

Margaret did not reply. Her speculation, at the moment, was indeed bold. Alcott is one-sided, she was thinking, but it is profitable for me to acquaint myself with one who can see Heaven in an apple and Christ in an acorn.

On two afternoons of the week Latin recitations in Alcott's school were suspended for recreation and duties at home. On those days Margaret occasionally walked to her uncle's office on State Street, there to wait until he had completed his day's work. Then they would walk together, nodding to the Boston merchants who had just left their countinghouses or insurance offices. Sometimes Margaret would speak of the news she had received from home. The new hired man, dubbed by Arthur "the elephant," was reading Scott's *Napoleon,* marking all the long words he could find in the book, and was resolved upon becoming an itinerant phrenologist. The boys had begun their winter skating and Richard and Arthur were tending to the three cows and pair of oxen. At the head of State Street Uncle Henry paused to make his purchase of food—a fowl occasionally, which he would carry under his arm, wrapped in fresh paper. Sometimes they would stop at Mrs. Nichol's confectionary shop on Court Street and sit together in the small parlor over a cream cake.

On February twenty-seventh, instead of spending a free afternoon with her uncle, Margaret had arranged to meet her friend Sarah Clarke at the Athenaeum. The air was clear and the houses bright and gay as she plied through Washington Street to the Common. The white stone and red brick glowed; the green blinds twinkled as they flapped under the winter sun. The gilded letters of the signboards shone merrily, and the clown and pantaloon swung in the wind. When Margaret entered the Athenaeum she picked up the pen to write her name in the Visitors' Book and noticed the inscription, Mr. W. H. Clarke, Chicago. Sarah had surprised her then. The brother of whom James had said so much was here. She

bought the catalogue of the eleventh exhibition of paintings for twelve and one-half cents and walked into the
Gallery.

Sarah was happy to greet her friend, brimming over
with her own studies under Washington Allston, eager
to hear of Margaret's work with Bronson Alcott, impatient to present her brother.

"William," Sarah explained, "has built a store on
Lake and Clark Streets in Chicago, for the sale of drugs
and medicines. He says nothing can induce him to return
East."

Margaret looked at the tall figure and the open, ruddy
face. James had said he was like her and would understand. His eyes were gentle, though not black—the color
of conquest.

"Do you plan to stay in Boston long, Mr. Clarke?"

"No indeed," he smiled. "This is a brief visit. But I
hope that one day you will visit my city."

Margaret felt a slight twinge of disappointment. This
man was so different from Uncle Henry or Bronson Alcott, so different indeed from his brother James.

Sarah drew Margaret and her brother to Benjamin
West's "King Lear" and Margaret raised her new lorgnette to examine the painting.

"Look at this Guido Reni, " Sarah called. "The lights
are not led along in waves, as they are in Raphael, but
Judith's hands! They seem to move!"

"That is decidedly Italian," Margaret commented.
"The body becomes intellectual and all the limbs take part
in the expression of feeling."

"Is not that true with all the arts?" asked William
Clarke.

"All high works of art," Margaret returned, "are a
reflection of human nature. The plastic arts, however,
are especially busied with the human body."

"You have been reading Bell's *Notes on Anatomy of Expression in Painting*," Sarah murmured wisely.

"You must not give away my secrets, Sarah. But see how different those Copleys are from the Domenichino 'David.' To the Saxon the body is a convenience, to the Italian a thing alive with beauty."

Le Baron Russell of Plymouth passed the Copleys at that moment and paid his respects to Margaret. William Clarke wandered off with his sister to examine Allston's "Italian Scenery." Margaret turned to look at him. His hair was caught by a shaft of light. "Feathers and dust— today and yesterday," she murmured under her breath. Le Baron Russell was informing Miss Fuller of the new books that had been purchased by the Athenaeum. He was sure that she would be interested to know that Alcott's *Conversations on the Gospels* had figured among them. But William Clarke was still standing just where Samuel Ward had stood; his hair was caught by the light just as that other head had been caught. She turned toward the Domenichino again. "Feathers and dust—today and yesterday."

The dust of yesterday had been involuntarily stirred up and Margaret knew she must brush it away with today's bright feathers. The Clarkes would go on to Ashburton Place. Margaret would return to her room before her evening reading with Dr. Channing.

"His daughter Mary, whom I teach, has induced me to read German aloud to her father. I visit him one evening a week and this happens to be the evening. I shall not see you then," she turned to William Clarke, "unless I happen to journey West."

The elms and buttonwood trees on the Common were bare. Margaret wrapped her mantle closely about her and set her mind in order for an evening with Dr. Channing. He possessed the sense of the beautiful, but he held aloof. The readings in Herder must not be interrupted by any personal discussions. She walked up the dark, steep paths to Mount Vernon Street on Beacon Hill. At the four-story red-brick house, with its grilled iron balcony, she paused and raised the knocker. Then she ascended the stairs to the study. Dr. Channing was a little hard of hearing and Margaret had to knock twice at the door before he responded.

When she entered she found him seated before the fire, his gay plaid shawl thrown about his shoulders. His eyes glowed as if indeed he had been dreaming that the walls of Jericho would be razed by a silver trumpet instead of a ram's horn. Dr. Channing stirred, removing his Herder from the bookshelf. Margaret sat down and began to read aloud. She had not read long, when he raised a finger to question a point in Herder's philosophy. When Margaret tried to refute him he answered by a long silence. Then he spoke calmly,

"The truth is that our ultimate reliance is on our own reason. I am surer that my rational nature is from God than that any book is an expression of his will."

He may be the high priest of free inquiry, Margaret thought, but he is still deaf in one of his mind's ears. She turned again to Herder, Dr. Channing looking at her with his great devouring eyes—eyes that exaggerated the leanness of his face and the slightness of his form. Margaret remembered having been told that as a youth he had slept on the floor lest he become effeminate. There was about him, for all the ardent powers with which at the moment he was challenging slavery, a certain womanliness. Whatever she read, he was sure to look for a moral. Margaret felt she was not reading well, expecting any moment to be interrupted by the raised finger, the pause, and then the drawling ethical pronouncement. Then it came. The eyes glowed fire. The figure was lost in the shawl. The finger was raised.

"You see how even Herder leads one to the real idea behind atonement—the at-one-ment of God and man, manifest in Jesus."

"You will find the same philosophy," Margaret replied quickly, "in the poetry of Coleridge and Wordsworth—couched in lovelier phrases, perhaps."

"In the poetry of Coleridge and Wordsworth," Dr. Channing pursued carefully, "I find a theology more spiritual than in the controversial writings of either Unitarians or Trinitarians." He turned to his bookshelf and took down his copy of Coleridge. He opened to the soliloquy of Alvar in the dungeon, and read, prolonging every syllable, looking up at Margaret from time to time to make sure she understood.

"In Goethe and Schiller also, you will find such a philosophy," Margaret said when he had finished reading.

"In Schiller, yes. But not in Goethe. Goethe lacked the sovereign moral sense to read aright the riddle of the Sphinx. He wanted depth of heart and moral power. He was not capable of truth to woman."

"But he venerated woman none the less, Dr. Channing. His own personal life was too full of significant activity for us to cavil at a few lapses of conduct."

"Miss Fuller," he answered ponderously, "you blend a feminine receptiveness in your being with a certain masculine energy which permits you to view life differently from most people. You combine the fiery force of Northern and the soft languor of Southern races. You will find that most human beings are dominated by the one or the other quality; it is rare to find both blended as they are in you. Hence you know more of art, for example, than of Christianity."

Margaret was not sure whether Dr. Channing meant her to consider his remark complimentary. That was one difficulty of speaking with him. One could never be certain that behind his sweetest phrases there did not lurk a touch of moral disfavor. Dr. Channing was bent on continuing.

"You, Miss Fuller, would never, I am sure, be guilty of calling the leg of a table a limb, as most of our young ladies do. For the same reason you are incapable of finding the faults in Goethe's own moral system. You must surely come into your own in a day like ours, when Mary Gove is demanding the rights of women in medicine and the Grimke sisters are exhibiting themselves so nobly in the cause of anti-slavery."

"Nevertheless, Dr. Channing," Margaret replied, "I feel that the slavery of the South is merely one cause of many that men as well as women must struggle for. Have you heard, for instance, of the conditions in the Lowell Manufacturing Company, where the girls sleep six to eight in a room, and even three in a bed? We have our own slavery in the North, I believe, as well as in the South."

Dr. Channing was silent. His silence was almost formidable, Margaret thought. Then, at last, he spoke.

"Here in Boston, with our Odeon and our National Theatre and our art-loving Mayor Eliot, we are too easily diverted from the cruelties of existence elsewhere. We watch an equestrian performance at the Lion Theatre or listen with delight to Vandenhoff or Miss Ellen Tree and in our boxes we forget the world outside. As I have said so often at the Federal Street Society, the human soul is inherently good, but the atmosphere in which it lives is bad. We must abolish our national sin of slavery and be temperate and honest within ourselves. Then the Christian virtues will be practised, almost unconsciously."

He blows his silver trumpet well, Margaret thought, as

she turned again to Herder. But still it needs a ram's horn to topple the walls of Jericho. . . .

The walls of a nearer Jericho began to topple when on March 21, 1837, the editor of the *Boston Daily Advertiser and Patriot* decided to publish a review of *Conversations on the Gospels*. Mr. Alcott, Nathan Hale declared, invites his children to express "all their crude and undigested thoughts" about the Gospels and often excites them to a discussion of highly improper points. Alcott and his assistant read the lengthy criticism carefully. Beacon Hill at its worst had stormed the citadel of his new Jerusalem.

"Perhaps," Margaret tried to explain, "it is a result of the financial panic. When fortunes are lost and banks are unsafe, people forget to be liberal."

"Perhaps," said Alcott hopefully. "Let us wait."

They waited, only to read in the *Boston Courier* a letter from a "Parent" who believed that Mr. Alcott would bring the Scriptures into contempt and sap the religious sentiment of the entire community. "One would think," the Parent declared, "that nothing short of actual alienation of mind could have led any man to adopt the strange notion of making children the interpreters of the Scriptures." Mr. Buckingham, editor of the *Courier,* added his conviction that Mr. Alcott must be insane or half-witted and that his friends ought to take care of him without delay.

"Perhaps they will, Mr. Alcott," Margaret smiled wisely. "Let us wait."

They waited. And on April fourth Ralph Waldo Emerson made an attempt to stay the forces of State Street and Beacon Hill by a reply to Mr. Buckingham. "In behalf of this book," he wrote, "I have but one plea to make. Let it be read. Fragments out of a new theology of Christian instruction are not quite in the best place for examination, betwixt the price current and the shipping list. Mr. Alcott aims to make children think, and in every question of a moral nature to send them back on themselves for an answer." Alcott was grateful and Margaret reassured, but on the next day Mr. Eliot hastened to remind the readers of the *Boston Courier* that Mr. Alcott was still a humbug.

Together they walked through the high, square room with its Gothic window and gay carpet. The figure of Silence held his finger to his lip and Socrates looked down, wise as ever. But in the chairs there were only ten pupils left of forty and when Alcott counted his receipts he found they had dwindled to little more than one third of last year's. James Clarke and Margaret herself rose to his defense, but the last word had been spoken. Mr. Alcott was a humbug. Sadly he removed Shakespeare and Milton, Plato and Socrates from their pedestals. Krummacher's *Parables* and the black tablet still adorned with a diagram of the human brain were sold with the smaller slates and the little chairs. Only the Gothic window was left, and the light it cast was no longer bright, for the gay carpet had been stripped from the floor.

Alcott could no longer afford an assistant for his Latin and French classes. Indeed, he contemplated, he no longer needed an assistant.

"I have heard," Margaret informed him, "that 39,000 people are bankrupt. You must not consider this a personal defeat." But in her heart she knew that Bronson Alcott was destined for defeat. In the eyes of State Street he could never be anything but a humbug. In April he moved his family into cheaper quarters at the South End. He would continue to keep school, he said, in the basement of the Temple. It would still be the Temple, still dedicated to his beliefs, though the rooms were in the basement. It was really not defeat, he consoled himself, but a casual decline.

During these trying weeks, Margaret found it as difficult to think as if she had been a haberdasher's apprentice or the President of Harvard University. Yet the collapse of Alcott's Temple was not entirely unpropitious for her. It was not long before Hiram Fuller of Providence had invited her to teach at his new school on Greene Street. He must be a tolerant man, Margaret decided, for he had asked Alcott to deliver the dedicatory address and it was said he had modelled his new school on the Temple. Alcott declined the invitation, but Margaret did not. Providence was not Boston, but then the boys were growing up and Mr. Fuller offered her one thousand dollars a year to teach only four hours a day. She would have time to think, time perhaps to work on the biography of Goethe. Margaret began to look forward to exploring the fresh currents that were flowing into the stream of her life.

CHAPTER VI

THE GREENE STREET SCHOOL

THE TAG end of Margaret's sojourn in Boston was marked by visits to milliners, mantua-makers, and the shopkeepers of Washington Street. Notes were written, dresses adjusted by the deft fingers of the sempstress, and bonnets packed in bandboxes. It was the time for tying up loose ends, for fixing in her mind's eye the houses she would not see for a while. There were a few days for Concord, a few days to sit with Emerson in his garden among the lespideza and blue self-heals, reading *Vivian Grey* and instructing him, against his will, in German pronunciation.

"Now spite of myself," he remarked grudgingly, "I shall always have to thank you for a great convenience. I think you foresaw that, Miss Fuller."

Margaret had foreseen it; she had vaulted another buttress of his mind. That was return enough, but Emerson insisted also on lending her his Milton and Jonson, his Plutarch and Degerando. The Concord house, like the two towers of Masonic Temple, diminished in the distance. This was but a temporary leave-taking. Margaret was sure that Concord would be to her a welcome Lethe again. Yet she would be a different Margaret when next she walked through the open door to sit beneath the Fates.

There were a few weeks for tying up loose ends at Groton, for sipping lemonade on the piazza with William Henry, for admiring her mother's spring garden, and Richard's knack at milking cows. There was time to reproach Boss Rugg, the new hired man, for his drinking

habits and to commend the acres that Arthur had cultivated with corn, potatoes, beans, and pumpkins. There
were evenings to watch the boys play goal and high spy
till the nine o'clock bell rang in the village, evenings to
work over German translations and to read the journal
with which Alcott had entrusted her. Yet everything she
did was in the nature of a leave-taking. Her books were
rearranged, Scougal and Coleridge were returned to
Emerson, the traveling bookcase was packed. At last the
white frame house diminished in the distance and turned
into a bright dot as she waved good-bye and rode away.
After the many *Vales* had been spoken, Margaret was
ready for a new—a more jubilant *Ave*.

The Greene Street School was a white building also,
but how different from the rambling house on Farmers'
Row. With its six columns and simple cornice it looked
like a little Greek temple. Around it, the trees, each protected by an iron railing, sprouted tender leaves. Margaret opened the gate and walked in. As he escorted his
new teacher through the building Hiram Fuller was eager
to tell her the history of his little school.

"Last year," he said, "I had only thirteen pupils—all
boys—and we met in a small room at the corner of Mat-
thewson and Chapel Streets. When the girls began to
enter we had to fit up rooms in the upper story of a near-
by barn. Miss Frances Aborn, with whom you will room,
taught the girls in the barn."

Margaret was more interested in the little rooms for the
children's caps and coats and street shoes than in the past
history of the school.

"I require the boys to remove their ordinary footwear
and put on slippers before they enter the schoolroom,"
Mr. Fuller explained.

The carpet reminded Margaret of the Temple School.
But here all the rooms were carpeted, and every recita-

tion room had single desks and chairs for the scholars.

"There is my desk," Mr. Fuller pointed out. It was on a raised platform. Mr. Fuller, Margaret thought, would speak from above, not from the equal level that Mr. Alcott had assumed. Behind his desk was a bookcase surmounted, not by the head of Plato, but by a bust of Sir Walter Scott. There was a piano between the doors, and over it a portrait, not of Dr. Channing, but of Mr. Fuller himself.

"You see," he was expounding, "when I assumed charge of the school last year, I succeeded an antiquated teacher, a victim of minister's sore throat. It was not difficult for me to institute the reforms you observe, for the citizens were weary of old-fashioned methods."

Mr. Fuller was a practical man, Margaret perceived, for all his advanced notions. No one would ever dub him a humbug.

"Since Mr. Alcott declined my invitation," he was remarking, "I have asked Mr. Emerson to dedicate the school on Saturday. Now you will want to meet the other teachers and rest a bit."

At Miss Aborn's rooms Margaret was to occupy a common parlor with Mrs. Georgianna Nias and her children. Miss Aborn seemed pleasant, but rather commonplace. She was interested in the school above all things and immediately plunged into a discussion of the ways of the younger pupils. Mrs. Nias was different. English, French, and American blood had united in her to form a person of grace and beauty. She looked like a Peri, Margaret thought; that ornament she wore in her hair was charming; surely her smile had captivated the scholars already. Mrs. Nias mentioned her drawing and French classes, but when Margaret spoke of her own classical studies, she was silent, smiling, but never answering. She may be clever, Margaret concluded, but surely she has not had much training. Obviously she preferred talking about her two little boys, who attended the school, to discussing Virgil. Later Miss Aborn told Margaret that a third child had died and that Mrs. Nias was separated from her husband and never mentioned him.

The ladies watched while Margaret unpacked. Miss Aborn was impressed by the books and microscope she removed from her boxes and placed upon the table. Mrs. Nias was more interested in the bonnets and muslin gowns. Mrs. Nias, Margaret thought, would be a more serious rival in the Greene Street School.

On Saturday, June tenth, Hiram Fuller met Mr. Emerson at the cars and escorted him to the City Hotel. At four o'clock the pupils and teachers assembled at Mr. Farley's meetinghouse for the dedication. Emerson rose to deliver his good words, words about Mammon and chaste imaginations, immediate emolument and patient learning, Eastern mysticism, Kant and Fichte. "What is thrice-wreathed mysticism?" Miss Aborn whispered. Mrs. Nias shrugged her shoulders and mentioned something about Germano-Sartor-Resartus-ism. "Here in Providence, we have not acquired the taste for such verbiage." Margaret looked about her. The good words had fallen upon stony soil. Providence was a city of money-getting, where Mammon and not mysticism was master. She would find it difficult to enlighten its torpid minds. Professor Hansen seated himself at Mr. Farley's organ after Emerson's address. Then Mr. Fuller read one of his favorite poems, "We Are Seven." At this the children clapped their hands in glee. Their hearts were well-disposed at any rate, Margaret perceived, though they might lack the lively minds of the Temple School pupils. Teaching at Providence would be more difficult, but if she succeeded, it would be a greater triumph. She looked at Mrs. Nias, who was adjusting a flower on her bonnet. Mrs. Nias had triumphed, no doubt, with a smile. She would win with her mind. The Greene Street School had been dedicated. The children filed out and Margaret went up to Emerson to discuss his speech. Then he returned to his hotel, while she went back to her rooms to rest until classes met on Monday.

Margaret rose at five o'clock and carefully knotted a blue chenille cord in her red-brown hair. The flower or bright jewel in Mrs. Nias' dark tresses was worth imitating. It would be wise to dress carefully, for children, especially here in Providence, set great store by material devices that attracted the eye. Margaret stood before the long mirror in the parlor, adjusting the folds of her muslin dress, drawing the waist of her frock tightly, ruffling the wide sleeves. Every detail must be perfect. The blue chenille cord was striking, she thought. Even though it took an hour to dress, the time was well spent. The body was still the temple of the spirit and must be beautifully robed. There was time to arrange her papers before breakfast. For her classes little preparation would be necessary, but there were those notes on the life of Goethe that she wanted to work at in the afternoons. Margaret placed her books carefully on her table along with her little album of "Notes on Goethe." She would return to them after classes.

School was held from 8:30 to 12:30. Margaret understood, after a brief conversation with Mr. Fuller, that though she was to give instruction in composition, elocution, history, Latin, natural philosophy, and ethics, the classes would be so distributed that they would not fatigue her at all. She opened the gate of "the little Greek temple" and walked over the piazza and through the wide door. The children's hats, she noticed, were hanging on the pegs of the dressing rooms, the boys' caps at the left, above the row of street shoes, and at the right the girls' large bonnets. She walked through the main room, toward the two recitation rooms in the rear. There was a portrait of the poet Percival which she had not observed before. The walls were white, finished with pink; the ceiling was arched with a place in the center for a chandelier. There was a French clock also which had escaped her notice. How well the orange of the heavy carpet harmonized with the black and brown desks and chairs. On each side of the hall Margaret passed two rows of boys and girls, neatly dressed, waiting for Mr. Hiram Fuller to walk up the two steps of his platform. A little girl was filling the two vases on his study table with flowers. A boy was drinking from a glass goblet, having poured water from an urn in front of the platform. Margaret heard the voices of the younger children in the basement, where Miss Aborn would soon start the arithmetic lesson after the youngsters had left the washroom. She walked on to the rear recitation room and faced her class.

The boys in the composition group were eager to exhibit their journals, neatly bound in morocco and lettered on the back, "School Journal." Margaret spoke to them of the dignity of writing and soon entered upon a discourse regarding the style and the man. When one little boy took out his sack of marbles, she immediately awed him into stillness with an imperious gesture and he removed the offending sight from his desk. Then she continued, hoping that not only their thoughts but their grammar would improve during the months that would follow. Perhaps, she felt, she had been a bit too eloquent, for when the bell rang for a change of classes, some murmured "yes'm" and some "no'm" and all took a long breath as they filed out to the next recitation room.

On other mornings the Latin group met in place of the composition class. One tall lad, who had overgrown his tightly buttoned jacket, volunteered the information that the pupils were ready for Virgil. Margaret questioned the scholars and found only one who could translate a phrase into fluent English.

"You will be my leading man in Latin," she said smiling, nodding her head so that the blue chenille cord bobbed up and down. "But I fear the others must review their grammar and perhaps in about thirty weeks we shall be ready for 'Liber Primus.' " The overgrown boy looked disgruntled and began to whisper to his neighbor, but an imperious look was enough to quiet him. The class in Virgil turned into a group that plodded carefully through Latin grammar.

For Margaret the ethics class was more interesting. She soon selected Mary Allen, the eldest daughter of the Reverend Mr. Joseph Allen of Northborough, as the one possessed of the liveliest mind. On the days when even little Ann Brown and Harriet Taine, just of a size, affectionate and lively as birds, could not answer a question from Wayland's *Moral Science,* Mary would be sure to pop up with the correct response. One day Harriet Taine drew up enough courage to inquire why Miss Fuller's classes did nothing but listen to Miss Fuller talk. She said they all enjoyed it wondrously, but after all, was not reciting more important? Margaret swept the dozen girls of the class with a swift glance and replied,

"You must think as well as study and you must talk as well as recite. Above all, you must learn to listen."
Listen they did, their bright curls catching the sunlight through the open window, their young eyes opening wider as Miss Fuller spoke on, so eloquently, of the laws of conduct and right living.

On Monday and Friday mornings the poetry class gathered before Margaret's desk. And there again, the little girls listened. On Mondays they would hear their teacher read a tale, *Ferdinand,* or *Romeo and Juliet* from the Shakespeare stories. After she had read, pouring the lovely phrases into listening ears, the children would paraphrase the story and go home to rewrite it. On Fridays Margaret would assign to each pupil a modern poet, saying,

"Find out all you can about him. Where was he born, where did he die, where did he live, what did he write, what was interesting about him?"
Mary Allen had to be content with Chaucer, for by the time Miss Fuller came round to her, all the modern poets had been taken.

The next week, when Margaret again met the poetry class, she discovered that one of the girls had come unprepared either with a paraphrase or a biographical sketch.

"It is absurd," Margaret said, gazing down with austerity, "for you to attend a school of this kind if you do not expect to do your share of the work. Were you ill?"

"No," the child answered tremulously.

"Then you have no excuse whatsoever. You have simply made yourself ridiculous before all."
The little girl could not answer. She walked out dejectedly after Mary Allen had delivered her piece about the old gentleman called Chaucer.

When Margaret mentioned the child's defection, along with her own reactions to the school, to Mr. Fuller, he seemed less interested than she had hoped.

"You must not react so strongly," he advised, "to the trivial details that confront one in a classroom. After all, I expect to keep my school five years—income so much, outlay so much—and then I shall be able to go to Europe. The Greene Street School is simply a means to an end, not an end in itself." Margaret remembered with what high ideals Alcott had built his Temple. Indeed, he would have refused to exchange it for the Presidency of the United States. Mr. Fuller was without his practical defects, but he also lacked his poetic beauty.

"I am sure," she replied, "that the children take these matters seriously. You forget, Mr. Fuller, that school is life to them just now."

They did take the matter seriously. At the next meeting of the poetry class Mary Allen handed to her teacher a little triangular note signed as a round robin, in which Margaret read that she had been guilty of cutting a pupil into bits, a pupil of rare excellence and character, but so reserved and diffident that she would not explain for herself her failure to paraphrase *Romeo and Juliet*. Margaret took pains to reply at length to the round robin. She apologized for not giving more of her time to the girls, assuring them that she felt more regard for them than she usually expressed. Another teacher, she wrote, might have more time and better health, but she would always be willing to consult their wishes. She hoped she had not been too rough with the pupil in question. If she could but teach the girls confidence and self-possession she would be satisfied. She signed her letter, "Affectionately yours."

Mary went back to her aunt, Harriet Ware, with whom she was living in Providence, and said,

"Although Miss Fuller is very critical and sometimes cuts us up into little bits, I love her dearly."

Harriet Taine and Ann Brown rushed home to say,

"Miss Fuller treats us like human beings—almost like equals."

Margaret picked up the *Tales from Shakespeare* and Wayland's *Moral Science* and walked out slowly over the orange carpet. If the children, she thought, came from families where money-getting was considered more important than language and the cultivation of the imagination, still their minds were becoming less torpid. Somehow the routine of recitation and paraphrase had been elevated into a joyous experience. The portrait of Mr. Fuller looked down a bit skeptically, but the carpet glowed in the light and the blossoms on the study table opened to the sun. Scott gazed approvingly upon the scene. The French clock struck 12:30. Morning after morning it struck 12:30 as Margaret walked across the piazza and opened the gate of her little Greek temple on the corner of Greene and Washington Streets. She did not feel that these mornings were effecting any great changes within her. Perhaps she faced the Ann Browns and Harriet Taines with a little more composure than she had the Lemuel Shaws and Mary Bridges of the Alcott school. Teaching, Margaret reflected, could never be her shaper and moulder. At the moment the material gain seemed more important than the intellectual one. These mornings, after all, were but a part of the day and these days but a part of her life. The afternoons at least were hers, hers for thought and hers for writing.

Margaret's habit was to lie down on her sofa after dinner until three o'clock. Sometimes, after a particularly exciting morning, when her leading man in Latin had offered an interesting interpretation of a difficult line or Mary Allen had shown her a philosophic passage in her "School Journal," Margaret suffered from pains that shot from her spine to her head. On such occasions she resorted to a drop of opium and sleep would come, bringing fantastic dreams. But usually, as she rested, her thoughts turned to Goethe and before her mind's eye passed images from his life and writings. Werther's blue frock and yellow breeches, Goethe as the Weimar factotum, Goethe under the sway of his demon, Egmont led to the scaffold, Goethe with Frau von Stein, Goethe, a Roman in Rome—all moved before her in parade. If Mrs. Nias interrupted or Miss Aborn bustled into the parlor, it was no matter. The parade was endless; the images could always be invoked. These hours of rest, rest only to her body, were of greater significance, Margaret felt, than the Greene Street School. Did not Emerson consider her an astute critic of the German master? Had not George Ripley asked her to write Goethe's life for *Specimens of Foreign Literature?* In this work she would find herself. Even though she might be unable actually to write the biography, she would plan it; her studies would expand her mind.

At three o'clock Margaret arose, eager to think out her plans and write down her notes. She sat before the table near her bookcase where Emerson's copies of Milton, Jonson, Plutarch, and Degerando stood along with her own volumes of Goethe. She opened her album of notes. Definitely, she thought, Goethe's life seemed to parallel her own. His father had forced him to study, very much as Timothy had made her con Blair's *Rhetorick* when she was ten. In place of *The Chronology of the English Kings* Goethe had read a *History of the Popes.* At Frankfort he had organized an acting troupe among his friends. Margaret recalled the performance of *The Rivals* at Groton. When he was a student at Leipzig he had been interested in fashionable dress. Margaret touched her blue chenille cord and remembered the red sash she had worn at Miss Prescott's school. Surely, at Strasbourg, when Goethe had concluded that the rational was less important than the secret forces that permeate the universe, that the visible was as nothing beside the divine power that was only dimly perceptible to spirits in touch with nature, surely then, in his discussions over the table with Herder and Winckelmann, he had prefigured

Margaret conversing about demonology and the cosmos in Waldo Emerson's study. His love for Friederika, the noble woman of *Goetz, Clavigo,* and *Faust*—the *ewig weibliche*—did not this resemble somewhat her own feeling for Samuel Ward—for the *ewig männlicher?* Lying on his back among the trees, drinking philosophic draughts with his friends at Wetzlar, he had been a counterpart of Margaret, Margaret speaking with Sarah Clarke at the Athenaeum, Margaret walking to the Old Manse with Emerson. The golden heart that Lilli Schöne- mann had sent him—did it not bear comparison with the geranium leaf Margaret had given to James Clarke? After her meeting with Emerson how well she understood Goethe's friendship with those seven or eight years older than himself. Further, however, the analogies could not yet be drawn.

Goethe had accomplished so much. Margaret was still at the beginning of things. Perhaps her life would be patterned after his, as her past seemed to have paralleled his past. Goethe had written for a periodical, the *Frank- furter Gelehrten Anzeigen*—the organ of a new genera- tion. Perhaps Margaret would be able to establish such a journal in which her own generation would be given voice. In Italy Goethe had studied Michelangelo. Had not Mar- garet studied the Domenichinos in the Athenaeum? Did she not long also to journey to Italy, dearest to her heart? He had eaten figs on Lago di Garda and grapes in the market place of Vicenza; he had lived with the painter Tischbein and taken part in the Carnival. Margaret turned the pages of Goethe's *First Journey to Italy* and read, "God be thanked that I may again love what was so dear to my earliest youth! That the name of Italy is no longer to be a hollow word." One day, perhaps, she would write such words herself, eat the figs of Italy and drink the wine of the Italian grape. . . . The few Ameri-

cans who knew anything about Goethe called him immoral. But surely he had lived with Christiane Vulpius
only because of his conception of marriage as a sacrament
too holy to be profaned by an unworthy love. Never,
Margaret thought, was marriage more gloriously defended than in *Die Wahlverwandtschaften*. Never would
she wed unless in sacred marriage with one worthy. It
were better that the world cry immorality than that the
holy rite be debased in a degrading union. Then there
were Goethe's political views to be considered. He had
been convinced that the French Revolution had grown
out of the fault of those who governed. Yet he had worshipped Napoleon and considered the common people
unable to govern themselves or make use of their liberties.
From belief in revolution he had settled into contentment
with reform. Perhaps he had been right. The great masses
of people, Margaret thought, lacked the power of contemplation, and hence could not act with intelligence. Yes,
here too there was a parallel in their points of view, although Goethe had come to his convictions in his later
years and Margaret's opinions, she realized, might
change with growing maturity.

How intensely, purely human he had been. Like Wil-
helm Meister, Goethe and Margaret too, had been converted from a life of contemplation to a desire for activity
welded with contemplation. "Restless striving is man's
true sphere.

> *Im Weiterschreiten findet qual und Glück*
> *Er! unbefriedigt jeden Augenblick."*

So Faust had found redemption. So Goethe. So also would
Margaret. Most human of men had Goethe been. Had
not Napoleon said of him, "Voilà un homme!" And had
not Goethe himself said, "The more thou hast the feeling
of being a man, the more thou art like unto the gods."

Being a man, complete, intense, he had become a god. Margaret too would grow, and growing, find divinity within herself.

She opened her album and began the plan of her life of Goethe. She would begin with the preface from *Dichtung und Wahrheit,* with the martinet father and the Frankfort house. Her pen rushed along, carrying Goethe into his love affair with Käthchen, the little milliner, carrying him—or herself—to Strasbourg, presenting him to Herder—so like Emerson—the steady rock that stemmed his impetuous outpour. The outline grew. After Herder came Friederika. When Goethe loved her he was not quite twenty-two. How much he knew even then! Margaret thought of Waldo as a wonder, but at that age he must have been an infant compared with this man. The pen dashed on. Was not Goethe the thinker who made her think? the man of action who made her long for action? She was ready to write about his childhood at last. His childhood? or her own?

At six o'clock Mrs. Nias came in to give Margaret a letter. It was from Emerson and as she glanced down the page, one passage caught her eye. "Power and aim seldom meet in one soul. The wit of our time is sick for an object. Genius is homesick." Margaret smiled. In one soul power and aim had met—in a German soul. Perhaps they would meet again in a woman born in the New World, in a woman who carried the Old World in her heart. Mrs. Nias reminded Margaret that six o'clock meant supper and time to dress for the evening. The sun was low in the sky.

These afternoons, so short in time, so long in thought, were life to Margaret. The little French clock in the Greene Street School tolled her entry into a wider world every afternoon. Day after day at six o'clock she returned, refreshed and glowing, from another life. It was strange to live so many lives in one. The schoolmarm of the mornings became the scholar of the afternoons, who would in turn be transmuted into the lady of the evenings. From life to life, Margaret thought—such metamorphoses were life itself. The mornings might be tame, but the afternoons were sure to be fruitful. And the evenings, Margaret considered, as she restored her books to the shelf and rose from the table, the evenings were always entertaining.

One night Richard Henry Dana had given a talk on Shakespeare. It was strange to listen to the father of the boy who had been dragged by his ears across the dark schoolroom in Cambridgeport. When he lectured his gestures had been naïve, but the expression on his face rapt. His introverted eye and the almost infantine simplicity of his pathos had made Margaret re-experience all the reactions she had felt on first reading Shakespeare. Dana had merely elevated those emotions into a purer atmosphere. He seemed to have held one aim only before him—to preserve his own individuality unprofaned.

There had been another interesting evening, when Mr. Farley had escorted Margaret to a lecture hall to hear Mr. Whipple. Then there had been the time when Tristam Burges had spoken before the Whig Caucus and Mr. Fuller had been horrified that Margaret had attended. It had been heresy—delightful heresy. Providence society could not compare with Boston. But William Chace was always ready to discuss universal reform at Holly Home and his friend, Christopher Greene, could always be relied upon for exciting tales of his father's journey to Canada with Benedict Arnold. Then there was Sarah Pratt, always eager to spend an evening conversing about the Providence Ladies' Anti-Slavery Society, of which she had just become secretary. Then, of course, there was John Neal, and there was Sarah Whitman.

John Neal had come from Portland to give a talk to the girls of the Greene Street School, a talk about the destiny and vocation of women in America. Margaret soon discovered that he could talk about anything. He could be fallaciously witty about Richard Third, erudite about Whiggism, brilliant in a discussion of man, the whole or perfect man, the original or phrenological man. At the moment, phrenology was his great interest. He was eager to talk about Miss Brackett, the clairvoyant of Providence, who had "seen" the enlargement of a man's spleen before the post-mortem analysis proved her right. John Neal had arrived opportunely in Providence, for at the moment grocers, doctors, and factory girls were learning all they could about faculties and animal magnetism. Emerson would have scoffed, but Goethe would have listened. And Margaret was ready to listen.

One evening John Neal invited her to a soiree at the home of Albert G. Greene. Margaret had heard of his poem, "Old Grimes," for who in Providence could escape the principal creation of the town's scholarly judge? Her host was charming. As he led Margaret into his library, pointing out his volumes of English and American poetry, he remarked,

"You see I am the only American poet who has never—and will never—publish a volume."
Margaret thought it sufficiently remarkable that a judge of the municipal court should find time to write poetry. She seated herself in a large armchair, opposite her host, and was just ready to discuss the future of American literature when Hiram Fuller entered. Shortly afterward Mrs. Sarah Whitman came flitting into the room, looking, as John Neal had once remarked, as if she were in process of transformation either to or from the condition of a lapwing. Despite her birdlike flutterings Mrs. Whitman's slight figure and pale face cast a spell upon

the others. It was not inapt that she signed her poems, "Helen." Her deep-set eyes looked not at, but beyond the company. She was wearing a lace scarf and carried a fan which she held against her face as she tripped about the room in her dainty slippers. She spoke, winging her way from point to point, from the red house in which she lived—a color that most distressed her—to the floating veil she had just purchased, on to a poem she had written or a brief reminiscence of her husband John, who had died a few years before. But Mrs. Whitman's talk, however charming, was trivial, and when she mentioned the fact that Samuel Larned was living on apples after a year's consumption of crackers, Margaret broke in to speak gravely about Alcott's ethereal taste in food as an indication of his spiritual nature. He was, she said, as celestial a body as one could find.

Celestial bodies led Mr. Neal to the mutual influence that existed between the planets and the earth, and soon he was well off on a discussion of animal magnetism, from which he wandered on to his favorite topic, the faculties of phrenology. He discoursed at length about Amativeness and Adhesiveness, Ideality and Vitativeness, while Judge Greene raised his eyebrows and Mr. Fuller tapped his foot. Mrs. Whitman recalled her first meeting with John Neal, several years before, when he was selling India calicoes, practising fencing and boxing, editing a newspaper, and writing staunchly American novels like *Randolph*. He had grown older; he had studied law; but he had not changed. It was only his topics that had changed. The fire with which he discussed them was as ardent as ever. Margaret interrupted Mr. Neal's sally into Pneumativeness to remark,

"With your lion-like heart you can conquer the goblin brood. But what of those who allow themselves to be mastered by magic?"

Unconsciously, she smoothed her hair as she spoke. Mr. Neal did not answer. Instead, he arose abruptly from his chair and exclaimed,

"Let us have a topical illustration of phrenology this evening! Miss Fuller, will you be willing to be my subject?"

Margaret raised her head high and then slowly uncoiled the folds of her light hair. Mr. Neal approached her and felt her head with his long, thin fingers. Mr. Fuller and Judge Greene exchanged glances of amusement, but Mrs. Whitman gazed at the performance with deep interest, fluttering her fan in excitement. For a while Mr. Neal was silent. Then he muttered,

"Your character is complex and contradictory. It has heights and depths, nobilities and frailties. The faculties are at odds with each other. Parentiveness challenges Ideality, and Amativeness is struggling with Adhesiveness. You are a woman of contrasts, Miss Fuller; there is man in you as well as woman. There is scholar as well as teacher. There is child as well as mother. There is lover in you, too."

Mr. Neal removed his fingers. Quietly, Margaret pinned up her hair. Nobody spoke. Judge Greene looked up at his books, and Mr. Fuller down at his shoes. Finally Mrs. Whitman remarked,

"I feel I know you with greater understanding, Miss Fuller, than any conversation could ever give me."

Margaret was not sure she understood herself any better. The head that Mr. Neal had touched began to ache. The evening had been too entertaining perhaps. It was time to leave.

"In spite of the mistakes you probably made, Mr. Neal," Margaret said on the way home, "I like you very much. I know only three or four men whom I like better."

To herself she added, "He is so truly a man. Intensely human. Goethe would have approved of him."

Before she went to bed Margaret opened the *Zahme Xenien* of Goethe.

Je mehr du fühlst ein Mensch zu sein
Desto ähnlicher bist du den Göttern.

John Neal felt himself a human being; hence his power to act like a god. She had felt that power when he touched her head. Mesmerism—animal magnetism—demonology —second sight—how Emerson would have mocked. Margaret recalled little Anna Parsons, who had been able to perceive character. There was something genuine in all the experiments with which men were trying to explore the dark avenues of the inner life. People were weary of the tangible and the real. They felt the touch of unseen hands; they heard the ghosts of voices. Emerson did too, in a different way perhaps. Emerson found God in himself even though he shied away from the darkness of Limbo. Magic and reality—two faces on a coin. They must be welded in the perfect life, as Goethe had welded them, as Margaret might.

At any rate the evening had been intensely stimulating. Where had the schoolmarm and the Goethe scholar vanished when the lady had raised her head to John Neal's touch? How many selves there were, she thought. The self that did not approve of Emerson's airy vaultings into the cosmos; the self that scorned Alcott's simplicity; the self that listened, half amusedly, half sombrely, to John Neal's murmured analysis; the self that discussed *Romeo and Juliet* with Ann Brown; the self that had suffered at Groton and at Trenton Falls, who had wept over a heliotrope and conned Locke's philosophy. So many selves could be distinguished. Which was the real one?

During the August vacation of the Greene Street

School Margaret arranged to attend the Phi Beta Kappa exercises at Cambridge. One might study to become a citizen of the world at Providence, but one could not realize such an ambition without stepping forth from the microcosm of that city into the larger world outside. Emerson had told her that after the Reverend Dr. Wainwright had declined to deliver the address, Cornelius Felton had invited him instead. It would be interesting to hear the new thoughts that had been fermenting in Emerson's brain, and afterward she would go with him to Concord for another meeting of Hedge's Club.

On the last day of August, 1837, Emerson mounted the platform of Harvard College and faced a large concourse of spectators. Margaret looked about her. The faces had not changed considerably. The Farrars were there, though in place of George Ticknor there was a handsome young gentleman called Henry Longfellow, dressed as if he thought Cambridge was Heidelberg. Young Lowell sat back in his seat with the air of the cleverest scholar in Harvard. There were cambrics instead of muslins, and cauls instead of bonnets. But on the whole, no great change was perceptible, except perhaps the fact that Ralph Waldo Emerson, who had so disturbed the Adams family by his cosmic notions, had been invited to address the Society.

"Mr. President and Gentlemen:"

Margaret closed her eyes to the cauls and cambrics, to the velvet flowers and satin bands, and listened. No. So far Emerson's convictions had not changed either. He was discoursing upon the doctrine of the One Man who is all in one, priest and scholar, statesman, producer, and soldier. The scholar was merely Man Thinking. There was nothing new here, merely a variation on Emerson's favorite theme. Margaret recalled his beautiful phrases about Identity during her first visit to Concord. He was turning a page of his notes. Perhaps there would be a new thought. No, it was Nature again. "Every day, the sun; and, after sunset, Night and her stars." Emerson still went forth into the night to behold the stars, which did not change either and yet were ever new. The scholar and the flower proceed from a single root. Hence, "know thyself" and "study nature" become one maxim. Margaret wondered how the schoolmen would react to the elevated words about leaves and flowers, to the broad discussion about the mind of the Past. "Instead of Man Thinking," he was saying, "we have the bookworm. Hence the book-learned class, who value books as such." She glanced about. There was some head shaking already. Harvard would not like those words. But Emerson was soaring on, unmindful, or careless, of their reactions. "Books," he was declaring in that rich voice, "are for the scholar's idle times." Even the velvet flowers resented that as they turned toward the neighboring velvet flowers. Emerson should have been reminded that he was not addressing the lilies of the field, but merely velvet flowers purchased in Washington Street and sewed on new cauls. But he would not have been concerned.

Ah! Here was something new from that rock that had fastened on the soil of Concord. "Inaction is cowardice. The true scholar grudges every opportunity of action past by as a loss of power." Emerson had listened then, when she had spoken of Goethe, of the active life. The rock had flowered in the warmth of her rays. Those lessons in German pronunciation were bearing fruit. "Life is our dictionary." These were brave, new words from one who lived in the white, square house in Concord. Surely Margaret had given him this strange vocabulary. Now he was back again to his own thoughts about self-trust and self-reliance. The velvet flowers bristled. "In yourself is the law of all nature; in yourself slumbers the whole of Reason." Slumbers indeed, Margaret thought, as she glanced at Lowell's lifted eyebrows and Holmes' smile. "A nation of men will for the first time exist because each believes himself inspired by the Divine Soul which also inspires all men."

Emerson gathered his notes and retired from the platform. The words had been exciting indeed. But as she walked out to meet her friend, Margaret heard Holmes remark to his brother that the transcendental nose was one that stretches outward and upward to attain a foresmell of the Infinite! If Holmes had laughed, the others would frown. They had not agreed with Emerson's interpretation of the American Scholar. It would be a long time, Margaret thought, before the Phi Beta Kappa Society would invite him to the platform again.

Margaret met Emerson after the oration and they drove to Concord together. They spoke of the address, and then Emerson mentioned the meeting of Hedge's Club that would take place the next day. Elizabeth Hoar, he said, Samuel Hoar's daughter, had been betrothed to his brother Charles, who had died a year ago. She was more a saint than any one he had ever met—more a saint even than Lidian. She would attend the meeting this time. "The wise men in an hour more timid or gracious crave the aid of wise and blessed women at their session." Mrs. Sarah Ripley would be there also.

Margaret spoke of her meeting with John Neal, of the excitement over phrenology in Providence. Emerson calmly returned,

"Phrenology and animal magnetism are studied a little in the spirit in which alchemy and witchcraft or the black arts were, namely, for power. That vitiates and besmirches them and makes them black arts."

Margaret smiled, for she knew that Emerson's art of

tracing God in man and discovering the common root of tree and crystal was also magic of a kind. She replied,

"If the black arts can bring power, they are not black. Who would be a goody that could be a genius?"
She looked thoughtfully out of the carriage and went on more gravely. "Yet I know I cannot be a genius. If Corinna or de Staël or your Aunt Mary cannot satisfy the imagination, none can—certainly not I."

"You are a new woman, and you have a new, as yet inviolate problem to solve. Walk with erect soul serenely on your way. Accept the hint of each new pleasure that you find; try in turn all the known resources. You will learn from what you cannot as well as what you can do, the power and the charm that your new born being is."
If Margaret had beckoned Emerson onto the fields of action, surely, she thought, he had given her a place in the chimney corner of contemplation. Together they could hold the world in chains.

On September first the Hedge Club met again in Emerson's study. The old faces were there—James Clarke and Alcott, both eager to hear about Providence—Convers Francis and Henry Hedge, sucking transcendental doctrine out of theological straws—Ripley, eager to hear about Margaret's life of Goethe—Dwight, still singing his way to heaven. Cyrus Bartol, elfish as ever, was talking about Father Taylor, who had attended one of their sessions with his green spectacles thrown up on his forehead. There were some new faces also. There was Elizabeth Hoar's face, on which reposed an expression of unbroken purity. It was not strange that Emerson should have called her "Saint." She seemed to have joined herself irrevocably to the muses and the gods. She seemed not only holy in herself, but able to consecrate as well.

Brownson and Parker were missing, but David Barlow and George Bradford were there instead. Bradford, Margaret knew, was the son of Captain Gamaliel Bradford. It had been whispered of him that he would not be happy in heaven unless he could see his way out. Margaret wondered how long he would remain at the meeting of Transcendentalists that was about to take place.

Convers Francis started them off as usual. It was an unequal race of wits, for Alcott soared away on the wings of Plotinus, Dr. Hedge galloped his twin bays, Kant and Fichte, Mr. Ripley trotted gayly on the back of Schleiermacher, and James Clarke trudged behind on Jouffroy. Soon Emerson filled the air with the scent of the Hindu and Persian mystics, and Margaret thought him a citizen of the crystal palace, but of no country, because of all. He had never set a firm foot on Yankee-land, for all he had proclaimed that life is our dictionary. Through it all Elizabeth Hoar listened, a figure of immortality among those who, though not mortal, surely were not yet immortal. From Christianity to mysticism they veered, from the progress of civilization to the personality of God.

At one point the remark was made,

"It seems like going to heaven in a swing." Margaret gave the swing a push with a Goethean prod, and Alcott thought, "She is like a sacred bird, Indian or Egyptian. Yet though she is sibylline she has not fathomed my secret." Indeed she seemed to dominate the meeting to-day, divining oracularly what her friends would say, leaping to conclusions with her glancing logic. Emerson sat back in admiration of the darts of oratory she flung into the air. She had learned much from her study of Goethe; it seemed almost as if she had learned herself, from Goethe.

Suddenly, the horses that Hedge rode began to balk, James Clarke dismounted from the back of Jouffroy, and

even Alcott was thrown from the wings of Plotinus.
Emerson retired to his solitary intellectual grove, while
Margaret refrained from casting more darts into the air.
The head of Homer watched, impenetrable. The Flaxman
statuette was cold. The Fates looked on. The swing had
plunged to earth before it had quite reached heaven,
though Elizabeth Hoar seemed veiled in celestial sun-
clouds. One by one they descended from the swing. The
meeting was over. Again Margaret felt the discontent
that always troubled her after these sessions. Life might
be their dictionary, but they were still at ABC. One might
become a citizen of heaven here at Concord, but a citizen
of the world? One needed a special diploma for that—a
diploma not printed at Concord.

Perhaps in Boston one might con the dictionary of
life, Boston so full of activity that Providence seemed a
slumbering town by comparison. In November, Margaret
read of the reception granted to the Indians by Governor
Everett. In her mind's eye she pictured the Sacs and
Foxes, the Sioux and Ioways dancing a war dance on the
Common. She thought of William Clarke out West and
for a moment she longed to see the Indians in their own
territory—theirs no longer really, for had not the Secretary of War cheated the Sioux of their lands east of the
Mississippi? The desire to help them actively was there.
Inaction was cowardice. Margaret wrote a poem offering
a health to the Indian braves and treasured the hope that
one day she would visit them out West. There were other
meetings in Boston besides Indian delegations. Abolitionists were gathering to deplore Lovejoy's assassination
in Alton, Illinois. The West might throw the glove, but
the East drew the sword. At least Boston did.
During the winter of 1837 Margaret made several

short trips to the city from Providence. The Athenaeum Gallery and the Masonic Temple opened their doors to her. For her Emerson lectured on "The Head," John Vandenhoff played Brutus, and Joseph Gurney preached his Quaker doctrine. As Mrs. Fry's brother droned his placid gospel, Margaret prayed that the thick film of self-complacency might be removed from his eyes so that he would no more degrade religion. Neukomm's *Oratorio of David* was sung for her and she concluded it was to music what Barry Cornwall's verse was to poetry. She longed for deeper chords and richer harmonies. This music might answer the dictates of taste, but not the call of genius to recreate a world.

Her friends too opened their doors to the visitor. In December, after Emerson's lecture at the Masonic Temple, she walked with Caroline Sturgis to Alcott's home at Cottage Place. The eighteen-year-old daughter of Captain William Sturgis was filled with admiration for one who had attained the age of twenty-seven and who, though she numbered Mr. Emerson and Mr. Alcott among her friends, yet condescended to walk with her and listen to her quiet praise. Alcott had invited John Dwight also and both were ready to be entertained by Margaret's anecdotes about the animal magnetism that had attracted all of Providence. Dr. Channing was eager to receive her in his study on Mount Vernon Street, to hear her read bits of Dante or discuss the material sublime. She spent an evening with Theodore Parker, discussing Spinoza over an oyster supper. The whole gigman world of Boston passed before her gaze in those brief visits. It was refreshing after the recitation rooms of the Greene Street School and the long afternoons of solitary study. But Boston, for all its oyster suppers, its Athenaeum, its Vandenhoff and Channing, its Quaker preachers, was not quite the world. There was enough of the world in that city to make Providence seem tame by contrast, but no more. To be a citizen of the world, Margaret knew, she would have to venture farther afield. As yet the special diploma had not been printed in Boston either.

Nevertheless, those short excursions seemed to have changed Providence into a provincial town. The evening entertainments with Judge Greene and Mrs. Whitman were a little less amusing than the oyster suppers at Boston. The life of Goethe did not proceed beyond the outline of his childhood. Perhaps the Greene Street School did not demand enough thought.

It was as much to stimulate herself as to satisfy the children that just before the turn of the year Margaret formed new classes in the Bible, German, and rhetoric. When she opened Whateley's text and read a few passages at the first meeting of the rhetoric group, Harriet Taine asked,

"Shall we get the lesson by heart, Miss Fuller?"

"No," was the answer. "I never wish a lesson learned by heart, as that phrase is commonly understood. A lesson is as far as possible from being learned by *heart* when it is said to be, if it is only learned by *body*. I wish *you* to get your lessons by *mind*." Still lively as birds, Ann Brown and Harriet Taine, Mary Allen and the others set about learning Whateley's *Rhetoric* by mind. They wrote definitions of logic, rhetoric, and philosophy. When poetry arose as a topic of conversation, Margaret asked the class the meaning of the word. No one answered.

"Write it down, then," she said.

She looked at the children, a few biting their pens, one or two looking out of the window at the pale winter sun or down at the orange carpet, a few racing their thoughts along the page, all meditating upon the nature of poetry. This, Margaret thought, was teaching at its highest. Dr. Channing would call it creative. Yet, she felt she could never go beyond this point. It marked an end. It did not quite satisfy. Mary Allen brought her definition up to Miss Fuller's desk. "Poetry is a harmony of words." Margaret read it aloud and the children agreed that it was excellent. Then Margaret said,

"I regret to say that it is very incorrect."

Ann Brown asked Miss Fuller to give her own definition. Looking over the bright tops of the children's heads, Margaret defined poetry. It was a long definition and the girls had difficulty taking notes in their journals. It had to do less with words, somehow, than with life, less even with thought than with action. As she spoke the children experienced strange throbbings in their hearts, unfamiliar longings to escape the known and the commonplace. There was no doubt that this was teaching at its best. Mary Allen believed so, for she wrote to her parents, "It is worth a journey to Providence to hear Miss Fuller talk." Magaret felt it, for she saw the bright eyes widening, the grave eyes pondering. Yet it was not enough. Teaching was an avenue that had been explored; it did not open upon wider fields.

In the afternoons Margaret turned from Goethe to Körner. She sat at her little table with its microscope and Plutarch, its Milton and Goethe, and wrote an account of the life of Karl Theodor Körner, the poet who had prayed for the freedom of Germany, whose muse had ever sounded her silver trumpets. The trumpets of the outward world again. In days when worthless demagogues compassed their selfish ends by vaunting in every market-place sentiments fit only for the lips of saints and martyrs, it was good to read Körner. For he had said that a great day asks great souls; he had felt within himself the strength of a rock in a tempestuous sea. When Körner wrote, Prussia had armed herself against Napoleon. But Margaret's great day had not yet come. When it came

she knew she would meet it with a great soul. She sent
the article to *The Western Messenger* and in January and
February of 1838 James Clarke published it.

But Körner was not Goethe. And Mr. Fowler, who
examined Margaret's head phrenologically, was not John
Neal. Sarah Whitman's coterie seemed narrow. Their
habits of minute scrutiny, unknown in the wider circles
which Margaret had frequented in Boston and Concord,
began to annoy her. They jostled too closely to see one
another, or herself, fairly. Nor were they particularly well
informed. One day they babbled on about Schiller, calling
him Skiller time after time. Margaret could not restrain
her impatience and at last blurted out, "It is Schiller,
Schiller. Don't say Skiller; it sounds so like a vulgar
skillet." Mrs. Nias too, for all her beauty, had no great
understanding. Once after a particularly fruitless day
when neither Goethe nor Körner could stimulate her to
thought, Margaret entered the small assembly room to
find Mrs. Nias discussing mythology as if it were a new
phase of animal magnetism. Again the distaste mounted
within her. She could not check her tongue. Out they
tumbled, the words that could cut a human being into
little pieces.

"Why, Mrs. Nias, you would have been worth educat-
ing!"

No one was divine in Providence. Margaret felt that
she was more divine than any one she saw and that was
enough to say about the others. Emerson had judged
the world from himself. Emerson did not know the world.

The inadequacy of life in Providence was even more
noticeable after James Clarke visited Margaret from the
West. It was pleasant to discuss the Greene Street School
with him. She showed him two packages of letters which
she had received from her pupils, the first written after
they had been in school only a short time, all confessing
their ignorance. "Oh, Miss Fuller, we did not know, till

Teachers.

Miss SUSAN PRESCOTT,
PRINCIPAL, AND TEACHER IN THE FRENCH AND
ENGLISH STUDIES.

———

Miss MARY O. PRESCOTT,
ASSISTANT TEACHER IN THE ENGLISH STUDIES.

———

Miss ANN CATHARINE REED,
TEACHER IN DRAWING, PAINTING, AND NEEDLE-WORK.

———

Miss ELIZA H. HEWITT,
TEACHER IN MUSIC.

Two Pages from a Catalogue of the Young Ladies' Seminary in Groton, Massachusetts, conducted by the Misses Prescott.

(Courtesy Harvard University.)

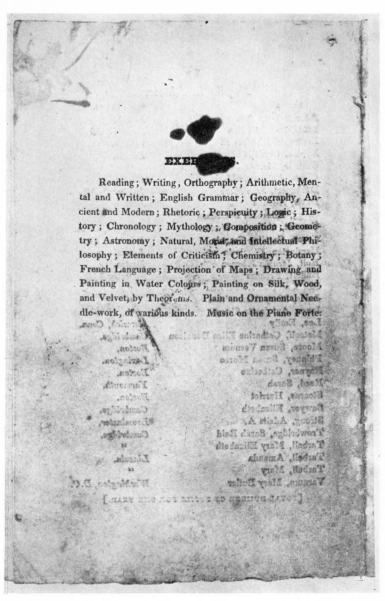

EXER.

Reading; Writing, Orthography; Arithmetic, Mental and Written; English Grammar; Geography, Ancient and Modern; Rhetoric; Perspicuity; Logic; History; Chronology; Mythology; Composition; Geometry; Astronomy; Natural, Moral, and Intellectual Philosophy; Elements of Criticism; Chemistry; Botany; French Language; Projection of Maps; Drawing and Painting in Water Colours; Painting on Silk, Wood, and Velvet, by Theorems. Plain and Ornamental Needle-work, of various kinds. Music on the Piano Forte.

In spite of the variety of subjects available, all offered for $15 the quarter, there were only four teachers.

we came to you, how ignorant we were. We seem to know nothing at all, and not to be able to learn anything." The second package contained the later letters, all acknowledging their indebtedness to Miss Fuller for "showing us how we can become something better. You have given us courage and taught us how to go forward." The first package Margaret labelled, "Under Conviction"; the second, "Obtained a hope." James Clarke was interested and thought that Margaret had accomplished a great deal at Greene Street. But Margaret, thinking of his *Western Messenger* and his activities in the West, felt as though her life in Providence had been futile. The afternoon with James was enjoyable. He brought her news from the West, where his brother William was selling drugs and medicine, where the Indians were being cheated of their lands; he brought her news from home, and said that Samuel Ward was expected to return shortly, that Washington Allston was dissatisfied with life in Cambridgeport, that Alcott had only three or four pupils left, but that he was grateful for Margaret's rejoinder to Harriet Martineau's tirade. The afternoon passed quickly. James Clarke had to leave. Margaret sat down to write a song for the May Day excursion of the school.

May Day passed quickly too. The children went a-Maying to the "Grotto" on Moses Brown's farm. Margaret's song was sung, to the accompaniment of a flute. There were dances and refreshments. Listening to the song she had written, Margaret felt ashamed. She who had hoped to lead the world in chains had written a song to lead little girls a-Maying. During the spring Hiram Fuller arranged other entertainments for the children. One day M. and Mme. Canderbeck came to amuse them with trained poodles. This was too much. Divinity might reside in a leaf—but in trained poodles? The growing inanity of her life at Providence bore down upon her. She would leave soon, she knew. But first she must return to Concord and see, after M. Canderbeck and his trained poodles, a man in whom the cold stars gleamed, in whom divinity still stirred.

Several times she went to Concord. She deplored with Emerson the news from Harvard, where Longfellow was telling his classes that he objected to Goethe's sensuality, that the old man had painted only sinful Magdalens and rampant fauns, and had written a monstrous book called *The Elective Affinities.* Caroline Sturgis and Margaret played with Waldo, a little boy now, the darling of the schoolhouse, shouldered and chaired at every recess. The lad told Margaret the names he had given the parts of his toy house.

"This is the *interspeglium* and this is the *coridaga.* The children cannot understand these names."

Emerson and Margaret smiled at the elaborate titles, but little Waldo did not mind. He was off, spinning his stories, telling how his horse went out into a long, long wood and how he looked through a squirrel's eyes and saw a great giant and the giant was himself. Cary Sturgis stooped to pet him and he told her how his little bell would sound in the middle of the night like some great glass thing which would fall down and break all to pieces —louder than a thousand hawks—heard across the water and in all countries and all over the world. As she listened, Margaret realized there was no Waldo in the Greene Street School, nor in the Temple School either. Waldo was one with leaf and crystal and flower.

"How in the right are children to forget name and date and place," she said, "to remember only that which lives."

After they had played with the child, Margaret confided to Cary that though she was a mutilated being in this life, in her bosom remained a faith that she would sometime see the reason; without throne or sceptre or guards she felt herself still the queen. Margaret knew it was Waldo or Concord perhaps that had restored to her her regal glory. She knew that when she returned to Providence and loosed her bolts of sarcasm at children who had not prepared assignments, there would be little left that was queenly. And so she stayed on at Concord or returned as soon as possible. She stayed to read to Emerson her journals and her poems or to discuss with him one of her own phrases, "One must live a great deal to think a very little."

"This," said he, "I prize."

Margaret recalled his words about inaction at the last year's Phi Beta Kappa ceremony. "I owe several things to your journal," he admitted, "things quite new to me." In his turn, he bade Margaret not to live as the servant of a visiting-card box. "Ten people," he remarked, "are a great deal better than a hundred." Margaret thought of M. Canderbeck, and Mr. Fowler, of Sarah Whitman's many friends, of Mrs. Nias—people who had made her the servant of a visiting-card box. Indeed, one phrase at Concord was better than a whole lecture in Providence.

With Emerson, Margaret also looked at the pictures in her portfolio, copies of Guercino and Piranesi. Together they sought the equilibrium of mind that he had said was the condition of right judgment. On another occasion Margaret brought with her a portfolio of Samuel Ward's. She said she had seen him in Boston, at the Athenaeum, and driven with him afterward. She did not say that he had not changed—that to him she was still one who might stimulate the mind, but never touch the heart. She did not say that in the years to follow she hoped he would change. She simply looked at Raphael's Sibyls and Thorwaldsen's "Entry of Alexander" with Emerson, and while he spoke of the grand style and architectural strength of the works before them, she saw, instead of Raphael, her own Rafaello, who had seen the originals and bought the copies.

"How much a fine picture seems to say," Emerson remarked. "It knows the whole world. How good an office it performs. What authentic messengers are these of a wise soul, which thus stamped its thought, and sends it out direct, undecayed, unadulterated to me at the end of centuries and at the ends of the earth." So far then, we are alike, Margaret thought. Rafaello has received the same message that I have from these pictures. So far only we have a common sympathy.

She stayed to look at the pictures, to hear about Henry Thoreau, who was teaching school with his brother, to smile with Emerson at Mrs. Russell's definition of transcendentalism. "Father Taylor's brilliant daughter did not flinch from defining the transcendentalists as a race who dove into the infinite, soared into the illimitable, and never paid cash." Margaret wondered how Alcott would react to such a definition. They laughed, and for once Emerson opened his mouth and betrayed his amusement.

They were delightful, these little excursions to the village of Concord, but too brief. One might look at a picture and consider a phrase or play with the wonderful boy—and then it was over. Back at Providence Margaret began to experience a definite antipathy to teaching. In place of the stimulation she had felt at first came the growing awareness that the self she gave to her children was not genuine. She was petty when the pupils neglected their assignments, and she was annoyed with her own pettiness. Her situation, facing group after group, day after day, was false. She could not think with more than a dozen pairs of eyes scrutinizing her every morning.

There was little reason now for staying on at Providence. Arthur was nearly ready for college. Margaret had saved enough out of the thousand dollars to pay for his tuition. Hiram Fuller's practical efficiency was becoming distasteful. He had rebuked her for attending the Whig caucus. Their cordial relations began to lapse. Margaret felt ill again. The headaches had returned and the tiny draughts of opium were the only means of release. Everything in her life seemed to have been marked by failure. Her love for Samuel Ward had been bootless. She could work no more on the life of Goethe. Even the little Greek temple seemed over simplified. Her own life was so complex. She realized that though she had learned much in Providence, she had thought little. She longed to think now as before she had longed to act. She was weary and she wanted rest. Yet, when she read Hugo's *Hunchback of Notre Dame* and considered that the Frenchman was only eight years older than she, she hoped to produce a similar work in the course of eight years. Here in Providence Margaret knew there was no time for tranquil meditation. She could no longer divide her day into three parts and expect the thoughts to flow. At the Greene Street School she was never alone and later in the day ideas would not come. It had been simple at first, but now impossible. One needed rest and leisure to think; one needed thought to write or act.

On November 15, 1838, the class in moral science met for the last time. Margaret began by reading the letters her children had written on how the Sabbath should be spent. Then she asked them to keep those letters and read them again one year from the coming Christmas. "Think of me when you read them; think whether you have been guided by the rules laid down there." Margaret extolled "sweet Mary Allen" for her devotion to truth, and bade the pupils good-bye. They trooped out quietly, subdued and moved by the simple farewell.

The rhetoric class gathered together for the last time in December. Harriet Taine carried to Miss Fuller's desk a copy of Shakespeare and a ring, gifts from the students. Margaret was touched and after she had thanked the pupils she spoke of her initial difficulties at the school, of her own teaching and her own manner.

"It has sometimes been harsh, sometimes too ironical,

but I have never really felt either toward you. If I have been harsh, it was to insure obedience, and if I have been ironical it was to awaken within you a sense of your deficiencies and to stimulate you to exertion. I fear I may have wounded many tender natures." Margaret remembered the round robin. "But for this I humbly ask your pardon and I can sincerely say that it was never intentional."

Again the winter sun cast its pale light on the orange carpet. It was the last time they would watch the carpet change its colors under the sunlight, the last time they would see the shadows climb the white walls. Margaret went on speaking of what she had done for her pupils, of how much more she had wished to do. She spoke too of her own trials, her own disappointments at Providence. There were tears in her eyes, and in the eyes of the children. At last, she said, "For the last time my girls, I say to you, you may go." No one moved. A few minutes passed. The orange carpet glowed in the midday sun. Margaret rose and walked to each girl, kissing her, bidding her good-bye. Then she left the room.

Miss Sarah S. Jacobs arrived to take Margaret's place in the Greene Street School. Margaret turned over in her mind her plans for the future. Lydia Child had written pretty descriptions of a South American oasis. It would be interesting to learn Spanish and establish a school in South America. She could maintain herself and at the same time experience new thoughts and new emotions. But founding a school was not really what she desired. One could not be one's self in a classroom. That was one of the things Margaret had learned from the Greene Street School. Her mother was ready to sell the Groton farm, but would not leave it until April. She would go home and stay three months. Then she would start out again, climb other promontories and look out upon other seas.

Chapter VII

INTERLUDE AT JAMAICA PLAIN

ALCOTT, Margaret knew, had the habit of making inventories of his intellectual real estate. This was surely the time, during the few months that she would remain at Groton, to estimate her own powers and achievements. She had always been precocious, but what had she gained by her precocity? She had never been happy. When she had sought action, her life had been uneventful; when she had longed for thought, trivial duties had been forced upon her. Through her mind the thoughts of Emerson and Alcott had filtered. Through her soul had radiated the shining beauty of Samuel Ward, the gentle light of James Clarke. Sarah Clarke had taught her to find richness in friendship as well as in painting, and in the gypsy charm of Caroline Sturgis she had found delight. Her friends were her sole achievements. Yet the page of her inventory was half blank. Margaret knew she had merely served an apprenticeship. The days of mastery were all before her.

Margaret embroidered her thoughts more readily than the needlework in her hand as she sat during the cold mornings in the winter parlor on Farmers' Row. It was Lloyd's turn now to be drilled in his studies and Lloyd was more of a recusant than the others had ever been. After the children of the Temple School, even after Ann Brown and Harriet Taine of Providence, it was obvious that her youngest brother was slow-witted. These lessons also marked an end, for Lloyd was the last child. There would be no more tutoring of Blair's *Rhetorick* or *The Chronology of the English Kings* in the future.

[167]

It seemed the time for answering letters and cogitating about friendship. It was the sort of life one led, Margaret thought, before one was ready to die—or perhaps before one was ready at last to live. When Emerson wrote that he had been unable to lecture on Genius because he had not slept the night before, she replied, "Lose a night's rest! as if an intellectual person ever had a night's rest;— that such an one should abjure a lecture on Genius because he had lost a night's sleep." How many nights of sleep had been lost to her, in the maze of nightmare or in the maze of thought. She had dreamed once of getting up and combing her hair. Her dressing box had been before her, but she could not find the hair ribbon. In the dream the hair ribbon had been as irretrievably lost as a soul groping in purgatory. Then there had been the dream about the Egyptian who sat by her side alluring a great butterfly to rest upon her finger. But the butterfly had settled instead on the left side of Margaret's forehead, plunging its bristling feelers deeper and deeper into her brow till her pain rose to agony. Another time she had dreamed that her body was a dungeon from which a beautiful angel escaped at the head. But what did Emerson, who lived ever in the light of day, know of such Limbo thoughts? She was the Pearl who lay at the beginning amid slime and foul prodigies from which only her unsightly shell protected her. Emerson knew nothing of this; he was the rock, untouched by the slime that clung to the Pearl. Her mother had sent him a gift of apples, food for the body. He had returned Plato's *Banquet* with which to feed Margaret's soul. So the rock answered the pearl. She would never possess his self-complacency. Though she comprehended his greatness, she would ever scorn the intellectual remoteness that made him great.

It was the time for rereading Jefferson and thus taking a last, indirect farewell of her father, who had first read the *Letters* to her. These were the afternoons to devote to Schiller, and pray again to write a *Wallenstein* and die. Margaret found a little book about the West by Mrs. Clavers and left her Schiller reluctantly to dip into the account of Michigan as seen by an actual settler. She felt she was leaving the past for the future when she turned from Schiller to Mrs. Clavers. One day she too might visit the West and view the scenes this book unfolded before her.

When Margaret left the Groton fireside for a brief visit to Boston she felt again as if she were bidding goodbye to the past. She spoke with Alcott, and it was as if she were turning the key on her memories of the Temple School. She realized for the first time that she had never grasped the complete man. He was still too close to his ideal, but he had range and power and precision. She would take him on faith. In the same way the book of studies from Salvator Rosa, which she saw in the Brimmer collection at the Athenaeum, reminded her of the past, of the Italian paintings she had seen in the galleries. Yet, it too drew her on to the future, to the paintings she hoped to see in distant galleries. When she met Washington Allston and found him so beautiful that she forgot to make herself interesting, she thought of all she had heard of him from Sarah Clarke, back in the past, and felt vaguely that he was but the first of many painters whom she would know in the future. It was strange thus to stand between the past and the future, to live an interlude, and know it was an interlude. . . .

At length, on March eleventh, the Groton house was sold at auction. Margaret visited Emerson to discuss the possibilities of purchasing a new home in Concord. The opportunities, he told her, were few. Mr. Gourgas was about to vacate his home, which could be rented for ninety dollars, but Mrs. Goodwin had already set her eye upon it. Henry Thoreau's aunts wanted to rent their house, but his mother said it was damp and she could not recommend it. Concord would never be more than a visiting ground for Margaret, but she would always make the most of her brief sojourns. She bewitched Elizabeth Hoar away from her needlework; she even started a smile upon that cold, saintly face. She amused Mrs. Ripley when she came for tea. In the afternoons she talked with Emerson, cautiously drawing out the man from the shell that encased him. There was talk of a journal, slight tentative talk, of some quarterly that might catch the thoughts of the Symposium Club and set them down forever. Margaret listened carefully; this had always been one of her cherished desires, ever since she had learned of Goethe's journal and James Clarke's *Western Messenger*. Some day perhaps she would establish an organ for the views of those who, like herself, were just emerging to mature life.

It was a happy farewell, that last look at the white frame dwelling in Farmers' Row and the blue hills beyond. Arthur would go to Harvard after a period of study at Waltham with Mrs. Ripley. He too was full of the future. Even the robins' blue eggs on the semicircle in front of the house were not hard to leave. They would hatch when the family was not there to see. Monadnock would lift its head above the mists when they were gone. Margaret did not care. With Groton she knew she was leaving her apprenticeship and coming into her mastery.

The house that Margaret finally rented was in Jamaica Plain and stood on the street between Forest Hill Station and Forest Hill Cemetery. It was tall and rather ugly, she thought, but the three-story wooden building was not far from Willow Brook and there were rocks behind it overgrown with cardinal flowers. It was but a short walk to Bussey's Grove, where she could gather great red bunches of columbine and in the garden Mrs. Fuller soon planted her Provence roses and her heliotropes. It was pleasant to sit at the little writing desk, looking up at the engraving of "Dante and Beatrice" or the "Madonna del Pesce," or glancing down at the work before her. She cleaned her pen with her little velvet pen wiper and plunged it into the ink. Though it was not the life of Goethe she was writing, it was a near approach. The master's conversations with Eckermann were a just index to the workings of his spirit. Translating those conversations meant conveying Goethe's mind to the Western World.

Sometimes, when her spine ached or her head throbbed, Margaret sat on the couch, holding her carbuncle or the seal her father had given her so long ago, dictating to Ellen. Then she thought of Eckermann, the poor boy who had learned painting from a horse drawn on a tobacco wrapper, and had walked to Weimar to show his treatise on poetry to Goethe. On she read, translating, omitting, turning the phrases into the English idiom. Goethe snuffing the candles and walking to the stove, Goethe believing with Kant that cork trees do not grow merely that we may have stoppers for our bottles, Goethe contemplating in the garden his life-enigma, the Dämonische, Goethe in his old wooden chair, pulling from his head the cap of bigotry and blind hatred—Goethe was here in these talks with Eckermann, the farmer poet, here in Margaret Fuller's translation of those talks.

On her twenty-ninth birthday Margaret sat down at her writing desk and wrote the preface to Eckermann. She wrote of Goethe as one who possessed the artist's eye and the artist's hand, but not the artist's love of structure. She found herself in union with him, for he was no idealist; he did not seek to alter or exalt nature, but merely to select from her rich stores. Therein, she

thought, he differed from Emerson who, endowing Nature
with his own Spirit, fallaciously believed that Spirit de-
rived from Nature. Goethe, she confessed, was an aristocrat. Her own sympathies were with the great onward
movement of democracy; her own hopes were with those
who trusted in a fair experiment to determine whether
men could be educated to rule themselves. Yet, she com-
promised, a minority was needed to keep these liberals
in check. As yet the caldron of liberty had shown a constant disposition to overboil. She thought of Harriet Martineau's dogmatic assertions about liberty, the dogma of
those who wished to destroy dogma. Goethe had drawn
her onto the fence of conservatism. It was well to rest
there and plumb the depths of the caldron before plunging into it.

Emerson approved, called the book a short way to
Goethe's character and sent it to Carlyle in Chelsea. The
translator, he wrote, was an accomplished lady whose
culture belonged rather to Europe than to America. Sarah
Whitman approved and sat down in her red house in
Providence to write her praises of German cosmopoli-
tanism for *The Boston Quarterly Review.* At Harvard
Longfellow thundered a little more vociferously about
the sensuality of the old man. Margaret felt that at last
she had aroused the New World to thoughts about the
Old.

She walked out into the woods to read about Frankfort in Goethe's letters to Meyer, to translate parts of his
Darstellunggabe, stringing, rather than melting, the
pearls of his thoughts. She carried the thoughts to the
woods and sat down with them. Wild geranium starred
the banks and rock clefts, the hawthorn flowered on
every hedge, the pines on the hill rose to the sun. She too
was in the sun at last. She had reached a few readers with
her written thoughts. Perhaps soon she would move a

larger audience with her spoken words. Often, as she sat
in the woods or at the writing desk she dreamed of voicing her own thoughts as she had translated Goethe's. She
was afraid to give too much time to the influence of another, no matter how great he was. It was time to shape
her own thoughts and to utter them. Had not Elizabeth
Peabody delivered lectures to the women of Salem; was
not Emerson sprinkling stardust in the halls of the
lyceums; was not Alcott "versing" rather than conversing
before all who would listen? Why not Margaret then?
It was a thought to be cherished—along with that other
fragment of a thought, the journal that had been wished,
though not yet conceived.

Margaret did not mention these plans to Richard, who
was eager to talk of his own life at Mr. Weld's school in
Jamaica Plain, nor to her mother, who was happy again
bending over her verbenas and Daphne Odoras. She expected Samuel Ward to visit her during the summer;
when he came she would skirt the idea, sounding him out.
If he were interested, his friends would lend an ear. Then
that eloquence she had coveted so long might be hers.

When Margaret entered her home one bright morning
after a ramble around the meadows and orchards and
wooded hills, she saw Samuel Ward standing in the parlor, looking out over the slope toward the south. She had
gathered flowers in the garden and offered them to him.

"The heliotrope is still my favorite—my chosen em-
blem, true bride of the sun that it is. Each flower is a
symbol to me of some emotion—there is a mythology of
flowers just as there is of gods. Are you interested in
mythology, Samuel?"
She led him around the room, showing him the "Dante
and Beatrice." "Approach and know that I am Beatrice,"

she murmured. "The power of ancient love was strong within me." She searched his face and then went on. "She is beautiful enough, is she not, for that higher moment. But Dante! Yet who could paint a Dante—and Dante in heaven? They give but his shadow as he walked in the forest maze of earth." Samuel Ward followed her to another corner of the room where she pointed to her Raphael. "His eyes," she remarked, "are softly contemplative, yet lit with central fires." Like yours, she longed to add, but did not. Margaret turned back to her writing desk and showed him her medallions, her seals, and gems. "Each," she said, "is enigmatical. Each proposes an enigma in me. Gems have their mythology too, Samuel."

They sat down before the window and Margaret spoke on. She discussed the mythology of Greece and the statue of Minerva-Polias, cut from an olive tree. "There is one wooden column left standing from the ruins of the first temple to Juno. This is a type of the glorification of life's earliest experiences by our perfecting destiny." Our perfecting destiny. She was leaning forward now, gently drawing in the reins of her own destiny. If Samuel Ward were interested, she could speak her thoughts aloud to a host of listeners—discourse with them about mythology and destiny and life. Then too, if Samuel were interested in her mind, he might lose himself one day in her heart. "In the temple of love and Graces, one Grace bore a rose, a second a branch of myrtle, a third dice. Who can read that riddle, Samuel?" Samuel Ward, looking at Margaret's rich hair—a little darker than when she had stood under the moon at Trenton Falls—at her gray eyes that still flashed fire after the eyelids had contracted almost to a point, at the light complexion, so much fairer than when he had first met her at the Athenaeum, thought, surely you are the sibyl who can read that riddle. Margaret bent toward him. He was interested, she knew. The perfecting destiny hovered near.

"I think you will be able to cast your net of words and gather all the fish in the Boston seas with your conversation," he said smiling—but not me, he whispered to himself, not me.

He spoke of their friends, the Clarkes, and of Emerson, who had been writing to him, of his portfolio of pictures, of Goethe's *Essays on Art* which he hoped one day to translate. Then he spoke of Anna Barker.

"You have been to me, Margaret, as a mother. She is more nearly at my level."

He had not meant to be cruel. He had merely wanted to disengage himself from the glance of those dilated eyes, the sibylline air, from the hand that grasped the arm of the chair, from the net of words, from the net of Margaret. She rose and walked toward him.

"You do not wish to be with me," she said. "You come here to go away again and make a call upon me in the parlor while you stay. You send me pictures and ask me what I think of them. Your mind is dissatisfied with its own pursuits. I will be as indulgent as a mother to you, as delicate in my vigilance as if I had borne you beneath my heart instead of in it."

Samuel Ward was moved. The woman before him was no longer the girl who had stood beneath the moonlight at Trenton Falls. He would not be bound in her net. He would not be unriddled by a sibyl. Anna Barker was beautiful, and Margaret, standing there so dignified, so aloof, was not beautiful. Anna was at his own level while Margaret, erect, magnificent, arching her neck, was far beyond him. She was one of the rare flowers in her mother's garden, one of the gems on her writing desk. She was Margaret, but she longed to be Beatrice. The power of ancient love *was* strong within her. Samuel Ward was afraid of that power. He turned to leave. He looked back at her and saw her standing before the window, a gem glittering in her hair. He closed the door gently. Margaret knew he would never return. This too was past—this interlude. Another door had closed. She groped in the corridor of her heart and found all doors were closed.

On the eighteenth of September Margaret met the gentlemen of the Symposium Club at Cyrus Bartol's home on Chestnut Street. Emerson was not there, but Margaret was happy to see William Channing again, as well as Theodore Parker and Henry Hedge. Most of the talk this time centered about the periodical to be designed as the organ of views that were in accordance with the Soul. Alcott remarked offhandedly,

"I call my own Scriptures—that is, my own Diaries— the Dial. Why not call our journal by that name?"

Much was said about *The Boston Quarterly Review* that Orestes Brownson was editing and about Heraud's journal across the seas. Margaret said that if she were organizing a new quarterly it would be the medium for the freest expression of thought on every question of interest to earnest minds in every community. She liked the title Alcott had suggested, for her magazine would occupy a position on which the light might fall, open to the rising sun, able to report the progress of the hour and the day. Theodore Parker was not quite sure whether a periodical edited by a woman would be virile enough for his taste. Miss Fuller he thought a good enough critic—but no creator—no *vates*. George Ripley considered that in such a journal he might find excellent opportunity to publish the ideas that were hatching in his brain—ideas about social communities, more exciting by far than his simple pastorate. No action was taken, however. But the seed had been sown.

The next day Margaret made a pleasant party of transcendental lords at Jamaica Plain. Emerson came, to

hear the news about yesterday's meeting. Theodore
Parker, listening to his hostess discuss *The Dial* began to
think that she resembled Mme. de Staël more than any
woman he knew. That power of hers for putting into
speech the thoughts that peopled her mind was matchless.
Did she say that she had outgrown Carlyle? Well, she was
a prodigious woman. She might put herself upon her genius rather too much, but there was no denying that she had
genius. Mr. Calvert of Newport was introduced and immediately proceeded to discuss his drama, *Count Julian,*
which he had nearly completed. George Ripley was eager
to discuss his reply to Andrews Norton's attack on the
transcendentalists. The pamphlet was already in the press,
and Ripley was in high spirits about it. Jane Tuckerman
sang *The Delicate Stem,* but Margaret made no effort
to recall the similar vapid melodies of her childhood. The
past had no place in her thoughts as she sat with her
elbow on the arm of her chair, discussing the Allston
Gallery or Papanti's new dancing school on Tremont
Street. New sculptures by Greenough and Crawford had
been added to the Athenaeum collection and Margaret
discoursed at length about the busts of Byron and Napoleon. She had also seen the Allston exhibition at Harding's Gallery on School Street, she said, and agreed with
Emerson that it was an altar without fire.

"The impression the gallery made on me," Emerson
explained, "was that whilst Homer, Phidias, Dante,
Michelangelo, and Raphael make a positive impression,
Allston does not. It is an eyeless face, a cultivated mind,
but no man."

"I think," Margaret suggested, "that Cambridgeport
has rotted the man's soul. He cannot finish his 'Belshazzar's Feast.' A man must go forth into the world
before he can paint the world."

"My young friend, Henry Thoreau," Emerson replied,

"believes that one may find the whole world in Concord. This summer he spent a week on the Concord and Merrimac Rivers with his brother, and I am sure he found the cosmos in those streams."

"The cosmos perhaps," Margaret murmured—"but not the world." She rose as if the final word had been uttered. "Tonight we shall eat cake instead of Plato's *Banquet*." She walked about with the cake plate in her hand, but the others, who had listened carefully to the dialogue between Margaret and Emerson, were not ready to be thus prosaically diverted.

"At Papanti's new hall," Jane Tuckerman persisted, as she reached for a slice, "one sees a goodly portion of the world. The fond mothers sit on the sofas, the musicians play in the gallery, the girls admire themselves in front of the huge mirror, the boys stumble about on the new spring floor, and Mr. Papanti in his dress coat and curly wig calls out directions over his bow."

"That is Carlyle's gigman world at Papanti's," Margaret replied loftily, "not our world."

"Our world," George Ripley observed, "will be found in the pages of our new journal, *The Dial,* will it not?"

"So much thought has accumulated that it must find an organ for self-expression," Parker asserted thoughtfully.

"Let us hope it will. But first, I want to launch my conversations."

Margaret told her friends of her new plans, plans to array her own world in a setting of words that would dazzle the ladies of Boston. The ribbon in her hair fluttered as she spoke. She twirled her carbuncle ring round her finger. She arched her neck and moved her hand restlessly on the arm of the chair. Her eyelids closed; everyone was drawn to her as if by a loadstone; the very air seemed magnetized. To Margaret this evening presaged the future, when larger audiences would be attracted by her powers. After they left Theodore Parker observed to Emerson,

"She is more like Mme. de Staël than any woman I have ever met."

"There is some Récamier in her too," he replied.

During the autumn months Margaret planned her Conversations, contemplated the new journal, and occasionally entertained her friends. Anna Barker visited her once when Emerson was at Jamaica Plain. Looking at her, a woman without particular talent, without great dignity of manner or expanse of intellect, Margaret felt that none the less she had a complete beauty. There was no single feature of conspicuous charm, but Anna Barker had developed into a woman altogether lovely. It was not remarkable that Samuel Ward had been captivated. Soon, she knew, they would be engaged. She does not sit at home in her mind, Emerson mused, but goes abroad into the minds of others. Margaret seemed to guess his thought. She knew that Anna Barker had gone forth into the mind of Samuel Ward and bewitched it. There was no breaking the spell. When Anna left with Emerson, Margaret understood that she would always love Samuel Ward, for his nature had become a part of hers. The love he had excited would accompany her through eternity. But it had become a quiet love. It would trouble her no more.

Margaret sat down at her writing desk to outline her Conversations and write a letter for Mrs. Ripley to circulate among the ladies of Boston. Once again she cleaned her pen with the velvet pen wiper and began—not to translate the thoughts of others, but to phrase her own. She wrote of the advantages of a weekly meeting for Conversation and of her ambition to pass in review the departments of knowledge, to systematize thought with a precision and clearness in which her sex were so deficient.

She would open a discussion on such subjects as the Life of Man, Literature, the Fine Arts, the History of a Nation, and lead others to express their thoughts upon those topics. The actual design would look too grand on paper. It would become apparent as the ladies met and conversed. The meetings would be held in Miss Peabody's rooms on West Street and would start in November.

There was *The Dial* too to be considered. It was strange that when two great interests of her life had been abandoned—the biography of Goethe, her hope for Samuel Ward's love—two others were beginning. She would concern herself with the Conversations first. Those other seas she had watched for were in view.

CHAPTER VIII

CONVERSATIONS IN WEST STREET

O N WEDNESDAY mornings the descendants of
Boadicea—for to her the Peabody clan traced their
ancestry—rose earlier than usual. Dr. Nathaniel Peabody had given his daughter Elizabeth permission to
straighten out the shelves where his homeopathic medicines were stored. She moved about briskly, adjusting and
rearranging. That copy of Dr. Kraitsir's *Lectures on
Language* must be removed from the chair where Theodore Parker had left it the day before. The bookshop
which she had established at number 13 West Street was
holding its own, even against the competition of James
Fields' Corner Book Shop. She smiled at the recollection
of Emerson's remark that her rooms were turning into
Margaret Fuller's "Parlatorio" at St. Paul's. The view of
the Church from the front windows was charming, but
today there was no time for window gazing. She hoped
the noise from Washington Street would diminish a little
—for Margaret's sake. Elizabeth's red and black petticoat hung down untidily as she reached for General
Joseph Bem's Historical Chart which had fallen from its
peg.

Sophia Peabody's face was less alive and translucent
than usual as she stooped over the painters' materials that
Washington Allston had helped her purchase. It was very
disturbing, she thought, to be aroused from a nervous
headache to arrange chairs for Margaret Fuller's Conversations. Dear Nathaniel Hawthorne had not been entirely unjust to call her a persecuted little dove whose
abiding place had become a Babel of talkers. She did not

wish precisely, as he did, that Margaret Fuller might lose her tongue, but she did long for the golden silence that enwrapped her prince. Her chin was more tender than resolute as she thought of the letters he had been sending her. She smiled and Elizabeth, catching a glimpse of her younger sister, thought how nobly shaped Sophia's head was, how gray and soft her eyes had become. She was less of an invalid now than she had ever been. Her diet of bread and milk and chickens must be effective—or else it might be the influence of that mysterious and haunting gentleman who told stories so delightfully.

As the two sisters arranged the chairs, they left spaces between the sections where the various contingents were certain to seat themselves. The ladies from West Roxbury were sure to want a row a little apart—and the Boston abolitionists would never be content in the more rarefied atmosphere of the ladies from Concord. It was wonderful, Elizabeth thought, that Margaret could address them all and make them for the time being, one, uplift them from the petty hostilities of party into purer regions. Margaret must also be expanding under the influence of these Conversations, she reflected, as well as increasing her income. Twenty dollars for a course of conversations was a high fee, considering what one could do in Boston these days for far less. There was the Allston gallery; there were the lectures of Everett or Webster or Emerson; one could dance the pastorale at Judge Jackson's for nothing but an invitation, and right here, she meditated, she allowed her patrons to borrow Strauss' *Leben Jesu* or the English quarterlies for nothing if they had not had enough time to read them through. She looked around the room. Schubert's *Geschichte der Seele* had fallen from the shelf and Constant's *De la Religion* lay on the arm of the chair where George Ripley had left it. The box sofa must be brushed and that wood-top table cleared for flowers. Elizabeth removed her sister Mary's *Flower People* and Leroux's *De l'humanité* to make room for the bouquet of chrysanthemums that were to Margaret a symbol of power. She was just in time. The bells of St. Paul's were sounding the third quarter. At eleven Margaret would arrive. Even now the ladies had begun to enter.

As Elizabeth had foreseen, the West Roxbury contingent came together and sat together. Anna Shaw's bright eyes were even brighter than usual, perhaps by contrast with her modest alpaca, or more likely because of her anticipation of the pleasure before her. Her sister-in-law, Mrs. Frank Shaw, was wearing a pin with a Mercury holding the head of a goat, which she exhibited to Elizabeth Peabody.

"In case Margaret should mention Mercury I shall have an apt illustration in jewels instead of in words."
The Russells sat with the Shaws, their black silks vying with the alpacas of their neighbors. Lydia Parker ambled slowly toward them. It was no wonder, Sophia thought, that her husband called her "Bearsie"—she looked like an amply stuffed bear.

Elizabeth turned to greet Mrs. Farrar and Anna Barker from Cambridge. As she discussed the sale of Mrs. Farrar's *Young Lady's Friend,* Elizabeth could not help noticing how very beautiful Anna Barker looked in that *pou de soie* with her green velvet scarf, just the right shade to set off her gray eyes. Miss Burley bustled in from Salem and pounced upon Mrs. Farrar to compare the literary lions they had been entertaining in their respective salons. Elizabeth detached herself from the group to welcome Mrs. Horace Greeley, in Boston on a trip from New York, and at the moment less interested in discussing her husband's journalistic enterprises than Sarah Shaw's mythological pin. Mrs. Sarah Ripley's lace cap soon dominated the scene and Elizabeth at last found a moment's rest in a discussion of Chinese grammar with her learned friend. In her turn, Mrs. Ripley was eager to pour forth the information she could only trickle for her rusticated boys at Waltham, and pour she did—huge doses of Euripides and Spinoza into Elizabeth Peabody's listening ears.

Sophia walked toward the door to escort the Concordians—Lidian Emerson and Elizabeth Hoar, along with Belinda Randall, to her sister. Lidian had a daughter now, named after her husband's first wife, and Elizabeth did not marvel that Emerson called her his "Asia" and claimed her the incarnation of Christianity. "Elizabeth the Wise" discussed the latest sayings of young Waldo with "Elizabeth the Learned," while Belinda Randall conversed with Sophia Peabody about the tonal reaches of the new song she was learning. Maria White and Jane Tuckerman wandered into the bookshop, chatting together about their "Band" which, they thought, made the White home a fit comparison with Margaret Fuller's house at Jamaica Plain. Indeed, Jimmy Lowell, whom Maria referred to as the King of Cambridge, had warned her against Margaret Fuller who, he said, would label her every component with a Latin appellation, and turn her into a fossil like herself.

Last of all, the Bostonians began to stroll in and Sophia Peabody left Belinda Randall to greet them. Louisa Loring sat next to Ann Phillips and confided to her that her husband had taken a boy of color into his office to be trained for the law. Ann applauded the good work, replying that although ill health had overtaken her and soon she would have to confine her rovings to walks from the bed to the sofa, and the sofa to the rocking chair, her husband Wendell would carry on the cause of abolition. They were soon joined by Marianne Jackson, who defied her father's hostility to the abolitionists by accompanying Lydia Maria Child to the Peabody bookshop and seating herself next to Louisa Loring.

Sophia disengaged herself from the incendiary group to hasten over to Mrs. George Bancroft still puffing a bit after her journey from Winthrop Place. Mrs. Bancroft adjusted her pink satin bonnet and prepared herself for a talk about Nathaniel Hawthorne, her husband's assistant at the Boston Custom House. Though she would have preferred to converse about Daniel Webster, whose junior partner her first husband had been, she was ready enough to answer Sophia's eager questions with the little information she had gathered about weighing and gauging.

Mary Peabody descended the stairs, looking slightly annoyed to see that on the wood-top table a huge bouquet of chrysanthemums had been substituted for her book, *The Flower People*. She joined the Sturgis sisters fresh from a stroll round the Chinese porcelain wall of John Cushing's Summer Street home. As daughters of a merchant prince whose firm, Bryant and Sturgis, had long dominated the Boston trade, they thought Mr. Cushing's taste too ostentatious, but the walk had been delightful and Caroline was sure it would lead to Elysium. She wondered what Margaret would say, while her sister, Ellen Hooper, wondered what Margaret would wear. Sophia had wandered to another corner of the room and was busily engaged in discussing the cast of Michelangelo's "Night and Day" with Sarah Clarke, who kept one eye turned toward the door in expectation of Margaret's entrance. Mary Channing approached them and turned the talk to the West, for now that her cousin Ellery was living in a log cabin near Cincinnati she felt a common bond with Sarah Clarke, whose brothers had blazed the trail before him.

"Margaret's sister Ellen will probably go West also to teach school," Mary remarked. "She may live near John Keats' brother, George, but I'm sure she will not get along with him—or any one else. She's like Ellery in that respect."

The room was filling now. Mrs. Thomas Lee entered with as much pride in her pelerine cardinal as in her *Life of Richter*. There was Mrs. Samuel Putnam, Lowell's sister, looking slyly at Maria White. Mary Haliburton and Ednah Littlehale stood shyly in a corner, for Mary was squint-eyed and Ednah was the youngest of the company. Sophia grimaced when she heard Ednah tell Mary that Margaret had once asked her whether life was rich to her. Her answer had been, "It is since I have known you." Mary looked radiant and turned toward the door. No, she was not there yet. It was just Julia Dorr and there was Sophia Ripley colliding with Mrs. Barlow. Surely, Mrs. Barlow thought, as Sophia plunged into a discussion of her husband's dissatisfaction with his Purchase Street Congregation, she is losing the gracious composure that her Dana and Willard ancestry should have given her. Had not her own husband left not only the ministry, but his wife and three children?

Elizabeth Peabody looked about quite satisfied. The ladies were all seated. There was more of a murmur inside the bookshop than outside on Washington Street. The stage had been well set, she complimented herself. If only General Bem's Chart would not tumble down. She turned to fasten it securely on its peg. The voices died down. Suddenly, Ednah Littlehale called out,

"Oh, I do wonder what she will say!"

The ladies veered around to look at the excited youngster. They all began to wonder what she would say, how she would look, whether she would wear a cape or a scarf, how far aloft she would carry them. The sunlight glowed

on the chrysanthemums. St. Paul's pealed the eleventh
hour. The door opened and Margaret entered.

She strode toward the front of the room, nodding con-
fidently at Sarah Clarke, glancing brilliantly at Caroline
Sturgis, both seated near her, smiling vaguely at the
Concord group and the West Roxbury contingent, for her
nearsightedness made her uncertain which was which. She
carried herself, she was sure, like a queen—a queen who
at last had found her kingdom. Her new black mousseline
dress with the purple sleeves had been well chosen. The
tight, smooth coiffure must be becoming for she had
labored over it an hour before leaving Jamaica Plain. The
color of the chrysanthemums would blend with her light
hair. She walked toward the wood-top table and stood
near it. She placed her copy of Wordsworth's *Tour in
Greece* and Heeren's *Mythology* on the chair, raised her
pince-nez with their spherical lenses, and looked at her
audience. Mrs. Bancroft was murmuring behind her hand
that her husband had started work on a translation of the
Heeren, and Margaret paused till the interruption had
ceased. She looked for a moment at Sarah Clarke, who
seemed to cast the mildness of a moonbeam on the parti-
colored scene of pink satins and green velvets and black
alpacas. She raised her hand, allowing the carbuncle ring
to glitter for a moment near her hair. Then she began.

"In the business of life," she said, peering through the
pince-nez, "women find themselves inferior to men. All
our studies"—and she looked pointedly in Sarah Ripley's
direction—"have not given us the practical good sense
and mother wisdom which grew up with our grand-
mothers at the spinning wheel. Men are called upon, from
a very early period, to reproduce what they learn. But
women learn without any attempt to reproduce. Their
only reproduction"—and this time she glanced toward
Elizabeth Peabody's drooping eyes, "is for purposes of

display. It is to supply this defect that my conversations have been planned. I am not here to teach, but to provoke your thoughts." That should set them at their ease, she considered, except perhaps Mrs. Parker, who had very few thoughts to be provoked. "The Grecian mythology," she continued, turning toward the female abolitionists, "is quite separated from all exciting local subjects. It is serious without being solemn" (this should appeal to Mrs. Barlow) ; "it is playful, as well as deep. It is sufficiently wide, for it is a complete expression of the cultivation of a nation. It is also generally known and associated with all our ideas of the arts."

"What exactly are our ideas of the arts, Miss Fuller?" The determined voice from the corner was Sarah Ripley's. How tiresome to be interrupted just when she wanted to speak of the Greeks who saw the oreads and naiads, personifying all they beheld. But Mrs. Ripley must be assuaged.

"There is, for one, the art of the dance. The impassioned bolero and fandango are the dances for me."

Ednah Littlehale looked up as if she were magnetized by the presence before her. She could not exactly see Miss Fuller with her pince-nez dancing the bolero on Boston Common—but still, in another climate perhaps, her curved neck and beautifully moulded shoulders, those graceful hands, might move to the soft Spanish rhythm. "These dances are not merely loving, but living; they express the sweet southern ecstasy at the mere gift of existence. I love. I live. I am beautiful! I put on my festal dress (everyone glanced at the black mousseline) to do honor to my happiness. I shake my castanets. (The heads bobbed in the direction of the waving purple sleeves and the glittering carbuncle ring.) I—*felice—felicissima!*"

How wonderful she is, sighed Ednah Littlehale. Sarah Shaw glanced down at her Mercury pin, and thought, she

is all in all to me. She is at her best, considered Sarah
Clarke.

From the abolitionist corner Lydia Child popped a
question.

"Cannot sculpture as well as painting and the dance
express the idea of immortality?"

Margaret was grateful that Lydia had given her a chance
to return to the Greeks. She probably wanted to discuss
immortality for her own sake as much as for Margaret's,
for she was interested in planning a book on the progress
of religions.

"The Greek art," Margaret replied, "expressed immortality as much as the Christian art, but it did not
throw it into the future. The Greeks expressed immortality in the present, by casting out of the mortal body
every expression of infirmity and decay. Their color expressed passion, their sculpture thought. But perhaps,"
and Margaret allowed herself a little sally away from
Heeren's *Mythology*—"perhaps life is the finest of all
the arts." That would surprise Sarah Ripley and make
them all think. "Now I shall propose a question for you.
What is life?"

Caroline Sturgis felt as if she had heard three syllables
emanating from the mouth of the Sphinx. The velvets
and satins scarcely rustled. Nobody answered. Anna
Barker looked out toward St. Paul's, thinking life was
Samuel Ward, whom she would marry soon—Samuel
Ward whom Margaret had loved—Samuel Ward who
had rejected her for Anna Barker. Over in her corner
Maria White thought of her King of Cambridge and his
sonnets to his queen. Galahad, who rode a white horse
over the fields of the New World. James Russell Lowell.
He was life. Sophia Peabody, seated next to her sister
Mary, was contemplating life in the form of the gentle
youth who nibbled on a bag of miseries and transmuted

them into stories. The prince of princes. Nathaniel Hawthorne. He was life. Her sister Mary was thinking of life
in a long black coat—life emerging as fire from the
square jaws of a young widower who was secretary of the
Massachusetts Board of Education. Life, solid, emphatic.
Horace Mann. He was life, the life she had found in
Mrs. Clarke's boarding house and would treasure always.
Even Mary Channing was meditating less about her
father, who knew all one could of life, than about Fred
Eustis, for somehow the Reverend Mr. Eustis held more
of life for her than the Reverend Dr. Channing.

"Caroline," Margaret prodded, "what is life?"
Caroline Sturgis attempted to answer the sibyl.

"It is," she said hesitantly, "to laugh or cry, according
to our organization."

"Good!" Margaret declared, "but not grave enough.
Come, what is life? I know what I think. I want you to
find out what you think."

From the rear of the room a red and black petticoat
swished. Elizabeth Peabody opened her eyes and remarked categorically,

"Life is a division from one's principle of life in order
to a conscious reorganization. We are cut up by time and
circumstance in order to feel our reproduction of the
eternal law."

That, Sarah Ripley reflected, must be the effect of Chinese grammar, while Mrs. Barlow concluded that the
stout, ungainly descendant of Boadicea had lost herself
in Basque. From the Concord group there was a rustling
of silks and Mrs. Emerson spoke mildly,

"We live by the will of God, and the object of life is to
submit."

Submission was hers, Margaret considered. Was it possible that with a husband like Waldo Emerson, Lidian
could still believe in Calvinism and at the same time sub-

mit to transcendentalism! Mrs. Barlow interrupted to forestall a debate on Calvinism, for Mrs. Parker looked restless and might at any moment repeat her husband's last sermon. "The object of life is to attain absolute freedom," she announced quickly. Susan Burley could not down the thought that the beautiful Mrs. Barlow could ill afford to tread the dangerous soil of freedom after her husband had left her with three children. Margaret kindled at her words, raised her finger—the one with the carbuncle ring—and spoke,

"My opinion is that life and creativeness are dynamic forces out of which we, individually, go forth. Within our being is some dynamic force by which we also add constantly to the sum total of existence, by which we shake off ignorance and become more ourselves. So we do attain to absolute freedom. In short, we become gods, able to give the life which we now feel ourselves able only to receive." Margaret was satisfied by her inversion of Emerson's theory of God dormant in man at the beginning to God attained by man after the working of life's dynamic forces.

She was dynamic at that moment, as she stood before them with lifted head and raised finger. Nothing like that, Susan Burley reflected, had ever been seen at her salon in Salem. Sophia Ripley felt herself irradiated in a flood of light—she had found her true relation to the universe. She has broken her lance upon their shield, thought Sarah Clarke. Their outworks are falling before her assault. Margaret Fuller is not exactly agreeable, Elizabeth Hoar considered. One might prefer Emerson's garden or a solitary walk on Fairhaven to a room shaken by this vivid lightning bolt. But she is just. Lidian Emerson also might have found a circle of spiritual beings more congenial than Margaret's flesh and blood, but there was no denying her power. That raised forefinger was uncomfortably like the rod of Jehovah; those words were thunder that would crash upon the deafest ears. Mary Haliburton and Ednah Littlehale, Caroline Sturgis and even Sarah Clarke had no thoughts at all. They were bespelled, as if indeed a sibyl had unsealed the wisdom of the serpent or showered fruits from the tree of life.

"The best that we receive from anything," Margaret continued, "can never be written. The best part of life is too spiritual to bear recording."

But the best part of life, Caroline Sturgis thought, can be spoken—if Margaret is speaking. Her eyes are almost dark now, blue-gray, the color of genius. How beautiful is the shape of her hands, mused Sarah Clarke, and those gestures, how Italian. "Women, true women," declared Margaret, "know this. Growing in self-reliance and self-impulse, they find that virtue has flowed into their souls. But today," and Margaret swept the room with a disdainful glance, "there is no woman, only an overgrown child." Some day, she reflected, she would write of the true woman, of her significant part in the nineteenth century. But she had digressed too far from the gods. Soon Sarah Ripley would accuse her of inability to pursue one thought to its end.

"Let us return to our mythology, ladies. To understand the Greek mythology, we must denationalize ourselves, and throw the mind back to the consideration of Greek art, literature, and poesy. Only then can we perceive that Jupiter is the symbol of creative energy, Apollo of Genius, Bacchus of Geniality. When I was a child this mythology was very real to me—more real than Christianity. I remember that I once prayed to Bacchus for a bunch of grapes."

How thrilling, thought Ednah Littlehale. How pagan, thought Lidian Emerson. Theodore was right, reflected Mrs. Parker. What transcendental nonsense she can twaddle. Sophia Ripley decided to interrupt Margaret's recollections of her childhood with a question.

"Do you think that mythology was a prophecy of the Greek mind to itself or that the nation had experienced life in any wide or deep sense?"

Elizabeth Peabody tried to recall the book that George Ripley had borrowed recently. Such a preposterous question must have come from some socialistic interpretation of Greek mythology. It was no wonder that Margaret seemed out of patience.

"It does not matter which," she declared, staring icily through the pince-nez at the questioner.

But Mrs. Ripley was not willing to surrender.

"Do you not believe," she pursued, "that the Hindus were more virtuous than the Greeks? The virtue of the Hindus lay in contemplation. If a man had seen God, he was exempt from the ordinary obligations of life and allowed to pass his life in quiet adoration."

Emerson must have been reading passages to her from the *Bhagavad Gita,* Margaret decided. But she saw her way clearly out of the problems of Hindu contemplation.

"The Greek," she answered archly, "knew better than that. He felt the necessity of developing the Infinite through action, and embodied this necessity in his art and poesy as well as in his myths." She smiled wisely, for at last she had been able to weld her own definition of life with the Greek attitude.

"The mind," she continued, "cannot receive this thought —or any thought—unless it is excited. I must, for example, go through all the intellectual experience of a Plato to be as great as he. Then I may go forward to still greater results."

"But," and with Mrs. Ripley's "but" the Shaws and Russells twitched their black silks, and Mrs. Barlow's pink satins rustled impatiently. "But in the first case, you would be nothing *but* Plato."

Margaret willingly acceded to this pleasant proposition and quickly went on to a discussion of Greek fables.

"A fable is more than a mere word. It is a word of the purest kind rather, the passing of thought into form. The age of the Greeks was the age of poetry; ours is the age of analysis. We cannot create a mythology."

"Why," interrupted Mrs. Russell, for Sarah Ripley looked as if she were preparing herself for another question, "why do you find so much fault with the present?"

"I have no fault to find with the present," Margaret replied. "I take facts as they are. Every age does something toward fulfilling the cycle of the mind. The work of the Greeks was not our work. I accept the universe." And here she raised the threatening carbuncle and arched her neck toward the ladies. What a noble statement, considered Ednah Littlehale, nudging Mary Haliburton. Rather patronizing of her to accept the universe, mused Susan Burley. The universe should be obliged to her. "I accept the universe," Margaret repeated, "only because I believe that evil is good in the scheme of things. It is no blunder. Its scope is a noble one. I would not accept the world—for I feel within myself the power to reject it—did I not believe evil working in it for good. Man has gained more than he lost by his fall. God is simply the background against which all creation is thrown. The past is a curtain on which every nation has embroidered its pictures of the present. Through every age evil has worked for good. Through every period a single thread can be traced. The Olympian deities are like modern men who talk to women forever about their softness and delicacy, until women imagine that the only good thing in man is a strong arm. The girl elopes with a red coat and the indignant lords of creation wonder why she did not appreciate their modest merit and unobtrusive virtues. Poor beauty weeps out the crimson stain upon her escutcheon in a long age of suffering. It is still the same. Even Yankee philosophy has its roots in the Greek attitude toward life. We find beauty where the Greeks found it; we are indignant when the Greeks would have been indignant."

"Divinities, it seems, still have a right to be indignant," Mrs. Barlow whispered noisily.

But Margaret did not blush, Ednah Littlehale noticed. She was riding her Pegasus now at a gallop.

"Like the Greeks we still have our unanswered riddles; like the Egyptians we still have our Sphinx."

She paused now to propound her question—the question toward which her whole conversation had been moving. She had asked them to define Life. Now she had a more searching problem for them. "Ladies, what is the Sphinx?"

Again no one answered. Surely, Margaret thought, Elizabeth the Wise, Elizabeth the Saint, can tell us what the Sphinx is. But Elizabeth Hoar would not answer. The Sphinx, she thought, was probably one thing to everybody. Yet, why did the word bring before her eyes the image of Charles Emerson—dead, but always alive to her. Then, for no reason at all, she remembered having seen a letter on Emerson's desk, a letter from Carlyle stamped with the new penny postage from England. Now thoughts could cross the seas more quickly. Just as in her life she could communicate with the dead, a single thought could span the ocean. Perhaps that was the meaning of the Sphinx. Margaret turned to Elizabeth Peabody. If Elizabeth the Wise could not answer, surely Elizabeth the Learned could reply. But she lowered her eyelids and remained silent. She thought, somewhat irrelevantly, of how she had looked out early that morning through the back windows of the West Street bookshop and seen the towers of the Masonic Temple. Alcott had been driven from there when he persisted in teaching a little girl of color. Now Theodore Parker would mount the platform in the Masonic Temple to seize the listeners' ears with the fangs of his oratory. Alcott had given way to Parker. Perhaps that was the meaning of the Sphinx. Margaret was looking at Sophia Ripley. But Sophia Ripley could not answer. She was thinking of her husband George and his new interests in socialistic experiments. She was wondering how far from Purchase Street they would lead him —and her. She was thinking how far she had already been led from her Dana and Willard background. Her past had been embroidered over by her present—hidden almost. Was that the meaning of the Sphinx? Lidian Emerson, herself the wife of a New World Sphinx, surely knew the answer, Margaret reflected. But Lidian did not know. She saw her husband's face, impenetrable, enigmatic. She saw him talking with Come-outers and Millerites, with Baptists and Abolitionists, with philosophers and madmen—ever proposing, but never answering the riddle. Margaret swept her audience with a questioning glance. Maria White—could she answer? Maria was thinking of James Lowell and of James Lowell's poor opinion of Margaret. There was irony there that might bring her nearer the meaning of the Sphinx. Caroline Sturgis, looking more like a gypsy than ever, would not reply, though she believed that a picture of Black Hawk which she had seen in George Catlin's Indian Gallery resembled the Sphinx more closely than anything she had ever seen. She dared not utter so trifling a comparison however. Anna Barker—could she answer? Could her beauty and grace find the answer? Anna was thinking of a chorus from the *Mount of Olives* that she had heard at the Boston Academy of Music, a chorus that always reminded her of Samuel Ward. But that really had nothing to do with the Sphinx.

"Incomprehensibility," Margaret remarked somewhat impatiently, "exists only in our want of the power to comprehend."

"Tell us," Caroline Sturgis called out, "tell us your definition of the Sphinx."

Margaret hesitated a moment, twirling her carbuncle ring. Then she spoke.

"To me it represents the development of a thought, founding itself upon the animal until it grows upward into calm, placid power. I revere our good ancients who did not throw away any of the gifts of God, who were neither materialists nor immaterialists, but who made matter always subservient to the highest ends of the Spirit. Matter, like the past, is a curtain upon which we must embroider the Spirit. Matter, like God, is the background against which our souls are thrown. To me this interrelation solves the riddle of man, the riddle of the Sphinx."

No one stirred. St. Paul's boomed the first hour after noon. The chrysanthemums nodded in the winter wind. Here, thought Ednah Littlehale, in this little room at number 13 West Street, in Boston, in Massachusetts, in America, in the New World, the problem of the Sphinx has been solved. Sarah Shaw looked down at her pin of Mercury. Mrs. Barlow adjusted her pink satin bonnet. This was the signal for the ladies to return to earth. They had been lifted far aloft. The rustling of alpacas helped to carry them back. Margaret swept her books from the table and removed her pince-nez. Elizabeth Peabody bustled to the front to take Margaret's hand and lead her to the box sofa. The ladies gathered around, murmuring congratulations and appreciation.

"You must undertake an evening class to which gentlemen may be admitted!"

"Our husbands will want to hear you speak on the humanizing of the old Earth-worship by the Greeks."

"You have outdone even yourself, Margaret."

"Tonight," Elizabeth Peabody said, "I shall write an extract of this Conversation."

"You were like the Sphinx yourself, Margaret."

"You have irradiated us all with your light."

Margaret could not listen to the talk. Her head began to throb and she leaned back on the sofa. Elizabeth Peabody brushed the ladies aside and amid murmurings and rustlings the room was finally cleared.

Margaret lay back on the sofa. A flame seemed to shoot up beneath her in wild, beautiful jets. Sometimes the flame sank again and all was a black mass, unsightly and forlorn. But not today. Today the fire beneath persisted and conquered. The black dead mass had become radiant, life-giving, fit for the altar. The flames seemed to shoot into her head, up from her spine. She twirled the car-buncle ring thoughtfully. She had found her kingdom. The serpent had sloughed off its dead skin. The phoenix had risen from the ashes. In Margaret's mind many images flashed in confusion. The most vivid of all was of a sea on which the sun shone, the undying sun of life whose shadows were cast behind.

CHAPTER IX

SHADOWS ON THE DIAL

THE WEST Street Conversations alone would have made the winter of 1840 a full one for Margaret. When she returned to Jamaica Plain she could have satisfied herself by writing her account of the *Chat in Boston Bookstores* between Professor Partridge and the Reverend Mr. Nightshade, both leaning over the counter, discussing the Muse in her petticoat, the sonnet, or *Vathek*, or Henry Coleridge's wife. It would have been enough merely to muse about the West Street bookshop and dash off a literary notice for *The Boston Quarterly Review,* signing it "Dahlia" and cloaking her thoughts on *The Fairie Queene* and Jouffroy in a flowery anonymity. It would have been sufficient just to sit and look at the fire, scribbling pencil notes in little books or contemplating the destruction of the steamer "Lexington" by a less beneficent fire in Long Island Sound. Had she wished, she would have found enough to do in the house near Willow Brook, seeing that Lloyd had his figs and bag of crackers, writing detailed instructions to Arthur to teach geography by means of vivid word pictures. Recommending books to Richard, who was sweeping and dusting the store of a dry-goods jobber in Kilby Street, and supervising the cooking of pork at home would have occupied her time quite completely.

It would have been sufficient almost during the spring to watch the blooms in her mother's garden—the multifloras, the verbenas, and lemon branches, to associate each with a friend and herself with hothouse plants innumerable. To Emerson belonged merely a sweet pea or laven-

der because he was only a philosopher, not a hero. Her
walk through the woods would have been eventful enough
when she read his letter about the jaunty tassels of last
year's grass on the top of a New York wall. There was
even more food for thought in her copy of *Nature,* which
she carried to the woods and read through for the first
time on April eleventh. As she laid the book aside, recalling Emerson's voice when he had read it to her, she
felt herself approaching the City of God. She remembered the story circulated after its anonymous appearance. "Who is the author of *Nature*?" someone had
asked, and the answer had been, "God and Ralph Waldo
Emerson." The bluebirds would have returned by this
time to their box in his barn. Surely the Orphic poet he
had described was none other than Alcott. He too would
be in Concord now, in the new house where Mrs. Alcott
would sing as she swept and her husband would mistrust
the step he had taken because of its very popularity.

The days in Boston too would have been full. She could
have gone forth from the rooms she had rented again at
2 Avon Place to see Forrest in *Metamora* and meditate
about the Indians. One day she would visit the tribes, face
the dirt and discomfort and melancholy to behold their
stately gesture and concentrated mood. It would have
been sufficient after a Conversation to discuss the latest
reports of the Woman's Rights Movement in London
and smile at Ann Phillips' remark to her husband, "Now
Wendell, don't be simmy-sammy today, but brave as a
lion." Brave he had been, when the American women were
denied entrance to Freemason's Hall at the convention
of friends of the slave. And from such discussion she
might have turned to gossip about Oliver Wendell
Holmes' bride, Amelia Jackson, niece of Wendell's
teacher of medicine, or to ground nearer home than
Montgomery Place in a more private talk with Caroline

Sturgis about Samuel Ward's illness and broken engagement to Anna Barker. But this touched her too closely. It was well that she had other work to do.

The other work was great in comparison with such minor pursuits as these. It was the labor of introducing a new age through the pages of a new journal, of giving utterance to the boundless aspirations of the time. When Margaret assumed the editorship of *The Dial* she assumed at the same time the power to protest usage and to search for principles, to make new demands on literature and let the American bluebird take the perch from the English skylark, to point out the true office of the critic and the position of the thinker, to clear the ground for the first appearance in print of the younger generation. *The Dial* would measure no hours but those of sunshine. Let it be one cheerful, rational voice amidst the din of mourners and polemics. With George Ripley, who had consented to act as business manager, she agreed on the editorial policy of the new publication. It was to furnish, as she had proposed at the Symposium Club, a medium for the freest expression of thought; it would discuss principles rather than promote measures. The contributors would be united by sympathy of spirit rather than by agreement in speculation; their hearts would be in the future rather than in the past; their trust in the living soul instead of the dead letter. *The Dial* must occupy a position on which the light might fall, from which it might report the progress of the hour and the day.

It was all very well to contemplate the higher natures of ideal contributors. Margaret discovered she would have to angle for the real ones. William Henry Channing was preaching in Cincinnati. Once he had prophesied a new literature. Margaret must write to him to contribute to that literature. Henry Hedge was preaching in Bangor and Margaret wrote, begging him to be good and politic, assuring him that she depended upon him for solid bullion. James Clarke must be induced to write a piece, and Albert Greene from his bench in Rhode Island cajoled to turn his pen again to verse. Alcott would more easily be persuaded to cast his bit of light upon *The Dial.* From his thoughts on Swedenborg and on the spine he would be able to make Orphic utterances on the pantheon of the mind. Emerson too could be relied upon for a reprint of a lecture, or a new pearl dissolved in the crucible of his mind. He would also be able to obtain contributions from others who represented his own tastes. Theodore Parker would surely gather his ideas together from the tomes he had been consuming and offer solid pabulum for the thirty actual subscribers and the thirty thousand hoped for. Christopher Cranch out West must be dissuaded from drawing pictures on the margins of his books and urged instead to pen some verses about his inner world. George Bradford could be trusted to write on abolition, for though he was a little of a Whig, he was altogether a gentleman. There were the ladies also who must be induced to contribute—the ladies whom Margaret had uplifted in her Conversations and who must now return bits of the star dust with which they had been sprinkled. Ellen Hooper must write Hellenic verses and Caroline Sturgis Carolinian ones. Lights from all corners of the New World must shine on *The Dial,* lest a shadow cross its face. Lights from the West were warmer and more persistent than from the North, for Henry Hedge had put up a fence between Bangor and Concord and would have nothing to do at first with the enterprise.

To make up for his defection, however, there were volunteer contributions. Emerson had apparently been successful with his young friend, Henry Thoreau, for he had been persuaded to copy poems from his big red journal and despatch them to Margaret. Even James Russell

Lowell, on the point of publishing his first volume, *A Year's Life,* decided to offer a contribution. Anna Barker also had written poem after poem, and now, after her link with Samuel Ward had been knit together again, was ready to offer the results of her meditations to the new periodical. Really, more volunteer contributions were coming in than could be printed, and Margaret was forced to adopt some policy regarding their acceptance or rejection. When, through lack of time, she failed to answer every contributor, those who were thus rebuked were never heard from again. Any contribution, she decided, that combined individuality of character with vigor and accuracy of style would be published. If young Thomas Wentworth Higginson sent in a manuscript not without merit, yet without that vigor and accuracy, it must lie unprinted.

It was necessary for Margaret to sit for hours at the desk in Jamaica Plain or Avon Place, reading manuscripts, making criticisms, deciding upon final rejections, and sifting the best work. The velvet pen wiper was busier now than it had been when it cleaned the pens that translated Eckermann or planned the Conversations. Margaret pored over the essays and poems, making pencilings in the margins of the manuscripts. A sentence here must be marked "good," a phrase there "*bella.*" Emerson's grouping of the words, "eloquence" and "wealth," in his essay on *Modern Literature* had rather an "air bourgeois" and must be corrected. His expression, "dreadful melody," did not suit her. The "dreadful" had become vulgarized since its natal day. He repeated the word, "whipped," too often; the offense should be removed. Elizabeth Peabody could never be clear and accurate in a brief space, and though her thoughts on Christ's Idea of Society were illuminating at a time when Ripley was so engrossed in communities, they must be condensed. Lowell's sonnets, after all, seemed too eclectic. They had a Tennysonian flavor; though they had merit, it was not a poetical merit. The last one, perhaps, might be accepted. Alcott and Parker could always be relied upon for contributions, but Margaret could not quite overcome her distrust of Alcott's mind and was unwilling to make Parker the leader of her journal. Those poems that Ellery Channing was sending from the West might be inserted. How much they reminded her of her sister Ellen! Now she must return to Thoreau's manuscript. The second reading confirmed her first impressions. His essay, *The Recruit,* was rich in ideas, but they seemed out of their natural order. She could not feel herself in a stream of thought; she seemed to hear the grating of tools on the mosaic. The article was so rugged that it ought to be commanding. Truth was seen too much in detail; there was a want of fluent music. It must be rejected. Thoreau said too constantly of nature, "She is mine." Margaret knew she would not be his till he had been more hers. William Story's piece was too long and must be omitted. Finally, after the sifting and second readings, after the pencilings on the margins and the revision of words and phrases, Margaret established her regular platoon of contributors and made space for a few first appearances. Alcott, Parker, and Emerson formed the trio whose words the reader might always expect to find. Thoreau, Dwight, Cranch, Dana, Ellery Channing, and young George Curtis would make their first appearance in print in the pages of her *Dial.* It was not an uninteresting assemblage, she reflected.

Margaret looked once more over the articles she had determined to insert in one issue. Would *The Dial* find its place in the sun? There was the lengthy essay by Thomas T. Stone called *Man in the Ages,* which would reflect the transcendental light. Stone might speak once and then be heard no more, but it was fitting that his con-

ception of the divine element in man, evolved from man's
sensualism, should appear in her pages. It was well too
to include Dwight's short account of the *Ideals of Everyday Life,* to proclaim to State Street and Beacon Hill (if
they would but read) that the end dignifies the means,
that the meanest occupation through which shines a lofty
purpose becomes glorious. Parker's lengthy essay on German literature was strong meat and should appear before
Alcott's tidbits. It was timely to remind Boston that the
Germans had sat on the brink of the well of Truth and
continued to draw for themselves and the world. Parker
must know that Beauty and Truth were but two aspects
of the same idea, two sides of the same diamond. She
would speak to him about this when next they met.

Margaret chewed the tidbits next—Alcott's *Orphic
Sayings.* "The trump of reform is sounding throughout
the world for a revolution of all human affairs. The issue
we cannot doubt." That would set the axe at the tree of
idolatry. "Reformers are the noblest of facts." Beacon
Hill would shake its stolid head at that and at this gem
too, "In the kingdom of God are love and bread con-
sociated, but in the realm of mammon, bread sojourns
with lies, and truth is a starveling." Even the Federal
Street Society would not like to hear that "the current
version of all sacred books is profane," and Harvard, if
it turned the pages, would laugh aloud to read that
"facts reported are always false." But the *Orphic Sayings*
must be uttered. They would go forth bearing Alcott's full
signature, uncloaked by the anonymity that the other contributors preferred, who hid their names under letters of
the alphabet.

Sophia Ripley, well obscured by the sign, "W.N.," had
heard enough at the Conversations to contribute a short
essay on *Woman,* announcing to the world that in the
present state of society, woman possesses not, but is under

possession. Before Emerson's *Thoughts on Art,* Lowell's *Sonnet to a Voice Heard in Mount Auburn* might serve as herald. After the world of reformers had been given voice, it would be fitting to hear Emerson's characterization of art as the conscious utterance of thought to any end. Here was transcendentalism at the very fount. "Nature paints the best part of the picture. . . . The mind that made the world is not one mind, but the mind. Every man is an inlet to the same, and to all of the same. . . . The delight which a work of art affords, seems to arise from our recognizing in it the mind that formed Nature again in active operation." Those were draughts from the deeper wells. They might gag in the throat of Beacon Hill, but they would soothe the palate of West Street. The Italians must be represented also. Samuel Ward's letters from Italy on Dante, Petrarch, and Boccaccio would sound the southern note and remind the New World of the Old. In between the essays there were poems to be inserted, lines by Caroline Sturgis, who loved to sign herself, "Z," stanzas by Thoreau, verses about violets and sphinxes.

Even then, the copy would not hold out. Margaret would be forced to bridge the gaps with her own writings. She would use her fantasy of *Klopstock and Meta* to fill the empty pages, along with her flowery exhalation from Lake Pontchartrain about the magnolia that knows the secret of the stars. This sentence was not bad, she considered, "The stars tell all their secrets to the flowers, and if we only knew how to look around us, we should not need to look above." It would go unsigned, nevertheless, but she would add an "F." to her essay on *Menzel's View of Goethe.* She was glad to proclaim to Boston—and to New York and London if they would listen—that Menzel judged Goethe as a Philistine who looks at a master from without and tests him with a rule by which he never lived.

These phrases about Goethe carried a certain dignity: "See how he rides at anchor, lordly, rich in freight, every white sail ready to be unfurled at a moment's warning."

The *Record of the Months* would fill the last seven pages. The select list of publications would include a remark about Bancroft's *History of the United States* and this would be followed by the announcement of Hawthorne's *Grandfather's Chair*. Margaret was happy to scribble a note in praise of Sophia Peabody's friend and indeed it was true that no one of all the imaginative writers had indicated a power so peculiar in making present the past scenes of American history.

Margaret thumbed the pages. This was *The Dial: A Magazine for Literature, Philosophy, and Religion,* a journal in which the isms of the new day were reflected and the older tendencies still cast light. She was fatigued and quite unfit to hold the pen any longer, but surely, she considered, *The Dial* must find its place in the sun.

Proof must be corrected, either at 121 Washington Street, where the office of *The Dial* was located, or in Avon Place. It was better to proof read in her own room, where George Ripley would not be rushing in for a financial discussion with Weeks and Jordan, the publishers, and where printer's ink was not so indissolubly associated with the writings of her friends. After the proofs had been corrected, she had only to sit back and wait. Would shadows fall on the face of *The Dial?*

It was annoying, but not very important, to find a few printer's errors when the issue was published, and to hear that Emerson did not like the appearance of the word "Dial," and wished strong, black letters in place of the cautious, palefaced ones that had been used. Other attacks on the journal were more violent than that. *The Knickerbocker* poked fun even at Emerson; *The Philadelphia Gazette* called Margaret a zany and bedlamite, considerably madder than the Mormons. But most of the periodicals seized upon Alcott with the cruelest delight. *The Post* remarked that the *Orphic Sayings* resembled a train of fifteen railroad cars with one passenger, and many rising young journalists found keen pleasure in writing parodies of his utterances, which Alcott calmly cut out and pasted into his diary with the appropriate index.

Even the loyal supporters out West could not refrain from drawing caricatures for private circulation. James Clarke and Christopher Cranch joined forces to paint their friends as others saw them. In one, James sketched Margaret driving a carriage and Emerson riding behind her. The editorial remark emanating from Margaret's mouth was,

> "Our Dial shows the march of light
> O'er forest, hills, and meadows.

To this a critic trudging by replied,

> "Not so, and yet you name it right
> It marks the flight of shadows."

Those drawings from the West were not in earnest; they cast no shadow on *The Dial*. But Margaret had no doubt when she listened to the chat in Boston bookstores, that it was Theodore Parker's articles that carried the quarterly and not her own or Emerson's. No one read the poetry at all; the new contributors were overlooked. They could all digest Parker's meat, but Alcott's tidbits stuck in the throat.

For all the storm at his own work, Alcott did not hesitate to tell Margaret that the periodical was but a twilight "Dial," measuring not the meridian, but the morning ray. The nations, he mused, still wait for the gnomon that shall mark the broad noon. Emerson also considered the journal too timid and did not believe it would scare the tenderest bantling of conformity. It was too literary, he said; it should contain the best advice on government, temperance, and trade. It should be nearer to the hodiurnal facts than his own writings were. Without bruising the whims of others, it should discuss property and land. Margaret knew that Emerson's opinion was the result of the essays he was writing at the moment on labor and reform, but she felt a certain justice in it none the less. The public that had stood before their doors in the highway were no longer on tiptoe for the coming of the new organ. Perhaps Emerson was not wrong in calling *The Dial* a herbarium of dried flowers. Yet at the same time, he felt that it did report the progress of the day, and that all who wrote and sang for it were clothed in white garments. Possibly their garments were too white. Even Sarah Clarke thought the pieces a little lonely, and Carlyle began to write maledictions from Chelsea to the effect that *The Dial* was spirit-like, aeriform, aurora-borealis-like. Where, he demanded, was the stalwart Yankee with color in his cheeks and a coat upon his back? Parker, being the most stalwart of the Yankees associated with *The Dial,* wanted the journal to grow a beard. It lacked fire and flame; it lacked strength. Ripley and Margaret agreed and began to run it down themselves. When Ellery Channing complained of her disposition to mysticism and Germanity, Margaret made no denial. The periodical did not seem everyday enough. It might mark the flight of ages, but not of hours.

Some favorable opinions, however, did begin to be heard. In New York, Thomas Delf, a young Englishman in the employ of Wiley and Putnam, was reading *The Dial* with interest, though he was still seeking articles more solid and distinct for the advancing evolution of truth. And in Louisville, John Keats' brother George found much in it to please him. Though Emerson's hope that the whole world would be its final audience was not fulfilled, the glance it cast upon books and things of the age was a broad one. It had touched a spirit in New York and one in Louisville, and the reposeful spirits of Beacon Hill had been shaken if not profoundly moved.

There was another side of *The Dial* to be considered, a side that reflected more shadow than sun, Ripley's side. The circulation, he was quick to discover, would never include more than three hundred names. Weeks and Jordan were loath to allow the contributors more than twelve free copies for all. Instead of the two hundred dollars that had been promised for Margaret, she found herself the possessor of two free copies of *The Dial*. The expenses of publishing, Ripley estimated, would amount to seven hundred dollars, while the three hundred subscribers would yield only seven hundred and fifty dollars. Margaret realized that she would be unable to continue long without remuneration. In addition to all the monetary difficulties which Ripley had disclosed, Weeks and Jordan were on the point of failure. The Cambridge firm of Metcalf, Torry, and Ballou might print *The Dial* privately for a while and then Elizabeth Peabody might undertake publication. Elizabeth could be relied upon for disinterested support, but never for accuracy in writing. She might wrap the issues of the quarterly, but beyond that Margaret would not trust her far.

There were shadows indeed on *The Dial*. But though it lacked fire and power at times, and though it was failing financially, Margaret comforted herself with the thought that perhaps it was a dial in advance of its times, a dial that marked the sunny hours of the future and hence bore the shadows of the present on its face. Though it did not satisfy the man of the age with its report of the progress of events, it might be to a later generation a history and a sign. It had given her an opportunity, at any rate, to give voice to those of her friends who seemed destined for larger audiences. It had given her exercise in criticism. If it had not yet found its place in the sun, perhaps it would one day. "*The Dial* that marked the flight of shadows." When the shadows had passed, the light would fall upon *The Dial*.

Often during the summer of 1840, it was relief to lay down the pen and the *Dial* proofs to hear Rakemann play or Knight sing Beethoven's *Rosalie*. At Chickering's Rooms Margaret listened to the finest piano she had ever heard, and if she tired of music there was the Athenaeum Hall of Sculpture, where Sarah Clarke was eager to point out the contours in Clevenger's bust of Washington Allston, or the marble Raphael which Mr. Perkins had lent to the gallery. Before the bust of Nicholas I of Russia or the cast of Dr. James Freeman, Margaret could forget the smell of printer's ink or her post-Conversation headache.

Back at Jamaica Plain a visit from Charles Newcomb was excellent excuse to let the velvet pen wiper lie idle. Watching his strange vacillation of mind, his inability to rise above his doubts and fears, Margaret could thank heaven that she was made of firmer fibre and more resolute mind. Yet this young apostle of obscurity, who hated intellect and had no employment beyond his readings in Aeschylus and Calderón, had a subtle influence upon Margaret. He could speak for hours, his puny body crouching on the forest floor, about Being and Reality and Consciousness. Margaret recalled her own ecstatic state on that Thanksgiving Day so many years before, and felt again a restlessness and fever, a mid-summer madness that drew her into strange cosmic relations.

It was not at all the kind of state that Emerson would approve; yet when he invited Margaret and Caroline Sturgis to Concord during the month of August she was

glad to come. Anna Barker was there also, happy in anticipation of the saffron light of October which would soon
make Samuel Ward her husband. With his friends Emerson was far more remote than with his little daughter, his
"honeycomb." For Margaret he led out his winged grif-
fins to take her into the empyrean, and she taxed him with
inhospitality of soul. She offered friendship, she said, and
he gave in return literary comment. Caroline was eager
to give him of herself, but he remained apart, critical,
still a stranger.

"You count and weigh," Margaret reproved, "but you
do not love."
Waldo listened with humility, confessing to the fact of
cold and imperfect intercourse, but not to the impeach-
ment of his will or the deficiency of his affections.

"I count and weigh," he said, "but I love also. I cannot
tell you how warm and glad the naming of your names
makes my solitude. You give me more joy than I could
trust my tongue to tell you." But as he spoke Margaret
knew that if he loved, he loved in a flinty way and that
his thoughts on friendship were even at the moment being
shaped into phrases for an essay on that subject. Margaret was weary of essays, and Emerson, hearing that he
was cold and unkind, retracted his feelers and became a
cake of ice. The crystals seemed to shoot about him, and
the drops solidified. "There is a difference in our constitu-
tions," he explained. "We use a different rhetoric." His
Genius warned him away from so personal a topic. It was
not for him to bring his friendship to speech. Little
Waldo, he said, was the same, for when he asked the
child in the midst of a dialogue with his hobbyhorse if
he loved his father, the boy turned mute and stupid.
"Speak to me," Emerson begged, "of everything but
myself."

Margaret wanted to persist. Emerson, the man, was

more interesting than Emerson, the essayist on Friendship. But she must acquiesce. And indeed there was no want of subjects for discourse. Waldo was eager to talk of his walk with Alcott, Parker, and Christopher Cranch to the Millerite Convention at Groton. A disciple of William Miller had approached them with the words, "Gentlemen!—do you know—do you realize that the world is coming to an end today?" The gentlemen knew that the disciple was anticipating his master, who had postponed the millennium till October 22, 1843, and Parker had replied gruffly, "It does not concern me, for I live in Boston." Emerson had said calmly, "The end of the world does not affect me; I can get along without it." At Groton they had sat in the strange-looking building, one part of which was reserved for women and one for men, listening to Benjamin Hall, the fire eater of fanaticism, and gazing at the white ascension robe of Aunt Betsy Farnsworth, who had bought a new set of false teeth and a green umbrella in preparation for her coming elevation. Margaret smiled, for Aunt Betsy recalled to her mind that other original, the hermitess of Groton. They had all enjoyed the disputes between the Comeouters and the Millerites and had stared transfixed at the beard of Joseph Palmer from No Town. What was more important however, the Friends of Universal Reform would be ready for a convention in the fall, and then, Emerson declared,

"Alcott will come into his own."

The fall of 1840 was an exciting time, for Margaret as well as for those who were sewing their ascension robes. She knew that in spite of his flinty way Emerson was understanding her more completely. Though he did not quite speak her language, he comprehended it. He had thought her a great lady with a Louis Quatorze taste for diamonds, but he had found her with a Bible in her hand, faithful to the new ideas, beholding undaunted their tendency. She held herself aloof from the tendencies, establishing her own equipoise, though she found a place for them in her weekly Conversation or her *Dial*.

The tendencies were in the air, and she sniffed, if she did not breathe deeply. The Ripleys were always ready to discuss their social plans. George Ripley hinted that he might abandon the Purchase Street parish for a community of his own. Emerson began to weigh and count.

"I do not wish to be removed from my present prison to a prison a little larger. I wish to break all prisons."

"You are a little too sanguine," Margaret told Ripley, thinking that though he had the mind of a captain, it was not that of a conqueror. She would look on and see the coral insects at work, though she was not ready to work with them herself. She might give a perch to the fledglings of Community in her *Dial* or let them preen their feathers at a Conversation, but she knew they must be willing to fail before they could succeed. Besides, Margaret felt, every man must struggle with his own ills. It would be no different if many individuals grouped together to struggle *en masse*. Emerson went home to dig his garden—or, as little Waldo said more accurately, his leg. He also preferred a community *en famille* to one *en masse*.

It was almost as exciting, Margaret reflected, to observe experiments as to take part in them. There was a little pain intermingled with her speculations about that more personal experiment—the marriage of Samuel Ward and Anna Barker. It was easier to contemplate Ripley's social plans than to resign without a sigh those two friends to each other, to cover up this fact with roses and myrrh. Samuel would spend his evenings now, sketching in Anna's chamber. Each evening he would conceive a design and draw it—in Anna's chamber. It was less painful to cogitate about other experiments, such as the one on Chardon Street. There the Friends of Universal Reform met to discuss, they said, the Sabbath. Yet, from Emerson's account, Margaret gathered that the assembly of Dunkers and madmen, Muggletonians and Groaners, Agrarians and men with beards soon departed from a consideration of the day of rest to chide or pray, preach or protest their own conceptions of universal reform. There Alcott had his day, speaking in lobbies and halls, while Garrison sat behind his eyeglasses in a corner and Jones Very ascended to the rarefied atmosphere of his own thoughts and Dr. Channing looked on, musing about atonement, and Captain Maria Chapman laid plans to expose the ministry as poor ambassadors of Christ.

The fall fled into winter. Between Conversations on mythology and proof sheets of *The Dial* Margaret found time to discuss Joseph de Maistre's *Soirées de Saint-Pétersbourg* over a cup of tea with Emerson. There was time to lay aside the manuscript of a new contributor and ruminate about a letter George Keats had written to James Clarke, which hinted that Margaret's sister Ellen was not getting along as well as she might with the Keats family, and that her work as a teacher must be postponed because of her neuralgia. Flowers lay dormant under the snow at Jamaica Plain. It was pleasant to return home after a stimulating Conversation and feel the glow of Italy beneath her Saxon crust or to drop the proofs of *The Dial* and thumb through the copy of *Essays* which Emerson had sent her.

Slowly another revolution was completing itself, as winter thawed into spring. Between West Street and Jamaica Plain the tendencies of the age had their span. Greeley had just announced a new morning journal, the *Tribune,* which would labor to advance the interests of the people. Margaret wondered how it would compare with *The Dial.* Greeley wished to avoid servile partisanship and gagged neutrality as much as she did. A daily newspaper would reach a wider public than a quarterly. It would be interesting, Margaret considered, to voice her views in such a journal. Instead of fifty readers she would have fifty thousand. . . . Closer at home, Theodore Parker was reaching another audience with his sermon on *The Transient and Permanent in Christianity.* At the same time that he was preparing for *The Dial* his article on the pharisees of the fireside, the printing press and the street, he was annihilating the pharisees of politics and the church who had sold their Puritan heritage for trade profits. Emerson would be interested in discussing Parker's statement that the germs of religion were born in man, that God was a fact, given in our nature.

Emerson was interested. Working five or six hours a day in his garden, he cherished his own thoughts on labor and on pharisees. Margaret was glad to forget the Peabody bookshop and the *Dial* office among the wildflowers and singing birds, the hens and cows of Concord. Now Waldo had a friend with him, Henry Thoreau, who was acting as his workingman. It was strange that though this gaunt, angular man wished to be a farmer, he should be so earnest a thinker. He seemed to have all the natural history of Massachusetts at his fingers' tips, and as he rowed Margaret across the pond in the boat he had made himself, she planned, not only to ask him to write on that subject for *The Dial,* but to know him better. In this short May visit there was scarcely time to discover the honesty that hovered about his long nose and queer mouth; he paddled so perfectly—almost with the skill of an Indian —perhaps nature *would* be his one day.

But even Thoreau's paddling could not completely dispel the strain of a winter of Conversations and proof sheets. The headaches still tormented Margaret at Concord and Parker's views on Christianity and Greeley's journalistic plans became a throbbing nightmare. One evening as she groped about for her medicine in the darkness, Margaret opened a phial of camphor by mistake and swallowed it all. When Elizabeth Hoar discovered what had happened she raced to Dr. Bartlett to inquire how much camphor one might take without fatal effects. The gruff Dr. Bartlett looked out of the window and demanded, "Who has taken it?" "Margaret Fuller," responded Elizabeth. The foundation of Dr. Bartlett's character was absolute honesty—in speech as well as in action. As he ducked back into his room, he called out, "A peck!" Then he slammed the window.

Margaret had a lordly appetite and could take a peck of activity as easily as a peck of solitude—or of camphor. When Caroline Sturgis suggested that they spend part of the summer together near Dr. Channing's home in Newport, Margaret dropped her *Dial* sheets and her plans for next winter's Conversations to go to Paradise Farm. The house was about a mile and a half from Newport on the second beach. The shore was bounded by rocks and very few of the Newport fashionables ventured near it. Margaret was glad to doff her white cambrics for a savage dishabille and race up the slope of the hill on which the little white farmhouse had been built. She need not rise early to coil her braids or prepare her thoughts for the ladies of West Street, but could lie in bed, watching the glitter of the wide, blue waters. A farmer prepared a bathing house for the two guests and every morning Margaret put on her bombaset for an ocean bath. Then she walked back slowly to the house with its scarlet honeysuckle trained over the door, and its little window stands with greenhouse plants.

In the afternoons she drove with Caroline to Oakland, where Doctor Channing spent seven or eight months of the year. Sometimes they would all go out together in a rough wagon or a chaise and Dr. Channing would point out a bird's nest, or a flower, the roll of the surf, or a cloud that passed in the skies. He liked to call Margaret's attention to Washington Allston's haunts, for as a boy the painter had studied in a Newport school. There was tea after the drive and then everyone must gather in the garden to look at the western sky, for the house was too embowered to admit a view of the setting sun.

After sunset Dr. Channing left the outer world for his parlor, and then at last he would consent to talk with Margaret about *The Dial*. He too was disappointed in the periodical. It did not display the ability he had expected. It was a pity that Henry Hedge had not had more to do with it, for Hedge was conservative and might have made Transcendentalism appeal even to Beacon Hill. Here the Doctor would smile archly, for he too had dwelt upon that promontory. Then he would shift the talk to the Conversations, advising Margaret to ignore whatever ugly things might have been said of them. Caroline rushed to their defense, praising Margaret's bursts of eloquence. The Doctor nodded agreement. He knew Margaret's conversational talents well, he said. Had he not listened to her three years before when she had discussed Herder and Goethe? Margaret considered that she had done most of the listening then, but perhaps Dr. Channing was forgetting. He was growing perceptibly older, and though he had heard the torrent of the times he wished to stem it. Margaret had no wish either to stem or force the torrent. She longed only to hold her ear close to the ground and listen. From that sound one day the music of the spheres might rise. All things seemed possible in this fourth decade of the nineteenth century.

The torrent of the times rushed no more forcefully than the torrent of Margaret's own life. The winter Conversations must be planned. For the October *Dial,* which

Elizabeth Peabody was to publish, Margaret gathered together Emerson's *Woodnotes* and Cranch's poems and polished up her own *Lives of the Great Composers* after a study of Schindler's *Beethoven* and Forkel's *Bach*. Yet, when Phi Beta Kappa day rolled round once again she found time for a visit to Cambridge. The Farrars had invited her and Julia Ward to pass the day at their home, and together they walked to the meeting to hear Henry Hedge deliver his first Phi Beta Kappa address. As Margaret listened to the steely ring of his voice and his clear-cut sentences, she reflected that the Society had not recovered sufficiently from Waldo Emerson's *American Scholar* to summon a more radical speaker than Henry Hedge. When Julia Ward later asked Margaret whether she had not found Dr. Hedge's discourse very good, she replied,

"Yes. It was high ground for middle ground."
She would have preferred a speaker who could have taken a more pronounced position with regard to the torrent of the times. Shortly after dinner, while Miss Ward was seated on the piazza with Margaret, a carriage drove up before the door. It was Mr. Ripley, who had come to take Margaret to Waltham.

Margaret's camp chest was a roving one these days. From Newport to Waltham, from Concord to Cambridge, she wandered. But if she could forget *The Dial* for a few weeks, news from home pursued her wherever she retreated. The news that followed her to Cambridge was sudden and not entirely auspicious. Her sister was engaged to Ellery Channing. His poems indeed had suggested her beauty and the possibility of such a union had flitted across her mind when Ellen had gone to Cincinnati. Still, in its suddenness, the news came like a blow. From what she knew of Dr. Walter Channing's son, she recognized Ellery as a capricious creature, who would follow any will-o'-the-wisp into fairyland. His study of law had been as desultory as his excursions into medicine. Her sister was in her way no more reliable. They were so young. Had it not been for the expense involved she would have packed the roving camp chest once again and set out for Cincinnati. But Margaret knew it would have done no good. There was moonlight in Cincinnati no doubt as there had been at Trenton Falls. . . . The news about Richard was more hopeful. He had left the Kilby Street jobber and was determined to enter Harvard as a sophomore next February. Margaret must write a note of introduction to Emerson so that the boy could study at Concord while he lived in true transcendental style on milk and brown bread.

After the October *Dial* had been safely launched, Margaret packed the roving camp chest for another visit to Emerson. Yet again she felt that inability to receive him —his inability to give himself. She walked into his library one day when he had wandered off alone into the fields. It seemed to her a sacred place. She had come to find a book so that she might feel more life and be worthy to sleep, but there was so much soul in this room that she did not need a book. She stepped off the library steps and glanced away from the Plotinus and Milton, the Scott and Herschel. She could not reach Emerson, the man within the shell, but as she wandered about the room, looking again at the head of Homer, the Parcae over the fireplace, and his papers upon the floor, the beauty and permanence of his life came to her.

She sat down at his table, drew a paper from his leather portfolio, and took up his pen to write to him. Poetry had ascended from the depths of nature, and only at a similar depth should she be apprehended. Margaret would tell him, while she felt it, how long it must be before she could meet him truly. "I see you," she wrote, "and fancied it nearer than it was; you were right in knowing the contrary." How much more she would have liked to say, but could not. She was too powerfully drawn while she was with him and could not advance a step. But when he was gone, she had learned something. She had learned that their friendship would grow, though her own affections were more household than his and her ebullitions burst over his calm surfaces. She stopped and looked at her note. She knew that Waldo would endorse it carefully, "Letter written at Concord from room to room." He would agree that when they promised to come nearest in their relationship, they froze one another to silence. . . . Indeed, after Emerson had read her letter, their conversation, he thought, was strange, cold-warm, attractive-repelling. Yet he always admired her, revered her almost, and sometimes, he confessed, he loved her. That must be enough. To tread beyond were hazardous.

The ground near Alcott's home was less dangerous. As they walked to Dove Cottage, Emerson told Margaret of the plays in the barn with which the Alcott children were amusing themselves. Once, when "Jack" cut down the squash vine running up a ladder that represented the bean stalk, the "giant" had come tumbling from a loft. Little Louisa was very ingenious. She had provided a vast pumpkin for Cinderella, and a long black pudding to fasten on the nose of the woman who wasted her three wishes. At one of Alcott's strawberry parties, she had ambled about with a cockleshell in her hat, while her father had sat beneath a tree asking Emerson, why, since he wrote on the genius of Plato and Pythagoras, he did not write on the genius of Alcott. Alcott's biography was his favorite subject, Margaret considered. His topic yesterday was Alcott on the sixth of October; today it would be Alcott on the seventh.

Margaret had not been entirely correct. His topic today was not Alcott, but Alcott's children. He was eager to show his guests the little pictures he had been using to illustrate the girls' lessons. For Louisa there had been a child playing on a harp, beneath which were the words: Love, Music, Concord. The contrasting picture was of another child drawing an arrow, and beneath this he had written: Anger, Arrow, Discord.

"Well, Mr. Alcott," remarked Margaret, "it is fine that you have been able to carry out your methods in your own family. Now I should like to see your model children."

No sooner had the words been spoken than they were answered—by a wild uproar, and the approach of a wheelbarrow holding baby May arrayed as a queen. Louisa, it became apparent, was the horse, who bitted and bridled, while sister Anna did the driving, and sister Lizzie played dog, barking under the wheels of the chariot. As they approached the steps of Dove Cottage, the car jolted, Louisa's foot slipped, and down came all in a hilarious heap.

"Here," Mrs. Alcott said, waving her hand, "are the model children, Miss Fuller."

It had been a long way, Margaret reflected, from Dr. Channing's home at Newport to Alcott's model children. There was poetry in both and she meant to drink deep of it. The Conversations, now in their third year, were fatiguing, and it was annoying to find that the printers had cut Cranch's poem in half in the last *Dial*. There was more poetry in a few days at Newbury than in weeks of West Street or Jamaica Plain. With Caroline Sturgis Margaret visited that pleasant spot, forgetting the proof sheets in her little room over the mill, as she had forgotten them at Newport during the summer. She rose later than her brother Richard would have approved and then Caroline rowed her about the river in a little boat

painted green with an orange rim. In the evenings they
sat before the bright wood fire, looking at Cursen's
sketches of life in the West, planning one day to visit
that part of the country. Those three days at Newbury
made Margaret understand why Goethe had limited the
days of intercourse to three in the *Wanderjahre*. They
made her long for a community of friends settled on the
banks of a stream like this. Here the weight of the social
contract could be thrown off. Perhaps George Ripley had
not been too sanguine when he bought Brook Farm.

It must have been the poetry of Newbury that lived
on in Margaret's mind during the winter. For the first
time in her life she awoke from a dream saying three
lines of verse:

> "Where man never came
> And no song of blame
> Attends in the course of the stars."

The stars of winter looked kindly down after so full an
autumn. The camp chest roved no more. From Jamaica
Plain Margaret launched the seventh issue of *The Dial*
and from her "Parlatorio" at West Street gave to the
ladies of Boston a new interpretation of literature. Yet,
no sooner had the New Year turned than the stars retracted their kindly influence. Poetry was hidden in a
shroud. Death had come to Concord, and Emerson's
beautiful, blue-eyed Waldo had turned into a statue. Why
he, she asked, why he, who bore within himself the golden
future? His father no doubt would meet his boy again,
but for Margaret he was irrevocably lost. Waldo was the
only child she ever wished she might have called her own.
His beauty could not save him. Emerson must struggle
with his own farewell.

Beauty could not save—but work might. *The Dial* was
faltering and though Margaret felt she could not edit

another issue without recompense, there was other work
to do. There had been no compensation from Hilliard
and Gray for those Eckermann Conversations. Perhaps
another translation might bring better success. Though
the life of Goethe had never been completed, the master
still would lead the way. His correspondence with Bettina
Brentano had been translated and recently reprinted in
Massachusetts. Margaret knew of other letters, almost
as interesting, between the child Bettina and the canoness
Günderode, which had never been translated. Margaret
would give to the world the ideal Günderode who had
thrown herself into a river because the world was too
narrow, and the natural Bettina who lived to follow out
every freakish fancy. Again the velvet pen wiper was
busy, wiping away the pain of Concord along with the ink
that stained the pen. She would direct her mind to the
exact transmission of thought, the thought that had
passed between two girls in Germany at the dawn of the
nineteenth century. As she bent over the letters on her
desk, Margaret became Bettina, the worshipping child,
became Günderode, the soul so delicately apparelled, the
woman so tenderly transfigured. The canoness was about
eight years older than Bettina. Margaret understood their
relationship well. She had been the Bettina to Emerson's
Günderode; she had been the Günderode to Caroline
Sturgis' Bettina. The action between the two was the
action of the ideal upon the natural and was of the highest
poetical significance.

Margaret slipped into Bettina's mood. In the girl's
history lessons she rediscovered her own childhood. When
Bettina's tutor opened his mouth he opened an impenetrable gulf which spewed forth the mammoth bones of the
past, not unlike those found once in *The Chronology of
the English Kings*. Herr Hoffmann explaining the mysteries of thorough bass became Mr. Taylor at a piano in

Cherry Street. Margaret sat with Bettina alone in Meerholz, writing to her friend that she longed to take root in her, that death was a chemical process, a separation, but not annihilation of powers. Margaret could understand Bettina's notion that out of the power to discern connections, the gift of prophecy arose. But the connection between life and death she could not perceive with the hopefulness of the sixteen-year-old Brentano.

She visited the canoness with Bettina and left her shell box with the sepia saucers on the floor. How long ago it was, really, since she had built castles out of shells on her father's whatnot. The flageolet she played for Günderode, as she had played the piano so many lives ago. She walked with the canoness on the hill in the night dew, and then lay down to rest with her, talking as the wind rose, holding grand and profound speculations. How strange that Bettina should have thought each man had a demon that would answer only to unprofane questioning. Bettina's demon held her firmly bound to the canoness. Margaret hovered near while the girl braided her friend's hair and Karoline von Günderode composed Ossianic songs. Günderode was the seer, while Bettina regarded only the shadows of those spirits that consorted with her friend. Man was nothing but the desire to feel himself in another. As the two were drawn upward in the soundless, silver night, almost touching the centre of truth, Margaret remembered other silver nights with Samuel Ward at Trenton Falls, with Caroline Sturgis on a green river boat at Newbury. In the work she had forgotten and yet rediscovered herself. Through the work she had given to the world a Bettina who drew new tides of vital energy from man and tree and friend, a Günderode who harmonized all objects into their true relations, extracting from every form of life its eternal meaning.

Emerson too had found release from pain in work and

thought. He had said his farewells to his boy, and though he would never cease to say them, he could hold discourse in more earthly language now. On Staten Island he had met Horace Greeley, the young man with soft white hair who was listening after all new thoughts, who declared himself a Transcendentalist, yet was a Unitarian and a defender of miracles at the same time. Emerson had dined with Greeley and Brisbane, the socialist, in a Grahamite boarding house and had heard the trumpets of Community's advance guard. He too was watching the progress of the hour and the day and was willing to take over the editorship of *The Dial* to report that progress. He too knew that work would save where beauty had failed to save.

But after work came the demand for rest; the body must be served as well as the mind. Again Margaret's camp chest roved, to Canton in the spring, for she was ready to visit her uncle, Charles Crane, and rest for a few weeks in the red farmhouse. It was pleasant to contemplate nothing but stacks of crockery, blue plates, and silver spoons after she had soared with Bettina to the empyrean. The kitchen, with its salt box full of eggs, was a comfortable place after the crowded West Street bookshop and if the shingles of the farmhouse peeled before the winds, it was a fine off-shore breeze to inhale after the smell of printer's ink. If she longed for books, there were the dramas of Euripides and the works of Xenophon. Within the house nothing but the sound of the wind or the scratching of the chickens interrupted the silence. It was a bower of solitude after the rooms at Avon Place. It was Lethe and a bed of asphodel.

Yet the outer world tapped even on the windowpanes of the Canton farmhouse. Letters must be acknowledged; Margaret's brothers must be told to buy linen for their shirt bosoms; Emerson must be given instructions about

The Dial. Though Margaret refused to be disturbed by the trumpets of the outer world, she heard their blast. Alcott had sailed for England and not long after, seven hundred and fifty copies of his *Conversations on the Gospels* were sold to the trunkmakers for wastepaper at five cents a pound. Margaret hoped that England would receive the gentle philosopher more cordially than America had. Young Thomas Higginson, she heard, was promenading the streets of Boston in a new flash vest, and the ladies of Washington Street had taken to long sleeves in place of bishop's sleeves. Margaret preferred the roaring of the wind in Canton to the gossip about Boston fashions, but to other news she could not turn so deaf an ear. Sophia Peabody had written a letter to her "dear, most noble Margaret," announcing her engagement to Nathaniel Hawthorne and suggesting that she visit them when they set up house in the Old Manse. Margaret was glad for Sophia's sake, for she knew that her love had been freely given, that it had grown not from wants and wishes, but from the demands of her character. Hawthorne had enough woman in him to understand his delicate Sophia. The whole earth was decked for their bridal. Sarah Clarke had gone to Concord with Sophia to help her measure her house for carpets and papers. They had had time to speak of Margaret and to hope that she would visit Concord before long. Sarah had measured Emerson no less accurately than she had measured the floor for carpets and perceived that he was beginning to find in the eyes of little Edith, his honeycomb, the eyes of Waldo.

There was yet another visit for Margaret, however, before she could contemplate a journey to Concord. If she had found rest in Charles Crane's farmhouse, surely she could find even more relaxation at the New Bedford home of Mary Rotch, the Quaker. Had not Emerson suggested that it was the vision of Mary Rotch leaving church when the Last Supper was to be commemorated which first cast a blight upon that rite in his eyes? Even her humor was quiet, for she was ever listening to the voice within. Though Miss Rotch was entertaining other guests, Margaret could sit alone in her room several hours every day, and then could converse with her "Aunt Mary" (it was pleasing to be allied with Emerson in the possession of an Aunt Mary) about the "leading" and "oracles" at the latest meeting of Friends. It was new for Margaret, a stranger quiet than the howling of the wind had afforded at Canton. And in that quiet she was finding new thoughts. Though it was nobler to live than to think, one must think in order to live, and the thoughts were taking shape at last.

If Margaret had found thoughts of poetry in Caroline Sturgis' rowboat at Newbury or in the red farmhouse at Canton, it was not strange that she should find them in the dances of Fanny Elssler which she saw with Emerson. It was pleasant to forget her Conversations on the Fine Arts in a performance of one of the finest of arts. She shows us freedom, Emerson mused. Elssler is bewitching because most of us are pinched and restrained by the decorums of city life. They walk through their cotillions in Papanti's assemblies, but Fanny's arms, head, and body dance as well as her feet. Bewitching! he thought, in that arch "Cracovienne" and in "Natalie." How charmingly her partner, Sylvain, responds to the call of her castanets. If Margaret found poetry in Fanny Elssler's dancing, Emerson perceived a kind of religion.

Religion, Margaret was beginning to understand, had a common root with poetry. In the summer of 1842, she paused to gather her thoughts together and find her exact relationship to the universe, to examine the philosophy which her thirty-two years of life had given her, and write her "Credo." First there was a force—a spirit, uncontainable and uncontained, within which dwelt good and evil. This spirit it was that evolved the suns, the plants, the animals, and man, and an infinity of forms not yet visible to Margaret's horizon. It generated, she pondered, and conquered obstruction, working ever for good, even through evil. Man was its Hallelujah, who must at once be imbedded in nature, and yet rise above nature, publishing spirit in the human form. Man was the rivet in the great chain. Man interpreted and cast light upon darkness, at the same time posing another mystery yet to be penetrated. Man was a tree in the garden of the spirit, from whose trunk grew the branches of art and literature, of the social contracts and religion. As the oak desired to plant its acorns, so did souls become the fathers of souls. Some did this through the body and these were the citizens. Others did this through the intellect and they were the philosophers, the poets. All were anointed, all Immanuel, all Messiah, if they were true to the law of their existence. The spirit gave laws with Confucius and Moses, tried them with Brahma and lived its life of eloquence in the Apollo. It wandered with Osiris and lived one life as Plato, another as Michelangelo.

Margaret searched her mind and found that she believed in the long preparation of ages. So Jesus came, when the time was ripe. His miracles were of no consequence; of consequence only was the ideal truth they illustrated. The Jewish nation who passed their children through the fire to Moloch were as pious, but less superstitious than the exclusive devotion to Christ had made many of his followers. As Apollo was the representative of his age, so Christ was of his. Yet he would make himself known only to those who had freed themselves from him. Margaret discovered that she believed in Christ only because she could do without him; because the truth he announced she could see elsewhere intimated; because it was foreshadowed in the very nature of her own being. Let men who could do so with sincerity live in the church. For herself she would not, for her belief was a wider one than that of any body of men she knew. The blue sky preached better than any minister. Apollo, a beautiful child, the summer's earliest rose, Jesus—all were modifications of the same harmony. She would not loathe sects and persuasions and systems, though she could not abide in them one moment. Most men still were in need of them. Even Henry Thoreau worshipped with his Sunday-walkers.

From all the sects Margaret would seek the Father of her soul, learning from them all, from the countless ages that had passed, and from the Word that yet would come. The very greatness of the manifestation of Spirit in Jesus called for a higher manifestation. We want a life more complete and various than his; we look for one who will live out all the symbolical forms of human life with the calm beauty and physical fullness of a Greek god, with the deep consciousness of a Moses, with the holy love and purity of Jesus. The soul must do its own immortal work. "It is expedient for you that I go away; for if I go not, the Comforter will not come unto you; but if I depart, I will send him unto you." Margaret's soul was doing its own work. She was breaking the idols of the mind. She knew, as Emerson himself did not know, that man's spirit and body were interrelated; she felt, as Alcott could not feel, that the Golden Age lay beyond in the future, more glittering than that in the past. She looked upon the ages with an eye more universal than that of the Unitarians or the Quakers, or the Transcendentalists. In no sect would she put her faith, but in man who could free himself from sects. Hers was a credo, she reflected, not for the New World—but for some newer world, where planet was generated from planet and sun from sun. The stardust that had been sprinkled upon her at Cambridge on Thanksgiving Day, in another age of her life, the stardust that she had sifted with Emerson at Concord—these were but signs. The star itself was there—far off—in the future. But before man could tread its shining surface, he must walk on the earth erect and filled with courage.

Margaret was never reluctant to leave off star-gazing for earth-treading, especially when the earth was that of Concord. Concord had always been close to heaven, but now that Nathaniel Hawthorne had carried his bride, Sophia Peabody, thither, the village gave promise of approaching the empyrean. Ellery Channing had also decided to take his wife, Margaret's sister Ellen, to live among the rarefied spirits of the town. Concord might not be a star, but it lay nearer to the celestial regions than any other spot on the map of the New World.

Margaret invited herself to Emerson's home on condition that she might put on sulkiness as a morning gown and he might wear sulkiness as a surtout, that speech be contraband and the exception not the rule. Emerson admired the terms of her treaty and on August seventeenth Margaret boarded the fly for his home. It was a different Margaret, she reflected, from the one who had driven in impetuous haste to Concord six years before. It was a Margaret who was holding, if not the world in chains, at least twenty-five ladies who assembled for the West Street Conversations, a Margaret who had roused Beacon Street from its slumbers by her *Dial,* who had gone abroad, if not in Europe, in New England, and had found in Newport and Newbury, in Canton and Cambridge, ground for the sowing of seeds and water for their growth. It was a Margaret who had suffered and conquered her pain in the work of translating the letters of two German girls, a Margaret who had gathered the strands of her life together in a Credo and had at last begun to know herself.

In the downstairs bedroom of Emerson's house or in his study she passed the days by preparing a paper on the Rhenish and Romaic ballads for the next issue of *The Dial*. She lay on the large mahogany poster bed in the guest room and looked up from her papers to the Sistine Madonna on the wall. Sometimes in the study she turned from her essay to Emerson's journals, or flipped the pages of Ellery Channing's poems, finding in his "soft breathing of mid-summer wind" a tribute to his wife, her sister.

Ellery was at Concord too as a guest and Margaret soon decided to remove her morning gown of sulkiness for a robe of sociability. She wanted to know him and that other poet too, Emerson's workingman, young Henry Thoreau. Already she knew a great deal of Ellery from his poems. They were full of freakish fantasies. It was as if he would never study the harp of his mind, but would always improvise. He thought himself a genius whose verses were too sacred to be sold for money. So he said as he hovered about the study like a hobgoblin, full of indirections. But outside of the study his vagabond nature came into its own. He had the gypsy talent and knew how to take a walk. When Elizabeth Hoar called him a wood-elf, Margaret replied, "He reminds me of a great Genius with a little wretched boy trotting beside him." Yet when he walked the little wretched boy trotted far behind, and the great Genius stalked ahead, manifesting itself in Ellery's phrases. "I hope there will be no cows in heaven," he said, "for I have discovered what cows are for. They make easy walking where they have fed, and they give the farmers something to do in summer time. Thus intemperance and the progress of crime are prevented." Margaret kindled, but Ellery could never stay long with a cow. His perpetual *non sequitur* was disturbing, but delightful. The Genius was running on, now, catching life in a butterfly net. "Life is so short that I should think that everybody would steal." Margaret had no opportunity to ask him to explain, for as he had snared life, he would snare his friends in his net. "Alcott has caught the universe on his thumbnail, and cracked it; he has been at the banquet of the gods, and borrowed the spoons." Ask him to pursue the subject of Alcott, and he darted off to Hawthorne. "He is a lucky man who can write forty pages on a hiccough and ten pages on a man's sitting down in a chair, like Hawthorne."

It was strange, Margaret thought, that Ellery and Thoreau should be such fast friends. But both were poets and both were walkers, and those were broad enough grounds on which to meet. When Ellery spoke, it was as if one listened to the sharp taps of a woodpecker, but when Thoreau spoke it was like hearing the wind among the boughs of a forest tree. There was more honesty in Thoreau's ugliness than in Ellery's elfin beauty. Ellery did not see as far as Thoreau, who could see the horizon and therefore had earned the right to say what he pleased of any tree or twig between himself and it. It was amusing to walk with the two together. Margaret noticed that Ellery had begun to carry a little pocketbook as Thoreau did, but where Thoreau gazed with his enormous blue eyes upon a woodchuck and transmuted every aspect of its hide into crystal clear words, Ellery darted his gray eyes from twig to flower and only affected to write down their names. Ellery always seemed to be looking for clues to himself. Margaret felt that Thoreau might well have found the clue to the universe. Elizabeth Hoar had said that one would as soon take the arm of an elm tree as Thoreau's, and her mother had concluded that Henry talked about nature just as if she'd been born and brought up in Concord. Concord was nature to Thoreau.

On his favorite walk, for like Emerson he had his favorite walk, he tired even Ellery with his diligence. Under his long arm he carried his father's *primo flauto* with which to press plants, and his short legs strode the old Marlborough road as if he wore seven-league boots. He felt in his pocket for the diary and pencil, the spyglass for birds, the jackknife and twine. In his strong gray trousers and stout shoes and straw hat he would brave every shrub-oak and smilax in the woods, and while Ellery was musing about a phrase he would climb a tree for a hawk's nest or wade into a pool for a water lily. His shoulders sloped as he walked, a little like Emerson's, Margaret thought, and sometimes he would stop sharp, looking more like a bird than a human being. He had a little boy in him too, she perceived, not Ellery's wretched boy, but the wide-eyed boy who could never pass a berry without picking it, who could make a basket out of a square of birch bark, who would never grow up. He too had his Genius—and Margaret suspected it was greater than Ellery's. He knew that the truth he would write would be the tougher for the callus on his palms. He had set his traps for facts and not for fantasies, and he too could transmute them into a phrase. The bluebird, he said, carried the sky on its back. The wood-tortoise and the turtle were his friends. The song of the thrush was as familiar to him as *Tom Boline* or Moore's *Canadian Boat Song*. He knew the otter's tracks; he had sounded the deeps and shallows of the Concord River.

At rare times he would speak to Margaret of the journey he had taken on the Concord and Merrimac three years before with his brother, and of the boat they had made, green below with a border of blue to correspond to the two elements in which it was to spend its existence. He would turn his ruddy, weather-beaten face toward the river and tell how one morning before sunrise he had passed down the stream between fields of lilies that flashed open before him as the flakes of sunlight fell upon the surface of the water. He had heard the telegraph harp singing its message through the country; he had heard the screaming of the fish hawk and the sound of rain on the roof of a tent. He had heard silence, but that was all he would say of silence, for she could not be done into English. Thoreau stopped talking as suddenly as he had begun. His brother John, with whom he had explored the rivers, had died of lockjaw in February. Of John he could not speak, but it was hard to look at the Concord without thinking of him.

At night the four would sometimes walk together to the hill, Emerson, Thoreau, Ellery, and Margaret. Emerson watched the stars, while Ellery whipped out the latest phrase he had coined, "How well they wear!" Thoreau said nothing. Margaret understood that in the fluttering of a leaf he had heard his Christianity preached. That too could not be done into English. There, on the hilltop, with his collar turned over like Emerson's, and his huge nose casting shadows on his chin as Emerson's did, he was still himself. His life was the poem he would write. Emerson had gone forth to love nature as one would go to a book to learn a new language. Thoreau was nature itself. The best part of an animal, he said, was its *anima,* but the scientists never got any further than the shell. Emerson had penetrated the shell, but Thoreau, Margaret knew, was himself the *anima.*

Often Thoreau and Ellery would leave the house early in the morning and walk by themselves. On the evening of such a day, Emerson and Margaret strolled together to the river to see the moon broken in the water. They spoke of their friends, of Ellery, who had written a charming poem to Elizabeth Hoar, calling her Una, in whose silver network play thoughts that to the gods aspire. It was little wonder that Ellery should kneel before Elizabeth's pathless mind. He was so full of cunning contraries himself. If he had not considered himself so great a genius, Margaret thought, he might perhaps have been a little one. Emerson agreed, adding that Ellery's oddity occasionally amounted to comedy. One day he asked Henry Thoreau to tell his mother not to appear when he came to his house. Thoreau of course had refused, saying it was his mother's house. The next time Ellery went there, Mrs. Thoreau opened the door and he turned his back to her. Mrs. Thoreau, in her lace cap with long strings, immediately turned hers, and there they had stood, back to back. Yes, Ellery's wretched little boy would always trot behind him. Margaret wondered whether her sister would ever trap the boy and free the genius. In a way, she thought, Ellery himself was a tendency of the times, of a capricious age that lent its ear first to one and then to another party.

"I feel myself in the midst of tendencies," she said, looking up at Emerson's face, on which the moon cast its interrogating beams. "I do not regret life nor accuse the imperfections of my own while these strong native tendencies appear. In the children of us all they will be ripened."

Emerson looked at the moon that questioned the waters, and did not answer.

It was easy at Concord to don the morning gown of sulkiness again after the evening robe of sociability. Two days after her walk with Emerson Margaret went alone to Sleepy Hollow. It was the coolest spot in all of Concord, and there, near the low wooded ridge she could sit down among the wildflowers on the hillside and read the copy of Kant's *Pure Reason* which she carried under her arm. There she sat, meditating the tendencies of her day, turning the pages of Kant, but thinking more of practical than pure reason. It was pleasant, after the noise of Washington Street, to listen to the wind, to the birds, to the silence that could not be done into English.

As she sat, she saw approaching her a man in a blue frock such as she knew the Brook Farmers were wearing at Ripley's community. He looked down at his boots as if he were shy even of sunlight, and Margaret recognized him as Nathaniel Hawthorne. He sat next to her, glancing at her book, the title of which he did not seem to understand. He looked at the curve of Margaret's shoulders and at the partial closing of her eyes, feeling that they penetrated his own through their narrowed apertures more deeply than if they had been wide open. Hawthorne feared that history would begin to drop from her fingers' ends, but Margaret was less interested at the moment in Kant or Plato than in the proposal that Ellery and Ellen board for a while with the Hawthornes at the Old Manse. She had written to Hawthorne, suggesting such an arrangement, and he had replied that Adam and Eve would not have received two *angels* into paradise as boarders. He was still averse to the thought of living with the Channings, and his conversation with Margaret was somewhat strained. Soon, an old man passed by and smiled to see her reclining on the ground with Hawthorne sitting beside her. He remarked upon the beauty of the afternoon and then withdrew into the shadow of the wood. It became easier to talk. Autumn would soon brood over Concord; there was its beauty to be discussed; there was the pleasure of being lost in the woods to be spoken of. When a crow perched upon a twig, there was a lovely image to transpose into phrases. They spoke of mountains and the view from their summits. Hawthorne spoke briefly of his experiences at Brook Farm and again suggested that Margaret visit Sophia at the Old Manse. Margaret told him she had just sent her youngest brother Lloyd to Brook

Farm and was about to mention the boy's backwardness when they heard footsteps above them on the high bank. A voice called, "Margaret." Out of the green shade emerged Emerson, a pure gleam diffused about his presence like a shining garment.

"There have been muses in the woods, today," he said, "and whispers in the breezes."

The shadows on the woods were six-o'clock shadows. It was time, Emerson said, to return. Lidian's face was swollen after a dental operation, and though he hated to leave the woods for the house, he could not forget his Asia in the midst of Sleepy Hollow. Hawthorne walked away, disappearing into the shade. "He holds a dark steed hard," commented Emerson. "His reputation as a writer is a pleasing fact because his writing is not good for anything and this is a tribute to the man."

Margaret was inclined to disagree. She felt he rode the steed of words far more gallantly than the steed of life. But since she had seen Thoreau in his Concord setting, she thought it would be interesting to watch Hawthorne nibble on miseries in the shadow of the Old Manse.

Before she could visit Hawthorne's home there was Phi Beta Kappa night to be celebrated at Ripley's house in Waltham. On August twenty-fifth the Concordians descended on Waltham Plain in solid column. There was much to be discussed at the soiree. Sarah Ripley was eager to talk of Sophia Ripley's metamorphosis into a laundress at Brook Farm, and Emerson was ready to impart the news he had just received about Alcott. Mr. Alcott, he said, had written to his wife that he had quarreled with Carlyle and Emerson quoted his friend as having declared, "Greatness abides not here. Her home is in the clouds, save when she descends on the meadows or treads the groves of Concord."

"Alcott will never recognize a world outside of Concord," Ellery remarked. "Even his collection of diaries is his Encyclopédie de Moi-même en cents volumes."

"Yet," Thoreau returned, "he is the best-natured man I ever met. The rats and mice make their nests in him." Mrs. Ripley thought that Alcott would surely be interested in the community at Brook Farm, but Ellery considered that no community would interest Alcott unless it were his own.

Margaret looked from face to face. Thoreau would surely prefer a community of one, she decided, and Emerson, for all his faith in the Universal had not yet enough faith in society to take part in any association. Ellery might enjoy a visit now and then, but Ellen surely was waiting for him to find a home for her in Concord and not a community dining hall in West Roxbury. As for herself, she would wait. Her brief visit to a masquerade at Brook Farm had not been enough to acquaint her with the new philosophy. Hawthorne, who had lived there, would know more than those who looked on from a distance. It was another tendency, she considered, one that she would observe with interest as she had observed so many others.

On September fourth, Samuel Ward appeared at Emerson's home for a brief visit, and was glad to accompany Margaret to the Old Manse. As they walked she confessed that she had longed to see him a painter rather than a merchant drudging in a broker's shop. Yet, he seemed happy enough, dividing his day into merchant hours and painting hours. Perhaps his sketches in Anna's chamber made up for his notations in the broker's shop. Perhaps he was strong enough not to disintegrate under this division of his life.

They walked on through the avenue of sombre black ash trees that led to the Old Manse. The house was set back from the road, its entrance guarded by two tall granite posts. Margaret knew that the gate itself had fallen from its hinges years before. On one side of the house she saw the apple orchard that Dr. Ripley had planted, and pointed out the blue pearmain, the dark red autumn apple with the purple bloom upon it. They walked toward the manse, catching a glimpse of the Concord River sweeping in magnificent curve by the broad meadows and hills that led up to the pale blue outline of Wachusett in the far-off western horizon. The whole wheel track along which they passed was overgrown with grass; an old white horse was nibbling a mouthful. There were shadows among the ash trees. It was as if Hawthorne had drawn a shade between his home and the outer world.

As they entered the doorway, Mary Bryan, the cook, called Mrs. Hawthorne, and Sophia came forth to greet them. "My husband," she said in a whisper, "is writing entries in his journal, but he will be down shortly."
She escorted her guests around the house.

"Boston could not afford so charming a drawing room as your parlor," Samuel Ward remarked.
It was true, Margaret thought; even the astral lamps and card tables, the silver taper stands and gilded Cologne bottles did not seem at all impertinent in this dark and ghostly parlor. There was a music box to which Sophia said she often danced.

"But there are stranger sounds to be heard here. My husband says that a ghost rustles papers in this corner, as if he were turning the leaves of a sermon."

Sophia would not have dared lead her visitors to her husband's study had he not appeared and invited them in. There were golden-tinted hangings in the room and the shadow of a willow tree swept against the eaves. Margaret walked about while Samuel Ward pointed out to her the head of a Raphael Madonna and two little pictures of the Lake of Como. Margaret noticed that the bronze vase she had given to Sophia had been filled with ferns and placed in Nathaniel's sanctuary. Hawthorne's books, she observed, looked as if they had never been disturbed. There were three windows, each with a little crack across it. Margaret looked out toward the orchard; through the willows there were glimpses of the river. Here, she thought, Hawthorne could drive his dark steed hard. And it was here, she reminded herself, that Emerson had watched the Assyrian dawn and the Paphian sunset and written his essay called *Nature*.

They walked down to the orchard and Sophia proudly pointed out her husband's hill of beans. She could have looked no happier had she pointed to the Tree of Life in the Garden of Eden. At the river's banks they rested, Hawthorne and Ward lying on the grass, while Margaret and Sophia sat on the rocks. Samuel Ward wanted to hear everything that the Hawthornes were doing in their Elysium and Sophia was eager to tell how her princely husband split wood every morning and then ascended to his study to write until dinner time. Sometimes he even helped wash the dishes.

"Your honeymoon, like mine, will never end."
As Samuel spoke Sophia looked at her husband and thought, he is a kingly man. Margaret was talking to him now, trying to draw from him his reactions to Brook Farm. But Hawthorne would not be drawn today. He had been in the midst of writing about his love of the Sabbath when it was not spent in church; his thoughts were on the elms below the bridge at Simmons' Landing. He had been disturbed and would not shake off his annoyance. He wanted to vanish into the house and would not speak about Brook Farm.

Margaret left Hawthorne to his pocketful of miseries and returned to Concord. After Ward had left there would be greater opportunity perhaps to discuss Community. Yet Emerson's spirit was detached from all associations, except the universal one in which Margaret claimed no membership. Many other voices were calling for Union—Ripley's, Owen's, Fourier's. But Emerson insisted that if a man kick a fact out of the window, it will return through the chimney. The individual was of greater significance than the community. Reform was futile unless the inner self subscribed. Emerson's inner self would not subscribe. He would reform the world by digging his own garden. If Margaret wanted to understand Community she knew she would have to go to Brook Farm for a longer visit.

On the dressing table of her bedroom at Concord, the "Pilgrim's room," she left a penknife and key as symbols. By the stroke of the clock she knew the meridian hour sat full upon the fields. It was the meridian hour, perhaps, of her life. She had advanced beyond Emerson's studied love of nature, beyond Thoreau's knowledge of the woodchuck, beyond Ellery's capricious whims. She would leave them together in Concord. The village was not broad enough for her to live in. Margaret was ready to buy for her family a new house in Cambridge, the one that stood on Ellery Street in the orchard of the old Dana house. Dr. Wesselhoeft lived next door, and his little daughter would be an avid listener to her stories. From there they could see the sunset over Mount Auburn instead of the blue Wachusett. Cambridge might be a den of narrowness, but it was easier to withdraw from it than from Concord. Concord intoxicated; Cambridge sobered.

At the meridian hour it was time to pause, to look behind and then beyond. Margaret knew she had emerged from a groping girl into a commanding woman. Had not Thoreau said, thinking of her, that fire was like old maids, the best company? She had bewitched Thoreau, she had discovered Emerson's inability to go forth and learn of the world, she had scrutinized Ellery and found the flaws beneath his elfin charm. She had met Hawthorne and knew that though he might ride well the dark steed of words, he would fall from the steed of life. She had observed the tendencies no less carefully than the men of her day. She had heard the torrent of the times; she had opened channels for it in *The Dial* and in her Conversations. This other tendency, called Socialism, was still to be considered. To Brook Farm then, where this other torrent of the times could be examined at the source.

Chapter X

RECALCITRANT HEIFER

MARGARET boarded the Brook Farm omnibus at Brattle Street in Boston and sat back while Jonas Gerrish cracked the whip. The nine-mile drive gave her time to consider the little she knew about Ripley's Association, as well as to look upon the pleasant farms and stone walls that dotted the Roxbury countryside. She knew, and admired, the fact that George Ripley had abandoned his Purchase Street parish to buy a milk farm from Charles Ellis. Ripley had even gone so far as to pledge his library in place of a four-hundred-dollar subscription and Marcus Spring was beginning to take stock in the Brook Farm Community. Nevertheless, they needed whatever money they could earn. Her own board would cost four dollars a week. But this sort of information revealed very little, she knew, about the inner workings of the community. Nor had her own brief visit to the masquerade at Brook Farm given her any real insight into the philosophy of the fledglings of Association. It had been nothing more than a picnic party in the woods in honor of Frank Dana's sixth birthday. The Brook Farmers had arrayed themselves as gypsies and as Indian chiefs, and Ellen Slade had been metamorphosed into Diana for the occasion. But, after all, there had been no indication of a social revolution in the woodland gambols and collations of fruits and cakes at Frank's picnic. Margaret had heard of other such occasions, when the lovely George Curtis had pranced about in a muslin dress in the style of Fanny Elssler, and Ora Gannett had romped about the woodlands in white Turkish trousers. But John

Dwight need not have joined the community to don a sky-blue frock coat and wander about with Little Nell and Hamlet in a fancy-dress party. As Margaret glanced out at the white houses with their green window blinds and the little front flower gardens with their pudding-stone ledges, she realized that she had seen Brook Farm only in masquerade. Now she would see it in undress.

It was dark when Jonas Gerrish drew up before the Hive. Margaret wrapped her cloak closely about her and stepped out. There was a gray barn that she could barely make out to the south of the Hive; the gurgling of the brook was almost lost in the whipping of the wind. It was a bleak place, she thought, gray, with the wind moaning and the trees sighing. It was no wonder that people turned to communal life here. One needed the warmth of human sympathy in such a place. She buried her face in her cloak and walked quickly toward the dining room.

Nearly everybody at the tables must have recognized her tall, stately carriage and arched neck. She walked like a queen, wandering incognito among her subjects. Her hair glinted in the lamplight and seemed more red than brown; her eyelids were almost closed as she peered near-sightedly at the benches. But though everyone knew Margaret Fuller had entered the dining room, no one rose to greet her. Indeed Carlo, the large Newfoundland dog, was the only member of the Community who stirred himself. He ambled slowly around the long pine tables, sniffed her cloak, and then retreated to the brick fireplace.

Margaret removed her wraps and looked about her. There were no curtains or carpets in the room; yet the white linen and tableware, and the bright fire of oak logs gave it a friendly air. Margaret saw many familiar outlines on the white, backless benches, but still nobody seemed to recognize her. Perhaps it was one of the customs of Community not to acknowledge the presence of a *civilizée*. In annoyance she pulled at the long gold chain reaching to her waist. There was nothing to do but to take the empty place near Mrs. Ripley. Margaret sat down and greeted her friends.

As she looked down at the long pine table, she saw a line of blue frocks, brown tunics, hunter's blouses and gay chintz garments. This was Brook Farm in undress, then. The costumes looked like a compromise between the peignoirs of novices and the blouses of Paris workmen. Some of the men wore their hair parted in the middle and falling over their shoulders. There were a few beards on parade. On the floor was an array of broad hats and little vizorless caps. One gentleman had placed his cow-hide boot, crusted with peat bog, on the white bench. Margaret looked at the place that had been set before her. There were heavy white mugs on the white linen tablecloth. There were plates of potatoes, turnips, squashes and brown bread boiled in milk.

"That," Amelia Russell whispered to Margaret, "is brewis!"

"Take some pandowdy," Mrs. Ripley offered.
Well, at least they had begun to speak, Margaret considered. She tasted the brewis gingerly. The table next to hers, she was informed, was for the Grahamites who fed on cold water and unbolted flour. The dismal fare had been brightened somewhat by the bouquet of wildflowers with which John Codman had ornamented the Graham table. At last the talk which had diminished to whispers at Margaret's arrival rose again; the word "affinity" especially was caught and tossed like a boomerang.

Mrs. Ripley raised her gold-bowed glasses and addressed herself to Margaret.

"We are glad to welcome you to Brook Farm. No doubt, you will want to hear first about your brother, Lloyd. Frankly, he is extremely slow. It will be very dif-

ficult to fit him for college. I hesitate to tell you this, but
he is a refractory member of our community and scatters
pages of his diary about where those whom he dislikes
may find them. One leaf of his journal informed me the
other day that I had not baked the apples well, and that
Mr. Dana was no gentleman."

To herself, Mrs. Ripley commented, he has all the Fuller
faults and none of their merits. Margaret replied that she
regretted to hear of this, but when she thought of her
sixteen-year-old brother, with his large head and loose
joints and the down showing on his upper lip, she knew
that she too would have little success with him. Perhaps
it would be wise to send him to a printing office. But after
all, Lloyd had not been her principal reason for visiting
Brook Farm. She wanted to acquaint herself more thoroughly with the fledglings of community, to know whether
they were learning to fly.

She glanced about her again. At the far end of the table
a few Brook Farmers were reading notes that they had
discovered folded under their plates. There was Charles
Newcomb, his prominent nose turned to his plate of
brewis, his hand brushing back a lock of dark, unkempt
hair. He shifted his slight body in Margaret's direction
and peered at her mysteriously.

"He changed his seat," Georgiana Bruce confided to
Margaret, "because he resented the profound exactions of
a feminine vis-à-vis." Now he was seated next to the
Curtis boys; suddenly his cachinnatious laugh roared
across the table.

"He has hung a picture of Fanny Elssler between
Loyola and Xavier in his room," remarked Mrs. Ripley.
Margaret looked at him. She smiled, remembering that
Ellery Channing had said they used Curtis and Newcomb
as decoy ducks at Brook Farm. John Dwight glanced up
at Margaret shyly when Almira Barlow addressed him

as "the Poet." Margaret wondered how he was getting along at Brook Farm. She had heard from Theodore Parker that Ripley had said Dwight would hoe corn all Sunday if he were permitted, but all Massachusetts could not make him do it on Monday. Almira Barlow was still very beautiful. She was looking at Dwight rather strangely. Could that be one of the affinities that Brook Farm seemed to foster? Margaret wondered. But Almira was beautiful and always liked the society of men even after her husband had left her. Orestes Brownson broke into her thoughts by demanding,

"Miss Fuller, is the butter within the sphere of your influence?"

Margaret wondered whether it was Brownson's St. Simonianism or Unitarianism or Associationism that made him speak in such an extraordinary way. Apparently Brownson liked to change everything but his attire, for whether he became a Buddhist or a Catholic he would always clothe his tall thin figure in that wrinkled swallow-tailed coat with the large white handkerchief folded in front of his neck. Margaret passed the butter into his broad hand, and turned again to look at the Curtis boys. George and Burrill were both so lovely that it was impossible to decide whether she favored the blond, god-like air of the one or the softer beauty of the other.

Suddenly, Isaac Hecker walked from the chimney corner, his baker's cap on his head. Margaret studied his pockmarked face while Mrs. Ripley told her that Hecker made the bread for the community. Margaret was curious to know if his ideas were better baked than his bread.

"Cut the pie," he announced to the entire table, "from the center to the periphery. There you have the doctrine of the Transcendentalist. The Transcendentalist has keen sight, but little warmth of heart. He is *en rapport* with the spiritual world, but unconscious of the celestial one.

He prefers talking about love to possessing it. Nature is his church, and he is his own god. Cut the pie from the periphery to the center and you approach the celestial god, unknown to the Transcendentalist."

He pressed his baker's cap down on his head and walked back to the chimney corner.

"I have heard," Georgiana Bruce remarked to Margaret, "that he was crazed by the rays of the moon which enter the three windows of his room."

This must be Brook Farm in undress, Margaret thought. It was rather disconcerting. Surely Christopher Cranch over there would speak more soundly. He was a visitor like herself, a *civilizée*, as they said. She looked at his dark, curling hair, his broad forehead and delicately cut features. He was slight and very graceful. He would be interested in the latest developments of *The Dial,* although while he had given her poems with one hand he had caricatured her with the other.

"You are enjoying your visit here?" Margaret began. Cranch played with the white mug in front of him and replied that he did. Brook Farm nourished one side of his personality.

"I am a bad mixture of the oyster and the spirit, the unexcitable and the excitable, the sluggish and the impulsive, the lymphatic and the nervous."

Margaret had no opportunity to inquire which portion of his nature it was that Brook Farm fed, for John Cheever, the Irish valet, was approaching Mrs. Ripley and addressing her as "Your perpendicular majesty." She could not hear what message he was conveying to her highness, for suddenly the whole table cried out, "Here comes the Professor." It was Charles Dana, carrying a plate of pandowdy in one hand, and a Greek book in the other. Margaret knew he had ruined his eyes by reading *Oliver Twist* in candlelight, and had come to Brook

Farm for his health. He wore a full beard, auburn, like his hair, which gave him a firm and professorial look.

"He is working here as a waiter," Mrs. Ripley explained. "He reads his Greek between courses."

At last, Margaret felt, this was a clue to Brook Farm. The initial inhospitality of the members, Charles Newcomb's oratory about butter, Hecker's rhetoric about pie —all might be regarded as display. But this, this reading Greek between the courses, seemed to condense Brook Farm into a phrase. Margaret believed she was beginning to touch the center of the Associationist's philosophy. She looked at the mug, full of milk, and asked whether she might not have tea. Georgiana Bruce told her she must place one cent at her plate for that service. Margaret reached into her purse, determining that in the future she would sup in her room. Yet she was glad she had seen the Brook Farmers at table. As men ate, so they lived. Beneath all the display, beneath the facetious puns and the cachinnatious laughter, beneath the brown tunics and vizorless caps there was a principle, a way of life. She would unearth it on her visit. She was tired now; the journey had been wearisome and this dinner had supplied more food for her mind than for her body.

Margaret went to her room. As she undressed, she heard the sound of dishes being washed to the chorus of *O Canaan, bright Canaan*. Before she fell asleep she heard George Bradford's voice exclaiming about the constellations. Later in the night, her sleep was interrupted by the sound of Charles Newcomb reciting the litany. It was a place peculiar to itself, she decided, a place where all creeds could unite under the cover of Community— hardly a place for sleep, but then without losing a night's sleep who could find thoughts for the day to come?

The day at Brook Farm began earlier than Margaret had anticipated. It seemed as if the five o'clock rising horn followed immediately upon Newcomb's recitation of the litany. Even though she would have liked to rest after that trumpet of dawn, it was impossible to do so, for a singing group had begun to chant under John Dwight's windows. Margaret roused herself for a breakfast of griddle cakes made under Dana's supervision, and determined to roam about Brook Farm to see the buildings and then wander off to the woods.

Margaret's impression of the night before did not change as she strolled toward the barn and approached Marianne Ripley's school building, the Nest. The wind still howled above the murmuring of the brook, above the voices of the Spanish pupils from Manila, above Lloyd's declamations. The houses were dismal and gray. Even the Eyrie, with its pudding-stone ledge, had been painted the color of gray sandstone. As she passed the high point of land on which it had been built, she heard John Dwight strumming the piano. The view was wide, frightening almost, on this chill morning. Here was high ground indeed, from which to look upon the distant hills, misted in the gray light, on which to stand, whipped by bleak winds. Margaret walked on to the Cottage, which had been built in the form of a Greek cross with four dark brown gables. She heard the voices of the children inside at their lessons. On the meadows near by the tunics of brown holland cloth and the blue skirts paraded; tarpaulin straw hats and large black hats bent over to the soil. As she approached the Pilgrim House, which looked as if twin buildings had been placed back to back, she saw Thomas Blake, the "Admiral," stroll by in his nautical hat and rolling collar. She turned back again in the direction of the Hive. Beyond the wooden fence and row of mulberry and spruce trees the blue tunics dotted the embankments. Under the elm beside the gateway, John Cheever, in his green plaids, was conversing with Peter

Baldwin, who had adorned himself in a green jacket. Water carriers were bearing their pitchers from the pump. There was John Chiswell, the carpenter, carrying part of a portable stage to his shop. Apparently there was a place here for the hewers and drawers as well as for the idlers, Margaret thought.

Minor Pratt, the head farmer, was supervising the weeding of the garden. Margaret listened and heard him reciting Tennyson as he stooped over the ground. Brook Farmers seemed able to scratch out weeds to the music of Tennyson. Pratt, she had heard, knew all the plants and flowers in Concord, and obviously knew his Tennyson as well, for his calm, soft voice intoned the musical phrases as his large frame bent down to the soil. Margaret saw the cobbler advance toward the Hive, repeating bits of Shakespearean verse to himself. This might not be a new world order, she reflected, but certainly it was the scholar-farmer's paradise. The clue that Dana had given her the night before seemed to lead in the right direction. He read Greek between the courses while he waited on table, and here a Shakespearean cobbler toted shoes to the rhythm of glorious pentameters.

Beyond, near the barn, Mr. Ripley, in his high boots and wide straw hat, was calling to Daisy and Dolly, his cows. Margaret crossed over to him and Mr. Ripley pointed out Prince Albert, the bull.

"I like to milk cows," he said with a twinkle in his eye. "Such occupation is eminently favorable to contemplation, particularly when the cow's tail is looped up behind."

"You seem to combine meditation with farming very well, Mr. Ripley," Margaret commented.

"That is one of our purposes here. Over there George Bradford is wringing out clothes. He will shortly hang them out on the line while he discusses abolition with Tom Allen. Right here in the barn we like to read Dante aloud while some of us do the milking. Beyond the field, you see a few ladies who have combined science with meditation, for they have just come from the water cure and will contemplate its virtues after they have doused themselves with ice water. But now that you have seen our outside world, Miss Fuller, why not go into the kitchen and dining room and see the indoor activities of Brook Farm?"

Margaret thought it might be more difficult to scrub floors to Dante than to scratch out weeds to Tennyson, but it would be interesting to see for herself.

She walked over to the kitchen. Ora Gannett was standing on the brick-paved floor, preparing bran bread and baked beans. Above her head were shelves lined with earthen jars of pork and brown bread for the Sunday dinner. Georgiana Bruce sat below the tins of rice pudding, cleaning vegetables. Amelia Russell was near them, clearing starch. Georgiana addressed her jocosely as "Miss Muslin" while she discussed Amelia's dancing classes. "Miss Muslin's" pleasant smile dimpled her cheeks as she amused Georgiana with stories about the dancing aptitude of George Bancroft's sons. Others were scrubbing the floor, scraping potatoes, washing dishes. But above the kitchen noises, Margaret heard a rarefied conversation about Transcendentalism as applied at Brook Farm.

"Transcendentalism," she interrupted, "we interpret as above mere reason, freely, religiously, intuitive, spiritual; at one with nature. You Brook Farmers may be able to combine reason with floor scrubbing but I doubt if you can combine Transcendentalism with it."

Margaret pulled at her gold chain and walked about the group, while Georgiana listened to her remarks respectfully and Amelia Russell began to giggle behind her hand. Perhaps, she thought, she would try to combine meditation with manual labor, and find by experience rather than observation how it worked.

Margaret left the kitchen and carried her book of German poems to the dining room. Mrs. Ripley was stitching the hired man's socks, and smiled as she saw Margaret turn to the ironing board, prop her open book between two forks, and proceed to iron Community collars while she committed German poems to memory.

> Zerraufte sie ihr Raabenhaar,
> Und warf sich hin zur Erde,
> Mit wüthiger Geberde.

The collar began to burn. The work did not proceed very well. If she watched the collars she could not recall the lines, and if she learned the verses the collars turned brown. Besides, Margaret reflected, this combination of efforts was not very different from her activities at Groton. There she had had enough of uniting needlework with a translation of *Tasso*. Either iron collars or learn German poetry, but if you do both at once you will do neither. Charles Newcomb, she considered, might recite the litany in more admirable Latin if he paid less attention to weeding the garden. She removed the book from the forks.

"I am off to the woods, Mrs. Ripley. I think the Community collars should be grateful."

Margaret walked through the dim groves toward the sunny uplands and the denser woodlands. The brook ran slenderly through the meadow. She decided not to venture on the great boulders that formed Eliot's pulpit, but instead to stroll on to the distant woods surrounding Muddy Pond. It was good to find solitude after so much society. She sat down under a great sycamore and opened her book. It was almost as difficult to think in the woods as before at the ironing board, but at least here she found herself expressed. She leaned back and looked at the snatches of sky that flickered between the leaves.

Suddenly she heard the tread of feet, and looked up to see Brownson's great figure in his swallow-tailed coat, with John Dwight in his tunic, and young Georgiana Bruce between them.

"Are you interested in the idea?" Dwight began immediately.

Margaret wondered for a moment what the idea was, but soon realized that there was only one idea at Brook Farm that a *civilizée* could be interested in, namely, Brook Farm. He did not give her an opportunity for answering, however, for as they seated themselves next to her he went on. "I came here because West Roxbury was my mother's home, a refuge in days of distress, but my other reason is that I have full faith in Mr. Ripley's idea."

"I have as yet full faith in no single idea," Margaret replied. "All are interesting to me, but none has engrossed me utterly."

"You look too far ahead, Miss Fuller. No 'Dial,' " Dwight remarked, smiling, "should tell the time of day so far ahead."

"What exactly are the purposes of Brook Farm?" Margaret asked. Brownson stood up suddenly, raising his huge bulk to emphasize his answer to this comprehensive question. He drew his long broad hands through his black hair while the swallow-tailed coat bulged about in the wind.

"We Brook Farmers," he began, "are a self-supporting group of men and women; all of us share in the manual labor, as well as the leisure and educational advantages of the place. We live in fraternity, free from the burdens of civilization. By doing this we shall lead in the end to the formation of a perfect society. We have introduced community feeling without destroying the individual. When we eat at a common table and labor together, the individual desire to encroach on the social body is destroyed, but it is suffered to remain as a spring to industry."

Brownson stopped speaking and sat down. Margaret felt as if he had been addressing a congregation.

"Hawthorne," she objected, "left Brook Farm apparently because he felt his own individuality was being annihilated."

"Hawthorne," Brownson returned grumpily, "cannot understand a tendency till it is at least a hundred years old. He admitted that himself."

"I think Mr. Hawthorne had a literary purpose in coming here," Georgiana contributed. "He used to sit on the sofa beneath the stairs at the Hive and hide behind a huge book while he listened to every remark that was said. By the way, Miss Fuller, do you know that he spread a story that the cow you contributed to Brook Farm was most recalcitrant? He claimed it was a transcendental heifer, that was very fractious and apt to kick over the milk pail. The cow made itself the ruler of the herd, but I am sure," Georgiana hastened to add, "that it bore no resemblance to its mistress."

Margaret flushed and dismissed Nathaniel Hawthorne's transcendental heifer with a wave of her hands.

"Any heifer, or any contribution I may make to Brook Farm, must remain recalcitrant. I am here as an observer, not as a member, except possibly of the opposition. There are other tendencies and indeed other similar associations that interest me almost as much."

"The experiments at Zoar and New Harmony," Dwight returned, "are less indigenous than ours. The only source from which we have borrowed is that which flows from the plains of Galilee."

"You have read Miss Peabody's article in *The Dial* then?" Margaret interrupted, " 'A Glimpse at Christ's Idea of Society.' I believe that Owen had Christ's idea as much in mind when he began New Harmony as Mr. Ripley has now. Owen borrowed his communism from the Rappites, did he not? Outside of his theory that man's character is formed by his circumstances, he believed with Christ that we must be good. And when the Shakers shake off their sins in their dances I am sure they too believe that they are enjoying a glimpse of Christ's idea of society."

"Perhaps Fourier will give us a closer glimpse of that idea," Brownson suggested.

"From what I have read of Fourier," Margaret replied, "he starts with the repellent conditions of labor and tries to make them attractive. His battle cry, however, is not justice, but order. Fourier says, 'as the institution, so the men.' Goethe believed, 'as man so the institutions.' I myself favor a union of the two systems."

"This reminds me," Georgiana contributed, "of the sermon that Theodore Parker delivered when we all went to his church and ate lunch in the pews. He said that some believe a man's soul makes his circumstances, and others that the circumstances make the soul. Mr. Parker thought the truth was that they acted and reacted upon one another, generating the character of the man together. He clothes his philosophy in a common dress," she added shyly, "and makes it more understandable, I think, than Fourier or Goethe."

"I have chipped marble with Emerson from the same tower of thought," Margaret returned. "He seems to think that one may arrive at similar results without a community, and believes that you Brook Farmers are making life more complex by banding together. He has always dreamed of a small family of ascetics instead of a large society. Indeed he has tried to have one table in his house for the help and the family. He longs for the solitude of his library, and says it yields a more precious fruit than the barn yards of community. He thinks you Brook Farmers obey impulse without being guarded by the bounds of intellect."

"Before I came out of civilization," Brownson interrupted, flourishing his broad hands, "I believed that too. But now I find my ideas have changed considerably."
Brownson's ideas, Margaret thought, might be an accurate barometer for fluctuating atmospheres, but not for steady weather.

"William Channing is very much interested in our idea," Dwight persisted. "When he visits us, walking in his stately way down the paths, and preaching to us in those burning, eloquent words of his, we all join hands in a circle to cement our solidarity. I hear that your friend Mr. Alcott has been hatching some Community plans of his own since he returned from abroad."
Plato Skimpole, Margaret thought, cannot have more than one idea, no matter how he garbs it.

"Don't forget," she remarked aloud, not wishing to continue the talk about Alcott, "that you may trace your communities to a source nearer home than the plains of Galilee. The Panic has given you a chance to grow, and financial prosperity may mark your end."

"Financial prosperity will not end slavery," Dwight returned. "Society itself must be reorganized, possibly in the way we have adopted, before slavery can be abolished."

"Mrs. Ripley," Georgiana ventured, "always says one must shriek at wrongs if they are to be overcome."
Margaret remembered that Mr. Ripley, for all his glimpses at Christ's society, had refused to admit Caroline Henshaw to Brook Farm, the poor girl who mar-

ried the murderer John Colt a few hours before he killed
himself in prison. Lydia Child had pleaded for her and
been refused.

"Fourier," she said, "is shrieking at wrongs too—with
Albert Brisbane and Horace Greeley as interpreters. I
have heard of Brisbane's articles in the *Tribune,* but I cannot help feeling that though Fourier may organize
wrongs into orders and series, he will not destroy them.
As Emerson says, he leaves out no fact, but one—the fact
of Life."

"Greeley may destroy them," Brownson commented.
"He looks like a spectre when he comes to visit us, with
his light hair and white hat and drab coat, but the
spectre soon shoots fire. His pockets are always bulging
with clippings and memoranda, and I have always felt
that one day he would take out the solution of our problems from one of the scraps of papers he carries in them."

"When I read Brisbane's *Social Destiny of Man,*"
Dwight continued on his own line of thought, "I felt that
one day perhaps we Brook Farmers might adopt Fourier's
philosophy of Attractive Industry and Association in
groups and series."

"Fourier is much more interested in establishing groups
among the constellations than among human beings,"
Margaret considered. "He is too mystic, even for me,
when he demonstrates how the sidereal universe moves to
the rhythms of ut, re, mi, fa, sol. And Albert Brisbane is
not reliable either. He slides from animal magnetism to
Fourierism and will soon slide off into another ism unless
you chain him down."

"If we Brook Farmers become Fourieristic," Georgiana smiled, "we shall have to start with something
extraordinary, like a Rejected Lovers' Sympathizing
Group."

Suddenly, Margaret thought of Henry Thoreau—in

himself a practical answer, almost a refutation of the theories of the Brook Farmers. He carried all of Brook Farm in his breast; he lived extempore, like the animals he loved; his revolution was perennial; it would not shift with shifting times. He needed no society, for unto himself he was society. His independence made the Brook Farmers look like slaves. Yet his answer was not hers. She could not live as he did any more than as the Brook Farmers lived. There was no need to do so. She had come to hear the torrent of the times, not to plunge into it. One must be patient; one must grow and slough off many selves before one could find one's own self. One must not catch at straws. There were firmer reeds on other banks,

In the evenings the tunics and blouses of Brook Farm trooped from the Hive to the Eyrie. The fledglings of Community seemed able to overlook the dismal smooth boards of this square wooden house when they gazed down from the high point of land on which it had been built. But for Margaret the view recalled that wide expanse she had seen from the back of her home on Farmers' Row; to her the wide, gray sweep was melancholy and the gray Eyrie depressing. The Brook Farmers passed the orchard, walked up the long flight of steps from the road, and turned into the parlor on the left of the hall. John Dwight immediately seated himself at the piano, though he had no intention of playing before Margaret Fuller had fulfilled her role of conversationalist. Georgiana pointed out to Margaret the little flower vase on the study table which Mrs. Hawthorne had sent to Brook Farm before her marriage. Mr. Ripley, still wearing his farmer's blouse and high boots, walked in from the library opposite. His black eyes peered through his spectacles as he glanced nearsightedly about the room, beckoning Margaret to the sofa under the stairs. Charles Newcomb and the Curtis brothers sprawled upon the floor, while Christopher Cranch and Amelia Russell draped themselves on the stairs. Margaret wished they had seated themselves on chairs; she would find it difficult to address a group already prone. But apparently this sans-culottism was a characteristic of Brook Farm. Horace Sumner, Charles Sumner's younger brother, sat on one side of Margaret, while Georgiana Bruce quickly claimed another vacant place on the sofa. Everybody, even Orestes Brownson, looked up at Margaret expectantly. They had been told that her Conversations would be held on alternate evenings with husking parties. They were waiting for the lady of West Street to begin.

Margaret pulled at her gold chain and raised her lorgnette. "Let us speak," she began, turning toward the group on the stairs, "of education in its largest sense—of what we can do for ourselves and others. My opinion is that perfection is our aim, patience our road. Your present object is simply to give yourself and others a tolerable chance. Let us not be too ambitious in our hopes as to immediate results. Our lives should be considered as a tendency, an approximation only. Most of us expect to do too much." George Ripley glanced at his wife a little restlessly. He hoped Margaret would not cool the high ambitions of the Brook Farmers. A sound was heard from the group on the stairs and Margaret glanced over to see Amelia Russell's plump face trembling in a stifled yawn.

She would view the subject from another angle. "I do not believe that by excluding evil you can attain good. Evil is a growth of nature and one condition for the development of good." Margaret looked up to see Charles Newcomb rise from the floor and walk out of the room. It was disconcerting, this license. But nobody else seemed to notice it. Brook Farmers simply left a room when they had heard enough. Margaret took a deep breath and continued. "That is one of my reasons for objecting to Association. Another reason lies in the difficulty of allying labor and capital to secure the hoped for co-operation. You also face a danger when you attempt to merge the individual in the mass to such a degree as to paralyze energy, heroism, and genius."

A host of idiosyncrasies was not genius, she reflected. One must distinguish between the pseudo-heroic and the heroic. Georgiana Bruce looked up at Margaret worshipfully. She seemed to her the embodiment of wisdom. How rich and varied were the intonations of her voice. Georgiana was sure Margaret could interpret the inner life of every man and woman there. Horace Sumner gazed at her in adoration. Burrill Curtis' long golden curls gleamed in the lamplight as he nodded understandingly.

Suddenly, Orestes Brownson stood up to interrupt. Horace Sumner looked at him in annoyance, but he did not notice.

"You are too consistent, Miss Fuller. You lack that glorious inconsistency which does honor to human nature and makes men so much better than their creeds."

Mrs. Ripley remarked quietly,

"When you speak of inconsistency, you must speak only for yourself, Mr. Brownson."

George Curtis laughed and said,

"If a preacher invited the members of all Christian churches to a communion table, you would be the only person who could fill the bill. I am sure you must have gone through every sect by this time, except Catholicism, and I do not doubt that one day you will walk backward into the Catholic Church."

"If I ever enter the Church," Brownson thundered, "it will not be a backward step."

Margaret interrupted,

"Let us not slide off into discussions of our personal natures. There is a more comprehensive nature that waits to be mentioned—the nature through which spirit ascends, the nature that spirit does not supersede."

Horace Sumner did not take his eyes from Margaret's face. He hung reverently upon every word. How wonderful Brook Farm was, he thought, where he could rake hay and learn to pick cucumbers, and hear this great and noble lady. He looked up shocked, hearing Amelia Russell whisper, "I wish her English were plainer." Margaret went on with her defense of nature. After a few moments George Bradford stood up, and as he did so several clothespins dropped noisily from his pocket. Margaret decided to conclude her talk quickly. She finished with a flourish and removed her lorgnette.

One or two, she felt—Georgiana and Horace—had enjoyed the new light she had cast on Association; the others had not listened or had not understood. The yawns became audible from the group on the floor. Christopher Cranch picked up his guitar and prepared to strum Schubert's *Serenade,* taking out of his pocket a manuscript copy he had made of the composition. Margaret wondered what the West Street ladies would do if suddenly one of them began to strum a guitar after a Conversation. Here, apparently, they could shift from a discussion of Nature and Education to Schubert's *Serenade* as easily as they turned from milking cows to reading Dante. Christopher's dark brown hair was ruffled as he bent over his guitar; Margaret thought the thick whiskers which met under his chin entirely out of keeping with the Byronic shirt collar he was wearing. After the *Serenade* he smiled, raising his good baritone voice to *Here's a health to ane I lo'e dear,* and would have gone on to *Take thou, where thou dost glide,* had not Amelia Russell begged him to give them a taste of his ventriloquism instead. Margaret watched as he distorted his broad forehead and delicate features in his imitation of the denizens of the barnyard.

Apparently Cranch could do everything well—write, paint, sing, and now ventriloquize. No wonder the Brook Farmers delighted in his presence.

After Christopher had stopped, the group considered whether to hear Mr. Ripley elucidate Kant or Cornelia Hall recite *The Ancient Mariner*. Cornelia won the evening and recited the stanzas delightfully. Finally George and Burrill Curtis walked over to the piano and sang the *Erlking* to Dwight's accompaniment. Margaret thought George's beauty almost feminine; no wonder he had masqueraded so charmingly in a green skirt like Fanny Elssler's. Dwight played the chords resoundingly on the Currier piano, while the Curtis brothers sang the ballad dolefully. It had been a full evening for the Brook Farmers, though Margaret was still somewhat disconcerted at the turn it had taken after her Conversation. George Curtis withdrew from the piano and began to trim the lamps. It was the signal for the Farmers to disband.

As Margaret walked down the steps of the Eyrie, Georgiana Bruce ran after her.

"Please don't go, Miss Fuller. I wish you would take my room here at the Eyrie while you are visiting us." Margaret hesitated, but remembering Charles Newcomb's recitation of the litany at midnight, decided to accept Georgiana's offer. The girl looked so grateful, as if a privilege had been granted her. Margaret fetched her clothes and her copy of the del Sarto Madonna and then followed Georgiana up to her room. She placed the Madonna carefully on the dresser and watched her young friend burn the pastilles she had begged from Cornelia Hall. Georgiana glanced back at Margaret reverently as she shut the door. In the morning she would carry breakfast to the room and instead of a white mug, she would borrow the one china cup from the Hive closet for Margaret's coffee.

So the days passed, the mornings punctuated by Georgiana Bruce's breakfast tray; the afternoons by strolls to Cow Island or the woods; the evenings by husking parties or Conversations. Margaret had seen Brook Farm, had heard the torrent of the times at its source. Before she left she drew her conclusions together, not in a lengthy Credo, but in a poem, which she called *Sub Rosa, Crux*. The age had lost the password of the Knights of the Rosy Cross; the undying lamp flickered. Everywhere, in Cambridge and in Boston and in Groton, even in State Street, and surely here at Brook Farm, they sought the password, to learn to feed again the dying lamp. In place of the ruby cross, the knights of Roxbury and Concord bore a cross of ebony. Yet, why wear a cross at all? Why seek the password? Why bind oneself to any central doctrine? Association might be the great experiment of the age, but still it was only an experiment. One could not build Utopia. Human nature stood in the way. Margaret recalled a picture she had seen once outside a door in Boston. On it was painted a flaming yellow sun, at the centre of which were the words, "Universal Unity." Beneath the picture was an inscription in black and white letters, "Please wipe your feet." One must indeed wipe one's feet before one could tread the ground of universal unity. Yet every noble scheme prophesied to man his eventual destiny. For herself, Margaret preferred the hell of the free soul to the heaven of the slave. But play out the play, gentles. The time might come, she hoped, when the curtain would fall upon this play, as upon all others; when rosy and ebon cross might both be cast into the sea and no password needed to kindle a dying lamp. On such a day a rosy dawn would light the waters. "No lamp is needed, for the night has died."

CHAPTER XI

PROLETARIAN SUMMER

EVER SINCE the death of Timothy Fuller had denied Margaret the opportunity of going to Europe, she had played with the idea of visiting the West. The news of William Clarke, who seemed to have found himself in Chicago, James Clarke's own reactions to Cincinnati, and Ellen's meeting there with Ellery Channing, all gave to the Western part of the country a glamour which Margaret longed to experience for herself. She remembered the poem she had written when Governor Everett had welcomed the Sacs and Foxes to Boston. Catlin's Indian Museum had whetted her taste for seeing the tribes in their own setting. For one who wished to observe the tendencies of the times, the West was an exciting region, teeming with refugees and immigrants who were taking the place of the vivid Indian tribes. Women pioneers had gone West and written of their travels. Margaret recalled Mrs. Clavers' account of her home in Michigan. Harriet Martineau had spoken of the feathered Indians and wide prairie lands, and Dickens had recently returned from Kentucky and Ohio. The West was changing far more quickly than the East. To see the real West before a mushroom growth had transmuted it completely, Margaret realized she must go soon.

She had observed other tendencies of the times and found them wanting. She had scrutinized the flaws in transcendentalism and given her conclusions to the ladies of West Street and the readers of *The Dial*. She had found that Brook Farm gave no glimpse into Christ's idea of society. The winter that had passed had not differed greatly from other winters. From Cambridge or Avon Place she had gone to West Street and had returned home to write for *The Dial*. Margaret felt she had been too much in the East. With a land to the West driven by changing forces, she could not remain seated at her desk in Cambridge, even though her article on *The Great Lawsuit—Man versus Men, Woman versus Women* had interested her far more than any other essay she had written for *The Dial*. The East was a quiet place compared with the stories she had heard of the West, and when the opportunity came for Margaret to accompany the Clarkes to Chicago, she did not hesitate. By reverent faith she determined to extract the mighty meaning of the scene that would pass before her, perhaps to foresee the law by which a new order, a new poetry, was to be evoked from its chaos.

For a journey of this sort Margaret realized she must prepare her mind. Early in May she began to read Catlin's book about the Indians, Murray's *Travels*, Schoolcraft's *Algic Researches*. She even returned to her Cooper and found Uncas, after Catlin's Indians, merely the white man's view of the savage hero. Irving's Indians were academic figures and M'Kenney's tour to the lakes dull next to Adair's account of his travels or Carver's trip through the interior. As she read in the library at Cambridge, Catlin's rational enthusiasm seized her and she decided to observe the tribes as he had, with large views of manliness and a deep feeling for their beauty. For Margaret the Indians took the place of the masses of factory workers at Lowell or the Irish immigrants in Boston; all were downtrodden, but in their brilliant feathers and stately stride, the tribes carried a pride of race with them, a beauty which was lacking in the workers of the East. They were comparable also with the slaves of the South and the North. They too had been cheated of their heritage—but the heritage of the Indians seemed more noble, their loss of it more grievous.

Into her roving camp chest Margaret packed, besides the black dress that Aunt Mary Rotch had given her and her ruffs and purple muslin gown, a copy of Kerner's *Seherin von Prevorst* and *Philip van Artevelde* to read during one of the intervals of travel. On May twenty-fifth she boarded the train for Niagara with James and Sarah Clarke, and Caroline Sturgis, who would accompany them no farther than the Falls.

On the steam car James forgot his Church of the Disciples, which he had inaugurated in Dr. Peabody's house on West Street, to point out with an almost child-like enthusiasm the charcoal stove in the centre of the carriage door or the conductor who stalked up and down in ordinary street dress. Sarah opened her sketchbook and began to draft rough pictures of two gentlemen engrossed in a discussion of politics or of one whose nose was buried in a newspaper. Caroline Sturgis watched the incessant shower of sparks on the railroad, while Margaret looked out at mile after mile of stunted trees, of mechanics working at their trades, of boys flying kites and playing marbles, of pigs burrowing and horses rearing, men smoking and women carrying baskets from the market. After a while they nodded off, only to be awakened by the jolting of the cars, the shriek of the engine, or the sounding of the bell. There were at least forty people in each carriage; the air was hot from the coal stove and hovered like transparent smoke between Margaret and Caroline. It was insufferably close. The conductor leaned against the door with his hands in his pockets and stared at the travelers. The gentlemen wearied of discussing the banks and cotton trade; newspapers cluttered up the floor of the car. Margaret sat back and dreamed of Niagara.

When they arrived, the day was cold and rainy, the skies lowering with bleak winds. Margaret lounged about the rooms of the hotel, read the stage bills upon the walls, and looked over the register. Caroline wondered at her hesitation to go forth and see the Falls at last, but Margaret said she felt unworthy to enter the temple now that she had arrived at the gateway. She donned her black dress, as if to be in harmony with the rainy weather, and even then, sat down to write to Emerson about Carlyle's shortsighted view of democracy. She herself felt nearer to the Indians she had read about, who had made her consider democracy as the way to a new aristocracy, than to the great Falls outside.

At length her friends would wait no longer and they induced Margaret to enter the temple. As they walked toward the Falls they stopped at the store on the border of the forest, where glass and bacon, stay-laces and prints vied with drugs and crockery, bombazines and tin cans. They wandered through the wood on Goat Island and saw the wake-robin and Mayflower in bloom. Along the wild paths the belled heifer grazed while the swine gnawed at roots. Then they walked down to the bridge and from its frail support saw the Falls.

At first Margaret felt nothing but the tremendous power of the tumbling, rushing rapids whose roar dulled her ears. Confused feelings overpowered her; her throat was choked, and the thrill surged through her veins. She looked at Caroline, whose eyes seemed full of silver waves and lightning. Sarah's sketchbook was held, unopened, in her hand. James did not move. How strange a thing, this force of water! Margaret recalled the day in Groton when she had been tempted almost to fling herself into undulating curves of water. Before her lay a vision, vast and solemn, from which reality seemed barred. The gray clouds massed above the Falls; a few

fitful gleams of light startled the waters; the everlasting
roar thundered on. Still, reality could not long be barred.
It trespassed, in the form of the "guide to the Falls," his
title labeled on his hat, who came to offer his services.
Margaret murmured, "One might as well ask for a
gentleman usher to point out the moon. Yet why should
we wonder at such," she said, turning away from the
thundering cataracts of water, "when we have our Com-
mentaries on Shakespeare and our Harmonies of the
Gospels?" The spell was broken. Reality had intruded
upon the tearing, shapeless torrents of water. A damp
mist fell.

They wandered back along Table Rock, meeting Seba
Smith and General Porter. The General's temerity in
building the bridges to Goat Island had been punished by
deafness. One could not approach the grandiose mysteries
of nature too closely, Margaret reflected. Perhaps the
deafness had come upon him when he sank the first stone
into the rapids. Emerson, she considered, might find his
identity in a bobolink, but even Thoreau would flinch before these Falls. Seba Smith told them stories of the
battles that had been fought where they were standing.
It seemed strange that men could fight in such a place;
but no temple, Margaret commented, could still the personal griefs and strifes of men. Suddenly, Seba Smith interrupted to point out an eagle. In swift descent it
swooped down toward the water, its plumage brilliant,
and in its form all the king was visible. Margaret gazed.
Again the perpetual trampling of the waters seized her
senses. Over the crashing Falls the eagle soared, the royal
bird over his kingdom.

As she looked, she felt, rather than heard, the approach of a stranger. He walked up to Table Rock and
looked down at the Falls. Suddenly, he spat into the
waters. This was reality intruding in another guise. Util-

ity had found a home even in this watery vastness. Yet Niagara could swallow up this desecration as easily as it swallowed up the buildings that were encroaching on its margins. The great whole overwhelmed the petty deformations. America was large enough to overcome its little men, great enough to leaven the masses for purer bread. That America—that great expanse in the West—was what she had come to see. The Great Lakes waited after Niagara.

Caroline went home from Buffalo, full of disdain for the poor cold life of the East, where men lived like rabbits in a warren. The others boarded the steamboat at the wharf side, watching the baggage tossed on board, the passengers bustling about for their berths, the little boys hawking their newspapers and pamphlets. A heavy rain was falling. James, Sarah, and Margaret huddled in a corner behind a large trunk.

At last the boat moved and Margaret looked up at the long, black, ugly roof covered with feathery sparks. The iron chimneys towered above; the doors and windows of the staterooms were jumbled oddly together. She walked about, looking at the dirty beams and pillars of the barge. A group of New Englanders were commenting about the machinery on the lower deck. Near by a debate between Trinity and Unity was in progress. An old man was bending down to a little girl, telling her, not what they would do, but what they should get in the West. Margaret was weary of such narrow doctrine. New England must carry New England even to the West. Even on these free waters they must air their poor opinions. Earth was so much nobler than the people who inhabited it. As she approached her friends, she said thoughtfully,

"Earth is spirit made fruitful—life. And its heart beats are told in gold and wine."
James looked up in mock surprise.

"It is shocking to hear such sentiments in these times, Margaret. I thought that Bacchic energy of yours was long since repressed."

He looked up at the dark cloak wrapped about her. Even as he spoke he realized his judgment had been wrong. The cloak could not hide the fire that burned within, that sparkled through those half-closed eyes and glinted in the red-brown hair. Margaret was still the tall and regal lady who gestured eloquently as she spoke. The hand might be gloved, but on the hidden finger, there was the carbuncle. The body might be covered by a gray cloak, but underneath there was the bright sash, the golden locket.

"No," she was saying, "I have only learned to mix water with my wine, and stamp upon my gold the heads of kings and the hieroglyphics of worship."

No one answered. They sat quietly, looking about them at the baggage cluttering the deck, listening to scraps of conversation.

"Is he not a smart fellow?" asked a New Englander. The Westerner with him spat before he replied,

"He! he can't see through a ladder."

The damp mists fell. Soon James walked off, and Sarah and Margaret retired to their tiny stateroom to forget the wet, the chill, and the steamboat smell.

Up the lakes the steamboat puffed. The next day, when it stopped at Cleveland, the storm began to clear. As they ascended the bluff, Margaret saw the lake expand beneath her eyes between banks of red and crumbling earth. Here land and water seemed to mingle as they never did in New England; they rushed together and changed places. A new creation took place before one's eyes. Up the St. Clair the boat ploughed on. Sarah began to sketch the green ridges with the trees slanting over the water. In the background she drew the herds of cattle. The steamboat moved quietly, scarcely disturbing the gray surface of the still waters. Suddenly, Margaret rushed across the deck. "Look!" she cried, "our first Indians!" Everybody clambered to one side to see the blanketed forms encamped on the bank. It was twilight. With a wild proud stride a few mysterious forms moved along the bluff. The others slept rolled in their blankets. Margaret knew she was approaching the West.

The next morning they were off Detroit. Margaret caught a few glimpses of the wide streets and the wooden planks laid on the grass as pavement. The town seemed crowded, teeming with Irish and German settlers, who, one of the passengers remarked, were working their way into the back country. The scene was flat. The greatest hill near Detroit, a Westerner informed her, was only sixty feet high.

"If I built a house in Michigan, I'd build a hill first."

As the passengers looked back at the town, groups gathered together to talk about their observations. A lady approached Margaret and told her a story about a curious dinner she had once had in Detroit. She had been accompanied by her father and mother, and before they entered the dining room they met an old friend, Colonel Trumbull, whom they naturally invited to sup with them. The Colonel hesitatingly informed them that he was married and of course they invited his wife as well. Mrs. Trumbull's appearance accounted for her husband's hesitation. Her coarse and imperious expression reflected her low habits of mind, and her exaggerated dress and gesture betrayed her lack of education. At dinner Mrs. Trumbull drank glass after glass of wine and became abusive. Colonel Trumbull asked his host to forgive him. He had married, he explained, to atone for a sin. Margaret wondered why people always selected her as their confessor. She had heard so many stories about ill-fated marriages. Perhaps they too were a sign of changing times. Women must learn to think before they could learn to love wisely.

Margaret was glad when evening came and in the beauty of Mackinaw she could forget the unpleasant tale she had heard. It was too late and rainy to go ashore, but at last the Indians began to show themselves. They walked near the boat, richly dressed in blue broadcloth with splendid leggings and knee-ties. On their heads Margaret saw crimson scarfs adorned with beads. Their hair was long and fell over one shoulder. One or two wild figures strode by in white blankets. What a far cry, she thought, from an afternoon in Emerson's warm study or an evening at Mrs. Farrar's. This was the glimpse that made her long to see more of the Indians, to see them as they lived, in all their paint and plumage, in all their grandeur that was passing.

On the fourth day the weather was milder. At night the moon shone clear and on the next afternoon the passengers went ashore at the Manitou Islands where the boat stopped for wood. The islands were deserted except for the woodcutters, whose slovenly huts were almost invisible among the old monarch trees. These woodcutters, Margaret thought, lived the life that Thoreau would admire. They had profound solitude and joined with it service to the world. There was an ideal beauty here as in the lands where shepherds tended their sheep in ancient days.

Sarah sketched as they walked along the beach of smooth white pebbles, interspersed with agates and cornelians. One of the passengers asked a woodcutter what had become of the Unitarian tracts he had left a year before. The old Manitou looked at him indifferently. The tracts had been scattered along with last year's leaves. Margaret smiled at James; even the founder of the

Church of the Disciples saw the ludicrousness of distributing Unitarian tracts to men who were one with the woods in which they lived. They walked on through the forest, gathering the uva-ursi flowers, whose leaves the Indians smoked. As they wandered back to the boat, Margaret wished the passengers would imitate the smoking habits of the Indians, for their cheeks were rounded with plugs of tobacco and their eyes dulled with its fumes.

The boat creaked and ploughed on. On the next day they would reach Chicago. The five and a half day voyage had been varied, but above the memory of the passengers and their narrow Eastern doctrine, above the sight of Detroit and the short stop at the Manitou Islands, rose that glimpse of the Indians at Mackinaw. Soon they would be in the land of the prairies, which the Indians still called home.

When they descended from the steamboat, Chicago looked raw and bare. The houses seemed to have been placed in any location whatsoever, without direction or principle. James eagerly pointed out the busy streets crowded with land speculators. There was a Negro dressed in scarlet, bearing a red flag and riding on a white horse, announcing the time of land sales. Walking up toward Lake and Clark Streets, where James' brothers had established their drugstore, they passed men bearing the snipe and plover they had shot on the west side of the town, and bass they had caught in the river. Everywhere men were at work, developing the resources of the soil. Their energy was real; there was no aping of fashions here, no jargon, no burning out life as a tallow candle for a tawdry show.

When they arrived at Clarke and Company, William greeted them delightedly. He looked older, ruddier than he had in Boston. There was a self-possession about him that he had lacked then. He walked gayly with them to the hotel, eagerly calling their attention to a Hoosier wagon, a new wooden pavement or a native weed. The most trivial object was invested with significance when he pointed it out.

"There," he said, "is the flame-like Wickapee flower. It grows here in Chicago. The Indians use it as a remedy for illness." Anecdotes and tales fell from his lips with a quiet charm. In the afternoon he sat on the roof of the hotel with Margaret and Sarah, telling them of the pleasure that lay before them in their journey to the country round Fox and Rock Rivers.

"We shall travel by wagon," he said, for William had planned to accompany them through the prairies, though James would return East, "and stay with the farmers. You will see the West to better advantage in that way. One of the families we shall visit has had a land fight. Desperadoes laid claim to their property, but they have been finally broken up by lynch law. The mother of the family had to build shanties and she and her three daughters each took one to defend."

On and on William wandered, from the Hungarian count who had taken refuge in the West, to the paint on the Choctaw Indians and the bushes of the prairie lands. Margaret anticipated eagerly the joy of seeing the West with one who knew it so well, with one who did indeed seem, as James had said so long ago, like herself.

The week at Chicago was spent mainly in preparing for the journey to the interior. At the hotel Margaret looked over her notes on Catlin or listened to William's tales. She had no interest in hearing the talk at the hotel about land speculation, although one could be amused by some of the scenes that took place there. One hot Sunday about one o'clock a lady from Philadelphia rushed into the hotel, rang the bell, and requested a room immediately as she wanted to get ready for afternoon service. She hoped there would be no delay, for she had driven all through the night for the sake of attending church. Out she bounded to the meetinghouse, without dinner or repose.

Chicago had not come into its own yet, Margaret decided. At the moment, it was almost impossible to foretell whether the land-sharps or the church-goers from the East would conquer the town. She herself was more interested in the interior than in the mushroom city. William continued to whet her appetite for travel by his tales about the country, the hunting, and the roads through which they would pass on their inland excursion. It seemed quite natural that after James had left for Boston William should take his place, superintending the loading of the wagon and choosing a pair of strong horses that would force their way through the mud holes and stumps that lay before them.

It was a fine day when they set forth, William holding the reins, Margaret and Sarah seated in the strong wagon which was almost as large as those used for transporting caravans of wild beasts. They rumbled on through bush and plain and wood along the Des Plaines River through Wheaton and West Chicago. Now and then they could hear in the stillness the chorus of frogs. Sarah kept her sketchbook open, but the wagon shook so that it was almost impossible to draw the team of oxen that forded a stream or the broken down cart that had been abandoned in the swamp. William needed no road to guide him to all the spots where beauty loved best to dwell. Over his shoulder he would call out, "See that moccasin flower. Over there is the lupine."

Clouds began to gather across the sun's face just as they reached Geneva. After the thundershower had spent itself they wandered about the town and entered the Reverend Mr. Augustus Conant's church. As she watched the congregation Margaret saw many settlers from the East. The homesteaders here, she thought, seemed to have won from life truer values than the swarms of settlers in Chicago. When she visited the minister's home later in the day with the Clarkes, she found that the Unitarian clergyman was no less proficient as a carpenter than as a preacher, for every shelf and chair in his house bore the traces of his handiwork. The day or two at Geneva gave William an opportunity to fish with Mr. Conant in the Fox River, gave Margaret and Sarah happy hours in the woods that fringed the streams.

When they left the village the wagon clattered on along the river's banks across the south end of De Kalb County until William drew the reins in the afternoon at the home of an English settler. It was odd to see in this new country so large a dwelling surrounded by barns and a farmyard which housed cattle and poultry. There was a wood around the house, through which paths had been cut in every direction. The framed timbers harmonized better with the untouched country than the people within. Gwyntheon, the eldest daughter, aired the French she had learned in a convent school and spoke about music with Margaret. Nevertheless, she too had learned to take care of the milk room and kill the rattlesnakes that assailed the poultry yard. William called Margaret to the high, large window through which they could see Norwegian immigrants working in their national dress. From his rambles in the outlying country William brought back to her the blue spiderwort, and told her he had heard that many of the supposed settlers were merely biding their time before they would go forth into a wilder place, a post in the buffalo country. Margaret began to feel the strangeness of a land where an English girl named Gwyntheon, whose mother was of Welsh descent, could remember her music while she killed rattlesnakes. This, then, was what the settling of a new country meant; old England had its part here, no less than the New.

Next day they traveled farther through De Kalb County. Margaret and Sarah alighted to cross the river on a little footbridge, while the wagon churned through the waters at the ford. A black thundercloud was coming up over the stream; the air was heavy with expectation. Margaret realized that William was trying to calm their fears about the approaching storm with his anecdotes about deer and Indians. He drove admirably, with coolness and self-possession. He knew his path as a man, but followed it with the gay spirit of a boy. She had never seen such a person in the East. Yet William, for all his delicate perceptions and wit, could not prevent the shower from falling. They were forced to take refuge in a solitary house upon the prairie. As she entered, Margaret remarked that in this country it was as pleasant to stop as to go, to lose the way as to find it. The adventure of meeting new people in every hut was possible only in the West. In Boston or in Groton one could foretell exactly what one would find in each house, but here it might be a Hungarian count or a Welshman, a Unitarian from New England, or, Margaret secretly hoped, an Indian. Now it was an old, barefoot man who invited them into the hut, and pointed out the Provence rose that grew near the door, telling the visitors that many families had brought the locust with them and planted it in the prairies. So again the old had come to mingle with the new.

The violent shower soon exhausted itself and the travelers drove on to Ross' Grove, which they reached as the sun was setting. There were no families here whose hospitality they might beg and no hotels other than the barroom that had been built in Papaw Grove some miles beyond the village. Each bedchamber had been designed for twelve occupants and at the table Margaret drank her milk from a communal pitcher. The only napkin available was her own handkerchief. But Margaret enjoyed the lark and amused William with remarks about the English lady at the table who seemed unable to adjust herself to such indecorums. The only sleeping room for Sarah and Margaret, as well as for "Britannia," was the barroom, from which the drinkers could be ejected only at a late hour. The outer door had no lock to prevent their return and the host bade the ladies call him if any one disturbed them. There was a hard couch for Sarah, but Margaret had to content herself with a bed on the supper table. She was too fatigued to stand upon such a trifle and thought that as a Yankee she had been born to rove anyway. She lay upon the supper table with as much composure as if it had been the bigly bower of a baroness, and laughed to herself as "Britannia" sat up all night, wrapped in her blanket shawl with a lace cap upon her head. There she sat, shuddering and listening, but prepared to look the lady should any one enter. She seemed so well prepared, indeed, that Margaret thought she deserved some interruption. She watched, as her parent country watched the seas, that none might wrong her. There was no interruption, however, and Margaret, drawing her warm cloak over her, soon fell asleep on the supper table. The good bread and wild strawberries the next morning made up for the hard bed and refreshed the travelers for their journey to Rock River. Margaret wondered what the ladies of West Street would say if they knew she had passed the night on a barroom table. It was good, she felt, to take the West as one found it, and leave the East where it belonged.

They rumbled on in the morning through Lee County to Rock River, crossing at Dixon's Ferry. The river flowed sometimes through parks and lawns, sometimes between high bluffs whose grassy ridges were covered with fine trees or broken with crumbling stone. Swallows' nests clustered, thick as cities, along the face of the rocks; here and there deer stalked; an eagle soared. Alexander Charters' home at Hazelwood, where they had planned to spend three days, was a place of singular beauty on the bend of the river. Mr. Charters, the Irish owner, was absent, but he had offered the hospitality of his home through his deputy. The wildness of the place had not completely vanished. The deer chase had been there for ages; Mr. Charters had simply cut an avenue through it. William walked with Sarah and Margaret, calling their attention to the traces of the Indians. Margaret observed that they had chosen the finest sites for their dwellings. They must surely be the rightful lords of this beauty they had forborne to disturb. When the hog comes the rattle-snake disappears. The white settler pursues the Indian even so and is victor in the chase. But the hog deforms the country where the rattlesnake does not. Still, Margaret comforted herself, the pigeons remained. Every afternoon they returned in swarms to their home near Mr. Charters' poultry coops. Hazelwood had made no blot upon the scene. It harmonized with the country without desecrating it with "improvements." It deserved a poem, Margaret thought. On the last day of June she wrote a few lines about this Western Eden to leave at the house for Mr. Charters.

Margaret sat in the wagon once again, her muslin dress showing to advantage, for in the wide sunny fields of the prairie she needed no cloak. She waited with Sarah while William stopped at a cabin to ask the way to the village of Oregon. The master of the house proposed a short cut down an almost perpendicular hill studded with young trees and stumps. He even offered to free the wheels whenever that became necessary, but Sarah and Margaret could not persuade themselves to venture on such a descent. They rode instead down a less steep bank, William holding the reins as if he had been Rhesus in a chariot, and proceeded along Black Hawk's trail.

"How could the Indians let themselves be conquered with such a country to fight for!" Margaret exclaimed.

Sarah interrupted to point to a peddler who sat with his pack in the wild prairie, uncovered by tree or umbrella, waiting apparently for customers. Margaret descended to buy his wares, pins. What strange lives men led, she thought. There were the woodcutters at Manitou, the Norwegians in De Kalb County at work in their native costume, and here a peddler sitting in the wide sunny prairie, holding his pack of pins. On Black Hawk's trail they pursued their way, passing a little congregation just returning from services in a rude house in the woods. How Black Hawk would have scorned such worship, Margaret mused. William seemed to sense that she was thinking of the tribes, for he remarked,

"You have only to turn up the sod to find arrow heads and Indian pottery. It is not so long since they were driven away. You will see many more traces of them near your uncle's home in Oregon."

Margaret's uncle, William Fuller, had carried his knowledge of law from Harvard to the little village of Oregon, but as he showed his guests the wooden troughs in which the Indians had prepared their corn and their caches for secreting provisions, he seemed more interested in the tribes than in the legal disputes of the white settlers. Uncle William was aging, however, and was glad to let young Clarke show the sights to the ladies. A little way down the river was the site of an ancient Indian village with its regularly arranged mounds. On a soft and shadowy afternoon they wandered toward the inlet, treading the flowery paths that once bore traces of Indian feet. They might blacken Indian life as they would, Margaret thought, talk of its dirt, its brutality. She was convinced that the men who chose such dwelling places, who lived so familiarly with deer and birds, and swam that clear wave in the shadow of the Seven Sisters, were noble.

"I can believe," she said aloud to William, "that an Indian brave accustomed to ramble in such paths might be mistaken for Apollo."

Everywhere she went, every tale she was told increased Margaret's desire to return to Mackinaw and see the Indians who still roamed the forest. Back at the house her uncle told stories of the early settling.

"Once," he said, "we opened one of the tribal mounds and found three of their dead seated in Indian fashion."

"I was making bread one winter morning," one of the ladies began, "when I saw a deer from my window. I ran out, my hands still covered with dough, and called Mr. Fuller. We caught the deer before he could escape."

This, then, had been pioneer life. Margaret wondered whether Sarah Ripley would have dropped her Greek, as this lady had dropped her bread, to capture a deer escaped from the herd.

It was a glorious morning, that of July fourth, when Margaret walked with William and Sarah to Eagle's Nest near Mr. Henshaw's island. Margaret felt that she had never been happier to have been born in America than when she stood on the height above which the eagles massed and swooped down. Three feathers from their superb plumage fell on the ground. Sarah picked them up and gave them to Margaret. She would give one to Caroline Sturgis; one she would keep; the third she would send at some distant time to William Clarke to remind him of this Independence Day when they had seen eagles soar above a height in the Rock River country. Holding the feathers and looking at the royal birds, she felt as Ganymede must have felt—Ganymede in Thorwaldsen's sculpture.

Mr. Henshaw invited them to the island. It was only five years ago that the Indians had been dispossessed, he said, pointing out the marks of their tomahawks upon felled trees. He regretted that there was no room in his double log cabin for the guests to stay. Rather than remain at Mr. Fuller's home, which was a distance from the island, they slept in town, but spent most of their three days with the Henshaws, passing to and from the bank on a little boat, the "Fairy." On the afternoon of July fourth the Henshaws served ice cream to their guests after dinner. It seemed strange to Margaret, after supping on prairie chickens and white fish that had been drawn from the river, to eat so civilized a dish. There were fireworks in the evening and a little fleet passed over the stream, announced by drumming and fifing from the opposite bank. An orator from New England gave a speech which to Margaret smacked loudly of Boston, but the round Irish visages dimpled at his puffs of "Ameriky." Here in this Western island, the settlers gathered to sing *Hail Columbia;* the gay flotilla cheered the flag that Mr. Henshaw had raised from his cabin. In dance and song they celebrated the health of their country. Healthful it was, Margaret thought. With all its resources of fish and game and wheat, there was no need of a baker to bring "muffins hot" every morning to the door for breakfast. Here indeed, whole families might live together, coming from England and Ireland, from Hungary, from New England, settling along the banks of the stream.

"For the women," Margaret remarked to Sarah, "the work is more difficult. The ladies from the East feel they cannot degrade themselves. Accustomed to the pavement of Broadway, they dare not tread the wildwood paths. It is they who inject the fatal spirit of imitation, of reference to European standards into this new country. If only there were schools here, they would not give their children the ambition of attending college in the East."

As the last drum throbbed, after the flotilla had passed over the water, they turned to Mr. Henshaw's house. The subject of Western life was interesting to Margaret and she pursued it.

"Why," she asked, "do the settlers carry a piano with them? They merely imitate the habit of Europe there, for not one in a thousand can play, and certainly none can tune it."

"What would you suggest instead?" asked William.

"A guitar or any portable instrument. Bring to the West what the West requires; you cannot climb an Indian mound in satin shoes."

How easily, William thought, Margaret could doff her own "satin shoes" to climb an Indian mound. He felt that at any moment she could become a settler in a new land, could slough off her old skin as the snake did, and grow a new one. She could forget Cambridge and Boston in these Western forests. Even in moccasins she would walk like a queen.

She climbed into the wagon like a queen, he thought, when on July sixth, they left Oregon for Belvidere. Up the bank of Rock River they drove, crossing the Kishwaukee River in a ferry piloted by a girl. William pointed out the rattlesnake weed as they rumbled on through Winnebago County.

"The antidote survives the bane," Margaret commented. "Soon," she added bitterly, "the coarser plantain, the white man's footstep, will take its place."

No one answered and they rode on in silence until at Kishwaukee a ragged, barefooted man approached the wagon. He seemed to be the walking Will's coffee house of the place, for he told the travelers all the snake stories he could remember.

"Once," he informed them, his bright eyes glancing from one to the other, "I saw seventeen young ones re-enter the mother snake when a visitor approached!"

Margaret enjoyed his tales so much that she was almost sorry when William eyed him with scorn and raised the whip for the journey to Belvidere.

There, in Boon County, they rested at a hotel and heard eagerly the story of Big Thunder's tomb—now, alas, despoiled. At Belvidere Margaret thought it might be wise for her brother Arthur to buy one of the blocks near Newton Academy and set up a school. She determined to speak to him about this and lend him money for the purpose. It was a flourishing town, not more than two days' journey to Chicago. That journey lay before them, the devious circuit back to William Clarke's home.

The lumber wagon defied all the jolts of wood paths and mud holes. William drove admirably, animating Margaret and Sarah with his accounts of the habits of fish and fowl, and all the warlike legends of the country. He seemed equally at home with nature and with man. He knew a tale of all that ran and swam and flew or only grew. His was an unstudied lore, the unwritten poetry with which common life had endowed his mind. What a delightful contrast to the philosophic strainings of Concord or the subtle analyses of Cambridge! His was a beauty that could not be transplanted, that had grown in the West and must flourish there. It was he who had opened the West to Margaret, the tiny settlements, the traces of the Indians. If only he could go on and reveal to her ready eye the hidden details of Indian life at Mackinaw. If only he could go on and return with her to the East. . . . Margaret dismissed the thought as suddenly as it had arisen. William would not be William in the East. No, his beauty could not be transplanted.

The sun set calmly, splendidly, as they rolled into Chicago. The twilight afterward was soft, and just as calm. It was a glorious pageant painted on the skies to mark the end of so fine a journey. The evening of July ninth seemed to mark the end of one beauty and the beginning of a new.

William left his business long enough to show Margaret the Hoosier wagons on the inland side of town. She saw the rude farmers who traveled leisurely, sleeping in their wagons by night, eating only what they brought with them. They were the large, first product of the soil, so different from the Germans, the Dutch, and the Irish who poured into the city. In the evenings she watched them camping out, their horses grazing out of harness while the masters lounged under the trees. William escorted Margaret and Sarah to the wharf, where the whole town had thronged to see the "Great Western" embark. Under the moon Margaret listened. The French language rippled amid the rude ups and downs of the Hoosier dialect. Chicago seemed in a state of transition. It was a fitting place for her to rest, meditating on what she had seen, preparing her mind for the sights that lay before her.

Here too Margaret found time to open her copy of *Philip van Artevelde*. Reading it again, she realized that the country needed an Artevelde. Not the thin idealists who looked at the narrow Cambridge skies for signs and portents, not the coarse realists who fingered their money in the countinghouses of Washington Street, but a man whose eyes read wider heavens while his feet stepped firmly on the ground. Here in the West there was no Artevelde yet. There were the realists who had forgotten their ideals in politics and trade; there were the idealists, mainly the women, who could not adapt themselves to pioneer life. But there was no amalgamation of the two. There was none who could interweave the white and golden threads into the fate of Illinois. Perhaps the Indians had been like Artevelde. Perhaps they had scanned the wide skies and planted their maize, combining the ideal with the real. She would see. Margaret bade good-bye to William to go off with Sarah for two weeks in the territory of Wisconsin. They would return to Chicago again before Margaret went on alone to Mackinaw.

By contrast with the lumber wagon the boat that carried Margaret and Sarah to Milwaukee was well appointed. There were many fair sights to be seen on the lake shores, and on board children were playing about the deck while the ladies gathered together for a song. At the landing the Milwaukee settlers swarmed to greet the incoming boat, gathering round to receive and send their packages and letters.

To Margaret Milwaukee seemed better developed than Chicago. In place of Hoosier wagons and wooden houses there were buildings of yellow brick. There was a town band which beat a volley of drums whenever an archer shot his mark on the bank of the lake. Here, even more noticeably than in Chicago, the immigrants teemed. Refugees in their national dress arrived daily to pass the night in rude shanties in one quarter of the town before they walked off into the country. On her rambles through Milwaukee Margaret saw many settlers cleaning their door handles as they watched their children playing before the house. There were Swedes and Norwegians, Germans and Dutch, all of whom seemed happier in their new life than the Easterners Margaret had observed. At market she and Sarah saw a Hungarian count who had a large tract of land in Wisconsin and came to purchase supplies in town. Everyone called him "Count"; for the settlers in the West, he had no other name.

When she tired of the flatness of Milwaukee there was enough wildness with which to fill her eyes in the view over the lake. Above the lighthouse, the thunderclouds gathered, reflected in the waters, while the huge steamers loomed up. Often Margaret followed the margin of the lake beneath the tall bluff whose crumbling soil seemed to change daily. The colors of the water were as various as a prism, sapphire or amethyst or emerald. The old arbor vitae trees along the river watched, while a waterfall catapulted down the ravine.

From the log cabin where they slept, with its little flower garden in front, they often boarded a carriage to ride into the near by country. The coachman was afraid to tire his horses and his driving by contrast with William's was almost as tame as in New England. He could never be tempted to follow a strange wood path or leave the road in pursuit of wildflowers. Nevertheless, strangeness came to Milwaukee in the shape of a band of Indians, wild and grotesque in their paint and feather headdress. They had come to Milwaukee on a begging-dance and followed a chief whose deep-red blanket fell in large folds from his shoulders to his feet. He alone did not join in the dance, but slowly strode about the streets. In Margaret's eyes he wore his blanket as if it were a toga, and seemed more grandly Roman than Indian. He walked, unmindful of his band, unmindful even of the mosquitoes that swarmed about his head as he advanced.

Margaret had seen enough of the tribes to long to see more of them. When an excursion to the lakes was suggested, she welcomed the idea, hoping for a closer view of an Indian encampment. At Nomabbin Lake, however, there were only tales of the Indians; they themselves had vanished. A refugee who had settled near by told Margaret unwittingly of the white man's injustice to the Indians. He was lying beneath the bank, he said, when he saw a tall brave gazing over the knoll. He lay a long time, curious to see how long the figure would maintain its statue-like pose. When he moved at last, the Indian turned abruptly, gave a wild snorting sound of indignation and pain, and strode away. The white man laughed as he told the story. Margaret thought if she had been the Indian she would have shot him where he lay. But the power of fate was with the white and the Indian knew it. The man went on to tell of his travels through the wilderness with an Indian guide.

"I had with me a bottle of spirit which I meant to give him in small quantities, but the Indian wanted the whole at once. I would not give it to him, for I thought if he became drunk, there was an end to his services as a guide. But he persisted and at last tried to take it from me. I was not armed; he was, and was twice as strong as I. But I knew an Indian could not resist the look of a white man, and I fixed my eye steadily on his. He bore it for a moment; then his eye fell. He let go the bottle. I took his gun, and threw it to a distance. After a few moments' pause I told him to go and fetch it; then I left it in his hands. From that moment he was quite obedient, even servile, all the rest of the way."

He looked smugly at Margaret as he spoke. He had the usual aversion, she realized, for the Indian on whom he had encroached—the aversion of the conqueror for him he had degraded. "They cannot be prevented from struggling back to their old haunts," he continued. "I wish they could. They ought not be permitted to drive away our game."

Our game, Margaret thought. The divine right of the white man!

Near Silver Lake she saw at last an Indian encampment. She and Sarah crossed a wide field and came upon the Indians among the trees on a shelving bank. Just as the visitors reached them, the rain began to fall in torrents; thunderclaps startled the air. They turned to a small lodge for refuge, finding it crowded not only with Indians, but with other whites who had sought protection from the storm. Some of the Indians were sick and lay on the damp ground or on ragged mats. Yet all of them were courteous as they beckoned the strangers in, standing a little apart as if they knew that white people would not like to touch them. One sick girl insisted on moving to give Margaret a dry place, while a squaw kept the children and wet dogs from brushing the hem of her dress. Outside, their fires were smouldering, the black kettles, hung over them on sticks, smoking and seething in the rain. An old, theatrical-looking Indian stood with his arms folded, gazing up to the heavens. He seemed less genuine, less Roman than the leader of the begging-dance in Milwaukee. Excited by the thunder, the Indians' ponies careered through the wood around the encampment, now and then thrusting their heads into the lodges. Then, after a moment, they trampled off again into the rain.

A white man told Margaret and Sarah that the Indians were a wandering band of Pottawattomies who had returned on a visit, either from homesickness or in need of relief. The women had been trying to barter their headbands, with which they clubbed their hair, for food. Margaret looked around the crowded lodge. There was no food; there were no utensils, no clothes, no bedding—nothing but the ground and the sky, and their own strength. That was all the missionaries and the sharks of trade had left them. Margaret had no hope of liberalizing the one or humanizing the other; yet, she thought, let every man look to himself how far this blood shall be required at his hands. Let the missionary, instead of preaching to the Indian, preach to him who ruins him. The trader in the West had as much blood on his hands as the factory owner in the North, the plantation lord in the South. The storm abated. Margaret tried by gesture to wave her thanks to the Indians. She left the lodge with Sarah and walked on to the carriage.

They drove to a foreign settlement in the neighborhood of the lake and stopped at one of the dwellings. Though they saw books and pencils and a guitar in the house, neither wash tub nor axe was in sight. In the inner room the master of the house was seated; he had injured his foot on shipboard, and his farming was done by his young wife. The invalid sat on his wooden chair, dressed as neatly as if he had been assisted by a duke's valet. As he spoke he raised his clear blue eyes to Margaret. He had come from the north of Europe, he said, and was happy to show her an album of drawings and verses from his native land. She could not help feeling, however, that he was incapable of adjusting himself to life near a Wisconsin lake. She hoped at least that he would rear his children to be fitted for the freedom and independence of the West.

On the way home the fine carriage broke down and Margaret was greatly fatigued after her journey to Nomabbin Lake. Besides, she felt the need of digesting the sights she had seen and was glad for a day or two to rest in the Milwaukee boarding house before returning to Chicago. Here, she opened her copy of the *Seherin von Prevorst* and read of magnetic sleep and the revelations of dreams. Justinus Kerner's seeress was a far cry from the Norwegian refugees or the Pottawattomies. The character recalled to her mind Goethe's Macaria, who knew the life of spirit and soul as did the forester's daughter from Prevorst. Margaret remembered Anna Parsons, the little girl she had met at Cambridge so long ago, who seemed to have the second sight Kerner described. The magnet stone of red ochre with which the seeress was induced to sleep brought to her mind her own carbuncle ring and all her futile discussions of demonology with Emerson. Yet, the Seherin von Prevorst was after all not so far removed from the Indians and the Milwaukee settlers.

Every day of her journey, Margaret felt, had been touched by the supernatural. Standing at the pier, where the Swiss and Norwegians disembarked, she had been stirred, knowing they would carry their legendary lore to the forests of Wisconsin. The Old World had married the New in the West; their child was wonder, strangeness almost supernatural.

On the voyage back to Chicago, Margaret looked at Sarah's sketches of the Indian encampments, and as she turned the pages, summed up for her friend her thoughts about the West.

"Here," she said, "people are not respected merely because they are old; people have not time here to keep up appearances in that way. There is no napkin of precedent here wherein to wrap talent. What cannot be made to pass current, is not esteemed coin of the realm."
Margaret thought that Sarah had caught some of the feeling of the transient life in the uneven strokes of her pencil. She believed they were both wiser on their return to Chicago than when they had left.

At Chicago there were letters for Margaret, letters that brought all the news of the East into this Western town. It was strange to read, as she looked out at the crowds of land speculators bustling on the wooden pavement, of the Channings' new Red Cottage on the Cambridge turnpike with its neat slab fence and gate, of Ellen's five scholars, and the bitter criticism which Ellery's book of poems had received. Thoreau admired Margaret's article, *The Great Lawsuit*. Caroline had gone on to Nahant, still dreaming of Niagara. How unimportant, how trivial it all seemed. Margaret turned to the next letter. Richard had given a music box to Henry Thoreau, who had carried the condensed music of the spheres to Staten Island, where he was tutoring William Emerson's children. Thoreau had visited William Channing in New

York at his home on Fifteenth Street and had discussed *The Present,* the new journal which William intended to issue in the fall. Horace Greeley was shouting from the rafters of his *Tribune* office the glories of the Sylvania Association.

Margaret looked out of the window. How remote this news seemed. She turned to other letters. Charles Sumner had arranged for an exhibition of Crawford's works. Richard bemoaned his failure to conquer with spear or quill at Harvard. Mrs. Fuller was happy in her new garden at Prospect Street. There was another letter from Concord. Emerson and Thoreau were having difficulties in canvassing for *Dial* subscribers, though Greeley was advertising gratuitously in the *Tribune.* James Munroe had taken over publication. The Hawthornes had been interrupted in their Eden by visits from Emerson, whose face seemed to picture the promised land, and from Anna Ward, resembling the goddess Diana, in the full glory of her golden curls. Elizabeth Hoar had come too, looking like the rose of Sharon.

How pale, how vapid, the words seemed to Margaret, here where Indians were dispossessed by sharks of trade, where bread, not manna, was the hoped-for food. She reached for another letter. Here was news of the millennium. William Miller had capitalized on the great comet of the spring; Orion had helped him convince the world that the second coming was near. The Shakers had bestirred themselves; elders and eldresses were all turning into mediums, conversing with the prophets and martyrs of old. Alcott had gone off to Wyman farm at Harvard with Charles Lane and Christopher Greene and had called his community Fruitlands. Hecker had been won over from Brook Farm, and Samuel Larned, whom Margaret remembered from Providence, was roaming about with little Louisa May Alcott—all of them feeling of their shoulders to find if their wings were sprouting. Wings. The letters were so full of them. Margaret had begun to think that cowhide boots were more to the point.

Sarah came into the room.

"I have had letters too, Margaret. Washington Allston has died. It happened," she added gently, "the night we first returned to Chicago—that beautiful evening of the sunset when we drove into town with William."

"First, Dr. Channing," Margaret murmured, "and now Allston. Do you remember what Theodore Parker said when he heard of Dr. Channing's death? 'Why could not I have died in his stead.' But he could not. This is our generation, now, Sarah. The old ones are leaving. Their work is done. If only our generation would not think exclusively in terms of wings." She rustled her letters impatiently. "I want to see cowhide boots first."

She would see the cowhide boots, she knew, at Mackinaw. Here, on her last night in Chicago, there was time to soar a little way on wings. Good-byes were always painful, especially when there would be no return. She would not go back to Chicago; she would not see William Clarke again. They took their last walk together along the shore. Margaret wept, almost, when he told her that she had come to him in a season of melancholy and depression, the good genius of his life. She had breathed her energy into him and with her delight in his spirit of adventure had rekindled his powers. Margaret still knew his beauty could not be transplanted. His melancholy could never be perennial; it was a seasonal growth. His delicate perceptions would find roots here in the West and he would thrive. She looked at him, opening her eyes widely to penetrate his. She wanted to remember him as he was, the familiar of the prairie, lover of the country, its wild life and its legends. They had exchanged their gifts. To her he had offered his knowledge of the West; to him she had given a breath of new life. That was enough. There could be no more between them. He too would pass from her life though not from her memory, as Samuel Ward had passed. Others might come to whom she would be joined by stronger links, perhaps. They had touched the wings. Now Margaret was off alone for the cowhide boots.

Late on an August night she reached the island of Mackinaw. From the boat she could see thousands of Indians encamped there, representatives of the Chippewa and Ottawa tribes who had come to receive their annual payments from the government. As the boat puffed toward the shore, the captain ordered a display of rockets. The Indians watched, yelling and crying wildly at the sight. After the bursts of fire the night seemed darker than ever. Margaret left the boat. Walking in the midst of the shrieking savages to her hotel, she barely heard the pants and snorts of the departing steamer.

Here, as at Ross' Grove, she was forced to sleep in a common eating room and was eager when dawn broke to be out at last among her Indian neighbors. From the window of the boarding house she could see their canoes coming in, as one group after another set up a temporary dwelling. The women ran to erect the tent poles and spread mats on the ground, while the men brought chests and kettles from the canoes. Cedar boughs were strewed on the ground, the blanket hung up for a door, and in less than twenty minutes these nomads had found a home. How they chatted together! The Indians, Margaret thought, were anything but taciturn among themselves. They talked even while they cooked, learning, no doubt, the news of the day from their neighbors.

As she looked out of the window, a few traders from La Pointe and Arbre Croche commented cynically about her interest in the tribes. To Margaret the traders in the boarding house seemed wilder than the Indians. Two little girls bounded into the parlor, one an American, fair, with bright, brown hair; the other a French Canadian whose father and brothers were boatmen. The owner of the boarding house, Margaret discovered, was the widow of a French trader, an Indian by birth, who still wore the dress of her people. It was strange to hear her fluent French while her fingers stroked her precious beads. The whole garrison of Mackinaw, the soldiers, half-breeds, and Indians, gathered round the boarding house to pay her homage.

Interesting as the sights within the house might be, Margaret was sure that on the beach, where the Indian lodges honeycombed the sands, there would be more exciting scenes. Remembering that Mrs. Jameson had bedecked herself with a wampum necklace before meeting the Chippewas, she wore a golden locket; the occasion of her first actual visit to an Indian encampment should be honored by such a token. Margaret took her sun shade and walked off.

The Indians were out already, the children creeping from beneath the blanket door, the women pounding corn in their rude mortars, the young men playing on their pipes. Margaret had heard the Winnebago courting song before, but never had it sounded so like the call of a bird alluring its mate. She walked around Sugar-Loaf Rock through the old town, passing French and half-breeds as well as the Indians. Along the curving beach clustered the lodges of the tribes. There the women stooped over their kettles; the half naked children bobbed in and out of the water. A young woman with a baby on her back glanced at Margaret with bright eyes. Near by two girls were cutting wood, talking and laughing in their low, musical voices. Bark canoes were upturned on the beach; others were coming in, their square sails set.

Margaret gestured to one of the women, trying to explain that she would like to sit with her. The woman was ugly, like most of the squaws, except for her bright eyes. Her gait was awkward, contrasting with the noble stride of the men; she had been bent under many burdens. The woman answered with a timid gesture and pointed to Margaret's locket. Margaret removed it and let the squaw hold it. She shut her hand over it and then looked at it shyly. Then silently she returned it. Next, the woman pointed to the sun shade. By this time a group of Indians had gathered round Margaret. The woman then singled out an old squaw, sitting before the blanket of her lodge under an old green umbrella. We too have our dignified shade, she seemed to say. A younger woman, sitting near by, with a baby in a cradle at her feet, gestured for permission to hold the sun shade. Margaret showed her how to open it, and the woman put it into her baby's hand, laughing mischievously as if to say, "You carry a thing that is fit only for a baby." Margaret smiled, took her sun shade, and walked away. Some of the men, she observed, were drunk. Many seemed degraded, bearing but a faint impress of the lost grandeur of their race. Yet, as they stole along the heights or strode boldly forward, they reminded her that once there had been majesty in the red man.

As she walked on a white woman approached her and demanded,

"How could you endure their dirt and smell? Do what you will for them they will not be grateful. The savage cannot be washed out of them."

An Indian child approached them and the woman drew herself up, remarking, "Its odor is loathsome."

Margaret was outraged by the woman's lack of shame. The stern Presbyterian had degraded the tribes with their dogmas, their niggard concessions, and unfeeling stares.

The white man had sinned against the first-born of the soil. When they invoked the holy power it was only to mask their own iniquity. So the trader who has besotted the Indian with rum and red pepper, kneels with him on Sunday before a common altar and sins again by his hypocrisy. This woman was no different from the priest who bade his savage friends aim at "purity." Better their own dog feasts and heathen rites than the mockery the whites had taught them! Such women were called Christians, who found the odor of their brothers loathsome; such missionaries were called the representatives of Christ, who attempted by holding up the Cross to turn deer and tigers into lambs. Margaret walked silently away from the woman. She too was but a puppet of the traders, as were the preachers who tried to convince the red man that a heavenly mandate had dispossessed him of his home. Get you gone, you Indian dog, cries the pirate, for might makes right.

Margaret was disturbed from her thoughts by the shouts of an Indian orator who was addressing a congregation of Chippewas. She asked a white man who had strolled near by whether he could interpret his words. The man fortunately understood Chippewa and informed her, "The Indian began with the customary compliments about sun and dew. Then he explained the difference between the white and red man. The white man looks to the future, and paves the way for posterity. The red man never thought of this." He had made an accurate distinction, Margaret thought. At least she hoped, now that they had forfeited their virtue along with their lands, there would be some museum of their remains, some library of their customs, to recall their traits to posterity, and remind the white man of his sin. There was a captivity in a newer Israel that men must not forget. She would not forget it, and to cement her tie with the tribes, she bought a little Indian cradle to carry home as a memento.

Toward the end of August Margaret boarded the "General Scott" at Mackinaw to travel to Sault Sainte Marie. In her cabin were a Dutch girl and an Indian woman, both of whom spoke English. The Dutch girl was eager to tell of the shepherd's dance at Amsterdam and the Indian woman confided the story of her life to Margaret. She had left her husband, she said, and earned her living by going as chambermaid on these boats. The captain of the "General Scott" was a pleasant man. Yet, she added, he had never seen Sault Sainte Marie, though he had made the trip hundreds of times. Margaret went on deck later to watch the course up the river. The maple woods of St. Joseph's Island stretched before her. She could hear the rapids as they approached Lake Superior. At Sault Sainte Marie she left the boat and wandered through the old Chippewa burying ground. Seated on a large stone she could see, a little way off, the home-lodges, so different from the temporary tents at Mackinaw. The squaws trooped through the wood, stooping under the loads of cedar boughs that were strapped on their backs.

Margaret's main purpose in coming to Sault Sainte Marie had been to shoot the rapids. As soon as she arrived, therefore, she ordered a canoe, and sat down to wait for it. Soon she spied two Indian canoemen in pink calico shirts, moving the boat with their long poles. Now and then they cast a scoop net, and when they arrived at the shore, they spread a mat for Margaret in the middle of the canoe. In less than four minutes they had descended the three-quarter-mile stretch of rapids. As they went down the Indians caught a white fish for Margaret's breakfast. The whole experience had been so sudden, so brief, that she could scarcely realize it.

On the voyage back to Mackinaw Margaret passed her

time in the company of an Illinois farmer, whose solid talk was more enjoyable to her than the persiflage of the East. When the boat arrived at the island, Margaret looked down at the landing and saw Sarah, who had come to meet her and spend three days at Mackinaw before the journey home. They walked together to the Indian haunts, where the squaws showed less interest in Margaret's sun shade than in Sarah's pencil. The sketchbook was filling rapidly now with Indian scenes, though most of the lodges had been dismantled already and only rags and dried boughs marked the encampment.

Just before leaving for home Sarah and Margaret arranged for an hour's canoe excursion. The Indians who paddled them were richly dressed in blue and scarlet with scarfs of bright red round their heads. They carried them into the path of the steamboat, paddling with all their force, dashing the spume into the boat. The canoe sped over the waves, light as a sea gull. "Pull away!" one of the Indians shouted, laughing gayly, and the other answered, "Ver' warm!"

Pull away! Away from Mackinaw and all the northwest summer. The "Great Western" had landed and they must return home. The boat itself gave them a foretaste of the East, for a shabbily dressed phrenologist laid his hand on every head that would bend, recalling John Neal and Providence to Margaret. Here and there knots of people gathered to discuss theology. A bereaved lover sought consolation in Butler's *Analogy;* yet he had not turned over many pages before his eye was caught by the gay glances of a damsel who came on board at Detroit. Thereupon Butler was relegated to his pocket. At Detroit phrenology and theology were forgotten while the passengers looked out at the town. The "Wisconsin" was being launched and all of Detroit had arrayed itself in brilliant colors, while the band played. When the "Great

Western" moved on, the travelers went back to their doctrinal discussions. Some began to debate the merits of Fourierism.

Margaret preferred to sit quietly, deliberating upon the varied meanings of the summer that had passed. She had learned a great deal about the Indians. She believed she was familiar with the soul of the race. Recalling a conversation at Cambridge with James Clarke, Margaret turned to Sarah and said,

"I think I have the answer to the riddle I once propounded to James. We must not Christianize the Indians to civilize them, but civilize to Christianize."

As for the West, she disliked its "first rate," "offhand," "go ahead," instinctive existence almost as intensely as the petty intellectualities, the cant and bloodless theorizing of the East. She walked up to the bow of the ship and looked over the waters. Let me stand in my age, she whispered, with all its waters flowing round me. If they sometimes subdue, they must finally upbear me, for I seek the universal, and that must be the best.

CHAPTER XII

METERS AND PSYCHOMETERS

IN JULY, while Margaret was out West, Mrs. Fuller had moved from the house on Ellery Street, whose windows overlooked Mount Auburn and the slow, mild river, to one on Prospect Street. But Cambridge was still Cambridge and Margaret found that life in the new house did not differ greatly from life in the old. It was no longer possible to run next door to Dr. Wesselhoeft or to entertain his seven-year-old daughter Minna after she had crawled under Margaret's fence to beg for stories. The morning walks with Richard were over, for after he had received his degree, Margaret obtained a place for him in George Davis' law office at Greenfield. Yet Lloyd was at home again and though his lack of intellect made him a poor substitute for his brother, Margaret passed many hours singing psalms with him. Cambridge was still Cambridge for her, a pensioned sojourn in the outer porch.

Margaret had changed, she felt, far more than her house. It was of some significance that the Indian cradle stood below the del Sarto Madonna in her bedroom. To her love of Goethe and of Raphael she had added an absorbing interest in the oppressed tribes of the West. How often, as she looked up from her desk near the window, her eye wandered beyond the apple tree to scenes more remote, where refugees swarmed on wooden pavements, where Indians stole back to the lands that had once been theirs, the lands that haunted them. There was less time for such thoughts, however, than Margaret might have desired, less time also to watch the little yellow birds that perched for a moment on the window sill, to look at

[303]

her copy of Silenus holding in his arms the infant Pan, or to bury her face in the flowers she had picked early in the morning. It was well that she rose every day, as Emerson had said, with an appetite that could eat the solar system like a cake, for there was a whole solar system on her desk waiting to be consumed.

Once again the velvet pen wiper was on duty and from eleven o'clock till sunset the pen raced down the page. There were the winter Conversations to be planned. The year's topic of education would include discussions of Culture and Ignorance, Vanity and Prudence, Patience and Health. They must be illustrated by episodes on war; Bonaparte, Goethe, and Spinoza must provide the modern instances; Margaret must prepare for wide digressions. The chrysanthemums of West Street might delight, and the carbuncle ring enchant the ladies, but they must be supplemented with wide readings and adequate plans.

Then there was *The Dial*. As Margaret scanned the October issue, she realized how much the periodical had changed since Emerson had taken over the editorship. It was true that Parker was still given over thirty pages for his thoughts on the origin of Christianity, and Ellery continued to dilate upon the youth of the poet and painter, but now Thoreau seemed to have gathered as many flowers from the ethnical scriptures of China as from his walks in Concord, while Charles Lane had been allowed over fifteen pages to discuss the social tendencies of America. The magazine had changed, obviously, she considered, as she turned from *A Day with the Shakers* to the *Voyage to Jamaica*. When she had been editor, she had tried to make it appeal to more than one type of intellect. She had thought it less important that everything in it be excellent than that the periodical represent with some fidelity the state of mind in New England. Emerson worked on a different principle. Everything in *The Dial* now conformed to his taste. As far as it went, Margaret reflected, this was admirable enough, but it did not go far enough. His principle resulted in a narrower range. Rather expansive sympathies, she decided, than a limited, severe outlook. However, *The Dial* was Emerson's now, and since he had not failed it when it seemed as though it must go under, she would not fail him now, though indeed it looked again as though the quarterly could not continue.

The pen must turn from a Conversation on Education to a review of *The Modern Drama* for the next *Dial*. Here at least she would reiterate her belief that those who played a pipe cut from their own grove were far more admirable than those who displayed an ivory lute handed down from olden times. In the West the young people still acted *Tamerlane* and *Cambises* for the store-keepers and settlers, but the day must come when the fortunes of Boone or the defeat of Black Hawk would produce a dramatic form entirely new in America. We looked too much to the stars and forgot our private trust. There. Let that article come between Thoreau's extracts from Buddha's White Lotus and Charles Lane's vituperations against Brook Farm. Then there was a dialogue to be written for what might very well be the last issue of *The Dial*. There were lines in the conversation, which Margaret imagined between Aglauron and Laurie, that Emerson would not disdain. "Quiet thought always showed me the difference between heartlessness and the want of a deep heart." Ellery would like that. Even Thoreau would admit the precision of this sentence about Wordsworth, "whose wide and equable thought flows on like a river through the plain." And this idea would delight Emerson, "It needs not that one of deeply thoughtful mind be passionate, to divine all the secrets of passion. Thought is a bee that cannot miss those flowers." What would they say

of this: "Tragedy is always a mistake." Let the readers
of *The Dial*—of the last *Dial* if they would have it so—
take thought upon such phrases, as they turned from
Elizabeth Peabody's explanation of Fourierism to ex-
cerpts from the Chaldaean Oracles or Charles Lane's account of the Millennial Church.

It was always pleasing for Margaret to shift her attention from the moribund to the living. Somehow, she
felt, as she worked on her Conversations and *The Dial,*
that she was giving her mind to dying causes. This would
be the sixth winter of the Conversations, the fifth of *The
Dial.* The ladies of West Street, though animated as ever,
were straggling into the Peabody bookshop in smaller
numbers. As for *The Dial* there were so many shadows
on its face that it could not mark the time of many more
suns. But the West—the West was still alive; when Margaret could drop the pen for a moment, the Indians turned
the little path with its apple tree into Black Hawk's trail.
Underneath Del Sarto's Madonna surely the Indian
cradle rocked again. There was material in this past summer on the lakes for a book. Where her notes failed, her
memory served, and if memory faltered there was the
Harvard College Library. There she went day after day
to reread Catlin or Mrs. Jameson, Schoolcraft or M'Kenney, while the undergraduates raised their eyebrows at
the presence of a lady in their sacred precincts. Thomas
Higginson sat near her, proud in his proximity to one who
had already startled the world when he had been a baby
washed in his mother's brass-handled tub.

Back at Prospect Street Margaret assorted her notes,
inserting here and there a letter or a poem. There was
that copy of *Triformis* she must retrieve from Emerson
to incorporate in *Summer on the Lakes.* It would also be
well, she thought, to vary the accounts of the Indians with
a review of the book she had read at Milwaukee, the

Seherin von Prevorst. Here too, was space to include that autobiographical romance she had hoped to write ever since she had heard George Phillips' oration about "Incorporating Historical Truth with Fiction" at the Commencement of '29. How amusing it would be to watch the glassy eyes of a curious reader search for Margaret beneath the fantastic character, Mariana. All those pretty dreams of her childhood when she had walked through Tory Row, an abandoned princess, would find a place here. The English woman whom she had dreamed of as a star would be worshipped again in these pages. In this episode she would open again her father's closet of books and re-experience her delight in *Romeo and Juliet,* in Cervantes, in Molière. She would so interweave the true with the imaginary that none would be able to separate them. Those days at Groton when she had imagined herself dancing like a dervish would give color to the story. None would know whether it was Margaret or Mariana who wore the bright red sash and knocked her head in anger and remorse against the fenders. Margaret it was, but a dreaming Margaret—the Margaret who loved the heliotrope more than Colburn's *Arithmetic.* How many selves there were, and what delight to rediscover them, glorify them, incorporating truth with fiction.

The pen raced on. She would develop Margaret into a subtle, fantastic maiden who loved Sylvain. Sylvain. From what forgotten source had the name emerged? Yes. Sylvain had been Fanny Elssler's partner in the bridal dance. No man had ever realized his ideals any more than Margaret had ever really danced the dervish dance or swooned upon the hearth. Yet truth was there, the truth of dreams. It would be amusing to watch a reader seek reality in the dream. Truth was there, but touch it not, for it is protean. Seek not Margaret in Mariana, for she is only Margaret—is only everyman—in dream, a self that steps arrayed in jewels from a drab and homespun cloak, a bright splash of crimson between the pages of a book of travels. Before and after Mariana the Indians stalked, proud though oppressed. They too brought their color to the book, a color that had once been brilliant, but now was muddied from the white man's foot.

It would be spring, Margaret calculated, before *Summer on the Lakes* could be completed. She must verify her facts about the Indians; she must copy her notes, refresh her memories about the settlers. After a long day's work before the window, when Margaret had turned herself from the *Dial* critic into the fantastic Mariana and then into the observer of the West, it was exhilarating to go to Boston the next morning and shake the apples from her Cambridge bough at the feet of the ladies of West Street. After the Conversation there was much to be done in the city. There might be a tea at Mrs. Bancroft's, or a lecture at the Masonic Temple, or a soiree at the Peabodys' where Charles Sumner would tell his far-famed stories of Prince Metternich while James Clarke concocted bon mots in a corner. Sometimes there was so much to do that Margaret preferred working in her rooms at Avon Place to returning to the village after a morning's tustle with *Dial* proofs. She must dress carefully in her lilac satin before she would venture to discuss literature with Sir John Caldwell or shoot darts of rhetoric at such bulls' eyes as the Shaws or the Wards. Then there were the shopping days, when she must hasten across the smokers' circle on the Common to buy bombazine and black gloves on Washington Street.

It was for a special occasion that the bombazine had been bought at two dollars a yard. One must adorn oneself as magnificently to hear Beethoven's Seventh Symphony as to approach the Delphic Oracle, or, indeed, to interpret the utterances of that Oracle in West Street. Before this year, Margaret considered, as she fastened the tight-fitting sleeves, there had not been music of any great order in Boston. True, there had been the oratorios of the Handel and Haydn Society, but Mr. Braham had been able to shift too facilely from *The Messiah* to *My mother bids me bind my hair*. And if it had not been for Dwight's copy of *Fidelio* it would have been almost impossible to have heard any worth-while pianoforte work. Margaret recalled the depressing amount of Gyrowetz and Pleyel that she had herself played on the piano. Nowadays the pianists advertised the number of notes they could execute in a single bar, and the audience was as well pleased with a fantasy on *Bells upon the Wind* as with Rossini's *Stabat Mater*. Rakemann had done better things, it was true, and Margaret had heard Beethoven's Fifth, but it had been so poorly performed it was no wonder the Academy had almost limited itself to vocal music. They had an excellent chorus, she admitted, but their orchestra! Now it had changed, John Dwight had informed her. Professor Webb had come to conduct with a baton at the Boston Academy of Music in place of the tall Henry Schmidt who used to sway before his orchestra, violin in hand. Margaret placed on her finger the ring that Emma Keats, George Keats' daughter, had given her, with its inscription, "Feed my lambs." Tonight, the night of November twenty-fifth, in the year eighteen hundred and forty three, her lambs would be fed.

With John Dwight and Caroline Sturgis she climbed to the upper gallery, more like a sky parlor than anything else. Margaret looked up to see the stars shining through the semicircular window. She and Caroline placed their great muffs on the hard seats as cushions. As they looked at the program John Dwight chatted on about having walked from Brook Farm to see the willowy Schmidt lead his musicians in the days when the Academy had been called the Odeon.

"Nowadays," he continued, "we return to a different

Brook Farm from the one you visited. We have groups and orders under the auspices of Fourier, and I myself," he added with a blush, "am the chief of the festal series. The word 'mass' has crept into our language and Ripley is moving along Brisbane's Material and Aromal lines. There are scores of other communities that are doing the same thing, in Indiana and New York, Pennsylvania and New Jersey. Associations and phalanxes are dotting the whole country. I am not at all sure it will be for the best at Brook Farm. We have even turned music into terms of a Fourieristic gamut. Brisbane writes that the universe moves to the rhythm of do, re, mi. He even says that in thirty-five thousand years we shall all meet under Saturn's ring. But tonight we shall hear finer harmonies; we need not wait thirty-five thousand years to hear the music of the spheres."

Margaret twirled her ring. The lambs would be fed soon.

George Webb walked to the podium. He lifted his baton and Keyzer, the concertmaster, raised his bow. The orchestra burst forth with Hérold's *Overture to Zampa*. There were six short pieces that must be played before the Beethoven, Margaret counted, as she looked down at the program. After the overture, Mrs. Andrews billowed onto the stage, looking for all the world like the title of the Bellini song she was to sing, *Arrayed for the Bridal*. No wonder, Margaret thought, that Emerson in the midst of a solo plays tricks with his eyes, darkening the house and brightening the singer. One must have visual enchantment if there is no appeal to the ear. Kummer's solo on the flute was well executed by Mr. Werner, but Mrs. Andrews returned too soon to join Mr. Barker and Mrs. Kellogg in a trio from *Norma*. As soon as the trio strutted off the stage, Mr. Keyzer arose to render a solo composition by Lafont. This was charming. Margaret smiled at Caroline. Suddenly, a young lady and two gentlemen seated behind them began to buzz. Margaret turned back and tried to silence them with a glance. They stopped for a moment, but then the buzzing continued. They went on chatting and laughing through Mr. Keyzer's solo and Auber's *Overture to Zanetta*. Margaret was glad that the first half of the concert had concluded with an overture. She could forget that she had heard anything else, and imagine that the overture simply heralded Beethoven's Seventh.

During the intermission she turned to the trio behind her, and leaning across the back of her chair, caught the young woman's eye.

"May I speak with you one moment?" she asked in a bland and gentle tone.

"Certainly, with pleasure." The girl bent forward expectantly.

"I only wish to say," Margaret remarked emphatically, "that I trust in the whole course of your life you will not suffer so great a degree of annoyance as you have inflicted on a large party of music lovers this evening."

The young lady blushed and did not answer. Margaret murmured to John Dwight and Caroline, "At least we shall not be troubled during the second part of the concert. We shall hear—what we came to hear."

They sat quietly during the brief intermission. Anticipation filled the air.

George Webb entered again and raised his baton. He paused to glance at Mr. Keyzer. Margaret leaned forward. The baton was lowered and the harmonies of sound echoed to the far-off sky parlor. Melodies began simply and became complex. From the profound of affliction the music turned wildly into a mad dance. It was tragedy thundering from bass viols and trumpets, tearful sweetness disengaging itself from the haunting wood winds. Now it was triumph blown from a trumpet, reverberating to the upper gallery, where sound was transmuted to thought, as Margaret reflected, "It is the triumph of a noble democracy to which Beethoven remained ever true." It was fire on an altar—Beethoven losing his soul and finding it again, outpouring himself for a woman who sat in the sky parlor of an academy in Boston, listening to motifs that had been born in black and white dots on a score in Germany. Near the end of the third movement Margaret caught her breath as she listened to the succession of soaring passages, soaring, but holding on with a stress that almost broke the chains of matter to her listening ears. After the finale she sat back, depleted. She could not join the applause. A deaf man who lay buried in Germany had touched her through the medium of a conductor's baton here in a little corner of the New World, had stirred her to a point where words became meaningless. She felt her ring. The lambs had been fed.

Margaret picked up her muff and climbed down from the sky parlor with Caroline and Dwight. The stars still glittered through the semicircle of light. As they walked out onto the street, Margaret murmured, "After all, music is the best language known to man, the means of transmitting thought best calculated to meet at once the wants of both sense and soul." She need not have spoken. Caroline and John Dwight had both felt what she had felt. They walked on quietly, and as if by common consent, did not enter Mrs. Harrington's cake shop. After the sounds they had heard, silence was the only comment. Beethoven and silence—the antiphon of the true Mass.

When she returned to Avon Place Margaret stood long before the window, hearing in memory the chords that had been struck at the Academy, thinking again the thoughts they had touched off. She turned to her desk and wrote,

"Saturday evening, 25th Nov., 1843

My only friend,"

He was her only friend, this deaf man who lay buried three thousand miles across the water. She must write to him, to Beethoven, who had broken the chains of her sorrowful slumber and made her live again. "Thou, oh blessed master, dost answer all my questions, and make it my privilege to be. Thou art to me beyond compare, for thou art what I want." Yes, she thought, not Raphael, nor golden Plato, nor stern Angelo, nor the infinite Shakespeare can be seen in his presence. Shakespeare's creations are successive, but, she wrote, "thy fiat comprehends them all." In Beethoven, as in the woods, she found herself expressed. "Master, I have this summer envied the oriole which had even a swinging nest in the high bough. I have envied the least flower that came to seed, though that seed were strewn to the wind. But I envy none when I am with thee." Margaret paused and folded the letter between the leaves of her journal. She touched her ring again. The lambs had been fed; the lambs had prayed in thanksgiving.

It was strange that in the spring of 1843, when Beethoven had seemed to usher in a new beginning, and all the earth started awake in bud and brook and leaf, so much in Margaret's life should be dying. If the thought of William Clarke still persisted even that was given the touch of finality when she sent him a blank book inscribed with verses as sincere as those words that had passed between them amid the shadowy thickets that bounded the deer. In April came the last of *The Dial* and on the twenty-eighth of the month the last Conversation. After Margaret's final phrases the ladies had surrounded her, as she sat on the couch, loading her with gifts, presenting to her a bouquet of passion flower and heliotrope. On May twenty-third, her birthday, she wrote the last line of *Summer on the Lakes* and went to Mt. Auburn to walk among the graves. It was a spring when all things seemed to end for her. Only the proofs of the book remained to be read. All else had gone. Yet through it all those soaring notes of Beethoven leapt on, and seemed to Margaret to mark no end, but a beginning. If life should die in one way, it would spring afresh upon another bough. In Beethoven music born of death arose to life. In Margaret there would be such beginnings too. Having heard the coda, she waited for the overture.

It was not long after Little and Brown published *Summer on the Lakes* that Margaret, in July of 1844, accepted an invitation from the Hawthornes to visit the Old Manse. Hawthorne, she thought, looked more than ever like the "boned pirate" Tom Appleton had called him, as he sat weaving stories in the parlor or walked silently along the Concord River. He was interested in Margaret's book and wanted to hear more stories of Chicago and the West. As they sat one morning in Mrs. Hawthorne's room, looking at Thorwaldsen's "Night" at the head of the bedstead, Margaret spoke of the sculptor's "Ganymede," of Eagle Rock, and then of that evening, the ninth of July, a little more than a year before, when they had returned at sunset to Chicago.

"We later learned that that was the night of Allston's death," she said. "It was the night for endings."

Hawthorne looked up suddenly. On the wash stand was a picture of Venus rising from the sea, copied from Flaxman's illustrations of Homer.

"Here at Concord on that night," he said, "Martha Hunt was drowned. Channing, Buttrick, and I rowed about in the moonlight in the boat Thoreau gave to Ellery until we found the body. I shall never forget it. It *was* a night of endings." He looked at Margaret almost fiercely. Those hazel eyes of his were not always gentle. She felt that he was scrutinizing her for purposes of his own. She recalled a little uncomfortably his remarks about her transcendental heifer, and wondered, almost irrelevantly, whether it could have any connection with this drowning of Martha Hunt.[1]

"I do believe," Sophia remarked, "that my husband is planning another book."

That was how he wrote then, Margaret thought. She remembered Georgiana Bruce's description of him, sitting silently on the sofa under the stairs at the Eyrie, listening to all the talk around him, saying nothing. He picked up scraps of talk and isolated incidents; he clouded them over with a fantasy of his own; over flesh and blood he wove a ghostly veil. Before that stooping figure, before those hazel eyes and black curls, she suddenly felt unsafe. At length he walked out of the room and Margaret and Sophia turned the talk to Sarah Clarke's sketches for *Summer on the Lakes*.

On the twenty-second of the month Margaret had planned to return home, but Ellen was seized with a desire to visit her mother and consult Dr. Wesselhoeft about herself and her little daughter, Greta; so Margaret accepted her sister's invitation to keep house while she was gone. Ellery was in Berkshire and could not look at her, as he usually did, between his fingers, or talk in his mysterious whisper. The little Red Lodge on the turnpike was pleasant for Margaret. She arranged her books and writing materials on Ellery's desk, along with a bouquet of summer flowers. From the wall Julius Caesar and Domenichino gazed at her. Ellen's picture, which caught the purity of her brow and the peculiar shape of her eyelids, looked charmingly down. Margaret had only to go up the hill beyond the house to be in Sleepy Hollow. It was delightful to have Elizabeth Hoar and the Haw-

[1] It had—in *The Blithedale Romance*.

thornes within visiting distance, and to be Emerson's neighbor.

Through the arch of willows, beyond the bridge and across the meadows Margaret often wandered alone, but more frequently she trod a shorter distance to Emerson's house. Concord had not changed, she reflected; it had merely put on new clothes cut from the old pattern. The Curtis brothers had come from Brook Farm, both blooming with beauty and hard at work in the fields or at their studies. There was, in fact, a little delegation from West Roxbury; John Hosmer had come and Isaac Hecker too, to study Greek with George Bradford. Then there was the whole new world of infants who had been born in Concord, Emerson's little son, Hawthorne's beautiful Una, and Ellen's Greta. The trees of Concord had simply put forth new leaves.

At Emerson's house Margaret smiled to see the newness manifested in Lidian's door and dining room closet. In the study there was a new stove, but Margaret knew it needed more than that to kindle fire in Emerson's grave eyes. His fire would always be bright, but without warmth, for it came from too much gazing at the stars. Emerson spoke with Margaret about *Summer on the Lakes*, and its reception. There had been complimentary notices, she said. Most reviewers thought the book agreeable, full of touches of beauty and piquant sayings. But some, like Lydia Child, who was busy editing the *National Anti-slavery Standard* in New York, thought it had been written with too much effort. The stream had been pumped and did not flow.

"Perhaps she is right," Margaret added. "Perhaps there is too much furniture in my house."

"The same criticism," Emerson commented, "might be leveled at Sylvester Judd, who is still working on his book called *Margaret*. He takes the country from the time of the Revolution and follows it through, not to what it is now, but to what it should be. His Margaret is a flower, a flower drawn in a phantasmagoric perspective, an infinite, transcendental bloom."

Margaret wondered for a moment whether Sylvester Judd had had her in mind when he planned his book. It was strange that this thought should have cropped up directly after that curious conversation with Hawthorne. At least, she decided, if she was not great in herself, she might be able to inspire greatness in others.

"His picture," she added, pursuing her thoughts aloud, "is painted like that of an antique Venus, from a study of several models. Mr. Judd wrote to me recently to say he wished me to know I had one admirer in the State of Maine—a distinction of which I am not a little proud. He is a middle-aged clergyman, but he has not for that forgotten to be a man. Like William Channing he believes there is some connection between mind and body. But Boston folks seem to think the body is all a sham."

"What do you think, Margaret?"

She lowered her eyelids and moved her hand restlessly on the arm of the chair.

"My opinion is that there is a third thought which is to link each conflicting two. The third thought is the secret of the universe."

"I wonder," Emerson mused, "whether Alcott has found the secret. At Fruitlands he has been eating apples and biscuit, pouring cold water by the pailful over his body and rubbing it till he could shake flames from his fingers' ends, all to find the secret. His eyes have shot sparkles and he has heard the sound of many waters. I hope he will succeed in this and not be thwarted by any kindly Sam Staples who prevented him from remaining in jail when he refused to pay his taxes."

"We are all searching for my Third Thought," Margaret replied. She looked up at the Fates above the mantel, at the cold Psyche and the colder stove. "Even Horace Mann is filling his school reports with the laws of God and Nature."

"Closer home," Emerson returned, "we have our own Samuel Hoar. He has been appointed Commissioner to South Carolina to get information about the Massachusetts citizens who have been imprisoned without allegation of crime. I wonder what will happen when he confronts the Charleston mobs with that great frame of his, his fine gray hair, and forceful blue eyes. His head is like Dante's. Alcott once said that if he were nominated for governor, he did not know but he would recognize the State so far as to vote for him. I wonder if he will find the Third Thought in Charleston."

"We are all engaged upon our little reforms," Margaret remarked, remembering that Emerson was at work on his essay, *New England Reformers*.

"One apostle," Emerson replied, "thinks all men should go to farming and another that no man should buy or sell. Some find the mischief in our diet and make unleavened bread so that we shall not eat or drink damnation. Homeopathy, hydropathy, mesmerism, phrenology—they are all signs of rebellion, no less than the growth of free trade. Henry James has carried his revolt to England. William Tappan and Giles Waldo shot deer in Hamilton County to search out the answer to their problems, to express their own defiance. Henry Thoreau is planning to build himself a hut and unriddle the enigma in a community of one. For myself, I still believe that society will gain nothing while man, not himself renovated, attempts to renovate things around him. Friendship and association are very fine things and a grand phalanx of the best of the human race—excellent! But remember that no society can ever be so large as one man."

"Not even," Margaret asked, "your Social Circle here in Concord?"

"Harvard University is a wafer in comparison with the solid lands which my friends represent. I do not like to be absent from home on Tuesday evenings in winter when our circle meets. But it is still not as large as one man. Even when Thoreau, Hawthorne and I went skating together, we missed the fine fruits of solitude. I remember how Thoreau figured dithyrambic dances and Bacchic leaps on the ice. Hawthorne, wrapped in his cloak, moved like a self-impelled Greek statue and I closed the line, pitching head foremost, half lying on the air. But the skating would have been better done had it been done alone. So it is with all beauty, with all reform. We must renovate ourselves first."

"I think this smacks too much of Concord," Margaret murmured. Society interacts with the individual. We must renovate both or one will be neglected."

Emerson looked at Margaret.

"Beside your richness, which pours a stream of amber over all objects, I am taught how lifeless I am. Your growth has been visible. I shall know your star across the universe by the energy of its fires."

Margaret pressed his hand, and smiled.

"Why not venture into the universe with me, instead of watching for my star? Here in Concord life stumbles and steals on like the river. A very good place for a sage, but not for the lyrist or the orator. You are intellect. I am life. It is eight years, Waldo, since I first came to stay in your house. You remember I spoke of demons then? To-day I have brought you drawings of the sistrum, the serpent, triangles and rays, and here is one of the Winged Sphinx. Though you may scoff at the absence of intellect, you will find life in them."

She turned the pages of the sketches as Emerson looked

over her shoulder. "My growth may be visible, but I have remained faithful to some of my early notions. Look, Waldo, here is life, the life I have brought to Concord." Emerson stood up, strangely moved. He stooped a little wearily, as he rose from his rocker. He wanted air— Concord air—to restore his sense of balance. As he opened the door, he turned to look at Margaret. "Farewell," she called softly, "farewell, O Grecian sage, though not my Oedipus."

Margaret glanced out of the window at the pines and then sat down on Emerson's rocker. She picked up his pen, opened his portfolio for a paper, and wrote, "My dear Waldo." What she had not said, she must write to him. How could he expect the Muse to come to him? She hovers near. Often, Margaret thought, I have seen her, especially at evening, looking in at the study windows when they are not shut. Margaret grasped the pen and dashed off the rhymes that sang themselves in her mind:

> Seeing seated, pen in hand,
> By a gentle dubious light,
>   One whose eye beam, purely bright,
> Marks him of her chosen band,
>   She thinks, 'at last I may draw near
> And harbor with a mortal find
> In the wide temple of his mind
> No jangling notes can rend my ear.' . . .

But Emerson failed the Muse, as he rebuffed whatever interrupted the smooth flow of life in too peaceful Concord.

> But why sudden stops the strain
> Why backward starts that music-form
> Flutters up the heavens again
> With backward wings that rouse the storm
> Rouse thunder-peal & lightning glare
> In the repelled, earth-wooing air?

The Muse herself could not alter Emerson's belief that all is one, that one is all. By that conviction he would be marked, and so marked, excluded from all else. It would admit him into heaven, but hell he would never know. And how could he be brother to the Muse, when he had no knowledge beyond the heaven of Concord?

> In that temple so divine
> She sought at once the inmost shrine
> And saw this thought there graven,—
> 'Earth and fire, hell and heaven,
> Hate and love, black and white,
> Life and death, dark and bright,
> All are one
> One alone:
> All else is seeming
> I who think am nought
> But the One a-dreaming . . .
> All is well,
> For all is one . . .
> However voluble
> All life is soluble
> Into my thought . . . '

Margaret looked over her verses. She smiled to note how well she had aped Emerson's own runic style. She had breathed life for a moment into the airless tower of his intellect. He had been troubled by the breath. But now they must go their separate ways, he as intellect again, she as life. She left the page propped between two books on his table. He would read it, and endorse it with a title. She looked about the room as if in farewell. The little red rug before the fireplace, the round table laden with books, the shelves, the library steps, the Psyche, the Fates, the rocking chair still creaking—all would remain as they were, unchangeable. Margaret felt as if she might never enter that room again, or at least, that she would be a different Margaret when next she came. She turned to go, thinking that she was leaving the immutable for that visible growth he had spoken of, leaving the changeless and going forth into life, the ever-changing.

When Horace Greeley invited Margaret to New York to write for the *Tribune* she was not surprised. She had felt all through the year that she was about to step from an old life into a new. It was with such a feeling that she had composed her last article for *The Dial,* given the final Conversation, written the last word of *Summer on the Lakes,* waved farewell to Emerson's study in Concord. Yet before she could leave the life she had lived so long, she desired a foretaste of what was to come, a fore-warning. When the Clarkes invited her to Boston for a psychometric reading of her character by Anna Parsons, she realized that this was what she had needed; Anna Parsons would elucidate the mystery of sistrum and serpent, rays and triangles.

It had been an exciting year in Boston, and in October, when Margaret walked through the streets, she could feel the agitation almost in the air. All the reforms that Emerson had discussed had echoed from the sounding boards of the Boston lecture halls. People were still speaking of Dr. Buchanan's discourse on phrenology, of the Anti-Slavery Fair where Isaac Hopper had worn silver buckles and a costume modeled on that of William Penn, of the Total Abstinence Festival that had been held on the Common, of the Whig Mass Meeting, of Paulina Wright's course of lectures on anatomy. One woman, Margaret had heard, had fainted at the sight of Mrs. Wright's *femme modèle.* Yet Boston was changing, she reflected, more than Concord could ever change. She trod the streets a little proudly, knowing that she could walk from Allston's "Belshazzar's Feast" to Michelangelo's "Night and Day" at the Sculpture Gallery and then to a performance by Ole Bull or Professor Webb. They were all signs of the times, Ole Bull as well as Dr. Buchanan, and, Margaret added to herself, Anna Parsons as well as Ole Bull.

Anna had read Charles Newcomb's character, she remembered, by means of a poem he had written. Newcomb, sensitive as he was, had not been hurt by her revelations, for in his manuscript Anna had sensed the beauty of his soul. That early gift of hers was being fulfilled. She had read Fourier's character also, and, without knowing, of course, that it was his letter she was holding, had declared, "We shall not always eat so incoherently, but shall eat musically, harmoniously." Sarah had told Margaret that when Anna had tried to read Harriet Martineau's character, she had found so many entangled impressions she could feel nothing clearly. Emerson had scorned such experiments as peeping through a keyhole, but even he had been pleased at Anna's announcement, after she had felt a copy of *The Humble-bee,* that the author was holy, true, and brave. It would be interesting to see how he would react to tonight's psychometric reading.

She hastened her steps. When she arrived at the Clarkes' house on Mount Vernon Street, they were all there before her, James and Sarah, Caroline Sturgis, Emerson and Anna. Margaret walked in, her regal figure enhanced by the purple dress with its white muslin sleeves. She wore the carbuncle ring, for if her handwriting did not reveal her character to the new Ecstatica, surely the stone would send out sparks whereby they might communicate. After Margaret had greeted her friends, they all gathered around Anna Parsons, who, at the moment, looked more like a delicate girl than an Ecstatica with a gift for mesmerism. As Sarah handed a letter to Anna without Anna's knowing that Margaret had written it, Emerson looked on a little skeptically, but he too drew near when Anna held the paper in her hand and closed her eyes. No one spoke. Margaret withdrew a little way and toyed with her carbuncle ring.

Suddenly, Anna cried aloud, "A good deal of life in it —it burns." She held the letter as if it had shot forth flames. At the word, "life," Emerson turned to Margaret, remembering how she had said, "You are intellect. I am life." Anna continued, "It burns—not the outside skin merely, but deep into the bone. I can hardly hold it." Anna dropped the letter. Sarah Clarke immediately handed her another note Margaret had written. "This does not burn me like the other—in a different mood," Anna murmured.

"Is it sad or gay?" Sarah asked.
Anna held the letter to her forehead and gave herself up to the psychic impressions she received. After a few minutes she answered hesitatingly,

"It seems lively and sad."

"Has it thought or feeling?" Caroline questioned.

"It seems full of both. I like this person—one moment it seems near, the next distant."
Now James challenged the Ecstatica.

"Is it a large person or a limited one?"
Margaret looked over to catch the answer.

"Very different impressions this person would give me from different points of view. I can't take in the whole at once. You have seen a beautiful autumn day, with wind and shadows flying over the landscape. This person is like that."
Emerson stepped forward.

"Is the person solitary or social?"
Anna pressed the letter in her hands.

"Both," she answered immediately. "Solitary in society, and social in solitude. Every question you ask with two sides makes me want to say both."

"Does she neglect things not beautiful?" James demanded solemnly.

"She finds beauty in almost everything."

"Is it a musical soul?" Caroline asked suddenly.

Anna held the letter again to her forehead.

"A wild music!" she cried.

Margaret moved a little nearer Anna, and, rustling her white sleeves, twirling her ring, whispered,

"Is she the object of love?"

"Yes, I should think so."

Anna turned to Emerson.

"Do you love her?"

Emerson turned to Margaret; her eyes almost closed as they penetrated his.

"No, love is not exactly the word."

Anna felt the paper again, and shook her head.

"She would not care much for approbation."

"Does she desire love?" Caroline put in.

"She feels the want of it rather than the desire for it."

Emerson shifted the topic.

"Is it want of a sphere of action that makes her sad?"

"Perhaps it is. I have only taken an outside view. The whole life seems a prayer—pressing onward—a struggle. You have been up a high hill—seen hill beyond hill arise as you ascended. This character is like that."

Anna looked at Emerson. "You have had a great deal of influence upon her."

Margaret glanced up quickly.

"Is this influence reciprocal?"

"She has influenced him, not so much as he has her. Mr. Emerson does not understand this person fully. He says he does not love her, but I think he ought to. He wrongs his own nature and the writer also by not loving her. It seems as if she had toiled up an ascent with her back toward the landscape and when she reached the summit, she tasted of happiness—"

"Does she stay on the summit?" Margaret interrupted.

"No. She is not a stayer. She has a mind that would search and see things in their true relations—would see into the centre. She has high, very high hopes. At times she is transfigured. I don't see how she can be contented with the present state of society."

"Put your hand here." Caroline held out a page of Margaret's letter. "And tell us if she can love commonplace people."

Anna drew back.

"I don't like to put my hand there. I was in a higher state before."

Caroline chose her words carefully.

"Is she good for the sake of goodness, or because she wishes to perfect herself?"

"She can't understand weakness; she is so strong herself, I think she will. She goes backward to go forward. I think she is a very true person."

"Have you done with her?" asked Emerson finally.

Anna stood quietly, her eyes still closed.

"I have expressed myself very imperfectly. When I looked at Caroline Sturgis and she asked me if she loved, I wanted to say she loves you. When Sarah Clarke came near me I felt the love of the character more than when she was away. I think she loves her."

Anna dropped the letter and opened her eyes. Margaret knew that though little had been actually said, much had been suggested. Anna had been burned by the sparks of life that radiated from the letter. She had divined that Margaret was no stayer, even on summits, that in her search for the centre of truth, she would struggle on.

Nothing remained to be said. One could not leave the clouds of mesmerism for idle talk of earthly things. Anna's head began to ache. She was exhausted. Margaret too was weary. It was as though one part of herself had probed and analyzed another part. Emerson seemed a little less skeptical than before and James and Sarah looked as if they were trying to emerge from a sanctum. Caroline was sure she had beheld the unveiling of a sibyl. They all felt it had been a little strange, this psychometric reading in the heart of Boston. Somehow things had been revealed that might better have remained hidden.

"She is no stayer. She struggles for the centre of truth."

Margaret thought of Anna's words again and again when she returned to Cambridge. There was but a month between her old life and her new, a month before she would go to New York and struggle toward the centre of another truth. The end had led to a beginning; the coda had been followed by an overture. Before she left for New York, she would take a few weeks' respite with Caroline in the Highlands and expand her article, *The Great Lawsuit.* She felt the need of some transition before she could plunge into the life of a New York journalist. Work on her essay would serve as a steppingstone between the dead *Dial,* the dead Conversations, and the living *Tribune.*

She was life, as Emerson was intellect. Anna Parsons had sensed it too. Why was it, then, Margaret pondered, that with the intellect she had always overcome, but the life! the life! Oh, my God, shall the life never be sweet? As she packed her books, her Silenus, her del Sarto, her velvet pen wiper, her purple muslin dress, she thought of her own life, of its past, of its future. "Whither, oh, whither," she murmured to herself, "o *animula mea,* whither wanderest thou? Every hour is a death to the

THE LIFE OF MARGARET FULLER

past, and all the future lies in an unknown, untried world. With pervading eye and restless wing thou searchest the universe. Yet night comes, and thou pinest and growest sick. Oh, father!" she prayed, "purge thou away all mists that I may know myself what I am and with step assured and firm move onward on thy path." Surely from the sea the mists would rise, the night would die.

Chapter XIII

WOMAN OF THE NINETEENTH CENTURY

"THE MAN who clears the barnacles from the keel is more essential than he who hoists the pennant on the lofty mast." Margaret paused and raised her eyes from her journal. From the window she could see in line rising from line, the tops of trees, the river, and the purple Highlands beyond. The barnacles of her own life, she reflected, were being cleared, one by one. Now that she would soon be in New York, the house at Cambridge would be broken up, and her mother would wander about from Cincinnati to Boston—from Boston to Concord. Caroline had just brought a letter informing Margaret of the death of Grandmother Crane. The dear old lady would no longer nod over her *Saints' Rest* in Canton; would no longer raise her blue eyes to the rotting shingles of the next farmhouse. The barnacles were cleared, torn, one by one from the keel. Now to hoist the pennant on the lofty mast.

Day after day in those fleeting weeks at Fishkill Landing Margaret tried to hoist the pennant, when she read, and when she walked, and when she wrote. On the clear days of autumn sunshine she carried her copy of the *Four Books of Confucius* or of Fourier's *Nouveau monde* to the shore and sat with Caroline near the river. Yet her eye often wandered from the page. The books that Thoreau loved, that Brisbane had rejoiced in, were not good enough to read among these mountains. The eye found surer delight in the sails and steamers sweeping up the river, in the rush of waves, the red-gold leaves fallen on the paths. For a few days Ellery joined Caroline and Margaret, for he too was on his way to New York, to Greeley's *Tribune* office. Then the three walked along the paths, commenting on Taylor's Greek translations, on Scandinavian Mythology, on Moehler's *Symbolism* or Landor's *Pentameron*.

Ellery left disturbing news behind him. Sterling had died, died before his time, and Margaret felt how fast her own years were flitting by with nothing done. It seemed to her then a little simpler to clear the barnacles than to hoist the pennant. She longed for more now than mere self-expression. The time had come to participate in public life. Ellery had brought word of Polk's election. Polk meant the annexation of Texas, and the annexation of Texas meant a further encroachment upon human rights.

"I want to impel the general stream of thought," Margaret said to Caroline as they watched the steamers plough through the waters, "to share in public life. Might not we women do something about Texas, convene meetings, and take our stand at last?"

Caroline gently reminded her that women had taken their stand before this; Mrs. Jameson had fought for the rights of the Indians, the Grimke sisters and Lydia Child for the slaves; Georgiana Bruce had left Brook Farm to help the prisoners at Sing Sing.

"Yes," Margaret murmured, "and there was Countess Emily Plates who did so much during the revolution of Poland. Now, nearer home, the legislature of Rhode Island is trying to give property rights to married women. Perhaps I meant by my 'at last' that now *I* wish to join the general struggle. I have observed so long. I want to act now—to hoist the pennant on the lofty mast."

A white sail glowed in the sun.

"You have your book, Margaret. That may be your lofty pennant."

The morning after their talk Margaret rose early,

and after a long walk, sat down before the window to work. She reread her article, *The Great Lawsuit,* changed it, added to it, gave it bulk. She forgot the headaches and the pain in her spine. Never once did she lift her eye to the purple Highlands or the river behind the trees. It was of man and woman that she wrote, two halves of one thought, and of the oppression of the black man, of the Indian and of woman. The first two were the scoff of the world, the last a deed unchallenged. "We would have every arbitrary barrier thrown down. We would have every path laid open to women as freely as to men." The pen cried on the page, the pen tore down the page, storming for inward and outward freedom for women, a freedom that should be acknowledged as a right, not yielded as a concession. She paused a moment and took from her own life, from those very barnacles that had been cleared away, an instance and a sign. Call Margaret Miranda and let her speak through the thin veil. Let her tell of the high views of women she had found in the Bible, in Goethe, in the mythology she had preached at West Street. Let her stand at the head of her sex and announce to the world that woman too had her birthright of freedom, the intelligent freedom of the universe, to use its means, to learn its secret. Let Miranda remind State Street that it was Isabella who had furnished to Columbus the means for voyaging to America. This land must pay back its debt to woman, must pay for Isabella's jewels.

Margaret stopped for a moment to reconsider her own conclusions about Fourier, her conversations with Emerson about society. Then the pen raced on. There must be a parallel movement in the two branches of life; society and individual character must be renovated together. In such reform woman must be given her share. Her genius —she thought of Margaret, but wrote of Miranda—was electrical. Its sparks must purify, scorch out the wrongs. State Street might shake its head again, Mrs. Hawthorne might blush, and Sophia Ripley hide her head; Miranda would reveal the existence of ten thousand prostitutes in the city, of thousands more who were bondmaids in marriage. The pen dashed on. Leave out transitions, forget the niceties of style. It was all variation on a single theme, the theme a large one, woman in the nineteenth century. No artificial link was needed between the prostitutes and the annexation of Texas. Both were prostitution. Polk's election menaced a cause identical with the enfranchisement of the Jews, of the Irish, of woman, ay, and of Americans, for the choice of the people threatened to rivet the chains of slavery permanently on this nation. "Women of my country," cried Miranda, "have you nothing to do with this?" Let women think; let them act, till they know what they need. Let them be sea captains if they will! It matters not, if only the barriers are razed.

Margaret paused again and at last looked out of the window. The sun had set over the Highlands and the river lay dark under the autumn night. The darkness without made the glow within warmer. She had set her footprint on the earth. "I stand," she wrote, "in the sunny noon of life. Some fair effigies that once stood for symbols of human destiny have been broken." When barnacles are cleared away, she thought, the shells that protect pearls will be torn off with them. "But enough is left to point distinctly to the glories of that destiny, faint, but not to be mistaken threads of the future day." She placed the pen upon the desk. It was nine o'clock. All the day she had raced through a dark cavern and come forth at last upon the sunny noon of life.

On rainy days when the fire burned in the quiet house, she added a line, retouched a sentence, rounded a phrase. Finally, on the seventeenth of November, the work was finished. Woman of the nineteenth century stood at the head of civilization and pointed the way in which her daughters, her descendants of the twentieth century, must go. Margaret wrote to William Channing that she would be willing to spend a hundred or even a hundred and fifty dollars to pay for publication. She had set her footprint on the earth; its pressure must be felt.

It was not a far cry, Margaret thought, from demanding freedom for woman of the nineteenth century, to observing the women prisoners at Sing Sing. If she would impel the general struggle, she must continue to scrutinize the tendencies of the times. When William Channing suggested that she and Caroline visit the prison, Margaret—or the Miranda in Margaret—anticipated the journey eagerly. She dressed carefully. The pad she wore over one shoulder, so that it would not be lower than the other, was exactly adjusted; her plaid skirt hung neatly; her scarf gave a touch of color to the drab cloak. She arranged her hair, winding the brown-red braids into a knot at the base of her neck. Her pince-nez would be her only ornament.

When Channing arrived she was ready to climb into the little way-boat with Caroline and sail up the river. They passed in the line of the mammoth boats and arrived at Sing Sing in a resplendent moonlight. The prisons looked like palaces under the moon. But Mariana, with her palaces, must be off, for Miranda knew too well what was within them. When they arrived William addressed the male convicts in the lower prison, who listened with earnest attention to his soaring words. A few were even moved to tears, as much, no doubt, by his gentle eyes and searching looks as by his eloquence.

Afterward Georgiana Bruce introduced Eliza Farnham to Margaret and Caroline. Mrs. Farnham had recently been appointed head of the Female State Prison, and, according to Georgiana, had introduced far-reaching reforms. Mrs. Farnham remarked, almost offhandedly, that there had been rebellion among the convicts before she came. It was said that the stronger had tyrannized over the weaker and made night hideous with blasphemous and obscene songs. The matron had been attacked, her clothes torn from her body. The well-meaning, tightskulled little chaplain had prayed. Judge Edmonds, Mrs. Farnham said, was the most capable member of the board. It was he who had appointed her at Sing Sing.

"Now," she explained, "instead of reading the Bible to the women, I read *Oliver Twist*. We've introduced better sanitation and, as you will see, the walls are whitewashed."

She led the way to the lower building on the edge of the river, across the steep bank and highway to the smaller prison for the women. They walked through the gate beneath the tall, granite porch. On the stone balcony Margaret turned for a moment to look at the river. Then they entered the prison, passing the wooden kids which, Mrs. Farnham said, the rioters had once flung at Judge Edmonds. Sarah Mallory, one of the assistants, marched by with her nose in the air. She had been an evangelical sister, Georgiana remarked. Mrs. Farnham quickly ordered the women to gather together to hear Margaret's talk.

A far cry from West Street, Margaret thought, as she fingered the chain of her pince-nez and faced the sixty-odd women who stood quietly around her. Some were black, she noticed, and many looked dissolute; yet they listened almost with sensibility as she told them that she was writing about *Woman in the Nineteenth Century* and wished to gain information from those who had suffered more than she. Margaret spoke to them as a suppliant, she who had come again out of civilization to speak to another community, a different one from that of Brook

Farm. When she had finished many passed silently back to their cells. One or two approached her, begging her to speak to them alone, when she had time. Margaret promised to give them books and asked Georgiana to send her their journals—for some of them still wrote journals. She waved good-bye to the prison as if it had been a palace. But in the storm on the return trip the buildings looked less gentle than under moonlight. She would return as she had promised. For them, too, the fight must be fought, the struggle engaged in, as well as for the women who shopped on Washington Street, or loitered on the Common, or chatted in the Boston Academy of Music.

Back at Fishkill the days slipped quickly by. Soon autumn would turn into winter and Margaret must place the feet of her muse on the treadmill. It was a worthy treadmill, she thought, as she packed the roving camp chest once again, that *Tribune* office which was indeed a Tribune to America, a Tribune that cried for liberal thinking, whether in Transcendental or Fourieristic phrases. There, in New York, she would do her work, and find herself in the doing. No lofty pennant might wave— but she would climb the mast at least to trace a wider view. Though she might never impel the general struggle she would join it. So life grew out of death and a new self broke through the withered skin of the old. To know this alone were wisdom. Now—to act upon it!

CHAPTER XIV

TRIBUNE OF THE PEOPLE

IT WAS a cloudy, sharp December day when Margaret alighted from the stage on the Boston Post Road. She walked down the winding lane for a quarter of a mile, passing De Voor's Mill Stream that flowed silently beneath the bare trees of winter. Ascending a slight rise in the ground, she caught her first glimpse of Greeley's Farm. The rambling old yellow house lay before her, its box borders still green, its veranda fronting the East River. Greeley had been wise when he bought Isaac Lawrence's mansion in Odellville, for though it was two full miles from the city, Margaret knew that Murphy's hourly stage would carry her to town even from so remote a spot as this. Had she not been told that if one counted the streets, the Farm would be located at Forty-ninth and Third Avenue? She turned to catch a glimpse of a sail sweeping by. Not far from the gravel path on which she stood the boats lay round a rocky point below the banks of Turtle Bay. Opposite, she recognized Blackwells Island from William Channing's description. For all the wooded dells and white sails, that prison would ever lie before her; now was the time for a tribune of the people to see and write about such things.

Margaret walked down the piazza and knocked at the door. Her host appeared and after their greeting escorted her down a long hall into a bare room. Mrs. Greeley, Margaret concluded, did not believe in curtains or rugs, for the simplicity of the furnishings made the room cold and unfriendly. She was glad of the chair, however, after her journey, and sat down to take stock of her host.

Margaret felt comfortably that it was Greeley who

looked as if he had been traveling all day in a stagecoach rather than herself, for his shapeless trousers were tucked into the tops of his boots and his large neckcloth was awry. With a shambling gait he crossed the floor to a chair, but even when seated looked tall and gangling. He rumpled his pale silver-yellow hair while his collar retreated from sight. From behind his narrow spectacles he observed his guest, noting the way in which she had slid into her chair until she almost reclined. She was waiting apparently for him to have his say. In his weak, querulous falsetto he began.

"The gravest charges you have heard against me, Miss Fuller, are that I eat bran bread and believe in Fourier, that I wear a coat like Jacob's of old, and a hat double the size of my head."

Margaret wondered what charges he had heard against her, but had no time to inquire, for with a slight, awkward movement of his hand he continued.

"The Fourierism I have never denied, but Edgar Poe will testify that I eat boiled chicken at Sandy Welsh's, even though I do prefer vegetable food."

Margaret perceived that she would clash with her host at the dining table, for she definitely preferred condiments to vegetables and tea to milk. She said nothing, however, and Greeley went on in his thin, husky voice, saying that it was at a Grahamite boarding house that he had first met his wife.

"Had it not been for unsifted wheat I might never have known Mary Cheney."

In a few moments, Greeley's black-haired, animated, almost Oriental-looking wife entered the room, and Margaret was happy to greet her friend of the West Street days. Mrs. Greeley, she noticed, had not changed greatly. There was still about her that high positive purpose, that intensity that made her study passionately where others merely read. She carried baby Pickie in her arms, and presented him to Margaret, speaking abruptly, her words sounding like the report of a rifle.

"This is the Poet, our baby of the red-gold hair. He hasn't learned to walk yet, but he's been painted with a cluster of lilies in his hand."

Margaret smiled, and turned her attention from Pickie to his mother. She looked as disheveled as Greeley and seemed to move her hands constantly as if she were washing something. Her passionate intensity had grown into a fluttering nervousness. Margaret could not help thinking them an unusual pair, and concluded that, strangely enough, she would probably be the representative of conventionality at the Farm.

At length the talk turned to Margaret and her work. Greeley approved of *Woman in the Nineteenth Century,* although, he remarked rather pointedly, he did not approve of ardent feminists who needed an escort to walk down a dark lane at night. Here too, Margaret foresaw, they would be at odds. But Greeley said that as soon as the book appeared, in February, he would help it make its mark.

Though Margaret would have preferred discussing the coming Philharmonic concert at the Apollo or Luman Reed's collection of paintings at the Gallery of Fine Arts, Greeley gave her no opportunity for such talk. Her inquiry about the volumes of Goethe available at the New York Society Library went unnoticed, for the editor of the *Tribune* was bent upon discussing his newspaper. He had invited Margaret, he explained, to fill the post left vacant by Albert Brisbane. He knew, he remarked dogmatically, that Margaret would agree with the principles that had first incited him to the enterprise. The *Tribune* was a paper for the laboring classes, and it was for them that Brisbane's Fourierist articles had been printed, for them that Cassius Clay had written his letters on slavery. Soon they would be able to read the leading Whig paper in an enlarged format with new type.

"I have already stated," Greeley continued, rumpling his yellowish hair, "that the social conditions of the toiling millions must be improved. The Irish and the Negroes must recover their portion of the common rights of man. The slavery that exists in New York must claim our first efforts."

Margaret acquiesced. Was it not for this purpose that she had undertaken her work? Glancing at his wife from behind his narrow spectacles, Greeley went on.

"Do you realize that the average earnings of the laborers in New York scarcely exceed one dollar a week? This is news—and the Whig tariff theory must be invoked to protect labor by protecting capital. This will be a fighting year for the *Tribune*."

"How do you propose that I shall fit into your scheme of things?" Margaret spoke tersely, summing up her reflections with a sweeping gesture.

Greeley's weak falsetto became almost powerful when he replied.

"Whenever an opportunity offers we must encourage class harmony and, as I have said, ameliorate labor conditions by improving the products of labor. If this can be effected by advertising the hygienic virtue of daily baths— well and good. If it can be accomplished by revealing the socialism of Eugene Sue or dilating upon the New England Workingmen's Association, my policy will be upheld."

Greeley's collar was riding up to his chin. His neckcloth lay over one shoulder. But through the narrow spectacles his spirit gleamed. He had his dogmas, Margaret concluded, but they were the dogmas of the people. And if he was plebeian he was also a man of the people.

She rose and went upstairs to unpack her camp chest. From the window she glanced again at Blackwells Island, cold and sombre across the river. If plain puddings were to be her fare at the Farm there was stronger pabulum across the water to feed the mind. The tribune of the people had not reckoned without her host. She was eager to quicken the moving wheels at Greeley's office in Nassau Street.

Early in the morning—but not so early to claim Greeley as escort—Margaret hailed Murphy's hourly stage and the four horses clattered down Third Avenue. There were half a dozen country gentlemen inside, facing each other on long benches, ready to pass the time of day, but the sights on the outside of the window engrossed Margaret and excluded the possibility of light conversation. The coach soon joined the parade of hackney cabs and phaetons, tilburies and gigs and Margaret settled herself for the enjoyment of the colors and sounds of New York. There was a scarlet sleigh, drawn by prancing horses with gay trappings of little bells, and Margaret caught a fleeting glimpse of buffalo robes and French ribbons and tassels. Her eyes roamed from one sight to another, from the signs hoisted on poles advertising Oysters in Every Style to the black pigs eating their way through the streets. There was a flight of broad stone cellar steps leading to a Bowling Saloon or a Tenpin Alley, and near by were two Negroes taking water from a pump. As the coach wheeled toward the Bowery, clouds of dust arose, soot and ashes drifted about, a raw wind rushed through the narrow streets. Beyond, a leatherhead carrying a whale oil lamp announced that it was "a cold and frosty morning."

What pictures flashed before her eyes as the coach swung into the Bowery! A Tyrolese played on a street organ, a Negro beau glittered by with eyeglass and guard-chain, a barefoot girl swept the crossways with her stumpy broom. What cries sounded in her ears, mingling with the noise of a hundred wheels. "SweepO!" called the chimney sweeps; "Tea Ruk!" screamed the baker's boy, while the radish girl and scissors grinder, the clam men and sand peddlers shrilled their wares. Among the white and gilded omnibuses children trundled their hoops; ragged urchins hawked matches and newspapers. Bonnets and feathers and bright shawls vied in color with the green blinds of Jersey freestone houses. And the Bowery itself! What a kaleidoscope of fruit peddlers and auctioneers and chestnut vendors.

Margaret was shaken as the carriage swung into Chatham Square. There were no such sights as this in Boston. On Catharine Street, just off the Square, crowds fringed the sidewalks, jostling for tartan shawls and feather beds, hams and crockery. Peripatetic shoe dealers pushed their way through the throngs, their stock suspended on long poles. Poultry meandered in the gutters along with ladies in velvets and furs. At length the stage approached the great bustling promenade of Broadway with its red brick houses, its posters and placards. There a maid was sousing a black pig with a tubful of water. Margaret glanced at the shops, already prepared for the New Year with cakes in the form of pyramids and obelisks. And Maiden Lane—what a conglomeration was this of sailors and draymen, bricks and mortar! Surely no one had time to stand still in New York! What moving about, what bustling, what colors, what noise! Margaret gathered her cloak around her and pulled the leather strap to alight. She paid the driver her twenty-five cents, and thought the coin a fair exchange for her view of the roaring, dazzling metropolis.

Passing Mayor Harper's home on Rose Street fronted by the ever present pair of lamps, Margaret turned into

Spruce and looked up at the Brook Farm headquarters. From there it was but a short turn into Nassau, and at Number 160 Margaret stopped before the five-story brick building that housed Horace Greeley's thoughts. She climbed up the steep stairs, glancing at the stove filled with loose papers for kindling, looking in at the bustling publication office on the first story, mounting to the ware-room on the second. Breathing heavily, she finally arrived at the editorial rooms on the fourth floor. She pushed the swing door and entered the sanctum. Greeley was seated at his old, high desk, his nose nearly touching it. He himself was surrounded by files of correspondence, pamphlets, charts. Laying his pen on the ponderous inkstand, he glanced up to greet the latest member of his staff. He scarcely had time to introduce his clerk, Mr. Strebeigh, whose gold watch was much in evidence. Ellery, he remarked, between bawling a direction to a printer and supervising details on a newssheet, was doing well. He was amusing and lively, but Margaret found her brother-in-law nowhere in sight. Hurriedly, Greeley introduced his partner, Thomas McElrath, who placed his papers in orderly fashion on his desk and proceeded to show Margaret the sights of the office, the presses and engines, the countingroom and mailing department. McElrath, Margaret observed, seemed the antithesis of Greeley. He was a close calculator and, she noticed, as David the errand boy touched his hat to the master, a strict disciplinarian. In methodical fashion he pointed out the relays of riders who posted to the office with news, the printers who shuttled back and forth to Nassau Street.

When she returned to the editorial rooms, Greeley snatched up his huge white hat and slapped it on his head. "You think you have seen the *Tribune*, Miss Fuller, but, as I said to one country visitor, the *Tribune* is now inside this hat!" Margaret did not doubt the truth of his statement. Greeley was the *Tribune*. If the office was noisy and stimulating, it was Greeley who made it so—Greeley bawling in anger or jubilation, raging over mistakes, raising his husky voice to point out a faulty line or dispatch a rider for fuller accounts. He seemed to do everything at once, writing reports, reading correspondence, opening his safe, shouting instructions. His voice and his hand were everywhere. If, as Margaret had been told, he snoozed in his pew at the Church of the Messiah, he made up for lost time in Nassau Street. She left him, with his chin at the level of his desk, and seated herself in a corner to write her first article.

It seemed appropriate that her first review should be a criticism of Emerson's second series of essays. Opening her portfolio, she took out a sheet of paper to plead for a wider circulation of her friend's work. He was a man, she wrote, whose only aim was the discernment and interpretation of the spiritual laws by which we live. She glanced up to watch the printers at their work, another relay of riders with news, Greeley thumbing a report. Spiritual laws were not in the ascendant at Nassau Street. Hearing Greeley's thin tones raised in anger over an error, she minded herself of Emerson's grave, full notes, and proceeded to write of his voice, haunted by modulations, uttering words that take root in the memory like winged seed. Nor was the voice the only point of difference between Emerson and Greeley. Emerson was the man of ideas, but, she wrote, we want the heart and genius of human life. Could Greeley and Emerson but have united in a single person, she thought, that would have been a whole, a potent being. "We doubt," she continued, "this friend raised himself too early to the perpendicular"—had she not thought so long before she had met Greeley?—"and did not lie along the ground long enough to hear the secret wishes of our parent life. We

could wish he might be thrown by conflicts on the lap of
mother earth.''

She signed her review with an asterisk, and laid the
pen down. The office was so noisy she could scarcely reread the two and a half columns she had written. It would
be impossible, she decided, to think in the *Tribune* office.
David, she informed Greeley, would in the future send her
her books, and take her manuscripts and proof sheets
from the Farm. She herself needed peace for reflection
before she could criticize or write. Greeley looked up
amazed, but Margaret was adamant. If the editor was
stimulated by the noise and excitement of the office, and
could bawl out instructions while he buried his nose in
proof sheets, Margaret could not. If he had formulated
his principles overnight, she needed leisure to plan her
journalistic attitude and arrange her ideas for the press.

Gradually, in the quiet of the Farm, when Mrs. Greeley
fluttered out for an airing with Pickie, Margaret formed
her own critical policy. Since newspaper writing was next
door to conversation, she decided to use the first person
singular whenever she felt the need to be explicit. She
would say nothing, however, by which she was not prepared to abide. She would read every work she criticized,
for it was the work, not the private life of the writer,
with which she was concerned. Hence, the system of organized puff and venal praise which dictated the writings
of most critics, would be powerless with her. Criticism
with her would be a keen and delicate weapon, tempered
by manly judgment and imagination. She would not ask
how a phrase would sound nor what the gossips would
say, but is this the truth? The truth would be spoken,
and truth had nothing in common with slavish panegyric.
But with the breakneck speed that Greeley advocated,
truth could not keep pace. Its spur was calm reflection,
the quiet thought of many days. Margaret would write

no more than two or three articles a week; her ideas must mellow in her mind before she put them to the test of the public.

Along other lines, her policy agreed more closely with Greeley's. Though she might review William Hosmer's poem about the warriors of the Genesee, or announce a monument to Goethe, there would be another aspect to her criticism besides the literary. She would practise her preachment to Emerson, and lie on the ground long enough to hear the pulse of humanity. She would be more than a tribune of the littérateurs; the work that lay before her was that of tribune of the people.

It was in such a role that Margaret spent Christmas at Sing Sing, and for the second time addressed the women in the chapel. Her text was "the bruised reed he will not break." Ardently she trusted that the evergreen of hope would give promise to them of the eternal year, and bade them prepare under the good guidance of Judge Edmonds for a better course of life when they were freed. Love, she confided, was omnipotent—not fear, not force. Her *Tribune* column for the day was a plea for banquets for the halt, the lame, and the blind.

A week or two later Margaret arranged to undertake the trip to Blackwells Prison. With William Channing she was rowed across the East River to the island. It seemed a quiet, lovely place, with its open wells and shaded nooks, its willows and pretty boats. Here there was charm, but there was no charm in the heavy granite sea wall, nor in the grim Penitentiary building with its barred doors and grated windows. The stone with which it had been built and turreted had been quarried on the island and its cold grayness chilled Margaret's heart. William led her into the "shanty" where two or three hundred women mingled in confusion, screaming their ribaldry and profanity to the roof top. Surely, Margaret thought, this was a training place for crime. Unclean, unclassified, the women had no opportunity to reform. Mrs. Jacobs, the matron, approached and escorted the visitors down the long rows of cells with their grates and locks. Over the hard, paved floors they walked, catching a glimpse of the coarse plaid costume of the convicts. Finally they were led to the long passage that enclosed the penitentiary cells. There Mrs. Jacobs pointed out forty women, most of them black, engaged in picking oakum. In another building they were shown a group of forty-seven prisoners who took turns spinning at three or four wheels, while the keeper, the only other matron on the island, watched them from an adjacent room through an opening in the door, watched and did nothing. Their room was not ventilated. Margaret could scarcely breathe in the hot, close air. She was at a loss to know where to begin her task, for the whole place cried to heaven of its wrongs.

Among the women there was one who aroused Margaret's interest. Honora Shepard's husband was in the State Prison and she herself had spent her life among rogues. Margaret noticed that her eyes were young though they were artful, and believed that if Honora had erred she could still be redeemed. She determined to help the girl if ever she were released, to walk and talk with her, and by helping one make some attempt to help all. Channing, as chaplain of the socialist organizations in America, was grieved by what he had seen, but when Margaret spoke of her wish for a house of refuge for female outcasts, that radiant smile of his lit up his face. He knew that for one outcast Margaret herself might be a house of refuge.

Along with articles on Elizabeth Barrett's poems and Moscheles' *Life of Beethoven*, Margaret took time to describe her visit to the Bloomingdale Asylum for the Insane on St. Valentine's Eve. There, in the reddish brown building on Harlem Heights, she attended a dance of the inmates, while Dr. Earle in his stock and velvet lapels moved about conversing with hoidenish young girls and bluestockings, sarcastic observers and traveled Englishmen. Between offering sugarplums and exchanging repartees he told Margaret of his lectures to the insane on Intellectual and Moral Beauty or the Mechanical Properties of Air. While two elderly women improvised a peasant dance, Mrs. Hewlett, the matron, informed Margaret that among the causes of disease were disappointed affection, political excitement, and Millerism. The camisole was the only restraining instrument used; Dr. Earle of the curly dark hair and benign face preferred bagatelle or battledore to soothe the spirits of the mentally sick.

Between journeys to Blackwells Island and Bloomingdale, Margaret snatched time for still another kind of visit. Despite the fine weather at the beginning of the new year, she had suffered from influenza, back and eye pains, and a kind of *tic douloureux*. Ever since her experiences with John Neal and Anna Parsons, Margaret had believed in the possibility of intercourse between mind and mind. There was, she knew, a mysterious connection between the spiritual and the material. Her interest in animal magnetism deepened when she reviewed Grimes' book on etherology for the *Tribune,* and announced her belief in the influence that one being might communicate to another independently of the usual organs. She had herself used the triangle, a device for swinging with the hands, to relieve the pain in her spine, but Margaret preferred a human medium to a material one for establishing contact between the mental and the physical. Sherwood's Vibratory Magnetic Machine might be useful for some, but Margaret elected rather the services of Dr. Leger. Along Broadway she walked, as a Negro coachman wheeled by in a fur cap, and ladies in gaudy hoods stopped to chat with beaux whose whiskers met beneath their chins. She declined the hot spiced gingerbread that a vendor was bent on selling to her, and entered the office at number 74.

Dr. Leger had told Margaret that in six months she would be as straight as an Indian, and could remove the thick pad that she wore on one shoulder. The most satisfactory cures, he remarked, were effected in cases of spinal curvature. Margaret's dress was made to open at the back, leaving just the spine bare. She unhooked her gown and seated herself on a low stool. Dr. Leger held her thumbs for a moment until the necessary heat had been induced, and then sat down on a higher chair about a foot away from his patient. Margaret relaxed while the doctor held his right hand horizontally close against her vertebral column, his fingers pointing toward, but never touching it. Slowly and in complete silence he moved his hand from the end of her spine to the base of her brain, charging it with his own vigorous magnetism. His arm trembled slightly as he willed that his power flow into Margaret. She felt the sensation of having a rod of iron worked into her spine, though the doctor's hand never actually touched her. Finally, Leger wiped the beads of perspiration from his brow and shook his hands as if he were removing electric fluid.

After the treatment, the doctor discussed his methods with Margaret. The word he had coined to describe the technique was Psycodunamy—the power of the soul.

"I am a dunamiser, rather than a magnetizer."
Dr. Leger enjoyed recounting to Margaret the use of magnetic passes by the Indians and Hebrews, the Romans and Persians. He had lectured a year before, he said, at his office, and had successfully induced somnambulism in a patient by simply extending his arms before her. She

had expressed the thoughts of the audience in her duna-
mised state. Indeed, there had been an account of the
performance in the *Tribune*. Margaret herself felt as if
a vital energy had been communicated to her. She thanked
the doctor, knowing him to be a man of extraordinary
power whose spiritual vigor had been transmitted to her.
She seemed soothed and strengthened at the same time,
and was almost ready to walk the four miles back to the
Farm.

It was for a special reason that Margaret wished to
cure her spinal complaint and stand straight before the
world, for on the eve of the New Year she had met James
Nathan. Into the bare room where Greeley had welcomed
her, the newcomer had entered and while the dark-haired
Mrs. Greeley flashed upstairs to put Pickie to bed, and
Greeley himself toiled over his papers in an adjoining
room, Margaret entertained the guest. The lamplight
shone upon his gentle face; his blue eyes penetrated hers.
Almost instantly she felt as she had so many years before
when at the Athenaeum Samuel Ward had stood beneath
the shaft of sunlight, or when out West William Clarke
had charmed her. As simple as their coming was this of
James Nathan, who sat down beside her. Josey, his puppy,
curled up on the floor, and James laid his guitar on a
chair. His delicate, civilized face had a calm beauty, and
Margaret knew that he would show her how the sun of
today still shines upon the ancient Temple. She listened
while he spoke, telling her how he had come from Germany fifteen years before, a penniless boy. He had wept,
he said, when he told the ruthless landlord that he had
no money, and Margaret's heart sprang toward him
across the interval of years. Later in his loneliness he had
found friends among the Elm Street Congregation of
B'nai Jeshurun. And now though he preferred reading
a poem or playing a song on his guitar to delving into the

mysteries of business, he was perforce a wholesale clothier and spent his days on Cedar Street along with the merchants, lawyers and booksellers who plied their trades there. He bent down, as he spoke, to pet the Newfoundland puppy, and Margaret sensed his kindliness and longed to partake of the sun in his heart.

As he spoke she realized that he looked at things without their veils. He was calm and self-assured; he was the breast on which her wandering spirit would find refuge. Yet, at the same time, hearing him speak about his early days in America and his difficulties in adjusting himself to business, she felt like a mother toward him, and wished to protect his tender sweetness and sensibility. The force of kindred drew her to him. There were intimations of a deep mystic power at work.

Later in the evening, after Greeley left his papers and his wife returned from upstairs, James invited Margaret for a walk through the wood. Near a bed of myrtle they stopped and looked beyond over the rocks and the river. There, for an hour, they stayed, and mined each other's hearts. Margaret told him of her work in New York, and he of his native Germany. In his speech there were traces of his homeland, subtle reminders of the Old World. Then he gave her a flower he had brought with him, and its scent carried green wood and sunlight to Margaret. By such impromptu symbols they would worship. Though the night was cold, she felt the tender warmth of his blue eyes, the gentle loveliness of his face, the *ewig männlicher* that once again would draw her above. And after he left she pressed the flower in her hand and went to seek him in the land of dreams.

How many nights she sought him thus, after tea at the Cranches' or an evening at the Tabernacle. Though Mme. Pico found the contralto songs of *The Messiah* difficult to execute, and the tempo of the choruses was far too slow,

Margaret enjoyed the performance of Handel's oratorio since James was with her. Music united them, associated them in sympathy, stirred them, bound them together. She had no need to seek him in dreams, for could she not meet him at Mrs. Child's more earthly apartments in Isaac Hopper's house on Third Street? There they sat while Lydia discussed a caryatid that refreshed her spirit, or the *Anti-slavery Standard,* or her husband's interest in beet sugar. Margaret forgot Lydia's plain, unfashionable dress when her diminutive features became animated and her dark eyes glittered. Old Isaac Hopper in his Quaker costume was always a willing listener to stories about discharged convicts, while David Child could be relied upon for stimulating expostulations about the Texas conspiracy. Though they preferred to be alone, a meeting on Third Street was never without interest.

Dr. Leger's office was also a convenient place of assignation, where they need not linger as at the Cranches' or Mrs. Child's. A little foot-page was always ready to carry a note from Cedar Street to 74 Broadway, and so they could arrange to spend a day among green things or look at the moonlight from Margaret's window, or attend a performance by Ole Bull. The great Norwegian, fair-haired, robust, held the Tabernacle bespelled as he raised his bow. A juggler in the audience looked on, and moved not a muscle; the ladies forgot their velvets and furs; Margaret's eyes met James' and they smiled.

One day Margaret sealed her note with a flower, gave it to the little foot-page, and returned to the Farm to await Nathan's arrival. She chose the newest ribands and lace from her bandbox to add a colorful touch to her dress. At length he came. The trees had put on their white mantles and together they looked at the delicate traceries on the cherry branches near Margaret's window. Together they listened to the silence of the winter afternoon. Then James plucked the strings of his guitar and sang while Margaret yielded herself to a trance-like spell.

After his song, he held out his hand and let her over the wall to the little wood. As they stood there on the bare ground under the white and silent trees, he took from his pocket a package he had brought with him and gave it to Margaret. She opened it quietly and saw within a white veil.

"In your holy keeping I put my care,"
she murmured softly. By this impromptu symbol also she would worship. Margaret bent down to pluck a myrtle leaf that grew at the foot of a rock, and gave it to him. They held each other's hands and listened while the grass grew.

"Surely," she said, "we were born under the same constellation. I am the long, soft echo to your deepest tones."
He smiled and murmured,
"But you do not know me wholly."
She glanced at him quickly before she replied.
"To know the natural music of the being needs not long acquaintance."
She wanted to lay her arms about his neck and in her love find salt enough to keep the world from corruption. Softly she placed her hand upon his forehead, and he knit his brows. It was an immortal moment when her soul rushed out to him.

"I am with you," she whispered, "as never with any one else. With you I like to be quite still and have you be the actor and the voice. Surely you have life enough for both, *mein liebster.*"

As they turned back to the house she continued,
"You have had a portion of immortal love. Every hour you grow upon me and the root strikes to my inmost life."

This love, she thought, would blossom with flowers pure and fresh and if it never came to fruit would bloom forever in her memory. She held the white veil close to her; they were both within it, there together where the corrupt world had no place, in a land of stillness and frosty trees, where no footfall could disturb, no harsh color break the white radiance.

That evening James wrote to her, likening himself to the cherry tree by her window. Margaret placed the letter next to her heart. That winged feeling that came with early sunshine came now again to her in the cold, clear night. Surely twenty-four hours were too many, too long a time to fly alone on wings, too long to wait for him. *"Du Bester, mein Liebster, Lebewohl."* Across the night her love sprang forth to him.

Across the night, across the months her love sprang forth and ripened. As the months passed the beloved became the companion, sympathizing, listening to her words. So much there was to talk about with him. In February there was the burning of the *Tribune* office, when Mr. Graham and Mr. Strebeigh were forced to leap from a window into the snowdrifts below. The nearest hydrant was so frozen it had to be opened with an axe. In his light drab coat Greeley had trudged through the snow with McElrath to look at the fiery chasm that was all that was left of the Nassau Street office. Though the walls had fallen, the paper appeared as usual and Margaret told James that her admiration for Greeley's courage had greatly increased. She might quarrel with him, as she did nearly every morning, over her predilection for tea and spices, or her habit of writing only when in the vein, but beneath his prejudices there was a man of character. Besides, had he not sent a notice to Griswold about her book? Excitedly, Margaret told James that the first edition was exhausted in a week, and though she received only eighty-five dollars for the work, *Woman in the Nineteenth Century* was making a stir in the world. Together they scanned the reviews in the *Broadway Journal,* reading that Margaret was a contralto voice in literature: deep, rich, and strong, rather than mellifluous and clear. Though some thought she wasted the time of her readers since no unmarried woman could speak about marriage, and no true woman could desire the occupations that properly belonged to men, Margaret found that the favorable notices outweighed the unfavorable and that at any rate the newspaper sallies helped to sell the book.

James was a willing listener too to Margaret's condemnation of affairs in Mexico, and of that other blot on the American escutcheon, the annexation of Texas. It was with James that she deplored the Senate's decision thus to force the eagle to the earth. Lighter matters also they discussed, as they wandered through the wood or met at Dr. Leger's. If Margaret liked Mr. Hudson better than his lecture on Hamlet, it was James who listened eagerly to her opinion. If she wished to comment on a four-in-hand sleigh flying over the ice with carillons of bells tinkling from the harness, James was at her side, ready to hear and to smile.

When she visited Bellevue on Kips Farm it was James to whom she carried her impressions of old women enjoying their dish of gossip with their dish of tea, of a little Dutch girl, a dwarf who had been deserted by a showman, and whose glowering wizard eyes pursued Margaret as she left the Alms House. How different, she said, was the Asylum here from that at Bloomingdale. Here the mad crouched in corners. But Nathan helped Margaret forget the gray-haired woman wrapped in a shawl who never ceased chanting the church service, the brutal, stolid attendants, the pigeons that walked about among the violent, the black Judas that one of the inmates had painted. How well too he understood Margaret's desire to help Honora Shepard after her release. How sympathetic he was to her remarks about the Female Industry Association. Surely woman was finding her place at last in the nineteenth century when sempstresses and cap-makers and straw-workers could organize a society and declare their intention to get higher wages than ten or eighteen cents a day.

When Margaret heard that Thoreau had borrowed an axe from Alcott to cut the timber for his cabin on Walden Pond, or when Daniel Webster was seen on Wall Street wearing a bright blue satin vest sprigged with gold flowers, it was James to whom she told the news. If she found the heat and crowds intolerable at the Apollo Saloon where the Philharmonic Society played Beethoven's Eroica, or if she wished to discuss the opening night of Mrs. Mowatt's *Fashion,* or the rats that sallied out at the bell in the Park Theatre to scour the pit for peanuts, it was Nathan who heard, who smiled, who sympathized. When Cranch planned to exhibit a landscape at the National Academy of Design, or Crawford sent a bas-relief from Rome, Margaret reported the tidings to her companion. And as the news changed, the months passed, fled too swiftly, for all that the cherry tree was blossoming and the snow melted into the past. She told James that Greeley had decided to part with Ellery in April, and April approached quickly in all its freshness, its nostalgic bittersweet.

More bitter than sweet was April to Margaret, for on the seventh of the month James told her that he expected to return to Germany at the end of May. Did he not then prize her enough? Was there an ugly dwarf-changeling whose grave was hidden among their flowers? She did not understand, he said. He would come back. And she prayed him to be patient that she might understand. He feared she had hoped, and in her humiliation she drank a bitter cup. What part must common sense and prudence play in an affinity like theirs—in the kinship that she felt for him? Friendship would remain, but love's light wings were clipped since his heart hung cruelly out of reach. Pride, too, was left and Margaret told him that he had touched her heart and it thrilled to the centre, but she had been in her way a queen and her heart was a large kingdom. Then even pride faltered, for he had approached her more closely than any other. Oh, could he not stay at least to see her rose tree blossom, the rose tree that cast its shadow on the paper as she wrote to him? She leaned her aching head on the letter and with the last that she would send by the foot-page enclosed the pen with which she had written so often. When they met for the last time she gave him a small copy of Shelley, knowing well there was no poem like the poem they could have made for themselves. "I arise from dreams of thee," but no spirit now would lead her to his chamber window sweet. The ocean would stretch between them, and on another's eyes, perhaps, the blessing of his lips would lie.

The day before he left Margaret smiled ruefully to think that her criticism of Samuel Ward's translation of Goethe's *Essays on Art* should appear at that moment in the *Tribune*. How much there was behind the lines that called the precious gift to the attention of the American public. She had been a queen in that other farewell, and would be now again. But on the thirtieth of May it was hard to be queenly. She could not see him leave, but must stay at the Farm, entertaining James' townsman, Mr. Benson, who offered to take her riding in his gig, or sailing in his boat to Rockaway. He was kind, but she could make no music with him. In the evening at the Park Theatre with Lydia Child and Mr. Benson she saw not the actress robed in satin and crowned with flowers, but James, whose image rose before her. And the next week, returning from a Sunday on Staten Island, though she conversed mechanically with the people on the boat, it was James with whom she really spoke.

The summer shadows might lengthen as they would— his shadow eclipsed all others. For she had lost her dear companion who had felt every shade of life and beauty as exquisitely as herself. She kept his guitar by her window, and the white veil she placed with the dead flowers which in their bloom he had given her. Every object at the Farm was associated with him; at every turn in the garden his figure appeared. She could not go alone to the little wood where they had been so often together; the wall over which he had led her was painful to climb alone. Sometimes, though, she went to the rocks and wore her prettiest dresses to think of him. He had left Josey in Greeley's care, and the dog splashed salt water over her, turning his loving eyes to hers. If only she had a miniature of James or even a colored crayon drawing. There was so much she had meant to tell him. Could she wait till he returned to speak to him about the story of Isis and Osiris? They needed the suns and moons of this summer to ripen their knowledge of each other; then perhaps separation would have been less hard for her to bear. Now she must wait, watching the boats for his letters, the "Cambria," the "Great Britain." When he sent her Foscolo's book on Petrarch she kissed the pages and looked through all the margins for his pencil marks. Whenever she felt him close to her, she took out the white veil and looked at it.

Through the white veil she saw the life that moved about her. Her hammock was slung on the piazza and there she lay, swinging with Pickie in the summer evenings. In a white haze she played with the baby or bathed

at the foot of the tall rock, or dined with a set of Texas
distingués. Could she not learn the vanity of clinging to
shadows from the released convicts whom she visited at
the Prison Association on Twelfth Street? Could she not
learn the futility of death in life from the death of the
flaming old warrior, General Jackson? If he had been
unwise, still he had been sincere, and the golden urn upon
his bier had been deserved. Could she find no pleasure in
her mother's short visit, despite the fact that Mrs. Fuller
was appalled by the lack of harmony and order in the
Greeley home? Was there no delight in the news about
Eugene's marriage to Anna Rotta and his work on a New
Orleans paper, or in Richard's plans for law school?
Would she never cease to view events through a white
veil? Even the great fire in the city on July nineteenth
scarcely touched her, for James had been no loser by it,
though she would never forget the flames on Broad
Street, the broken windows, the explosive blasts. A man
sought his young wife amid the smoking ruins; a girl was
found in convulsions at the Fulton ferry house. Surely if
the people could suffer so in fortitude, she could find release in work, and look at facts without a veil.

Though Margaret continued to write literary reviews,
declaring Poe's tales a refreshment, or Longfellow's
poems the elegant museum pieces of a schoolmaster, her
emphasis in the *Tribune,* as the months passed, was not
upon letters, but the welfare of society. She was bent upon
tearing away the white veil, and the columns above the
asterisk were as good a place as any to find release from
sorrow. Even in Story Books for the Hot Weather she
found the solemn signs of revolution, and in Disraeli's
Sybil, visions of phalansteries in every park. As a proper
tribune of the people she appealed to all to help furnish
the Asylum for Discharged Convicts and employ the outcasts of society. On August first, the anniversary of the

emancipation of the West Indian slaves, she pointed out the serfdom that still existed in Poland, in England, in Charleston. In the poems of Thom and of Prince she found the spirit of the age working a revolution toward the glory of labor, and with joy greeted the emergence of poets of the working class. When the Prison Association met, Margaret was there with Catharine Sedgwick or Mrs. Cranch, ready to share her knowledge of the penitentiaries, glad to subscribe to the cause, and write her report as a Thanksgiving article in the *Tribune*. She returned again to Sing Sing to hear the female prisoners chant a choral on the words, *All is Well*. To the *Liberty Bell* for the new year she contributed words which she hoped would indeed make all well. It was not enough merely to free men from their chains; the errors that forged those chains must be wiped out. And to those words she appended a poem, proclaiming that our brothers *are* our keepers. If she were but patient, the strong winds of liberty might sweep even a white veil away.

Other ways there were also, to subdue her memory of James. The *Siciliano e Tarantella* which Ole Bull played by request, and Leopold de Meyer's interpretation of the *Danse du Serail,* were sources of delight. If the air was bad and the ushers missing at Palmo's Opera House, still *Der Freischütz* brought forgetfulness of sorrow, and Mr. Timm's performance of the Mendelssohn Concerto at the Philharmonic was balm to the soul. If music could bind capitalist and laborer in harmony, surely it could also dispel the discord of her own life. As she had plunged into social welfare during the summer and autumn, so now, at the approach of winter, she sought release in concerts and in friends.

In December Margaret moved to a boarding house on Warren Street, and though the expense was greater than at the Farm, she could enjoy the luxury of having meals sent up to her room. Later she found still pleasanter quarters in Mary Elwell's house at 4 Amity Place. There she could entertain her friends before her bright fire without the obligation of catering to Mrs. Greeley's whims or listening to Mr. Greeley's scornful remarks. Now it was pleasure indeed to don her light green silk dress and set a white japonica from Thorburn's flower depot in her hair, when she invited Cassius Clay or Harro Harring to her rooms.

Mr. Clay had been asked to discuss the subject of slavery at the Tabernacle, and Margaret found him a man who esteemed his own convictions more highly than partisan politics. To her he seemed to embody the freedom of the press, for had not his offices in Kentucky, where he published *The True American,* been destroyed by a mob? Ardently she agreed with him, that he who wrongs one wrongs all, that no part can be wounded without endangering the whole. It was the childish sweetness of Harro Harring that appealed to Margaret rather than his stormy moods. Like Clay, the Dane seemed to represent a lost cause, for at the last moment his publishers had refused to issue his novel, *Dolores,* and Margaret, in her green dress, with the white flower nodding in her hair, promised him help from her purse as well as her pen. Had he not declared in a novel that embraced such topics as Napoleon and Mazzini, marriage and magnetism, that the nations yet shall rise in all their might? Had he not written a defense of Garibaldi for the *Tribune?* Before her fireplace, Harring told Margaret of his expedition to Greece, his arrest at Alexandria, his commission in Grand Duke Constantine's Russian guards. His whole life seemed an attempt to unite poetry with politics. Freely, therefore, she gave him money with which to publish his novel, and in the *Tribune* proposed a congress of authors and publishers so that contracts would not again be broken. Margaret found Clay and Harring men of heroic blood, and happily entertained them as friends.

Though the blood at Anne Lynch's soirees was not always heroic, Margaret found the gatherings at Waverley Place as enjoyable as her own more informal parties. On February fourteenth she dressed with special care, trimming her green silk with lace and flowers for the occasion of "dear Lynchie's" Valentine party. This would be a far cry, she thought, from the Valentine's dance of last year at the Bloomingdale Asylum. She had gone a long way since then, but so had he—so had James wandered far off. Sometimes she doubted whether he would ever return, but perhaps one day she would go to him in Germany. She gave a last touch to the light green dress, glad that thanks to Dr. Leger she could now dispense with the shoulder pad. Now the cloak—and vanish all sad thoughts or good St. Valentine would frown upon her.

It was but a short walk from Amity Street to Waverley Place. Margaret caught a glimpse of Commodore Vanderbilt's miniature race course, and there near the brownstone fronts on West Washington Place was the school of the Misses Sedgwick. Margaret knew she would meet their aunt among the regiment of women who responded to the calls of their dear Lynchie. Catharine Sedgwick did not like the foggy Transcendentalists, but the author of *Linwood* and *Hope Leslie* would be ready with a clever bon mot about the novelists of the day or the female prisoners in whom she took a great interest. If Lydia Child could not afford the white gloves or the time for such gatherings Elizabeth Oakes Smith would take her place, escorted by her eldest son Appleton. How much water had flowed under the bridge since Margaret had met Elizabeth's husband, Seba Smith, at Niagara. But it was not Niagara that she would talk about tonight. Elizabeth would be eager to remark on the snakes she was so fond of or the reception of her poem, *The Sinless Child*. Poe had said many a kind word in praise of it. Poe—he would be there too. Margaret remembered how he had read *The Raven* at one of the Saturday soirees on Waverley Place. It might be scandalous, but not surprising that Mrs. Osgood's childlike face should have been suffused with tears under his wizard spell. When he read, from the long strips of blue paper, in that low, melodious voice of his, it was no wonder that delicate Frances Osgood "sparkled, exhaled, and went to heaven." Mrs. Ellet had had and probably would continue to have food for gossip if Poe persisted in gazing at Mrs. Osgood with his brilliant black eyes, or smiling so captivatingly at her pale, oval face. How different these soirees were from Emerson's rarefied conclaves! All the Gothamites—even to Mrs. Osgood, with her *Poetry of Flowers and Flowers of Poetry*—had lent their names to the annuals, but when they gathered together they traded in gossip rather than in heavenly discourse. Margaret passed Mr. and Mrs. Kirkland's School for Young Ladies, and at the next turn was on Waverley Place.

She knocked at the door of the brick house that bore the number 116, and a child portress admitted her to a dimly lighted hall. She followed her guide to a small room, where she left her cloak with the shawls and bonnets of the earlier arrivals. Then she climbed the dark staircase, walked along a hall filled with pictures and flowers, and entered Miss Lynch's drawing room. Posed near the bronzes and alabaster vases Margaret saw the hoop-skirts and ostrich plumes of the regiment of women who had already assembled. She approached her tall, slender hostess, who extended her tapered fingers in greeting. Dear Lynchie was receiving this evening in an elegant white dress that contrasted strikingly with the dark mantel and corded draperies near which she was standing. That white flower was a fine touch in her dark hair. Margaret seated herself on the sofa near Elizabeth Oakes Smith, observing that Frances Osgood had already taken her accustomed position on a footstool. Mrs. Ellet was standing in a corner with Anne Lynch, and Margaret heard bits of their conversation about gingerbread recipes, Delsarte's hygienic system, and Miss Lynch's contribution of "Bones in the Desert" to *The Opal*. Looking around, Margaret noticed that Greeley had preceded her, had in fact already taken off his boots and was drying his feet on the fender of the fireplace. Lynchie would forgive him even this, for his stand in opposition to St. Polk appealed to one who had been Clay's secretary. Catharine Sedgwick looked beautifully feminine as she discussed homeopathy and mesmerism with the black-eyed Mary Gove and in another corner Mrs. Stephens was making authoritative pronouncements about *Graham's Magazine* as she twirled her emerald ring and touched her gold filigree pin.

At first Margaret felt in a combative mood, for the conversation seemed to proceed in a low murmur that gave her no opportunity for self-expression. She smoothed her light hair, moved nervously on the sofa, and lowered her blue-gray eyes to Mrs. Osgood, who upturned her face, doing her infantile act. Her pallor, Margaret observed, was accentuated by her black hair, and the décolleté of her dress revealed her fragility. Someone perpetrated a pun and Margaret raised her upper lip in scorn, while Anne Lynch's short, odd, whimsical laugh rose above the light murmur of talk. Elizabeth Oakes Smith turned to Margaret to mention the fact that before her arrival they had been discussing Grace Church, and Margaret, though she despised puns, could not refrain from the comment that the Church would lack the grace of sharing its offerings with the poor. As she spoke, drawing out her words, she closed her eyes. Mrs. Osgood looked up in childish admiration, as Margaret continued. There might be ladies in mousseline de laine, she said, glancing at her shoulders, and dandies in high-heeled boots at Grace Church, but poverty was unfashionable, and would not be represented in the pews. Anne Lynch moved lightly across the room and approached the sofa, her arched instep showing to advantage in her slippers. Margaret drew herself up to answer with magnetic charm Anne's remark about the latest pronouncement of President Polk, and declared that war with Great Britain might be the outcome if he continued to assert a claim to Oregon. "But then," she added, smiling dynamically, "this is St. Valentine's day—not St. Polk's."

"I wonder," Mrs. Osgood murmured, glancing up from her footstool, "what verses Poe will favor us with tonight. I shall never forget how he looked at his desk beneath the picture of the loved and lost Lenore." Elizabeth Ellet moved nearer the sofa while Mrs. Osgood continued.

"For hours I have listened entranced to his strains of almost celestial eloquence."

"For hours indeed," whispered Mrs. Ellet to Anne Lynch. "And what does poor Virginia do when this fair visitor comes to Amity Street?"

Anne Lynch was saved from answering, for at that moment Poe appeared at the door of the drawing room. The eyes of the ladies turned now from Margaret's green silk dress to Poe's sober black suit. He held his head high, and under his broad forehead the lips curled in a sneer. Then he swept the room with his large, jet-black eyes and greeted his hostess. Mrs. Osgood, Margaret noticed— and so also did Mrs. Ellet, who watched every turn of the figure on the footstool—seemed unable to take her eyes from Poe's slight figure and pale, sad face. Virginia entered behind him, the pallor of her waxen face heightened by her black hair and fawn-like eyes. Surely, Margaret thought, she looked more like a child than a woman, in her simple crimson dress with a bit of yellow lace at her throat. How demure she seemed, lisping her greeting, smiling when Poe called her "Sis."

Margaret laid her head on the back of the sofa as Poe became the observed of all observers. His accent dropping like a knife through water, he uttered scornful remarks about the Bostonians whom he preferred to call Frogpondians, or the latest activities of the Snook Farm Phalanx. Miss Lynch moved about, serving grape juice, while the ostrich plumes waved and the hoop-skirts rustled, and the conversation turned into a steady murmur. Then she reminded her guests that this was no ordinary Saturday soiree. It was St. Valentine's Eve, and homage must be done to the good bishop. Valentines had been written and they must be read aloud. The guests proceeded to read their complimentary verses to one another and laughter and light applause followed.

Then Poe, standing in the centre of the room, his brilliant black eyes glancing from one to another, took from his pocket a strip of blue paper to read the Valentine he had composed.

"My verses," he said in his low, harmonious voice, "are enigmatical. They are addressed to her whose name is written within. If you can read the riddle, you may claim the Valentine."

Then he read, his gaze intense, his small hands holding the blue paper. Margaret looked from Virginia to Frances Osgood, both of whom seemed drawn to Poe, to his black suit, his thin face, his dark eyes. There was, indeed, an uncanny spell about him.

After he had finished, none could claim the Valentine,

for none could unriddle the name that was written within.
Poe smiled charmingly as he remarked,

"Perhaps you will find the key if the poem is published."

Margaret—and Mrs. Ellet too—had their own thoughts
about the solution of the riddle, but if Mrs. Osgood's
name appeared within, it was difficult to find it at the
moment. Perhaps Poe had written a diagonal acrostic, but
in any case there was little doubt as to the identity of his
latest Valentine.

The ostrich plumes nodded again; the grape juice reappeared, and at length the littérateurs proceeded to
claim their wraps, though none had been able to claim
Poe's Valentine. In the dressing room, Margaret put on
her cloak, and knowing that there had been no Valentine
from James—and seldom even a letter now, she sighed.

"Why do you sigh so deeply?" One of the rustling
hoop-skirts had heard her. The truth came to Margaret's
lips before she could think.

"I am alone as usual," she murmured, and turned
quickly from the room.

Back at Amity Street before her bright fire, Margaret
went on writing, as the months passed, articles that reflected the life she was leading. When Allston's painting
of Belshazzar's Feast was exhibited at the Granite Building, the painter's understanding of dress and jewels and
hair must be pointed out, and if Francisco de Noronha
composed a *Dolores* for the violin, his concert also must
be given space, especially since he was the husband of
Harro Harring's original Dolores. She did not, however,
abandon her role as tribune of the people, for such monstrous works as Cheever's *Defense of Capital Punishment*
must be attacked, and the activities of the city institution
for the deaf and dumb reported in the columns above the
asterisk. The newer literary lights must be extolled also,

and Margaret sent to Boston for a copy of Browning's poems so that she might diffuse the knowledge that Robert Browning existed and was writing subtle and radiant poetry. Now and then she devoted space to still another type of work, to the *Notes of a Journey from Cornhill to Cairo,* to Forsyth's *Italy,* Kip on *The Christmas Holidays in Rome*—to books that brought the Alps and the Rhine, the art of England and the color of Italy to New York.

For the hope that she had toyed with so long would soon become a reality. Not long after the Valentine's party at Waverley Place, Margaret was invited to go abroad with Marcus and Rebecca Spring. Margaret had known the Springs for some time, had met them at concerts, especially at the Philharmonic to which Marcus subscribed, had seen them with Lydia Child, at Waverley Place, or at committee meetings for discharged convicts. Marcus Spring was a benevolent merchant, and his name appeared on many a list of donations for the needy. Margaret spent the last week in March at his home on State Street in Brooklyn to round out their plans and arrangements for the summer.

Marcus and Rebecca, Margaret observed, had something about them remarkably simple and humane, serene and beautiful. They always called people by their first names. Marcus might be a self-made man, but he showed none of the acquisitive traits that ordinarily appeared in one who had hoisted himself by his own boot straps. His countenance was indeed a blessing. Rebecca was a Quaker and seemed always to glow with a quiet, inward light. Eddie, their son, might have served as a model for Cupid, for his calm, thoughtful face could light up most charmingly. They were eager to show Margaret their home, with its grape bower and garden porch, the pleached alley covered with vines, the veranda, and the weeping willows.

Marcus did not like to speak of what he did, but Rebecca found no greater pleasure than in telling others of her husband's interest in socialism and Brook Farm, of his horse Dolly, or his own soirees that rivaled Anne Lynch's.

On the garden porch they sat, while spring came on, discussing the journey that lay before them. They would leave in August, and stay for a year, traveling to France and Italy—to Germany also. Suddenly, Margaret trembled lest James Nathan should return to America just as she was leaving. But he had sent for Josey, and so perhaps he meant to remain in Germany. She would see him there; she would see the well beloved. And in Italy she would see the Raphaels; in the Italian soil she would take root; this, after all, was the hope that had always drawn her to Europe. If the Springs anticipated a tour that would add pleasure and variety to their lives, to Margaret it was a journey homeward to the land that had grown up in her soul—to Rome to which she had ever remained faithful.

Before August came there was work to be done. Nor was the least important to Margaret, the task of journeying to the cottage which Poe had rented in Fordham. A task it definitely was, for a purpose must be accomplished there in the most delicate way possible. When Anne Lynch had asked Margaret to accompany her to Fordham to retrieve the letters which Mrs. Osgood had sent to Poe, she agreed immediately. She remembered that James Nathan still possessed her own letters, and that the boats carried very few from him to her. Though the essence of her love was indestructible, the crystal that enclosed it might break and the perfume escape. Yes, it would be a good Samaritan who interceded between Poe and Frances Osgood, and returned the love letters to that childlike woman.

On the newly completed Harlem Railroad which ran

from City Hall through the Bowery and Harlem as far
as White Plains, Anne Lynch explained further to Margaret the circumstances that had necessitated their journey. Mrs. Ellet, she said, had chanced to see a letter from
Mrs. Osgood on one of her visits to Fordham. It was so
compromising that she had immediately called upon the
lady, remonstrated with her for her imprudence, and obtained her consent for a committee of ladies to demand
the return of the letters on her behalf. Mrs. Osgood had
diplomatically suggested that it would be best for Anne
Lynch and Margaret to undertake such a delicate mission.

"The gossip," Anne Lynch continued, "has become
notorious. I have heard that Mary Neal, John Neal's
daughter, has had the indiscreet audacity to write from
Maine asking Mrs. Osgood for a lock of Poe's hair!"
They would do their best, Margaret reassured her. Virginia would be restored to her own, and Mrs. Osgood's
letters returned to their writer.

They left the train at the northerly Dutch village of
Fordham to walk up the winding Williamsbridge Road
to the ledge where Poe's cottage stood. Margaret glanced
up to the summit of the knoll and around to the Harlem
River. A cherry tree was in full bloom and a rose bush
had been trained against the badly joined planks of the
wall. What a poor wooden cottage it was, low-eaved and
box-shaped. The long veranda was pleasant, though, and
the triangular plot of ground on which the house stood
gave a fine view of the rocky ledge crowned with cedars,
the flower bed, the vines, a farm across the Kingsbridge
Road. Poe appeared at the door in his threadbare black
suit and bade them enter the parlor. Mrs. Clemm was
seated on the box-lounge, knitting. Despite the worn black
dress she looked tall and dignified, and her snow-white
hair strayed out from under the widow's cap. She looked
up behind her glasses at the visitors and immediately

excused herself. Gathering her knitting together, she said she must go upstairs and sit for a while with Virginia, who was resting in bed.

Margaret looked about her. The room was so scantily furnished that she needed only a glance to note the table in the centre, the four chairs, the hanging bookshelf on which a volume of Poe's verses was conspicuously placed. She stood on the checked matting that covered the worn floor and walked up to the engraving and collection of sea shells above the mantelpiece. Then she seated herself on one of the chairs, a little dismayed by the cheap furniture, the lime wash on the walls, the four small-paned windows. She looked at Poe. His eyes were as lustrous as ever, his face as pale, and if the black suit had become a little worn since St. Valentine's Eve, he wore it with as much hauteur as ever. The mission, she sensed, would be even more difficult than she had anticipated.

Truth was ever first with Margaret. Briefly, she told Poe the reason for their visit. Anne Lynch presented the credentials that Mrs. Osgood had given her. They wished a packet made of the letters so that they could be returned forthwith. Poe's black eyes were fiery and he ruffled his dark hair. Then in his low, incisive voice, he turned upon them.

"Mrs. Ellet had better come and look after her own letters," he said scornfully.

Margaret moved nervously in the chair, and Anne Lynch lowered her eyes. They had not meant him to be so nettled that they would be greeted with reprehensible insults.

"You may tell Mrs. Ellet," he went on, "that I denounce her fair emissaries as busybodies."

"We are not interested in Mrs. Ellet," Margaret retorted. "We have come for Mrs. Osgood's letters."

Without a word Poe ran up the narrow staircase and

returned with the packet. He handed it to Miss Lynch and escorted the ladies to the door.

It had been an unpleasant affair and Margaret was glad to see the end of it. She felt indeed as if the Raven had perched upon the casque of Pallas and pulled all the feathers out of her cap. But the letters had been retrieved, and so perhaps the plumes of the Raven were more ruffled than the feathers of Pallas.

Margaret's other preoccupations in the few months that remained before August were more to her taste. At the end of April she had taken lodgings in Richard Manning's home at 43 Middagh Street. Brooklyn was quieter than the city, and in the loveliness of spring Margaret enjoyed being near the Heights and the Fulton ferry. The name inscribed on the door at Middagh Street was that of Hawthorne's third cousin, and Margaret found that if Mr. Manning had little in common with the gentleman of the Old Manse, he resembled Marcus Spring in being a benevolent merchant who fulfilled his obligation to society by serving on committees for discharged convicts. In his home peace, order, and kindness prevailed, and Margaret was happier than she had ever been at the Farm.

Bad news from home had preceded her, however. There seemed to have been a crisis between Ellen and her husband, with Ellery's decision that he must see Europe though his wife expected a child in the spring. In addition, he had expected Margaret to make up as heavy a purse for him as possible from her friends. His unnatural selfishness had been a little too much for her nerves. Besides this, after the fire at Brook Farm, Lloyd had been forced to leave. Charles Dana might have found immediate employment on the *Tribune* after the ruin of Ripley's phalanx, but for Lloyd readjustment would be more difficult. Bad news, it seemed, would continue to pursue her even to Middagh Street, for had not war been declared with Mexico? The people might rejoice and applaud the fireworks in front of City Hall after General Taylor's triumphs, but to Margaret the medallion of victory was inscribed on the reverse side with slavery.

Nobility still moved and breathed, however, when Thoreau could prefer jail to paying his tax, and so denounce the war in his own special manner. Brook Farm also might be ruined, but William Channing would still proclaim the unity of man with man, with God, with nature. Under this three-fold motto the white flag of the Associationists was still given to the breeze. Dearer to Margaret even than the news from Concord and Roxbury was the love that James sent from Hamburg. She recalled how she had lost the rose from Shelley's grave which he had enclosed in another letter. It had been sad that she could find only the green leaves. But could not a leaf grow and flourish, though it might bear no fruit?

There was so much to be done in the months that were left that Margaret had little time to think—even of a rose from Shelley's grave. Her critical essays must be selected from *The Dial, The Western Messenger,* and the *Tribune* and revised for publication as *Papers on Literature and Art.* Now that she had accepted Mr. Wiley's offer, she must gather together her thoughts on Crabbe's graphic skill and Shelley's delicacy of vibration, on Wordsworth, who dignified the petty operations of nature, on Coleridge, who could paint a single mood as if his colors were made of the mind's own atoms. More important than the article on the British Poets to Margaret was her essay on American Literature. She must remind her readers that an American literature cannot exist until an original idea animates the nation and fresh currents of life call unto life fresh thoughts along its shores. Emerson might deal with causes rather than effects, Longfellow might persist in artificiality and imitativeness,

Lowell might want the true spirit of poetry—still the desire for an American literature had shown itself. When this desire penetrated the springs of action, there would be poets—American poets. Such thoughts as these were worth gathering for the press, though Margaret would be allowed only twelve per cent on all copies after expenses had been paid. Some there were who appreciated her work. Despite the patronizing review of *Woman in the Nineteenth Century* that appeared in *The Southern Quarterly Review,* announcing that the female organization was characterized by a feebleness of muscle, an English edition of the book had appeared. Perhaps the miscellanies, too, would reach a wide public.

Margaret welcomed the appreciation, but, as she laid her plans for Europe, she could not help realizing that more monetary support would also have been acceptable. McElrath was making difficulties along financial lines, but Greeley finally arranged to give her one hundred and twenty dollars as advance payment for her articles from abroad. Richard had sent her an itemized account of her possessions, and the total came to $404.53. It was well that Marcus Spring had been willing to advance the money she needed; otherwise Europe would once more have become an impossibility.

June and July were busy months for Margaret. Work on the *Tribune* must continue as usual, though the lady of the asterisk thought more of the Colosseum than of the office at the corner of Spruce and Nassau. Her article on Hawthorne's pensive sense of the spiritual influences that haunt men's palpable life seemed to Margaret a farewell to the Old Manse and to Concord. The paper on M'Kenney's *Memoirs and Sketches of Travel among the Indians* was in its way, too, a farewell—to the West instead of the East. There was another farewell now to be written, the farewell to New York.

For the last time she walked among the jostling crowds on Wall Street, seeing the omnibuses, the street-sweeps, the gentlemen in silk hats thronging now on a baking and blistering thoroughfare. She entered the *Tribune* office and opened her portfolio to write her farewell to New York City, where twenty months had presented her with a richer and more varied exercise for thought and life than twenty years could in any other part of the United States. Where else, indeed, could she have condensed into so short a time her interest in the lame, the halt, the imprisoned, her concert-going, her visits to soirees, her love of James? Life rushed too fast perhaps, but wide and free, and to that pace her own life had kept time. She would go, she wrote, to behold the wonders of art and the temples of old religion. But she would see no forms of beauty beyond what her country was capable of producing in myriad variety, had she but the soul to will it. Then for the last time, she handed the short column to Greeley.

In the final weeks of bidding farewell to the past, Margaret went with Rebecca Spring to Plumbe's Daguerrian Gallery at the corner of Barclay Street to have her daguerreotype taken. She wrote to Richard asking him to look for her plates and have her cards engraved for her. The last-minute affairs were attended to. Farewells were exchanged with Greeley and his family, and the roving camp chest was packed again for a visit to Cambridgeport before she sailed.

On the afternoon of July thirty-first, Emerson journeyed to the Port to meet Margaret. He gave her a letter which he had written to introduce her to Carlyle. Margaret glanced through the note, reading that she was an exotic in New England, a foreigner from some more sultry and expansive climate. She looked up at her friend; she had thought herself a wandering intelligence driven from spot to spot, and now, as she read on, she learned that Emerson had dubbed her our citizen of the world by quite special diploma.

And so, the citizen of the world went forth to meet the world, bidding farewell to her family and her friends. The next day, Margaret journeyed to Boston to board the boat with the Springs. On August first, the "Cambria" cleared for Liverpool. Margaret raised her hand in farewell, and turned to look out over the clear blue waters. These, then, were the fresh currents she had waited for so long. Over the great expanse of sea the citizen would be borne from the New World to the Old.

BOOK TWO:
THE OLD WORLD

CHAPTER XV

WANDERJAHRE

AS SHE walked along the deck or sat of an evening watching the cold, black waters, Margaret recalled that Goethe had limited the days of intercourse in the *wanderjahre* to three. She wondered which three days would stand out in her mind after her *wanderjahre* had passed—which three of all the many bright and fleeting days that surely lay before her. Yet she could not think long, or even talk long with her friends, for she found the jar and smell of the machinery unbearable. The spectacle of ocean under a favorable wind was somehow more appealing from a firm, green shore. She passed the days, however, reading her copy of *Monte Cristo,* and chatting with the Springs, or occasionally with Captain Judkins. The commander, Margaret knew, had insisted that the Negro Douglass be admitted to equal rights upon his deck with the insolent slaveholders and it was with some pride that he told her that *The New York Herald* had labeled him "the Nigger Captain." Indeed, Margaret observed, he accepted the distinction with as much delight as Colonel M'Kenney had borne his title of the Indian's friend. Captain Judkins revealed his true democracy when Lord Falkland, the Governor of Nova Scotia, boarded the "Cambria" at Halifax. Though his lady was a daughter of William the Fourth, and he himself an aristocrat of the first order, the captain showed no more inclination to address his remarks to these notables than to Margaret. The summer passage gave the commander more time to chat than at other seasons, and Margaret found no one to sympathize with her distaste for the sea. The stewardess remarked to her rather pointedly that any one tempted God Almighty who complained on a voyage where they did not even have to put guards to the dishes. Margaret was grateful for the shortest journey ever made across the Atlantic—only ten days and sixteen hours—and, anticipating the glories of the Old World, she disembarked with her friends on a fine and shining morning.

Margaret and the Springs waited impatiently at the Custom House, where their baggage was detained while the officials gave preference to the mass of household stuff carried by Lord and Lady Falkland. At length they arrived at the Adelphi Hotel in Liverpool, where they passed the night. The next day they journeyed on to Manchester and Margaret was glad, especially for the sake of Mrs. Spring, who was too weak to endure the fatigue of hard traveling, that there was no rushing or tearing or swearing or snatching of baggage on the cars. In the evening Margaret observed the mill girls strolling bareheaded through the streets of Manchester with coarse rude airs and, noticing through the windows of the gin-palaces the women seated drinking, she began to think that the sweetness of the English homeside was melting into fable. There, too, Margaret met the editor, Alexander Ireland, and found him an excellent person, a devout reader of *The Dial* and, with his broad good-natured face and the comic tones of his voice, a fine antidote to the mill girls of the town.

Already one day of the *wanderjahre* had passed, and they must hurry on lest time fly more quickly than they. The very next day the travelers went on to Chester, where they visited a museum kept by a woman. Margaret happily observed to Rebecca Spring that apparently there were other ways for women to do good besides making clothes for the poor or teaching Sunday school. The

Chester inn was reminiscent of the saloon at Ross' Grove where Margaret had spent a night so many years before, for she was awakened from sleep by a loud dispute between her chambermaid and an elderly gentleman who claimed that he had engaged number 44, despite the fact that Margaret already occupied that room. The lock was a strong defense, however, and Margaret turned back to sleep, looking forward to her return to Liverpool for a longer stay.

The squalor and the shameless beggars of that city impressed themselves upon her mind during the three days she spent there. Nor was she greatly encouraged by the words she heard at the Paradise Street Chapel, delivered by James Martineau. He seemed over-intellectual, and hence partially developed. His half conservative, half reforming views lacked harmony, and seemed to Margaret best adapted to those who loved the new wine, but did not feel that they could throw away all their old bottles. The next day, at the Mechanics' Institute, she was pleased to learn that seventeen hundred pupils including girls could receive instruction there for a small fee. In addition, in the address given by the Director of the Institute, Margaret glowed when she read quotations from *The Dial*. Even in this murky and sordid city, *The Dial* had cast some sunlight.

For the trip to Kendal Margaret prepared by buying Bradshaw's Railway Guide, and on the road to Lancaster, read extracts in the handbook from Charles Sumner's writings on peace. At Lancaster the company boarded the canal boat where they passed some conversation with two cordial Englishmen and a smirking German traveler. Margaret preferred looking at a beautiful Bengalese youth who accompanied one of the Englishmen. Indeed she could scarcely take her eyes from his embroidered broadcloth robe, his rich shawl, and heavy gold chain.

The languid beauty of the Bengalese was a far cry from the crisp, fresh loveliness of the English lakes. At Ambleside the bluebell and campanula blossomed and the fuchsia grew magnificently in every cottage yard. Margaret immediately asked its mode of culture so that she might tell her mother how to make the bed of bog-earth and put down the fuchsia slips. The stone cottage where they stayed commanded a fine view of the lakes and hills, and Margaret looked forward to a week of happy drives and boating excursions.

It was Harriet Martineau who had arranged for Margaret and the Springs to occupy the little cottage at Ambleside, and to her new home they made their first visit in England. Margaret was particularly eager to renew her acquaintance with Miss Martineau, since she had heard that Harriet had recovered from an illness by means of mesmerism. It was pleasant to watch her hostess point out the many tributes that had been given her by her English admirers, but Margaret was disappointed to see that though her friend's health had been restored, she herself seemed commonplace and was not at all disposed to discuss her excursions into the land of dreams whither she had been led by Mr. Atkinson, the prince of English mesmerisers. Consequently, Margaret could not refrain from sending some unkind remarks through Harriet's ear trumpet, until she bustled about indignantly to her other guests. Margaret was a little contemptuous of a woman who looked the picture of rude, weather-beaten health after an experience in the spiritual world. She proceeded to harangue the drawing room party, thinking that Harriet scarcely looked as if she had been mesmerized at all, while Miss Martineau bounced about looking larger and more robust than ever, and directed her flowing discourse against lion-hunters to any who cared to listen. The bowl of her ear trumpet was passed from one to another, but

Margaret found that it resembled in no wise a pipe of peace.

On the excursion to Langdale that Harriet arranged Margaret was silent, scarcely speaking to anybody. She delighted in the sheep with their black leggings, the gray stones that dotted the hillside, the Pikes that recalled to her Wordsworth's *Excursion*. At steep and stony places the company alighted from the drosky while the driver led the horse, so that they took four or five hours to cover ten miles. Margaret was happy when they paused to look and she found in the free breezes and cold blue sky the sense of eternity that Wordsworth had conveyed in his poem. At a farmhouse in the vale they stopped to dine, and here too Margaret was silent, rejoicing in the stone floors and old carved cabinet of the cottage—even in the provision of oaten cakes. At Dungeon Ghyll Force and later at Buttermere she took deep pleasure in the comforting sight of green hills and summer flowers, valleys that were not too steep, lakes that were not too grand.

In all its gentle loveliness this was Wordsworth's country, and to the poet of the lakes they must make their pilgrimage. Margaret was disappointed in his habitation and could have wished a wilder spot for his home. Rydal Mount to her seemed a retirement for a gentleman rather than the haunt of a poet. Yet there was little of the wild in the reverend old gentleman who walked so cautiously along the garden path to greet his visitors. Apollo had vanished from Grasmere and left in his stead a man of memories clothed in black, a venerable cottager in a florid, fair old age. Wordsworth walked slowly with his guests to his haunts about the house, pointing out with pride his Rydalian laurels and hollyhocks. What simple tastes were these for one who had heard the voice of mountains. He who had seen cloudy visions on the lakes tended now an avenue of hollyhocks—straw-color and crimson-brown, rose and white—and bade his neighbors grow hollyhocks too. He led the company then into his house, showing them his portrait done by Inman, and Dorothy's picture.

> Five years have passed; five summers with the length
> Of five long winters! and again I hear
> These waters rolling from their mountain-springs
> With a soft inland murmur.

Five years? Alas more than forty-five had passed. Was his memory still the dwelling place for all sweet sounds?

Reluctantly the reverend poet turned from the past to the present, turned from the round ocean and the living air and the blue sky of remembrance to the Corn Laws of today. The principle that dictated the laws, he admitted, was right, though uncertainly he added that existing interests might not have been carefully attended to. It was no wonder, Margaret thought, that Wordsworth, protected by his gentle hills, isolated in the mansion of his mind, heard not the voice of misery which cried so loudly from Liverpool, from Manchester—the voice that would not be stilled by the persuasions of poetry or the balm of philosophy. Back at Ambleside she asked her landlady whether the countryfolk valued Wordsworth because he was so celebrated a poet.

"Truly, madam," was the answer, "I think it is because he is so kind a neighbor—and Mrs. Wordsworth too."

Such a visit was worth recording for the benefit of *Tribune* readers. Recalling her advance payment from Greeley, Margaret took time before leaving the lakes to sum up her observations of England, and dispatched them to Nassau Street from the little stone cottage in Ambleside.

On the coach to Edinburgh a rawboned Scotsman returning from a pilgrimage to Abbotsford took pains to inform Margaret that "Sir Walter was a vara intelligen

mon." She hoped for fresher news when she arrived at
the Scottish capital—for news of living men, for news,
perhaps, of James Nathan.

At Mrs. Cumming's lodging house at the corner of
Prince and Castle Streets there were no letters for Margaret. While below her windows women scolded their
dirty children and boys quarreled raucously and struck
each other she sat down to write a letter to James' friend,
Thomas Delf, telling him that she and the Springs expected to make a tour of the Highlands in Scotland, asking if Mr. Nathan were in London, suggesting that
perhaps James might come to her by rail and go "the
short tour" with them. If there were any letters from
Nathan, perhaps Mr. Delf would be kind enough to forward them.

Not long afterward she received an answer from Mr.
Delf, who enclosed a letter from James Nathan. The
letter stated quite simply that James was engaged to
marry someone else. She would not go to Germany, or
ever see him again. She could not bear just yet to recall
the stone wall and the little wood where he had led her—
his guitar, or his dog Josey, or a rose leaf from Shelley's
grave. There was too much pain in such remembrances.
She wished only that she might have borne a child. But
later on, she thought, perhaps she would be a worthy
object of love from one who would not disappoint or need
forbearance. Meanwhile, at least, there were no fetters on
her, no white veils between herself and the outer world.

There were ways of forgetfulness in the visits she paid
with the Springs to the notables of Edinburgh. For them
old Dr. Chalmers burst into indignant eloquence about
the Free Church and looked for all the world like a shepherd king while he raged on with his Scottish burr. For
them Dr. Andrew Combe left his invalid's chair to chat
for an hour or so about Mrs. Farnham's influence upon

the prisoners at Sing Sing. For them Dr. Samuel Brown expanded in his role of Paracelsus, speaking of the atomic theory and the mutual relations of God and man and nature.

Even De Quincey roused himself from his reveries to hold a *conversazione* with Margaret and her friends. He was a small, old man whose handsome face was marked by refinement, and he spoke with such deliberation and softness that Margaret forgot his plain, poor dress. He talked gently and pleasantly, and though he did not use the gorgeous style that she expected from the Opium Eater, his eloquence was subtle as the wind. His thoughts, like Wordsworth's, were of the past; he seemed a gentleman of urbanity, representing a day when men had time to do things more gracefully than now.

On September eighth they interrupted their visits for the short tour to the Highlands. After they had been carried in the boat to Rowardennan, Margaret's mind became the dwelling place of images from Sir Walter's *Lady of the Lake,* of purple hills and lochs and singing boatmen. Gaelic songs echoed in her ears while before her eyes reapers danced the Highland fling in a barn or the moon shone over Loch Earn, or a little boat was launched for Ellen's isle. Again Helen MacGregor lived; again Rob Roy unsheathed his sword.

Early one morning from the little inn at Rowardennan, Margaret and Marcus Spring began the ascent of Ben Lomond. Rebecca could walk only a few steps and hence remained at home with Eddie. Slowly they climbed the mountain on the clearest of days, stopping to look at the curving slopes below, and finally they reached the peak. Around and below were groups of hills purple with heather, among which the cold lakes gleamed. Peak beyond peak caught the shifting, lingering light of the late sun, while clouds gathered white upon the mountain top.

At about four o'clock they began the descent. Shortly afterward, the traces of the path became indistinct, there were no bridges over the springs, and Margaret remarked to her friend that she thought they had lost the way. Marcus left her to look for it and she stood still, waiting for his return. Soon he called, saying that he had found the path, and she followed in the direction of his voice. Somehow, she could not find him. She called, but there was no answer. She started to go down alone, but suddenly it seemed as though hills grew up before her whenever she had managed to climb down the slope of one. She sank to her knees in bog and climbed up again, seeking better crossing places. Twilight had come, and below she saw the lake and the inn of Rowardennan on the shore. If only she could get to the bottom of one high, heathery hill, she would be at the cottage before nightfall. She moved cautiously, clinging to the heather, trying to avoid the deep holes. By the time she reached the bottom, she was thoroughly weary. She must still cross the watercourse, and now, in her fatigue, it looked so deep in the dim twilight that she felt afraid. She threw down a stone, and the sound was so hollow she feared to jump. There was nothing to do but climb the hill again, but Margaret was too exhausted. Night had come. Below, a tiny light flickered. There was no sound but the rush of the waterfall and the sighing of the night wind. She drew her shawl closely about her and waited.

For two hours the stars glittered, but when the mist became heavy she saw nothing more, nothing but the visionary shapes that Ossian had dreamed of and that now rose from the gray mists. The grouse started in the heather. The moon rose to cast a dull silvery light. The hours turned into years. At last the little flies awoke from their bed amid the purple heather, and Margaret knew that day had come. She ascended the hill, crossed the torrent in the waterfall, and at about seven in the morning, drenched with mist and water, came upon the shepherds who had been searching for her all night long. They carried her to the inn, and there she rested from her night of fear and solitude.

The Scotsmen seemed closer to Margaret after her experience on Ben Lomond, for they were eager to exchange with her tales of hairbreadth escapes by flood and fell. She was almost sorry to return to Edinburgh, for had she not conquered the most majestic of hills, the deepest of the Scottish ravines?

There was time in the days at Edinburgh to visit Holyrood and to think, as she looked at the dull bloodstain and secret stair of the castle, of the sorrowful queen who had found so many champions once she was dead. There was time to write about Mary Stuart for Elizabeth Oakes Smith's edition of *The Mayflower,* and to send letters again for the *Tribune.* There was time to wonder what London would hold for her—whether one of those three days of the *wanderjahre* would be hers in the old gray city.

On the top of the stagecoach Margaret journeyed from Edinburgh to the island of Perth. Even in that fresh green country she observed such social inequalities that she could not but applaud the efforts of the Associationists to prevent those miseries in America. Through Birmingham they passed, and on to Glasgow, where the stamp of squalid degradation seemed even more appalling. The ills of poverty cried aloud and must be answered not in words, but acts. Margaret forgot the crowded, sunless cities at the Stirling inn, where she took up *The Scottish Chiefs* to read of lords and ladies gay. Late at night they reached Newcastle, and the next day descended into a coal mine to see the underground stables and narrow passages by the light of a tallow candle. Though Stratford was more hackneyed ground, Margaret found the

bare room where Shakespeare had been born more to her
taste and enjoyed handling the poker that Geoffrey
Crayon had used to such good purpose.

The first few days in London Margaret and the
Springs passed at Charing Cross on Trafalgar Square,
but later they moved into Morley's lodging house at 17
Warwick Street, Golden Square. From the little narrow
street she went to the offices of Brown, Shipley and Company to inquire for letters. There was news from home—
news mainly of Lloyd's infirmity. The *Anti-slavery Standard* had challenged Margaret's "aloofish thoughts" and
commonplace expressions, remarking that "those who are
elevated in a balloon by the aid of gas, are of course quite
conscious of soaring above the heads of their neighbors."
The Harbinger had rushed to her defense, lauding her
"disinterested advocacy of unpopular truth." In London
also Margaret saw Mr. Delf and on October twenty-fifth
she wrote a note of congratulation to James, giving the
final seal to a part of her life that belonged to another
world.

The London world seemed to Margaret a place of coal
smoke and fog, and John Bull a churlish clown with a
mug of beer in his hand or a man of honor prone nevertheless to solemn humbug. As at Perth and Glasgow
ruffianly, squalid misery walked the streets, walked next
to ladies in fine crinolines, walked even before the gates
of palaces.

Margaret was glad that in her round of sight-seeing
she had scarcely time to dress or sleep—and none at all
to think. The Murillos of the National Gallery flashed
before her eyes and the shining streaks of Turner's views
of sun and water. She sped through the galleries and the
British Museum along with a throng of nursery-maids
and men returned from work. In the rain at Hampton
Court she took shelter under the great yew trees; at the

Zoological Gardens she looked, with all the million, at the eagles and the lions. Soane's Museum was to her an old curiosity shop of jumbled treasures, sarcophaguses and manuscripts and the pictures of Hogarth. The cactuses and palms at Kew delighted, and the Reform Club in town amused her with its hierarchy of servants and cooks. On the Springs' wedding anniversary Margaret joined her companions for a Yankee version of John Gilpin's ride, going by coach through Cheapside and boarding the omnibus at the Flower-Pot. At the half-way house they took a carriage for the Bell at Edmonton, where they made their own fire and dined on tough meat and stale bread. In the evening there was English opera at the Old Drury or *The Patrician's Daughter* at Sadler's Wells, a play that seemed to Margaret a harbinger of the day when the noblest commoner would be the only noble possible in England.

In London, too, the notables remained at home for their American visitors. Margaret paid so many visits with the Springs that she felt driven from home to home as a renouncer who took from each the picture and the poetry. Joanna Baillie received her at her little retreat in Hampstead and Margaret found that the old lady still possessed the Roman strength which had dominated her series of plays delineating the passions of the mind. At Richmond, Miss Berry entertained the travelers, and for all her eighty years exhibited the same girlish charm and graceful manner that had delighted Horace Walpole so many years before. The elegant home of Mary and William Howitt was open to Margaret and the Springs and there they enjoyed many an hour of engaging conversation about *The People's Journal*. At Dr. Southwood Smith's they were interested not only in the philanthropist's plans of tenements for the working people, but in the skeleton of Jeremy Bentham which, fully dressed and stuffed out to a resemblance of life, leaned on a stout stick and sat as Dr. Smith's companion. After visiting one of her favorite poets of the people, Mr. Thom, Margaret was happy to meet his handsome son at a large party, where Goodwyn Barmby, an unclassed Unitarian minister in Suffolk, discussed his verses, *The Hand of Friendship*. Since W. J. Fox was present also, Margaret confined her talk to him, and while that gentleman ate sherbet and wondered when whist would be played, she conversed in a shining flow of words about Proclus and Plotinus. Margaret found that *Woman in the Nineteenth Century* had been read and prized sufficiently in London to open all doors to its author.

Another door, which Margaret had long wished to enter, was soon opened to her. Thomas Carlyle called at Golden Square to invite Emerson's friend to his home. Margaret looked at his blue eyes, at the thick thatch of dark, unkempt hair, the firm-set, deeply lined mouth, above all at the massive chin, and felt that here, too, was a face set in granite, but at least, unlike Emerson, Carlyle could laugh, openly and heartily. With his Scottish burr he sang his great full sentences, as if he were reciting the stanzas of a ballad, and Margaret listened while he roared on about a farmer who read Emerson's essays on Sundays, or the fanatics of England, or *Woman in the Nineteenth Century*, and the miscellanies. Now and then he gave Margaret a brief opportunity to free her lungs with mention of a laudatory criticism of her *Papers on Literature and Art* that had appeared in *The Democratic Review*, but soon he took up the cudgel of conversation again, giving her the news of the times. Naturally the Springs had found Wimpole Street deserted, for Elizabeth Barrett had eloped with Robert Browning and gone off to Italy. Tennyson was out of town, but Carlyle's house on Cheyne Row would be open to Margaret and the Springs for a dinner party.

Before the visit to Cheyne Row Margaret carefully

arranged her hair, and put on her lilac silk dress, trimmed with black lace. She arrived at Chelsea with the Springs in time for six o'clock dinner. While the maid served the soup, Margaret took time to glance about her at the company. Mrs. Carlyle, though neither plain nor beautiful, lent a vivacity to the table, while her dark eyes glittered from one to another, and her tall, slender form settled gracefully in her chair. George Lewes, seated near by, bubbled over with French flippancy and sparkled in a shallow manner about a life of Goethe he was preparing. Margaret might have replied more energetically to his irreligious sallies, had she not been so completely engrossed by still another visitor to Chelsea. By the time the fish had been served, she had studied every detail of Joseph Mazzini's long oval face, his olive complexion and delicate features, his fine forehead, his dark, piercing eyes. In his black, threadbare suit he seemed to mourn his country's lost cause, but when Margaret looked at his eyes, she knew there was hope in them. Over the meat and pudding they chatted about *The Daily News* that Charles Dickens had edited for a month, or Costa's programs at the London Philharmonic, while Carlyle pushed his chin out and, his eyes glancing like a falcon's, discussed Petrarch and Laura in the manner of a Teufelsdröckh vulture.

After dinner Mazzini drew a black cigar from his pocket and sat on the edge of his chair, wreathed in smoke, his doeskin boots oozing London mud on the carpet. Carlyle stood before him, a gaunt figure in his long smoke-colored coat, a clay pipe in his hand. Then Margaret listened. She listened to Mazzini's burning words of progress, and to Carlyle's scornful ragings about rose-water imbecilities. After Carlyle's thunder about the ignorant, blind, and vicious people—chiels and fools—she waited for Mazzini's lightning strokes about Young

Italy. The sad, grave exile had a curious way of speaking, with his "upon *my* honor," and his *"my dear,"* and his helpless *"what shall I say?"* He had his say none the less, and for all Carlyle's storming about Italian democracies and paper formulas, Mazzini was eloquent in the cause of revolution, lyrical in the name of progress. Mrs. Carlyle had no chance to speak at all, save with her black eyes, and Margaret seemed to have no wish to speak. Carlyle's volleys came too quickly to give her breathing space. Surely, she thought, his seal holding a griffin with the word *Humilitate* belied the hand of him who pressed it. Her host boomed on, even when he gave Margaret a note to Robert Browning, even when Mrs. Carlyle escorted the guests to the hall, but above the thunderclaps of his voice, Margaret carried in her mind the lightning flashes of Mazzini's burning eyes.

After several vain attempts to arrange an appointment Joseph Mazzini finally came to Golden Square with Harro Harring. With what lost cause had the Scandinavian poet not allied himself? Margaret was glad to greet him again, now as a member of Mazzini's Young Italy. She had given him a note to introduce him to Emerson, saying that he would tell all Concord of his Scandinavian runes. But the author of *Dolores* today forgot his toiling gods and heroes, and Margaret sat quite still in her chair, for both preferred to hear the exile speak of his home.

Mazzini held his cigar between his thin fingers, and, leaning forward, his black eyes flashing upon each, began. He told them how he had first studied the French newspapers when he found a bundle of them behind the books in his father's library. He told them how, at Marseilles, he had appealed to the youth of Italy to form a homeland, united, free from foreign rule or native tyranny, republican—as the French republic had been—Christian, but untrammeled by the Catholic theocracy. He told them of the *Giovine Italia,* and of the aid that Prince Belgiojoso had given him. His eyes darkened as he spoke of the Bandiera brothers who had been executed for their revolutionary attempts at Calabria. Between puffs at his cigar he spoke of Gioberti's *Primato,* in which the Turin priest argued, from his exile in Brussels, for an idealized Papacy.

"The moral man," he said softly, "cannot be sundered from the practical man. *Ernst ist das leben.*"
To Margaret's mind, he conveyed his own visions of a church of the future, and a state of free men, a holy alliance that had grown strong in his dreams.

When Margaret asked him of his life in exile, Mazzini told her of his home in King's Road, where cows grazed outside the gate, of his housekeeper, "waif" Susan, of the London climate that disagreed with him, and of his weekly dinners at Cheyne Row. He spoke bitterly of the violation of his correspondence two years before, but gently added that *The People's Journal* gave signs of fairer times in England now. His eyes glowed when he said that one day he would be able to return to Italy, with his canaries, and his Newfoundland dog, and all his hopes. He wished, he remarked, turning to Margaret, that he could go with her now in disguise.

Before he left, he invited Margaret to speak at the Free School for Italian Boys that he had started in London, saying that the Toynbees, William Shaen, and Harriet Martineau had supported him in his efforts to redeem the poor boys whom he had found selling images or grinding organs on the streets. Then the slender, black-clothed form rose from the chair, and he, with Harro Harring, was gone.

Shortly before Margaret left for Paris, she accepted Mazzini's invitation to the school at 5 Greville Street.

She entered the crowded room, glancing at the banners inscribed with the word, *Speranza,* that draped the walls and platform, at the youths in whose eyes an Italian fire burned. Prizes and bouquets were distributed, and speeches delivered by Mazzini, Pistrucci, Mariotti. Margaret rose to speak to the Italian refugees in English about the schools in her own country. Later they adjourned to another room, where the boys enjoyed a supper of fish, macaroni, and ale, and Margaret discussed with Mazzini his Sunday lectures to the boys on History, Morals, and Astronomy. William Shaen looked at her with frank eyes and resolutely told her how the boys had been exploited by their employers until he had at last brought the offenders to court. Finally, a lusty chorus of two hundred voices cheered everybody, and two hundred pairs of black eyes danced. Mazzini's sad face lighted up, and he smiled, glancing at the banner that fluttered with its brave token, *Speranza.*

Before leaving London, Margaret bade her farewells to Mazzini and the Carlyles, gave Mr. Delf a note of introduction to John Dwight, whom he expected to see in America, and, certain that she would return to London, took passage with the Springs for Paris. One of the three days of the *wanderjahre* was hers—the day that Mazzini had come, sitting on the edge of his chair, a mournful figure in black, whose eyes burned with visions of the future. Perhaps Paris too would yield another of the shining days.

The Springs engaged a suite of apartments at the Hotel Rougemont, Boulevard Poissonière. Margaret found her own small room quite to her taste, with its thick, flowered carpet and marble slabs. Above the fireplace was the French clock with its image of Cupid, and over the windows hung rich curtains. The room seemed to set the tone of a Paris of wax lights and mirrors, shrugs and wreathed smiles. Later on, at the Grand Hotel de Paris on the Rue Richelieu or the lodgings at 23 Allée d'Antin, the atmosphere of the Paris interiors was varied only slightly, and in every room Margaret's little oval pastille of Faust and Gretchen looked down from the mantel.

The outer world was different from this region of bright wood fires and vivacious ejaculations. Bad weather pursued Margaret through Paris, while an oily, tenacious mud made walking almost impossible, especially for Rebecca Spring. On the streets, Margaret encountered the glassy stares of men, half military, half dandy, who smoked bad cigars perpetually. Famine crept through the boulevards of Paris, and though it stalked less openly than in London or Liverpool, she sensed that the poor people suffered heavily during the winter. The signs of hunger might be suppressed, but the fact could not. It appeared even in the sham procession of the Fat Ox. The need of radical measures of reform was felt, and Margaret was glad that the propaganda of Fourier seemed to have an increasing influence.

She could not escape the mud or the hungry eyes even when she left her charming apartments merely to inquire for news at Galignani's. She was interested to learn, especially now, when Fourierist doctrine needed more support than ever, that a debate on its merits had been started between Greeley in the *Tribune* and Raymond in *The Courier and Enquirer*. Margaret found too that Poe's account of her work had appeared as a section of the "Literati" in *Godey's Lady's Book,* and the author had disclaimed responsibility for the condemnatory review of *Woman in the Nineteenth Century* that had been issued in the *Broadway Journal.* As for Poe, he found the book one which few women in the country could have written and no woman in the country would have published with the exception of Miss Fuller. Margaret was glad that Poe had apparently written the account before her little journey to Fordham. From her own letters Margaret gathered that her experience on Ben Lomond was being discussed in New York as a blessed mishap for an authoress. There was more disturbing news from James Nathan, who thanked Margaret for her note of congratulation and remarked that at the beginning of their friendship his anxiety to be clearly understood caused her much insult and himself much pain. Margaret was glad to turn to less personal matters and find that her essay on American Literature had been translated into French and published in the *Revue Indépendante*. Its reception counteracted the charges of mysticism, pedantry, and bombast with which *The Athenaeum* assailed her *Papers on Literature and Art*. It was more to Margaret's liking to turn from the work she had accomplished in the past to that which she hoped to achieve in the future, and she was indeed glad when Mazzini invited her to write a few of her impressions for *The People's Journal,* and thus to aid him raise the world from sterile Benthamism to the cult of the ideal.

By the time Margaret had received all this news, the French clock had ticked away many an hour, many a week. Time passed so quickly that there were scarcely enough days for her study of the French language, which she persisted in speaking like an Italian, for her letters to the *Tribune,* above all for her sight-seeing. After the Paris of wax candles and mirrors, after the Paris of mud and misery, it was a city of galleries and academies, museums and theatres that made a kaleidoscope of images in Margaret's mind. There was no need of analysis to grasp the thought of the Rembrandt at the Louvre, while the modern French paintings of nobles and generals mounted on excellent steeds, or of streams of blood and ghastly contortions hung before her in all the galleries. Margaret's mind became a storehouse of pictures and botanical models in wax, as she turned from one museum to another. When she was refused admittance to the Sorbonne to hear Leverrier (*Que voulez-vous, madame, c'est la règle.*) she passed an hour at the Cluny, looking at a jeweled dagger and the various Adorations of the Magi. At the Chamber of Deputies she saw and touched the Rousseau manuscripts, written on fine white paper and tied with ribbon. If Napoleon's tomb was not open to visitors, there was still another world for determined sight-seers in the crèches where poor women left their children while they worked, or the School for Idiots near Paris where the boys stood in a circle to dance or recite or sing. The evening schools of the Frères Chrétiens reminded Margaret of Mazzini's establishment on Greville Street, for there too errand boys and hardhanded porters studied and copied good models.

There was still another Paris that lived for Margaret in the evenings when Rachel played Phèdre with all the force of tragic art, or when Rose Cheny made pretty sentimentalities out of Clarissa Harlowe or *Le Protégé sans le Savoir.* If Duprez was a disappointment in *The Bride of Lammermoor, Don Giovanni* restored Margaret's love of the opera, and incidentally convinced her still further of the influence of mind over matter. She had taken ether to have a tooth drawn, and while the old dentist in his nightcap and dressing gown handled the tube and the instruments, she had wandered off in Oriental gardens among alleys of trees. Later on, however, the neuralgic pain returned, the taste of ether lingered, and it was not until Margaret went to hear *Don Giovanni* that her nerves were soothed by the music. Dr. Leger, she knew, would have understood this influence.

Two events of the time offered Margaret a glimpse

into still another Paris world. There was the ball at the
Tuileries celebrating the Spanish marriage, and Margaret
wandered among the throng of gracious French women
who made a flower garden out of the brilliantly lighted
apartments. While the fiddles played gayly, she saw
Leverrier dressed in his costume of the Academician,
looking as though he had lost the planet Neptune instead
of found it. When time came for the Dumas Trial, Margaret sent a message to Major Benjamin Poore asking
his help in gaining admission to court. She went early,
eager to hear Dumas defend his own case against the
editors who had sued him for evading his engagements,
but there was such a crowd that she saw nothing but endless staircases, dreary vestibules and gendarmes. The
treasures of the past, Margaret observed, might be offered most generously to the stranger in Paris, but when
anything of current interest happened, the French themselves took immediate possession of the ground.

There was many a notable, however, who did open his
door to Margaret, and in her brown merino dress and
blue shawl embroidered with white, her velvet bonnet and
muff, she entered a drawing room to hear Neukomm play
or a study to hear Lamennais speak with Béranger. If
the one seemed suffering and pale, and the other elderly
and citizen-looking, she nevertheless took delight in being
in the presence of the apostle of democracy and the great
French lyrist. Adam Mickiewicz gave her his time also,
and Margaret rejoiced to listen to one whose life was
part of the history of Poland and of France.

She took particular care in adjusting her velvet bonnet
for a visit to the Place d'Orléans. Though George Sand
had not answered Margaret's letter, she determined not
to leave Paris without a sight of the author of *Consuelo*.
Had not her review of the work in the *Tribune* entitled
her to a glimpse of the lady of the salon? A servant

dressed in a peasant's costume admitted her to the handsome modern house. Margaret threw her blue shawl back over her shoulders, sat down in the anteroom, and waited to be announced. In a few moments the servant returned, saying, "Madame says she does not know you." "Ask her," Margaret persisted, "if she has not received a letter from me." As she spoke, the door opened, and Madame Sand appeared. She stood looking at Margaret an instant. Their eyes met. The doorway made a frame for her large, well-formed figure, and Margaret saw at a glance her dark violet silk dress, and the black mantle on her shoulders, her beautiful hair dressed with exquisite taste, the strong, masculine mouth, the fine eyes. She seemed an exotic, even in Paris, with her olive complexion and Spanish air. Then she spoke, *"C'est vous,"* and held out her hand.

Margaret followed Madame Sand into her little study, and they sat together, talking of the letter that Margaret had written. Madame Sand explained the servant's mistake in announcing Miss Fuller as Mademoiselle Salère, and then mentioned her own realization that it might be *la dame Américaine*. She was busy, she said, preparing copy for the printer, but she would seize the present moment to speak with her visitor. Between puffs at her little cigarette, she spoke of the need of awakening ideal thoughts in the hearts of the proletarians. Had she not insisted upon that dream in *Consuelo,* in *Mauprat*? She spoke of Mickiewicz, who was carried to exaltation by his patriotism, of Mazzini and *The People's Journal.* God, she said, would work miracles in the church of the poor. It was more than a sect that the Parisians were forming; it was a religion that they hoped to proclaim. And as she spoke Margaret knew that like her work, her life needed no defense, since she had bravely acted out her nature. On a mountain top she had followed Cybele, the great goddess, the great mother. If there was something of the Bacchante in her, it needed only to be understood. From every wine press she had drawn rich drops.

Madame Sand invited Margaret later to her salon, and there, she saw the gentlemen lolling on cushions, smoking cigarettes, while Madame Sand sat like a queen in their midst, talking now to her daughter, now making some remark about her fantasy, *Tévérino,* to the entire circle. It was a far cry from Waverley Place, this strange home on the Place d'Orléans, and George Sand a nobler woman than Anne Lynch. She knew how to prize love's beauty, and if she had left a stupid, brutal husband, that act also needed no condoning. If she found delight in the love of Chopin, who could deny her right? She took rank in society like a man, and Margaret esteemed her for her courage, admired her for her nobility. When Margaret was invited to accompany Sturling, one of Chopin's students, to the master's room for a lesson, she eagerly accepted, and the frail man played for her with exquisite genius, filling the pearl-gray chamber with gentle echoes and subtle harmonies.

So much of Paris now was hers, the treasures of its galleries, its opera, its theatre, its hunger, its gaiety. The wax lights and shrugs, the vivid talk, the fleeting gestures were part of her life now, for all this she had condensed into a few months while the French clock on the mantel ticked on. There was time only to search in the shops for an engraving of Lamennais that would be as good as Charpentier's picture of George Sand. There were moments to snatch for a letter to Elizabeth Hoar about the visit to the Place d'Orléans or for a note to Emerson about Paris. She would return, she hoped, and one day write longer sketches about Béranger, and Lamennais, and Madame Sand.

She felt somehow that one whose aid she needed existed and was near her, but the time drew on for her to depart and they had not met. At least she had known George Sand, and that encounter surely made one of the three days of the *wanderjahre*. Mazzini, Sand, and who would bring the third of the immortal days? Perhaps in Italy, where Pope Pius the Ninth was kindling hope in hearts that longed for liberty, perhaps there the third day would be hers. As if to assure her, the sun at last shone bright and warm on February twenty-fifth, and Margaret left with the Springs for the Italy that had already grown up in her mind.

The journey from Paris to Naples was swift and varied. At Châlons Margaret and the Springs took the boat and reaching Lyons the same afternoon, sallied forth to visit the weavers' garrets. On one side the family had their looms, close to the door the stoves for cooking; the beds were shelves near the ceiling to which the weavers climbed on ladders. Turning from the garrets, Margaret thought bitterly, "And there are those who dare to say that such a state of things is well enough." On the steamboat she passed the time reading a pamphlet by a Lyons physician on the establishment of crèches. At Avignon the next day she varied her sight-seeing by wading through the snow on the banks of the Rhone to Laura's tomb. So poetry followed prose; after the stark misery of the living, the snow-covered grave of Petrarch's beloved.

On they journeyed from Arles to Marseilles and then by steamer voyaged on to Genoa. There Margaret took time to visit Mazzini's mother, who showed her around the house and led her to the balcony of her son's study. They chatted warmly of his school and his work and his hopes for Italy. Then Margaret plucked two leaves of the scented verbena that grew on the window of his library and pressed them in an album to send to the exile.

With the good wishes of Mazzini's mother she departed from Genoa and traveled on to Leghorn and Naples.

At last Margaret knew that she had found her Italy, that all the parade of brilliant colors that had revolved in her mind since she had first studied the Italian tongue, flashed living now before her. The women with their deep olive skins and black hair twisted and folded in heavy braids passed along the high-walled narrow lanes, decked in bright ribbons and gaudy bodices and glittering trinkets. The indolent aloe hung over the windows; orange and lemon trees gleamed in the sun; the leaves of the fig were freshly green. Troops of maidens clad in white walked with lighted tapers to sprinkle bay leaves on the streets or hang garlands on the altar of their church. Margaret warmed to the arch eyes that sparkled, to the sun that glowed upon the bay, to the rich and lilting voices of the Neapolitans. Surely if she had found *her Italy* in Naples, she would find *her country* in Rome. Eagerly she traveled on with the Springs, to the city that already lived in her mind, to Rome, the capital of the world, the Eternal City.

Up the dark stone staircase of her apartment on the Corso Margaret climbed with her friends, lighting her way with a coil of wax taper. From her window she could hear the twang of a guitar, laughter, and the gay talk of artists who, in velvet paletots and dusty boots walked along the narrow Corso with their camp stools and umbrellas. But Margaret could not long remain content seated at her window. The color, the warmth, the sounds of Rome waited below; she had but to turn west and follow any crooked street between high houses, to claim them for her own.

What a crowded city it seemed to her as she walked along the narrow ways. A woman brushed near her, and Margaret had a glimpse of her rich black knotted hair and low broad forehead. Wherever she turned there were the black figures of ecclesiastics, while the Capuchin friars in their brown woollen robes contrasted sombrely with the bareheaded damsels who strolled through the streets with silver stilettos thrust through their glossy hair. She turned to look at a Roman from *Trastevere,* his old cloak drawn about him like a toga as he wandered between the Tiber and the Janiculan hill. Near Santa Maria della Rotunda Margaret stopped to look at the vendors' tables on which their wares lay among garlands of laurel. The fire flickered under the pans while an old woman roasted her chestnuts; there was a cobbler working in his stall; beyond, a *segretario.* A man with a large hen in one hand passed by her shouting *"una bella femina!"* Artists in jaunty caps and velvet coats ambled along looking for "Il Cristo" or "Diavoli." Surely, Margaret thought, they had no need to look farther for a subject than that contadina from the Campagna in her scarlet gown or that white-bearded beggar beyond rapping his chin and twirling his hands before his mouth. How many beggars there were, rattling their little leaden boxes for a *bajocco!* Near the Piazza di Spagna was Beppo, the king of the beggars, whom Margaret recognized from the description in Andersen's *Improvisatore. "Buon giorno!"* he cried, as he sat with his withered legs crossed under him.

One could hardly hear him, for there were so many other street cries mingling with the noise of the green diligences and the scarlet carriages of the Cardinals. *"Un pauolo, un pauolo!"* filled the air, while the vendors stood at the street corners exhibiting their buttons and handkerchiefs, raising their arms and quivering their fingers over their heads. Hackney coaches and the chariots of princes rattled and flashed through the streets and Margaret hurried on, eager for yet another taste of Rome.

How many walks and drives there were to make her

dream of the city a reality. From the heights of the Janiculum on the terrace in front of San Pietro in Montorio, Rome lay before her. The yellow Tiber rolled beneath her feet, broken by dark masses of green pine and cypress or by shining cupolas and domes. From the Porta del Popolo it was an exciting walk along the Corso, and from there the Strada di Condotti brought Margaret to the Piazza di Spagna. She glanced at the hotels, Monaldini's bookstore, the print shops, stopped before the jewelry and mosaic establishments, passed on to Pakenham and Hooker's bank. From there it was but a short turn to Monte Pincio with its view of the Villa Borghese, the sea, and the city. Everywhere she saw the red earthen roofs, the ashen gray buildings that blended with the ground tone, the towers, obelisks and belfries that varied the sky line. The courtyards and ruins, the fountains and arches threw their magic spell upon her while the Borghese gardens flowered and two young monks passed leisurely along. Merry girls skipped by as she turned to look at the thick yellow Tiber and the black stone pillars of an old bridge. Along with urchins and idlers she wandered near the Fountain of Trevi. The warmth and color of the city grew in her heart.

Often in the evenings, she wandered amid the old walls and columns, or sat by the fountains in the Piazza del Popolo. The bas-reliefs and Obelisk, the terraces and villas lay about her, while the gate was crowded with dazzling equipages and water poured from the mouth of the stone lion. On Sunday mornings the English marched out of the gate, their Bibles under their arms, to their shrine outside the Porta del Popolo.

Many a Bible was carried, and many a bell tolled the Romans to church, for Easter was at hand and the cardinals rolled abroad in their gay carriages. In the Piazza di S. Pietro there was music and all Rome was on its knees.

Margaret saw the pomps of Holy Week at St. Peter's, saw its dome rising in the air, saw the lofty colonnade, and the cardinals in lace and scarlet. With the peasant girls in their white scarfs and the rustics in their tight stockings and steeple-hats, she too heard the ringing of bells, saw the illumination of the dome, and entered the Cathedral. Margaret watched while the worshippers kissed the well-worn toe beneath the High Altar; she looked down the long aisle and saw the bronze columns, the marbles, the lamps. There were the feather fans and triple crown and white robes of Pope Pius. How graceful and noble he looked; surely he was one who had set his heart upon doing good for mankind.

At the Sistine Chapel Margaret heard the *Miserere,* sitting next to Ottilia, Goethe's daughter-in-law. The magnificent boxes were hung with velvet and golden draperies; the papal Swiss guards stood in their bright array, the plumes of the officers' helmets waving above their light armor. The aged cardinals entered in their velvet cloaks with their white ermine capes; the Holy Father ascended his throne, in his purple mantle and silver tiara. The bishops swung the vessels of incense around them; the garments of Michelangelo's God fluttered above.

How strange it was, after Margaret's taste of the rich and dazzling city, after seeing the purple and scarlet robes of the Church, to hear that in New York ladies were wearing calashes. What a far cry from the crowded Corso with its cries of *un pauolo, un bajocco,* was the letter from Emerson telling of his lecture on Eloquence in Boston. After the Corso crowded with contadinas and *Trasteverines,* Elizabeth Peabody's home, where Anna Ward and Sarah Clarke had met after the speech, seemed farther than three thousand miles away. Thoreau's book, *A Week on the Concord and Merrimack Rivers,* was finished; he had given an account of his housekeeping at Walden Pond in the form of a lecture at the Concord Lyceum. Walden Pond—how different were the waters of the Tiber that rolled now before Margaret. Here, in a later letter, which she found at her banker's, Torlonia, was news of another journal that Emerson was planning. But Margaret did not care to dream the same dream over, especially now that an unexplored world lay about her. There was other news too, of Abraham Fuller's death, but apparently Margaret's inheritance would be small since there were so many to divide it.

The letters required answers, and there were others to be written also. While the carriages rumbled below, and dark-haired Roman women strolled along the narrow street, Margaret sat in her room on the Corso writing to Mrs. Howitt about her lack of time for preparing a memoir of George Sand, to Evert Duyckinck about Griswold's attack on her judgment of *Witchcraft,* to the *Tribune* about the illuminations of the Corso and the procession that streamed to the Quirinal with Bengal fires, about Michelangelo's Moses which had gone beyond even her hopes.

After she had paid her respects to the painters of old, Margaret often pased an hour at the studios of the American artists who had come to study the color and outline of Rome. In the spacious room that Thomas Hicks had rented on the Via Margutta she joined the loungers and youths on the grand tour who watched the artist standing before a canvas of Italia at Rome, or adding a touch to his Italian girl holding a mandolin. Sometimes Luther Terry came in to discuss the pigments of his own Fisher Boy, and Margaret listened while the painters exchanged ideas on coloring, or discussed the symposia at Hicks' rooms that had been enlivened by tea and spiced wine.

Christopher Cranch had come to Rome with his wife and George Curtis, and Margaret was happy to greet again her friends of Brook Farm days. Cranch had not changed; he was the same delightful young man of the curly dark hair and baritone voice, who brimmed over now with joy in his experiences at Rome, the Colosseum in the moonlight, the view from his rooms at Mme. Bordoni's house, his baby boy, the tomatoes and rice that his wife cooked on her little stove. After Margaret had chatted of her travels in England and France, he would seize his flute to play Schubert's songs, or speak of the night school he had joined, where students painted in water colors from costumed models. George Curtis was frequently seen at Mme. Bordoni's and he too reminisced with Margaret about Concord and Brook Farm, or spoke of the palms and orange trees that he had seen from a balcony at the Vatican.

Thomas Crawford had just completed a sculpture of his wife, Julia Ward's sister, and Margaret was interested in visiting his large studios on the Piazza Barberini. She watched with amazement while he pitched his clay together with a trowel, struck it first with his right hand and then with his left, turned it thrice upon its pedestal—and behold, a portrait bust! His thick chestnut hair was sprinkled with marble dust and with his modeling tool in his hand he stood before a head of clay upon which light fell from a candle fastened in his hat. Margaret enjoyed hearing him speak of Thorwaldsen, who had first welcomed him to Rome, of his statue of Orpheus, of the Pincian Mount, where he had stood so often watching the sun bid good night to Rome.

It was not long, however, before Margaret stopped passing an hour of the forenoon at the studios of her compatriots, not long, indeed, before she altogether ceased cultivating the society of Americans, for on the

evening of May thirteenth, she had met a young Italian
who introduced himself as Giovanni Angelo Ossoli. Holy
Thursday fell on May thirteenth, and even Mrs. Spring,
despite her delicate health, was bent upon hearing vespers
at St. Peter's to celebrate Christ's ascension. Margaret
and her friends entered the crowded vestibule and listened to the antiphonal choruses of the two great choirs
in different parts of the nave. Margaret later decided that
she would enjoy wandering alone among the different
chapels and suggested to the Springs that they meet her
afterward at an assigned place in the Church. When the
crowd dispersed, and Margaret had had her fill of images
and relics, she returned to the designated spot, but could
not find her friends. She walked about, raising her lorgnette to examine each group, but the Springs were nowhere in sight. Presently a young Italian approached her
and begged to be of assistance. Together they wandered
through the Church looking for the Springs, but since it
had become quite late, Margaret decided to go into the
Piazza to find a carriage. There they found that all the
diligences had been taken, and Margaret walked from the
Vatican to the Corso with the stranger.

It was a long journey by foot, and Margaret had time
to study the appearance of her escort. He seemed to her
very young, probably in his late twenties, and with his
tall, slender figure, blue-black hair, dark eyes and mus-
tache was an admirable representative of Italian grace.
Yet there seemed a melancholy expression about his eyes.
She answered his courteous remarks in her best Italian.
Then her glance shifted to a little scar on his face, and
laughingly he told her that it had been caused by a jealous
dog who had bitten him when his mother caressed him as
an infant. It was a blemish, he said, that he prized very
highly, for his mother had died when he was a baby.

Eagerly, he continued, telling Margaret of himself and

his family. She did not know why he placed these confidences in her, but she found it her natural role to act again the mother confessor. As they passed the Mausoleo di Adriano, almost deserted now in the quiet night, he spoke to her in Italian—for he said he knew no English—of his invalid father, who was the head of a Rione. His family, he admitted, was a noble one, though now impoverished, and they lived in the parish of Saint Marcellus. He pointed with his bamboo stick in the direction of the Villa Santucci, saying that it had been the property of his grandmother, who had given it to Santucci, her confessor and his own godfather. He himself, he went on, had no great respect for the Church, since an old priest had neglected his education and he knew no foreign language save a little French, and was quite ignorant of book learning. As they approached the Strada di Ripetta, passing a vendor going home with his wares and a man in short leather breeches twanging the strings of a guitar, he continued his story. He was very fond of his sister Angela, he said, but as for the others, he was the black sheep of the family. His three brothers, Giuseppe, Ottavio, and Alessandro, were in the papal service, one a secretary of the Privy Chamber and two in the Guardia Nobile. He himself could not follow such a career, for he had caught the principles of liberalism and hoped only for a way to free Rome from the shackles of tyranny. They had passed Bertini's café on the Corso and were near Margaret's apartment. She looked up at his deep-set eyes below the thick brows. Suddenly, it seemed as if Mazzini had spoken, and she realized that at last there was a point of contact between herself and this strange Italian. He was young and charming, but he could not speak her language, knew nothing of books which had for so long been her life, but if he hoped as she did for the future of Italy, perhaps they had a common language after all. Outside of that, surely his world was far removed from hers. He bowed farewell graciously and Margaret dismissed the encounter from her thoughts.

Giovanni Ossoli himself was not so easily dismissed. It was as if at last he had found one who could be companion to his thoughts, repository of his confessions. He called at Margaret's apartment on the Corso and invited her to see old Rome with him. Together they visited Monte Cavallo and as Ossoli pointed out the equestrian statues in the square and the streets that stopped short against a dead wall, Margaret found it pleasant to share her joy in Rome with one who knew the city so well. Together they wandered past Trajan's column to the silent Forum and the arch of Septimus Severus, where beggars now lay asleep, wrapped in their large cloaks. The tall columns cast long shadows as they walked through the spectral, ancient city. Together they heard owls hooting in the Colosseum by moonlight and saw its flattened arches overgrown with weeds.

This was a fallen capital, a dead city haunted by the past through which they wandered. But when they spoke, it was of a city that would rise anew in future triumph. While Ossoli pointed with the bamboo stick he liked to carry, to the Teatro Aliberto, or the Caffè Lepre, where Margaret's American artist friends enjoyed macaroni and cignale, he told her of the signs of a newer Rome, of the International League that Mazzini had established as a rallying point for democracy and Italian unity. As they passed the Casa del Scimia he spoke of the demonstration in Florence that had followed Cobden's visit. Reform was in the air, and though they strolled through a dead city of palaces with whitewashed colonnades and statues, the Torlonia, the Borghese, the Barberini, a magic wand would raise the city to life again. The Pope, Margaret agreed, had a definite tendency to reform, but she wondered whether that would be sufficient to affect importantly the state of things in Italy. Ossoli reassured her. If help did not come from the Pope it would come from the people. At his words, Margaret saw the future dawning.

Her own future seemed now less clear than ever. As the days passed she realized that the stranger whom she had met so casually was becoming a very thoughtful, a very close companion. He might lack vivacity and enthusiasm, but Margaret found that his excellent practical sense made up for those deficiencies. His sense of duty was so unfailing that it put most enthusiasts to shame. Who could resist his sweet temper, his delicacy in trifles. If he could not speculate about books his unselfishness and strength of character balanced his intellectual failings. After his first confidences to Margaret he seemed reserved, and longed to hear her speak. He himself said little, except about the future of Italy. When he loved strongly he could not speak, and Margaret perceived gradually that he had begun to love her with delicate tenderness. To Emerson he would be nothing, but to herself, she was not sure. After Samuel Ward and James Nathan, after the fire of too much bitter loving, it would be balm to be loved. At any rate it was comforting to walk abroad with a handsome young Italian who took such pains to lead her through the narrow streets so gallantly, or take her to just the right *trattoria*. Besides there was something warm and gentle in his nature to which she responded. There had been chills enough in the world, rebukes enough and to spare. Here was one who loved her, and who told her so, openly and with no fear lest he be misunderstood. Had she not, she recalled smilingly, always longed for a great Italian name to follow Margaretta? Yet there was nothing in Giovanni Ossoli that would make him her companion for life. There was

too much in her own life that he could never understand,
Cherry Street in Cambridgeport, Miss Prescott's School
for Girls, Alcott, and Emerson, and Greeley. Surely these
were a world apart from the life he offered her now. Was
there room for two lives in her own? Margaret thought
not. At least she needed time to consider. Soon the
Springs would return to America, and Margaret decided
to say her good-byes now and take another short tour by
herself in the summer, to enjoy the north of Italy and to
think quietly and serenely of one Italian who had offered
her his love.

In the early summer Margaret found Florence a mass
of flowers, and seeing the magnolias and jasmines in full
bloom, thought often of her mother and her garden.
From her room in the Casa Green on the Via La Apol-
lonia she went forth to visit the massive Palazzo Pitti,
the cypress-shaded Church of San Miniato, the Duomo.
New buildings had been erected on many a street and
everywhere smart omnibuses drove over the town. Yet
when she thought of Rome it was with the pain of Tan-
talus, for sometimes Florence, for all its summer blooms,
seemed lonely.

Margaret had friends there, however, for she introduced herself to the Marchioness Visconti Arconati, a
highbred lady from Milan, who helped her cultivate
spoken Italian. Margaret wished to master the tongue,
for otherwise she knew she could never be part of the
Italian world, nor could she speak fluently with Giovanni
Ossoli, who knew no English. With the Marchioness she
walked about beyond the Porta Romana, discussing in
Italian Verdi's new opera, *Macbeth,* or the agitation of
Tuscany that followed the assassination of a supposed
Austrian spy in Ferrara. All things, she said, seemed to
announce that an important change was inevitable.

Sometimes Margaret walked along the Piazza Sta.

Trinita, where the Caffè Donez sent forth fumes of coffee, hot punch, and cigars. She recalled the Lepre in Rome, for the Caffè Donez also catered to the artists. In Florence Margaret visited the studios of the American sculptors, and passed many an interesting hour opposite the Casa del Bello, where Hiram Powers welcomed her in his paper cap, linen blouse, and white apron. As he added a touch to his boy holding a shell he told Margaret of the Inferno he had modeled out of wax, or his portrait bust of Mr. Farrar, or Watson's clock factory where he had worked. His great black eyes burned beneath his impending brow as he beckoned Margaret to a secret room where he kept his tools and the machines he had invented. As he shuffled about in his slippers, his sculptor's cap tilted on the side of his head, he exhibited to the visitor his Greek Slave, his Eve, and the statue of Calhoun, at the same time making disparaging remarks in his Yankee twang about the work of all other sculptors.

Margaret could not agree with him, for when, armed with a note of introduction from Mrs. George Calvert, she visited the studio of Horatio Greenough on the Piazza Maria Antonia she found him seated beside a platform contemplating an unfinished model of David which promised high beauty. He too was glad to welcome his compatriot and told her of the wooden daggers he had carved as a youth or the pistol he had inlaid with flowers. Displaying his chanting cherubs and bas-reliefs he spoke to Margaret of his stonecutter's creed that embraced the three glories of beauty, action, and character. He reminisced with his visitor about George Emerson, who had fitted him for Harvard, and smilingly listened while Margaret told him that her father used to keep locks of his sister's hair in his desk.

Joseph Mozier was also to be seen at Florence, and Margaret was interested to learn that the sculptor had left his dry goods business in New York to follow the career of an artist abroad. He had, she learned, quarreled notoriously with Crawford when that sculptor had pointed out the impossible attitude of Mozier's Pocahontas. He still looked the shopkeeper, and seemed to display more of the characteristics of clay than of pure marble. He spoke shrewdly, running down the work of his fellow sculptors more maliciously than Powers had done, and seemed ready for any gossip, provided it was sufficiently meretricious.

Margaret felt little regret in leaving her artist friends, and was eager to be off for another short tour among the lakes and hills of northern Italy. She journeyed via Bologna to Venice and though she was ill the first week, she enjoyed watching the gondolas from her room at the Europa and liked to mark her window with a cross on the letterhead of the hotel. When she felt better, Margaret found Venice, with its canals and galleries and churches, a dream of enchantment where art and life were one. The work of Giorgione delighted her, and the view of the fete given by the Duchesse d'Angoulème was to her a fairyland of ladies elegantly dressed, rising from their gondolas, gliding up the stair, rustling their plumes. Through all of Venice there was one glow of joy and color.

There was excitement also in the news that greeted Margaret there. The ministry of Rome had decreed the formation of a Citizen Guard, and she wondered whether this would in any way affect Giovanni Ossoli. The news from Ferrara was more disturbing, for apparently the Austrians had made the rumor of a plot the excuse for occupying the town. It was pleasant to turn from reports of violence to Emerson's letter in which he said that Rome was keeping its old promise to Margaret's eyes, Rome which always kept its promise. Yes, she thought, Rome had, and would keep that promise. And here was

more news of the journal that Theodore Parker would
edit, of Henry Hedge, who had left for England. "O
Sappho, Sappho," Margaret read, "I would fain know
the best of your Roman experiences." She too would fain
know what Rome held in store for her upon her return.
Richard had sent a letter that made Margaret consider
still further the wisdom of any union with Giovanni Ossoli. Her brother was engaged to marry Anna de Reve,[1]
and Margaret quickly wrote to warn him that in the present arrangements of society the choice of a companion for
life would act as a Fate for the whole of life. The need
of love, she knew so well, might trick one into error.

At the end of July Margaret left the canals crowded
with gondolas and flashing gondoliers, for Vicenza, where
Goethe had eaten figs in the market place, for Verona,
and Mantua, and the island of San Lazzaro with its huge
oleanders in full bloom, where Byron had visited the
Armenian Monastery. In a tranquil room overlooking the
clear waters of Lago di Garda she listened to the waves
breaking upon the shore, and thought again of the dark
Italian who awaited her return.

Through Brescia she traveled on to Milan, where she
saw the white-haired lord of the domain, Manzoni, who
had exhaled his moral optimism in *I Promessi Sposi,* and
Guerrieri, the youthful lawyer who responded to her
hopes for Italy. Here too she took time to write another
letter to the *Tribune,* and was glad that she had done so,
for later Greeley sent word that she was to write as many
letters as possible, not merely fifteen as she had understood.

From Milan Margaret journeyed on to Lago Mag-
giore and Switzerland, a little romance in itself, of blue
skies and bluer lakes, and white clouds in the brilliant sunshine. Alone she crossed the Apennines under a crescent

---

[1]Really Adeline Reeves. Margaret misread the name.

moon that rose in the orange twilight, but at Bellagio Margaret found a companion in the graceful Polish Princess Radzivill who floated with her on the lake of Como and listened while Margaret spoke of Rome, of the exiles who pined for their natural sphere, of the winning sweetness of the Italians. She herself, she thought, as she sailed on the lake under the August sun, might do things that would invoke censure, but she too—like Goethe, like George Sand, like Mary Wollstonecraft, must act out her natural being and have no care for what the world might say.

Margaret returned to Milan for the Feast of the Madonna and then went south to Parma, losing her gold pencil on the coach, as she tried to jot down notes of her journey. After a taste of the Correggios and Parmigianos she traveled back to Florence, driven now by a desire to return at last to Rome, where she could read more closely the signs of Italy's future and her own.

At Florence, however, Margaret was ill, as a result of the Italian climate, and had to forget all thoughts of travel and take to her bed. For three weeks she lay, weeping and eating gruel, but in her despair there was much to console her. Italy, she knew, had received her as a long-lost child. Here at last she felt herself at home, and longed to drink deeper of the cup that she had sipped. News from home comforted her in her illness, Emerson's letter telling of his plans to go to England, of the success of Ellery's book on Rome, of Alcott and Thoreau, who were building a summerhouse of peristyle gables for their Concord friend. Mme. Arconati also sent her love to Margaret and the reports of Italian affairs were stimulating. Greenough, she learned, had taken a leading part in the fete in honor of the National Guard which the Grand Duke had conceded in defiance of the Austrian threat. The Brownings, she heard, had watched the procession

of banners and laurel leaves and had waved handkerchiefs from their window, and even Flush, their spaniel,
had been so intent upon the parade that he refused to
take his front paws from the sill. In her own room Margaret listened to the Roman hymn in honor of Pope Pius,
or read the liberal papers, *Alba* and *Patria,* that had been
established after the emancipation of the press. Mazzini,
she was informed, had written a letter to the Pope begging for alliances not with the princes but with the people,
and it had been flung into the papal carriage. Though the
Austrians tipped their arrows with poison, Margaret
knew that Metternich was trembling in his hole, and that
on his mule the Pope, the liberator, rode abroad.

Margaret had time in her weeks at Florence to think
of her own life too, of the *wanderjahre* that had passed.
Now she knew that she had experienced three immortal
days that would stand forever in her memory, the day
when Mazzini had spoken to her in London of his hopes,
the day when she had visited George Sand at the Place
d'Orléans, and that May thirteenth when a young, dark-
haired Italian had walked up to her among the crowds of
St. Peter's. In her *wanderjahre* also she had seen the
great past of Italy. She longed now to behold the great
future, when all of Italy would unite to send the gal-
leons of slavery from its shores. She longed to behold her
own future, when, with that very Italian perhaps, she
would find in life a tranquil sea at last.

CHAPTER XVI

ROME, MY COUNTRY

MARGARET returned to Rome in time for the
Ottobrate and immediately rented an apartment
on the second story of 519 Corso. The Springs had left,
and after all the rush and excitement of the last year she
was glad to be alone in her tranquil room. The total sum
of her expenses for six months, she calculated, would not
exceed four hundred and fifty dollars. She did not be-
grudge the portion of this that went to the Marchesa
from whom she rented her room. Though that lady was
an insinuating creature who did not always tell the truth
and had gained her title by forcing her lover to marry
her before his death, she took pains to serve Margaret
well. The black-eyed, red-haired Marchesa came in every
morning to place fresh roses and grapes at Margaret's
table. Besides, the house was centrally located, near the
Pincian Mount, the Piazza del Popoli, and the Villa Borghese, and Margaret's room was neat and well furnished,
with space enough for her bookchest. There were three
little black dogs in the house, however, whose barking
competed with the catcalls of the urchins on the curb-
stone and the *Copenhagen waltz* that the organ-grinder
of the Corso played in the hope of a few *bajocci*. The
handmaid was a little too free, Margaret thought, in per-
mitting cameo and mosaic peddlers to enter her room
and puff cigar smoke in her face, but the roses and grapes
made up for such disturbances.

There was one whose coming was never a disturbance,
for Margaret had thought enough about Giovanni Ossoli
in the months she had been away to know that despite
his intellectual failings he complemented a part of her

[419]

nature. He came often to Margaret's rooms and in his company she experienced a beatitude of rest after years of hurry. After his father's death Ossoli came to her even more frequently, telling her of his life at his sister's home, pouring out to her his difficulties with his black-hearted brother Giuseppe, who claimed that the house furnishings were his, discussing with her the patrimony that seemed encumbered with debts. She found joy in comforting him in his troubles, and gradually, out of their common need for companionship, their intimacy ripened. If she comforted him, he warmed her by his need of comfort. Imperfect as love might be, she suffocated without it. Her tie with Giovanni left her mentally free, and when she sought intellectual stimulus she knew she could find it in books. There were no books that gave her the stimulus that his presence did; his dark hair and olive skin, his handsome, youthful form attracted and charmed her. Now at last, after having searched so long for love, it was joy to be sought after, to be loved. His Italian nature made him different from any one she had ever known and Margaret found that she was gradually becoming divorced from that which was peculiarly American. Since life was, at its best, uncertain, she did not think it worth while to calculate too curiously. The touch of his hand, of his lips, set fire to a portion of her being that had smoldered for long. His answer to the girl's *"chi è?,"* the sound of his bamboo stick on the stairway, his knock at the door, his melancholy eyes burning momentarily as he greeted her, these were enough to kindle the flame again. It was not, she deliberated, the Margaret who had spoken with Emerson of the cosmos, nor the Margaret who had so carefully edited *The Dial,* but she who had, from her earliest days, sought the exotic in the commonplace, who had loved the fandango and built a Roman castle out of shells, who now, in the midst of a warm, colorful, and noisy city, found rapture in the arms of a dark-haired Italian. Rome had grown in her mind, and now, in her room on the Corso, a Roman was awakening her to a passion that had never before been fulfilled, to a love that had never before been answered. In this new channel of her life she found a buoyant happiness that she had never known across the sea.

At eleven every morning Margaret left 519 Corso and wandered through Rome, exploring with Ossoli a narrow street or the statuary of an ancient church, stopping on the way to buy sugar plums and a coral and gold cross to send to Ellen's little daughter, Greta. Giovanni could guide her to new Rome as well as to the landmarks of the old city and she found in him an uncommon means of observing the signs of the times. As they listened to the talk in cafés or glanced through the latest news report she realized how true was the hope that had always drawn her to Europe. This was the right soil in which she could grow; this was an age where all things tended to radical reform. Through Ossoli's eyes she perceived that young Italy now rejected Manzoni, feeling that his doctrine of "pray and wait" was not for her at this moment. As they watched the cardinals rattling by in their scarlet carriages they agreed that though the Pope was a generous man it would be difficult to pour new wine into old bottles. The people, not the princes, must press the grapes and mould the bottles for the time to come. Together they watched the noble Deputies for the Council riding in coaches of state, looking out of the windows like Whittington and his cat. Together they mourned when Parma fell into the hands of the Duke of Modena. Margaret especially rejoiced when Crawford joined the Guard and the sculptor of Orpheus left his studio to spend time on military exercises. Ossoli also planned to join and become an officer in the Republican service, though his brothers wore the white cloaks of the Papal Guard.

While Giovanni explained to Margaret the attitude of

a chestnut vendor or a waiter or a *Trasteverine,* she spoke to him of the Americans who thought that if a Lombard peasant could eat his fill of *polenta* he was happy enough, that because men were degraded by bad institutions they were not fit for better. The Eagle was betraying its high commission as humanity's advance guard. She listened, dismayed, to the same arguments against the emancipation of Italy that were used against the emancipation of the blacks. Everywhere the cause of tyranny and wrong was the same. Now at last, she said, she had come to see that the rabid Abolitionists at home had, after all, a high motive, one worth living and dying for. Before they realized it, the day had gone as they walked or drove about the city, speaking of a cause that was closest to their hearts, and at five o'clock Margaret returned to her room to read her books or write her letters.

The little black dogs liked to eat up her pens as she wrote to Greta, sending the sugar plums in a little shoe. Then she dispatched a letter to the *Tribune* or *The People's Journal* to declare that Mazzini was one of the men of Ideas, born to give impulse to a coming age. On Monday evenings she had less time for writing, for then Margaret held open house on the second story of 519 Corso.

She lit the salon and decorated it with fresh flowers before the arrival of her guests. Soon there was a loud barking below and Margaret knew that her visitors were at the door. Christopher Cranch came with his wife to amuse Margaret with his ventriloquism or flute playing, with stories of his night class or his wife's latest concoction on her little stove. William Story also came from the Piazza di Spagna with his wife Emelyn, and Margaret was glad to know them, for she had heard much in Boston of the grandson of a Tea Party "Indian" and the son of Judge Joseph Story. Besides she recalled the fact that he had submitted his work to *The Dial* and that she had seen him at Harvard Commencement many years ago. She found Emelyn a bright, sweet-tempered, intelligent person who knew when to talk about a bargain she had found in Roman vases, and when to be silent so that her husband might speak. William Story had a fund of bric-a-brac information and could talk about anything. Indeed, Margaret concluded, he was certainly as vivid and versatile a man as Christopher Cranch, for he wrote poetry, had studied the law, was a good musician, and now had apparently decided to lay aside all other possible careers for sculpture. Without seeming to make an effort, he amused and entertained the company, sparkling with a bon mot about the amateur who loves nothing and the connoisseur who knows nothing, looking grave as he deliberated with Cranch about the purpose of art, bubbling over as he spoke of the charm of a Rome where Alfieri still looked out of his window on the Villa Strozzi and Cicero and Horace walked the Sacred Way.

Giovanni Ossoli sat silent in a corner, looking on while Story spoke of a figure of Nero he would like to carve, of the Emperor hiding, listening for the steps of his approaching executioners. Margaret perceived in the sculptor a vein of melancholy beneath the coruscating surface, a dread of sorrow, a pain that seemed to arise from the very bounty of his gifts. In his courtly and distinguished manner he went on, turning from his sketches of old Rome to the subject of women's rights, mentioning that he was also a great advocate of men's rights. Ossoli looked up in admiration, as Margaret spoke of the emancipated Mme. Radzivill who was now in Rome and of Mrs. Trollope who, having violated America, seemed now bent on sullying the Eternal City. She mentioned a letter she had received from Mme. Arconati recommending the concerts of M. le Chevalier Landsberg, as well as the music in the Pope's Chapel to which a black dress and veil would admit any one.

The guests proceeded to exchange their views about the interesting spots of the city, and Ossoli reminded Margaret in Italian of her visit to San Luigi Francese where she had seen Domenichino's frescos. They spoke of the prayers for the dead at Santo Spirito and the festival at the Church of St. Carlo in the Corso, where Margaret had met an Italian child who had been brought to see the Pope. The ball at the Argentine had been as grand a festival as any, and Margaret spoke of the passionate *Saltarello* which she had seen danced by the *Trasteverini* in their brilliant costumes. She remarked that Rome at Christmas time was, except for the rain, as colorful as at Easter, for the *Pifferari* came down from the mountains of Calabria to wander about, piping through the streets in their high sugar-loaf hats and sheepskin coats.

Once they had spoken of the appearance of the city they could not long remain silent about affairs of the day. The times looked hopeful, they thought, for Austria trembled and the king of Naples was finding that he could not put down the spirit fomenting in his people, no matter how much of their blood he might shed. Though the long white cloaks of the Guardia Nobile stalked through the streets, the military frocks of the Guardia Civica appeared also, and Crawford still preferred "Mount Guard" to any of the other Mounts of Rome. As they spoke, the lights grew dim and the flowers wilted on their stalks. Soon Margaret's guests drew their wraps about them and she stood at the head of the stairs as they walked down, while the three black dogs barked their farewells.

Margaret was sorry when the Storys left for Florence, for she enjoyed her Monday evenings with them. Though Ossoli did not always attend her "at homes," since he could never share in the conversation, after the departure of her friends he was constantly with her, at her rooms where the red-haired marchesa served them cabbage and rice, at the cafés, at the fountains of the Piazza del Popolo. No longer, however, did the careless happiness of the fall surge through her; she who had not calculated too curiously deliberated now incessantly. For by the turn of the new year Margaret realized that she was entering upon a sphere of her destiny so difficult that at present she saw no way out except through the gate of death. She knew that in September she would bear Giovanni Ossoli a child. Her loneliness now bore down upon her; the beautiful forms of art charmed her no more, and Giovanni's love, in which there were fondness and tenderness, flattered in vain. She was alone, among indifferent strangers, and there was no friend to whom she could turn. Surely, she thought, she was a poor magnet, with power to be wounded by the bodies she attracted. Her room seemed empty now; the arias on the Corso and the barking of the dogs, the handmaid's *"Chi è?,"* the grapes and roses seemed part of an alien world. She suffered from headaches and fever, and despite Ossoli's devotion and delicate care, she lost her appetite for wine and meat, even for all their little excursions abroad. She needed money also, and in the night she lay awake in fear, pondering the dark enigma of her life, for in all the ancient city there was none now who could help her.

With the new year, Rome also was entering upon another sphere of destiny, and Margaret forced herself to leave the Corso and walk with Ossoli in the rain to observe the signs of the new day. It was a damp, dismal city they wandered through now, but wherever they went they felt the presentiment of change. In a searching cold, like that of a Scottish mist, the Pope had passed through the streets, blessing the people, while red and yellow tapestries hung from all the windows in his honor. He seemed the providential agent to work out the aims of Italy, but if he failed, the wave that had been set in motion would not stop until it cast up its freight upon the shore. Margaret went to the Quirinal to see him receive the new municipal officers whose black velvet dresses hung in folds as they bent to kiss his foot. Yet, for all the apparent calm, a cloud was swelling. Don Carlo Torlonia, commander in chief of the Guardia Civica, lay dead, and the advocates, Tommaseo and Manin, were thrown into prison for having dared to declare publicly the necessity of reform. At the Church of Ara Coeli the band played the Hymn to Pius and *Sons of Rome, awake!* In the gloom of the rainy city Margaret felt more than ever the impossibility of reconciling reform and priestcraft.

From outside of Rome more violent events were reported. The new year had brought the tobacco riots to Milan, where the military swaggered about, puffing smoke into the faces of those who abstained from cigars to strike a blow at Austrian revenues. The Austrians themselves had been guilty of murdering eighty people, and the butchery in Milan was followed by news of an outbreak at Palermo and an insurrection in Sicily, where even the women showered stones, furniture, and boiling oil on the troops. Ferdinand of Naples had been sufficiently impressed to offer his subjects terms of reform. The torch had been lit; Margaret waited for it to burst into flame.

From France too the news was ominous. After having given daily proofs of his apostasy, Louis Philippe was at last driven from his throne. Margaret hoped that whatever blood was to be shed, the social problems of the time would be solved, that the real meaning of fraternity and equality would be learned, that the world would in time come to reverence the true aristocracy of a nation, the only nobles, the laboring classes.

It was just after the close of the Carnival that the news of Louis Philippe's dethronement reached Margaret. Despite the torrents of rain, and her own fears for her future, she could not resist sitting before the open window of her room in her shawl and boa to watch the festivities.

Under the February mist the almond trees had blossomed
and the heralds with trumpets and velvet banners announced the approach of Carnival time. The servant girls
of 519 Corso promptly arrayed themselves in white
muslins and roses to venture out on the drenched street,
while Margaret sat coughing at her window and watched
the sights. The Corso was swept and she saw gay carpets
hung out from all the windows. Those who had chairs to
let cried, "*Luogi, Luogi, Patroni!*" and soon Margaret
saw the carriages rumbling through the narrow street,
their wheels covered with laurel twigs. The balconies were
filled with senators in purple and pretty little pages in
velvet caps, while the Papal Swiss Guard added their
touch of scarlet and gold to the spectacle. What a sight it
was! From her window Margaret saw the long narrow
street changed suddenly into a masquerade hall where
pantaloons and punchinellos jostled each other and char-
latan doctors and harlequins stopped at the booths to buy
red and white comfits. Confetti and flowers were flung into
the air. A Roman woman dressed as a mustachioed officer
threw sweetmeats to a masker wearing a fennel wig and
a bunch of salad in his shoes. Everywhere, in the mud and
rain, black eyes laughed and streamers of red and yellow
and blue waved gayly. Margaret caught a glimpse of
Christopher Cranch in a linen blouse and scarlet necker-
chief pushing his way through the throng. From the
Piazza Colonna she heard a band of music, while merry
doctors and shepherdesses danced and contadini beating
upon tambourines whirled madly in the *Saltarello*.

Toward the end of the Carnival Margaret saw from
her window the riderless horses goaded by leaden balls
racing from the Piazza del Popolo down the narrow
Corso to the Piazza Veneziana. The street was a glitter
of tinsel and ribbons, streamers and flowers. On the last
day the maskers laughed and danced and screamed; the
music sounded; the carriages drove up and down in a

climax of merrymaking. Soon, as night fell, everyone lighted his candle; in every window lamps appeared; paper lanterns were swung upon tall poles across the Corso. Wildly came the cry, "*Sia ammazato chi non porta moccolo!*" Paper balloons and lighted lamps came waving down from the windows. "Let everyone perish who does not carry a taper!" Suddenly through the flaming Corso came another cry, "*Senza moccolo!*" and the burning lights went out, one by one, in the narrow Roman street. The next day Margaret, peering from her window, saw the comfits lying in the mud, the torn streamers fluttering in the rain. Laughter and music and maskers were gone from the Corso and the Carnival of February 1848 became a memory.

After the color and noise of this mad, exciting month, it was stranger than ever for Margaret to read the news from home. As if in a dream she heard that American ladies had begun to cover their gray hair with frisettes, that Greeley had attended a meeting at the Broadway Tabernacle to offer a demonstration of sympathy with Pope Pius and Italy. There was more personal news in the report of Caroline Sturgis' marriage to William Tappan. Emerson sent a parcel of books from Manchester, and Mazzini thanked her for her lines to *The People's Journal,* saying that the *Times* of London was raging at the conquering spirit of democracy, that the Pope was a good man, *un buon curato,* but no more.

When she answered her letters, Margaret said nothing definite of her new way of life with Ossoli. Even after the Storys returned to Rome she kept her secret well. In March she joined them when they looked for rooms and saw them settled in an apartment on the steep Porta Pinciana. She met them in Crawford's home on the second story of the Villa Negroni, and while they sat together in the drawing room hung with dark maroon paper and filled with curious gems of art, she spoke, not of Ossoli, but of the Carnival and her news from home. Crawford's large black dog, Cato, dozed with his head on his paws before the bright wood fire and Margaret listened while her host chatted with William Story about mallet and chisel, plaster and marble. To the Argentine Ossoli accompanied Margaret for a performance of *Beatrice di Tenda,* but though the Storys sat next to them, Margaret breathed no word of her apprehensions for the future.

In her excursions with the Storys, in her breakfasts with Crawford at the Villa Negroni, even in her love for Ossoli the outer world seemed constantly to intrude. Margaret felt that she was seated in an obscure corner, watching the progress of events to record for the *Tribune* and for a book that she hoped some day would convey to the world the story of Italian liberation. She rejoiced to be in Europe at this moment, and was sure that she would return possessed of a great history. Now, instead of walking abroad, she waited in her room for Ossoli to bring her bulletins about the times, news from the Caffè delle Belle Arti. The torch that had been lit was bursting at last into a glorious flame that burned higher and higher in the heart of the nations. With every report that Ossoli brought to her, she knew that the flame could not be extinguished. The Grand Duke had given a constitution to Tuscany, with every religious distinction abolished at one sweep. Volunteers were pouring into Italy, Romans marching into Lombardy. Soon Ossoli came in, his eyes burning with joy, to say that Lombardy and Venetia had freed themselves, that Milan was encircled in smoke and flame, its church bells wildly clanging. The citadel had driven out Radetzky after a five days' struggle in which La Scala benches and court carriages had been converted into barricades, and nobles in velvet suits joined cooks in their aprons to expel the white-coated Austrian garrison. In Florence the crowds had seized and burned the Austrian arms, shouting curses under the palace windows.

Though Radetzky soon fell back into the Quadrilateral, Piedmont and Sardinia declared war against Austria. Sicily resisted the aggressor, Naples revolted, and Metternich was completely crushed. Ossoli took Margaret through Rome to see the Austrian arms dragged through the streets and burned in the Piazza del Popolo. Everywhere the Italians embraced each other, crying "*Miracolo! Providenza!*" Men and women danced in the streets. From the lofty portal of the Palazzo di Venezia Margaret and Giovanni saw the double-headed eagle pulled down and a white and gold standard raised in its stead, inscribed with the words ALTA ITALIA.

To celebrate the triumph and to snatch some moments of peace together while the world outside clamored and stormed, Margaret and Ossoli spent the early spring days in the near-by towns of Ostia, Frascati and Castle Fusano, Subiaco, Albano and Tivoli. There they reveled in the quiet days and tranquil nights. Margaret felt that she, like George Sand, had till now acted out her nature. Goethe and Mary Wollstonecraft, she recalled, had been true to their conception of marriage as an ideal union of two equal souls, until the outer world forced them to more respectable, but less holy ties. She too would have preferred the free relationship of the autumn had not her own circumstances made the adherence to convention a necessity. Her union with Ossoli would remain secret; otherwise his reactionary brothers would withhold Giovanni's share of the patrimony and society would scoff at Margaret. At least, she assured herself, no one would ever know when or where they had married.[1]

[1]It is the author's belief that Margaret Fuller and Giovanni Ossoli were married in a civil ceremony on April 4, 1848, in one of the towns near Rome. Since there is, to date, no actual proof of this, no definite statement has been made. The author's belief, however, is based on the following information:

    1.   The date, April 4, seems to have been an anniversary for the Ossolis. Their letters of April 3 and 4, 1849, express keen regret that they cannot be together on the fourth and hope that the next year will bring them better luck on that day. Margaret hoped that Ossoli

As soon as they returned to Rome, Margaret and Ossoli found themselves once again facing the great turmoil of events of the day. If her own life seemed now hazardous and unpredictable, Rome at least was keeping her promise. Official news had arrived that the Viceroy Ranieri had capitulated at Verona, that Italy was free, independent, united. It was to Margaret a time such as she had always dreamed of. Adam Mickiewicz arrived in Rome to enroll the Italian Poles and publish their belief in equal rights for all. Yet, though the Pope blessed their banner and had already granted a constitution, he seemed now to be abandoning the liberals in his refusal to declare war against Austria. At the Piazza del Popolo, in every market square, on every corner, the Italians discussed the Encyclical of April 29 in which he openly condemned the war and announced that he must embrace all nations in an equal paternal love. Mazzini had been right, after all. Here was no living soul, but the modern Lot's wife, a cold pillar of the past—a priest, *un buon curato,* not a man. Now at least, Margaret knew that the responsibility of events lay wholly with the people.

would see her in Rieti on April 4, 1849, and prepared blackbirds for a celebration dinner. When he could not come she left the dinner untouched. See p. 451 and Fuller MSS, Harvard College Library, IX, 196 and XVI, 141.

2. There is evidence pointing to the negative conclusion that Margaret Fuller was not married in Rome. In the Vatican Library, in the Protestant archives, in the Vicariate of Rome, no record exists of this marriage. For this information the writer is indebted to the Most Reverend Mr. Ralph L. Hayes, formerly rector of the North American College in Rome, to Mgr. Gustavo Tulli of the Archivio del Vicariato, and to Anselmo M. Alberedo, prefect of the Vatican Library.

3. The evidence does point to the fact that Margaret Fuller spent the days around April 4, 1848, in the near-by towns. It is quite plausible that, since she wished to keep the marriage a secret, she would have chosen a neighboring village rather than the city of Rome.

4. If Margaret Fuller as a Protestant wished to marry the Catholic Giovanni Ossoli in a church ceremony, they would have had to receive a dispensation from the Pope. There is no record of such a dispensation. The conclusion, therefore, is that they were married by a civil authority.

The people were ready. Fair and fresh, the legions marched through the Porta del Popolo while the trumpets burst forth the victory to come. The men of straw were going down—the Pope and the stout king of Naples puffing his cigar and driving about in his gig. The real men were rising to power, Montanelli preaching the Italian *Constituente*, Guerrazzi proclaiming the popular Moderate viewpoint, Mazzini returning at last to see what he foresaw. At Milan, Margaret heard, the exile had been rapturously welcomed. For the sake of unity he had accepted his old enemy Charles Albert as king of the freed provinces, though he continued his wordy quarrel with Gioberti. For all the factions and confusion, a noble spirit was struggling in Europe. Everything confirmed her in her radicalism, Margaret told Ossoli, and in the torrent of events she saw all her hopes about to be realized; she saw the Eternal City become the "City of the Soul."

The fire that burned in the hearts of men around her could not always keep her warm. Margaret's private fortunes seemed dark and tangled. In fear lest the world should mock her she continued to harbor her secret. Her way of life was so different from the days when she had held the ladies of West Street bespelled with her Conversations. She felt now more the child than the queen, and was tormented by the thought of the suffering that lay before her. Her strength was gone; in debility and pain she passed the days. Her financial affairs worried her also, for though Richard had paid two hundred dollars of her debt to Marcus Spring, after the sale of her property in America she would have left only six hundred dollars. Often now she awakened in the night harassed with fears for the future. Above her thoughts of what the world might say if it learned her secret, above her worry about approaching poverty, loomed the spectre of dread that she would not survive the ordeal that lay before her. One morning, after such a night of torment, Margaret went to Thomas Hicks' studio on the Via Margutta to ask him to take a box of souvenirs and letters with him to Paris and forward it to her family in case she died. It was mockery now to hear that Elizabeth Barrett Browning wished to meet her, that Emerson wanted her to return with him to Concord and live in Mrs. Brown's little house opposite his gate. The reunion which he envisaged was, she knew, impossible. Concord was not for her—not now, at any rate. She must go to the country, into wild and unknown regions, to bear her child in secret.

Before she left Rome, Giovanni had his picture made by Latilla, and Margaret packed it, along with her books, in her wicker basket. She stopped at the sign of the Sybil in Tivoli on the way to the country, and consoled herself with the thought that during the summer she would be able to write part of her book and explain in print the need of voluntary association in small communities to remedy the dreadful ills that consumed society.

By the end of May Margaret was in Aquila, hiding as Goethe had done, almost enjoying the fantastic luxury of incognito. The ancient village slumbered in the midst of the snow-capped mountains of Abruzzi, its white walls shining in the early summer sun. In the paths the olive and mulberry grew, the almond trees blossomed, the valleys were yellow with saffron flowers. Margaret saw the brilliant blue cornflower and the scarlet poppy splash their colors on the grain fields. In her little apartment she sat working on her book, and gradually the servants, Giuditta and Maria Bernani, learned her ways. Though Margaret suffered from headaches and the heat that oppressed the countryside after the rain, the book advanced rapidly. When she was not writing she spent her time in the open air, chatting with the contadinas, passing on the road the soldiers who had arrived in the village, meeting the principal lords of Aquila, the Marchesi di Ferres, whose castles were perched on the hills. The only distraction from her work was the news she received, lines from Newcomb informing her that Caroline was wearing Margaret's emerald ring and that the Pope's portrait was hanging in all the New York shop windows. She herself believed more strongly than ever that there was something fatal in a priestly environment. Greeley wrote also, asking why she continued to linger in Europe.

It was always a joy for Margaret to turn from her work, or from letters that disturbed her with their insistent questioning, to the notes that Giovanni sent with nearly every mail. She often found among the papers a gift he had enclosed, or copies of the *Epoca* and the *Italia del Papa* so that she might keep abreast of the times. By special post he sent her medicine also to relieve her headaches, and always asked for her mail at the Marchesa's or the post office. He hurried about Rome, hunting for the doctor so that he might be on hand when the time came. Knowing that she wanted to record in her book whatever important events occurred, he told her of the disturbances in Rome that had been caused by the news of Vicenza's capitulation. Mobilization had begun, and he himself, now as a member of the Guard, walked seven miles out of the city to meet a Vicenza detachment. Always as she read his letters she found word of his unhappiness at not being with her when she needed him. He begged her to leave Aquila for Rieti, since it was within the territory of the Papal States, nearer Rome, and nearer him. He hoped, he said, to come to her arms.

Before the three weekly departures of the post Margaret usually took time to answer his notes, to discuss with him the deplorable weakness of the Pope, to bid him exchange her notes for money at the bank or send her a bottle of eau de cologne from Louve's on the Piazza di Spagna. She too, she said, hoped he would be with her soon, and by the end of June decided to leave for Rieti so that Giovanni could visit her and return once again to her arms.

Since there was no room for Margaret in Renzi's lodging house at Rieti, she found a small apartment on the Strada Bondara in the home of Count Papetti, chancellor to the bishop. For nine dollars a month she had cool, spacious rooms with a loggia overlooking the river Velino and its hedge of willows. From the house she could hear the waters below and see on one side a ruined tower, on the other an old casino with avenues of cypress. In the distance the soft blue peaks of the Soutriana shimmered in the pale light, and at night the young moon trembled in the river.

When the troops who had just returned from Lombardy made too much noise at dinner, Margaret ate her figs and grapes, her salad and peaches alone in a little room adjoining her sleeping apartment. During the day she continued her work on her book, writing of Italy's struggle for liberation in her large, brick-paved chamber on the upper story of Papetti's house. The room was simply furnished, but if she tired of the lonely, bare apartment, she needed only to walk on the long wooden terrace to watch the river and the whispering willows, or to see her servant, Giuditta, washing clothes on a large stone below in the running water.

After the bells of the Convent del Purgatorio had tolled the morning hours, she went below to ride on a donkey or walk among the ancient red-roofed dwellings toward the town walls and the gates and the country beyond. She saw the snow lingering on the mountain tops while the grapes ripened and contadinas in red corsets and white head-clothes nodded gayly to her. With one contadina Margaret became quite friendly and looked forward to her Sunday visits when the native appeared in her red silks and coral necklace with a pair of chickens in

one hand for Margaret, to be eaten *"per amore mio."*
Margaret was *"simpatica,"* the Italians said, and they
freely discussed with her the price of figs, the probable
quality of the vintage, or the Pope, whom one declared
to be *"un gran Carbonaro."*

Margaret found that she was beginning to think now
in Italian, and when she thought, it was principally of
Giovanni, of a beautiful spot near the river where they
could go together when he came, of his devotion and his
love of her. Often now she took out the picture that he
had had made at Latilla's; she looked at his slender form
and dark eyes and hoped that God would keep him.

The only thing that varied Margaret's day was the
occasional arrival of the surgeon who came to bleed her.
Her head ached and she suffered from pains in her chest
so that often she could not sleep at night. Then she would
walk on the loggia, back and forth, watching the purple
clusters of the vineyard glimmer under the moon, catching the scent of the summer flowers from the gardens
below. The Convent del Purgatorio tolled the hours as
she walked in the windless night. The heat oppressed her,
and the continual boredom of waiting. Again the spectre
arose, the fear of death, the dread of her child's birth.
Surely, at least she could not die alone without the touch
of Giovanni's dear hand. In the silence of the night she
looked out over the loggia, beyond the red earthen roofs
of the mountain solitude and spoke in the secret darkness
to her mother, telling to her the strange story that she
had lived, whispering a farewell as the waters of the river
murmured and the convent bells tolled another hour fled
to the past.

Often she wanted to return to her home, but she would
be more rejected in America now, she thought, than ever.
The very letters that she received stirred her desire to go
back, but at the same time convinced her that return was,
now at any rate, impossible. Mme. Arconati wrote to her,

openly declaring that people were gossiping about her life in Rome, and Margaret knew very well that if the scandalmongers were wagging their tongues in Italy, at home they must be questioning her protracted stay with whispered words and raised eyebrows. Greeley, no doubt realizing her pecuniary needs, had sent four hundred dollars for her to Greene and Company, Paris, and Margaret received money from Mr. Hooker's office at 20 Piazza di Spagna.

The letters that disturbed her least were those that Giovanni sent so frequently in care of Trinchi at Rieti. After the *"Mia Cara,"* the *"Bene,"* came news quite different from that which she had found in the notes of another *"Liebster,"* in a city a world apart. Ossoli now was sending word of the war bulletin that had announced the victory of Charles Albert, of the throngs that had marched to the Campidoglio and rung the great bell at midnight, while volleys of fire and the bells from many churches continued the clamor till dawn. So that Margaret might record the most minute event for her book, he told her that a Civica detachment had been summoned to Monte Cavallo to hear the Pope, but Pius had merely granted the Apostolic blessing and announced that he had nothing more to say. To get news about Milan he went whenever he could to the Caffè delle Belle Arti, sending her word of the severe peace with Austria.

To his *Cara,* his *Bene,* Giovanni also sent news of himself and constant assurance of his love. Again he poured out to Margaret his troubles with his hated brothers and his implacable uncle, his difficulty in getting leave from the Guard, his fears that he might be ordered to the defense of Bologna precisely at the moment when Margaret needed him most. Fortunately, he later discovered that the Pope had postponed the departure of the troops and he looked forward to joining his beloved in Rieti.

After Giovanni had asked his uncle's permission to

leave Rome and had taken a seat on the *postino* for the day's journey from the city, Margaret prepared his coffee and watched from her window for his coach to come clattering over the bridge. At last he came. In the little eating room they sat looking at each other over the chicken and salad that Margaret had bought for a few cents, smiling to each other as they raised their wine glasses. Giovanni told her of her friends, William Story and Christopher Cranch, saying that they had gone with Jasper Cropsey to study the boats and fishermen and half-naked children at "Luna" in Amalfi. He spoke to her of Charles Albert's defeat at Custoza and his ignominious retreat on Milan. Yet, he said hopefully, God would watch out for the people. Margaret agreed that though Italy might not yet be ripe for republicanism the country would not find peace without it.

She herself found peace in the love that Giovanni lavished upon her during his brief visits. On the loggia at night they watched the waters together and in the sunlight she led him to her favorite walks among the gardens. Again it seemed as if they were snatching a few moments of tranquillity before the world outside rushed on to its new destiny, before Margaret herself faced her own approaching travail.

Whenever he could, Ossoli took time for these visits. Margaret was especially happy when he arrived before Tuesday, September fifth, for on that day her little boy was born. Signor Giovanni, the porter of the house, rushed about, while Giuditta hurried to Margaret's bedside. A woman from the sign of the Mater Dolorosa helped her in her labor. At last, after her long suffering in the distant mountain retreat Ossoli heard the baby's cry, and was proud. In her weakness Margaret smiled faintly to hear everyone call the boy "Angelino," and, looking at his fair blue eyes and light downy hair, his mouth so like his father's, a new gladness rose in her heart, a warm content unlike any she had ever known.

She resented the fatal destiny that always brought her evil along with good. After Giovanni's departure Margaret was ill with milk fever and she was in so much pain from a swollen shoulder that she could barely stretch her arm. Then too she had such trouble with the servants in the house that she felt she was in a den of wolves. First Giuditta proved so incapable and intractable that Margaret was obliged to discharge her. The baby refused to take suck from his mother and she was forced to engage Clara, a wet nurse whom Signor Giovanni found for her and promptly tried to seduce. Margaret tried to keep peace, but she herself felt that everybody scorned her even for so trivial a matter as buying her wine more reasonably outside the house.

Even the baby was the unwitting cause of trouble, for Dr. Mogliani was indolent about coming to inoculate him against smallpox and Margaret would not leave Rieti until this had been done. The doctor at last advised her to obtain the serum herself and Ossoli went to get it from Professor Bucci, the apothecary at the Spezuria di San Pantaleo. He packed it in a small wooden box together with Margaret's bottle of eau de cologne, and finally on October twenty-ninth, the little operation was performed so successfully that the baby thanked them all with a thousand smiles.

Meanwhile Margaret had come to know and to love Angelino's every mannerism. With a growing wonder she observed and almost anticipated his baby acts, knowing when he would be graceful or sportive, affectionate or obstinate. Every day he became dearer to her and she hoped that when Giovanni came he would be patient if Nino cried or was stubborn. She herself thought he had the delicate little ways of a ballerina. What a treasure he was as he bent his head for her kiss or lay looking at her on the loggia.

Now in her excursions Margaret had a new companion in Angelino. Together they went for a drive along the Litta Ducale, as soldiers hurried by and a gruff old officer shouted orders. In vintage time she delighted to take him to the bishop's gardens where they watched the asses and wagons being loaded with grapes that naked boys cut from the vines, while children frolicked on the grass. With deep joy she accepted a peasant's gift of flowers and a basket of grapes, while little Nino took stock of his mother's friends.

Sometimes Margaret thought it was a little doll that she held in her arms. Angelino slept close to her and she liked to awaken during the night to look at him. When he smiled in his sleep her heart jumped with a new, delightful rapture, and she doubted if she could ever bear to leave him in Rieti and go to Rome alone. Often during the night she got up to tend him, wondering if his nurse would care for him as well. Angelino awakened two or three hours before the sunrise and insisted on gazing at the lamplight, and Margaret awakened with him always.

Every aspect of his nature seemed now a part of hers. She could not keep her eyes from him when he played or kicked. She watched him to see if he gained weight. She looked carefully at his milk-white skin. She was sure that when she mentioned Giovanni's name the baby threw his father a kiss. Indeed, Margaret rejoiced as she began to see Giovanni in the child, finding the same love of warmth and heat in both. And as with every day she found something new to cherish in Angelino, she discovered also that she loved Giovanni more now than she had ever done before.

Eagerly she looked for his letters, noticing that he was careful to tear off the blank sheets to make the parcels less bulky. All the minute details she devoured, word of rain and chill in Rome, the remark that Giovanni was already wearing winter clothes or that he hoped to send her ten gold Scudi. He made light of his own ill-health, but Margaret anxiously read between the lines and was worried by the spasms that seized him at night. Once again she was torn between the desire to remain in Rieti with Nino, and the necessity of returning to Rome to be with Giovanni. From his letters she turned to her notes on the Italian struggle, recording the information he gave her. Always he was scrupulous in reporting the progress of the times, sending word that a regiment of the Civica from Frascati was stationed in Rome, that there was a rumor of the flight of the king of Naples, that he himself was on guard duty on the S.S. Apostoli Quarter. Throughout his letters she found a new note of resignation. We must yield to our destiny, he said. God would watch over their dear one. If they had trust, soon he would be able to hold her close again and shower her with kisses.

In order that she would find a home when she returned Ossoli looked for an apartment that Margaret might rent. Whenever he found a few moments to spare from guard duty, he wandered through the Corso or the Via Babuino, or the Piazza Barberini, searching for a comfortable apartment for a single person that she could afford. Finally, he rushed about, getting the *procura* for the baby's baptism, so that Margaret would at last be able to return to the city.

It seemed to her that there were almost as many difficulties connected with the baptism as with the inoculation. Originally Margaret had wanted Adam Mickiewicz as godfather for her child, for she thought he would befriend the baby in case some misfortune befell them. They had no time, however, to search for Mickiewicz, and Margaret did not consider it prudent to choose Signor Giovanni in his stead. As a last resource, they chose Ossoli's nephew, Pietro, for without a certificate bearing the godfather's name the baptism would not be legal. Ossoli at length arrived in Rieti and the priest,

Joan. Baptista Trinchi, performed the baptism on November sixth, christening the baby Angelo Eugene Philip, for his father, Margaret's brother, and his grandfather.

There was nothing further now to keep Margaret in Rieti except her dread of leaving Angelo. With a heavy heart she packed her trunks and put the baby's clothes in a wicker basket so that Clara could keep them. Knowing that the nurse came from an excellent family and seemed one who could be trusted, Margaret was consoled a bit at the prospect of leaving. After a month of writing and being near Giovanni in Rome she would return to her treasure. She gave Clara all the advice she could think of and, holding the baby close, whispered a farewell to little Angelo.

Margaret found a room on the upper story of 60 Piazza Barberini, which she rented by the month. The house faced the Piazza on the sharp slope of the Quirinal, and from the window of her large, sunny room she could see on one side the Barberini Palace and the Pope's gardens, and on the other the Piazza and the Street of the Four Fountains. It was, she knew, the tall corner house described in Andersen's *Improvisatore,* where the water poured through three pipes out of the wall down into a stone basin. Her own chamber near the roof was the one that Andersen had given to his Danish painter, and like her predecessor she enjoyed looking out at the neighbors' yards, and the wells inclosed with masonry and overgrown with Venus'-hair. Instead of the crafty Marchesa, Margaret was cared for by an old couple who saw that the furniture was gracefully placed and that the chimney gave off enough heat. Gradually, she came to know her neighbors in the house, the poor Prussian sculptor who had walked to Rome to wield his mallet, the priest who lived in the attic and insisted on making Margaret's fire when Antonia, the servant, was away. Below she could find a mustachioed Russian princess whose footman tied her bonnet for her, and a fat English lady who went to church in a fine carriage. Antonia grew flowers on a little balcony, and instead of the three black dogs of the Corso, there were birds and a huge black cat dubbed "Amoretto." Though the Padrone thirsted for money, Margaret screwed her expenses down to the lowest possible peg, spending no more than ten or twelve cents a day for her dinner.

Often instead of eating alone in her room Margaret made a little excursion with Giovanni. In spite of the rain and cold mists she rejoiced to hear once again the voices of many fountains, to see in the pale moonlight the obelisks and ruins of old. In the morning they went out, carrying roast chestnuts that they had purchased from a vendor; in a lonely little *osteria* they bought their bread and wine and reached Rome again just in time to see St. Peter's dome glimmering in the sunset.

When Ossoli could not be excused from guard duty Margaret spent her days walking, visiting the galleries, reading for an hour or two *Alba* and the newspapers that represented the Montanelli ministry. Most of the time she spent writing. It was nearly eight months since she had dispatched a letter to the *Tribune,* and both for Greeley's paper and her own book she must make her pen race with the progress of events.

There was much for her to write about as she sat in the quiet upper story, interrupted only by the birds or Amoretta's persistent mewing. Had she only been free from worry about Angelo Margaret would have rejoiced in times for which she had always longed. She thought, as she looked up from her notes, that if she returned to America at this moment, she would feel as if forced to leave her own house, her own people, and the hour for which she had ever prayed. After Milan's surrender to the Austrians—a bargain-price for the safe withdrawal of the Piedmont army—after Ferdinand of Naples won his title of "Bomba" by his treacherous destruction of Messina, there was a more auspicious event for Margaret to observe and record. Pellegrino Rossi, the minister who had renounced his country as an exile, dismounted from his carriage on November fifteenth before the Piazza della Cancelleria, and as he approached the Volunteers near the staircase, Luigi Brunetti stabbed him in the neck. The Pope, Margaret thought, had made Rossi a citizen, but the people had suffered him only one day. She had never thought she would hear with satisfaction of a violent death, but this act seemed to her one of terrible justice. The next day when the Romans fired on the Swiss Guard Margaret saw from her window a wounded man borne by. The drum beat called out the National Guard and Prince Barberini's carriage entered the courtyard gate with its liveried retinue. "Thank God we are poor," Antonia whispered to her; "we have nothing to fear!" The Padrone ran up and down, crying, "Jesu Maria, they are killing the Pope," while people shouted from their windows to learn what was happening. These were different sounds from the guitar that had twanged below her window on the Corso when she had first come to Rome.

Different sights too she saw now in her wanderings. At Monte Cavallo, where the Pope used to give his benediction, there were broken windows and burnt doors, walls marked by shot just beneath the loggia where he had stood so often. A few days later came word that Pius, disguised as a simple priest, had fled, imploring the protection of King "Bomba." Now Margaret felt certain that Rome could not stem the tide of innovations, let treacherous princes do their worst. She prayed that the people of America would send here a good ambassador, wishing indeed that it were another century that she might act as ambassador herself. Toward the end of November Margaret heard with joy the artillery discharges that

announced the opening of the *Constituente Romana,* saw
the Piazza del Popolo illuminated with lights and a great
fire shooting its flames to the crescent moon that hung in
a deep blue sky. On the platform of the Obelisk the
orchestra sat, the musicians' lamps reflected in the fountain. The casinos of the Corso added their share of light
to the fair scene, and Margaret felt that a great step had
been taken.

The only inauspicious news seemed to hail from France,
where Louis Napoleon was elected President of the
Republic. His maneuvers were assisted by "Plon-Plon,"
son of Westphalia's ex-king, and Margaret feared sometimes that her glorious hopes would be clouded in the
battle with giant wrongs.

There were pleasures in Rome, however, that made
Margaret forget her doubts. Though she missed her baby
and was often lonely when Ossoli could not be freed from
his guard duty, she enjoyed meeting Mrs. Crawford at
the Villa Negroni to chat about the Storys and Cranches,
who were wintering in Florence. Then too she found congenial society in the acquaintance of Germano, a poor
young student of sculpture who sold ornamental paper
boxes for a living. Margaret had met him in a diligence
and listened with sympathy to his tale of poverty and ill
luck, even lending him some money to help him in his
need. To none of her friends could she speak about
Angelo, however, and she missed him more and more as
the weeks rolled by. When Greeley sent word that he had
a new baby daughter she could not wait any longer to see
her own child in Rieti.

Despite the snow and gray skies Margaret had a comfortable journey and arrived in Rieti at 4:30 of a cold
December afternoon. She was sure that Nino recognized
her immediately when she picked him up and that night
he slept soundly in her bed. Margaret gave him everyone of the kisses that Giovanni had sent, and a goodly

store of her own. Had he changed? She looked at him closely, finding him only a very little bit older, though considerably fatter than the month before. As yet he had no hair to speak of, but his shining eyes made up for that lack. Margaret was told that Angelo had had the measles and that his head and body had been covered with spots; she felt that it was the grace of God that made him survive this disease, for Dr. Mogliani had never come to visit him. She was a little worried also because the house seemed drafty and the weather was unbearably cold. Nino did not mind, however, and had a grand time with his little toy doll. Margaret revisited her old haunts with the baby, and on Christmas Eve gave him a string of bells with the result that he refused either to go to sleep himself or to let any one else sleep. She received cheerful greetings from Giovanni, along with a *foglio* and letters. It was almost harder than before to leave the baby, but she had seen that he was happy and well and now must bid little Angelo another farewell. Before she returned she wrote to Giovanni, asking him to tell Antonia not to bother preparing much food for her, and to come himself to 60 Piazza Barberini after dinner. Then she would tell him a thousand things about their dear little one.

In the little upper room of her apartment they met, and Giovanni listened, drinking in every word that Margaret said about Nino's mouth and nose and hands and feet, about his little doll and his string of bells. When Giovanni went to his guard duty Margaret sat reading Didier's *La Rome Souterraine,* but often the memory of Angelo's chubby fists and little cries came between her and the picture of the ancient city. Mazzini's *Ricordi di giovine d'Italia* engrossed her more and she found it a word of fire, a thought illustrious as diamond.

Occasionally Margaret walked about the city with Giovanni as they had done when she had first settled in

Rome. Some of the old delight of discovering its treasures
came back now as they wandered together to the Piazza
Navona or examined the mosaics in the Church of St.
Lorenzo. The vendors still cried their wares on the narrow streets, the *Trasteverini* still walked in their old
cloaks along the Tiber, and they who had found joy in
each other a year before found again another joy born of
their separation and loneliness. Yet Rome was not the
same as it had been. A new spirit stirred, a restless anticipation that they felt as they walked about in the cold and
the snow.

More closely than ever before Margaret observed the
events of the time. She opened a new diary with the turn
of the year and, wondering what victories or failures
would lie between its covers, hoping at least that it would
be like the motto on her ring, "a possession forever for
man," she inscribed upon it the words "Rome, 1849."
Margaret never wanted now for exciting incidents to
record in its pages. On the evening of January second she
went to the Campidoglio to see the demonstration that
would usher in the year 1849. She watched as the troops
and a Civica detachment assembled in the Piazza del
Popolo and marched with arms and torches and a new
tricolor banner in the Campidoglio. The Rioni representatives gathered round when the banner was placed in the
hands of Marcus Aurelius. The bands played; the moon
looked calmly down; Bengal lights and torches shone on
the palaces and the Piazza was a fire of glittering lights.
A few days later Margaret saw the people of Rome tear
the Pope's manifesto from the walls and carry it in procession through the Corso round a candle's end. The
men from *Trastevere,* the vendors, the women ran along
mumbling in imitation of priestly chants, throwing the
scarlet hats of the Cardinals into the River Tiber. Such,
she thought, is the finale of St. Peterdom.

Everywhere now, Margaret was at hand, when a public

meeting was held at the Tordinona, or when suffrages were given for the Constituent Assembly. With all of Rome she went to the Capitol to see the procession carrying urns with Civica banners, to hear the music that heralded the Republic. Looking up at Marcus Aurelius, she found that the tricolor had dropped from his hand and thought it an evil omen in these fair days. The omen seemed alas an honest presage, for news had arrived that Radetzky was preparing for war and Margaret feared that the French would soon be at Civita Vecchia. To forget the monstrous treacheries that she dreaded she went to Ponte Molle to meet the first detachment of the legion from Venice. Margaret joined the throngs and followed the bands and banners of the Guardia Civica. She remembered well the time she had first seen the troops depart through this very gate del Popolo, and mourned that their banner now was worn and faded like themselves. "*In hoc signo vinces.*" The letters at least remained. Margaret remembered too that it was from this very point that Constantine first saw the fiery sign, and wondered what other signs the Romans would read in the blue Italian skies as spring came on.

Even the weather seemed different this year from last. February was as warm as May, and the Carnival ran its merry course from the trumpeting of the heralds to the Moccoletti without the rain of the year before. On February fifth Margaret saw the inauguration of the *Constituente Romana* and here too she perceived a contrast between the deputies walking on foot, ornamented only with the tricolored scarf, and the princely delegates for the Council who, over a year ago, had rolled into the city in coaches of state. Now the bands struck up the *Marseillaise* as they passed the Palazza di Bonizio where the Austrian arms had been torn down last spring. Now at last after long debate in the Palazza della Cancelleria where Rossi had been slain, Rome was declared a Repub-

The Greene Street School in Providence, Rhode Island. Here Margaret Fuller taught from 1837 to 1838. The picture is copied from the original in the Rhode Island Historical Society.

(*Courtesy of the Rhode Island Historical Society.*)

The Fuller Family. Standing are Eugene Fuller and Mrs. Margaret Crane Fuller. Seated, from left to right, are Arthur Buckminster, Ellen (Channing), and Richard Frederick.

Giovanni Angelo Ossoli.

lic. The great bell of the Capitol rang solemnly; the cannon answered; tricolor banners waved; *vivas* filled the air, *Viva la Republica! Viva L'Italia!* At St. Peter's Margaret saw all of Rome kneeling in a Te Deum for the new state. Finally, where the Pope had declared Rossi a Roman citizen, the people now proposed that Mazzini enter Rome, a citizen of the new republic.

Even the news that Margaret received from home seemed more remote than it had a year before. Lowell's taunts about Miranda in his *Fable for Critics* seemed scarcely worth her attention and now that her world was filled with the events of state, the poet's flippancies about her "capital I" and "sibylline tone" seemed no more important than the literary conceits of an ill-tempered rhymester. James Clarke still remained faithful and now bade Margaret to leave revolutions to revolve alone. "We want you here," he wrote. He did not know that there were others this year who wanted and needed her in Rome. Greeley, reading well the signs in the skies, had started his *Tribune* Association, but now Margaret hoped to see communities established on a larger scale than a newspaper company. In America there had been changes too, for sad news of death followed Margaret to Rome, word that "Aunt" Mary Rotch had died, Eugene's sweet baby, and Ellen Hooper.

To the Storys Margaret carried word of the news she had received, when in March her friends returned to Rome. Again, Ossoli escorted Margaret to the Storys' apartment, and she joined them for luncheon at Crawford's home. Again they visited St. Peter's to hear the music and walked about the Villa Borghese and saw the Vatican by torchlight. But when they spoke, it was no longer of balls and concerts and *Pifferari,* but of Rome, the new Republic, of Mazzini's election, of the placards posted all over the city bearing, in giant letters, *Giuseppe Mazzini, cittadino Romano.* The exile, Margaret told her friends, had thought once of entering Rome with her in disguise; now it seemed most glorious that he was about to enter republican Rome as a citizen.

On the eighth of March Margaret heard the bell ring and then someone called her name. The voice struck her immediately. She ran to open the door and admit her friend of more sorrowful times in London, to admit the exile returned in triumph. Mazzini seemed radiant, consecrated to a high purpose, as he sat on the edge of his chair, telling Margaret how he had come from the Albergo Cesari. The people, he said, had assembled under his windows and he had addressed them, assuring them that he would stay with them to the last. The holy alliance of God and the People would free Italy. Perhaps, he admitted, it would be impossible to save her from all her strong and subtle foes, but Heaven would help. After the Rome of the Emperors, he declared, his great black eyes burning fiercely, after the Rome of the Popes, there would come the Rome of the People. His slender form clothed as always in black, his melancholy face, his dark hair quickened in Margaret the memory of their first meeting. His voice stirred her as before. His own sense of consecration consecrated her life, and when he left she felt he could never be utterly defeated.

Margaret felt this again when she heard Mazzini speak in the Assembly; his fine, commanding voice filled the hall, and he himself seemed sustained by the fire of his soul. More than ever she longed to see the crisis to its end, and complete the work she had begun. Yet her interest in Italy could not still her anxiety about Angelo. She worried about him as much as about the news from Novara, where Charles Albert, mounted on a dark steed and cloaked in black, had met defeat at the hands of the Austrians. After his abdication, after the report that Genoa was not resisting for fear the city would be destroyed, and that France was sending her troops to restore the Pope, Margaret left Rome for another visit to her baby.

She found him looking plump and well. This time she was certain that Nino recognized her, for he rolled over the floor and banged his little head in joy. She was surprised to find, when she took off his tiny black cap, that he still had almost no hair, but he had begun to teethe and now slept all alone, sucking his chubby fist contentedly. After the melancholy news that had disheartened her before she left Rome Margaret found a sweet peace in bathing and dressing Angelo, in giving him the hugs his father had sent and kissing him to make up for all the months she had not seen him.

Yet trouble seemed to pursue her even in this mountain village, for no sooner had she seated herself next to the baby to watch him while he napped than she heard chairs and tables falling, and women screaming downstairs for help. She flew down and found the two men of the household, Nicola and Pietro, fighting furiously. The women held back Nicola's arms so that he would not fling his knife, while Pietro swung his club madly. If Angelo had been downstairs, she thought, he would surely have been killed. She dreaded the thought of leaving him alone again, though Clara was good and faithful as ever, and hoped that Giovanni would soon come to help her in her troubles and soothe her in her loneliness. Especially on April fourth, the day when, a year ago, they had sought peace together in the neighboring villages of Rome before Angelo had been born, Margaret hoped that Giovanni could be with her. She bought blackbirds for their dinner, but Ossoli was unable to leave Rome and Margaret could not bear to eat them alone.

When she left the house Margaret found no peace in the village either. Roman troops had been sent to reinforce Garibaldi's men who were stationed in Rieti, and more often than not the two forces indulged in quarreling between themselves before they took to fighting with their common enemy. Margaret heard that Garibaldi's long-haired, bearded soldiers had slain a priest and two citizens as well as nine of their own company. Everybody in Rieti was telling the story of how two bodies had been found in the river. As she wandered through the town, Margaret frequently encountered the fierce-looking warriors in their loose dark-blue tunics and green capes, their tall Calabrian hats adorned with black ostrich feathers. Ugo Bassi passed along the streets occasionally, his waving locks of hair clustering below his broad-brimmed black hat, his scarlet blouse flashing in the sun, and Margaret heard how Garibaldi had influenced him to change his clerical dress for the red shirt of an officer. Garibaldi himself in his poncho and black feathers dismounted from his white steed as he proceeded through the village, while his wife Anita remained at his side in the saddle. The quiet town of Rieti had changed its face since Margaret had first known it.

She dared not go out alone after a while, and merely took the baby to a small garden near the house. There she liked to read the letters that Giovanni sent, while Nino preferred putting them in his mouth. Shut off from the noisy streets, Angelo laughed and played while Margaret read the news of Mazzini's publication, *L'Italia del Popolo,* and Giovanni's decision not to subscribe any longer to the *Speranza del Epoca.* Ossoli sent word also of the Triumvirate that had been formed with Mazzini, Saffi and Armellini as leaders of the new state. The Civica, he wrote, had been called to guard their homes, for the reactionary party was threatening their lives in the hope of raising once again the Pope's standard and overthrowing the republic. War bulletins were constantly being published now, and Ossoli reported their contents in his letters, adding that he planned to come and tell Margaret the news himself.

Giovanni came for a brief visit, bringing books to Margaret from Arteman's, and thirty-one Scudi that he had obtained through his relative, Petrucchio, the bank clerk. After he had kissed and hugged the baby, examining his chubby little fists and toes, he told Margaret more about his guard duty and the war bulletins. They enjoyed a few hours of peace together in the tranquil garden, talking of the performances that the actor, Gustavo Modena, planned to give at the Teatro di Metastasio in the summer. Giovanni assured Margaret that the dressmaker had received her instructions from Antonia, and that she would soon have a pretty new frock. Margaret reveled in their quiet talk about trivial things and wished she might go on forever sitting with Giovanni in a garden, discussing clothes and theatres, while Angelo slept near them. Ossoli had to return to Rome, however, and Margaret followed him shortly after, holding the wide-eyed baby close in another farewell, glad of a bed and hot soup when after the day's journey she arrived at the Piazza Barberini.

If Rieti had changed from a quiet mountain village, Rome, in the few weeks that Margaret had been away, had turned into a barricaded city. From her window she saw now elegant ladies handling spades while men carried boards to support cannon. Often Margaret hoped, while the month of April ran its eventful course, that she would sit no longer, watching from her obscure corner, but take a part in the struggle that hourly was expected. From abroad the Pope sent his allocution, stating that the city of Rome had become a forest of roaring beasts, overflowing with apostates or leaders of communism or socialism. To Margaret, as she watched the review in the Piazza di S. Pietro, Rome seemed the dwelling place of *viva*-ing, clapping throngs intent upon a great cause. In the evening, after the great hymn had been played, the whole amphitheatre of the Colosseum was lit with the tricolor, the basement red, the next two stories green, and the top aglow with white. Giovanni, working on guard duty, Margaret wandering about with the crowds, Rome waiting in hope for a great future—all needed their courage, for on April twenty-fifth the news arrived that the French troops under General Oudinot had disembarked at Civita Vecchia. Margaret, hearing the addresses at the Piazza del Popolo, saw also the roads and houses decorated with notices bearing the fifth article of the French Constitution: France respects foreign nationalities; her might shall never be employed against the liberty of any people. Surely, she thought, the French themselves must be shamed by their own monstrous treachery.

Two days later Margaret stood in the street to see Garibaldi enter Rome at the head of his Legion. As the sunburned warriors rode through the Corso, their long hair falling over their shoulders, the black plumes of their conical hats waving, the Romans cried aloud for joy, "He has come! He has come!" Margaret among the great throngs of people saw him ride by on his white horse, his light chestnut hair framing his lion-like head, and all of Rome looked up at the white poncho and the sabre that he held in his hand. Next to him rode his giant Negro, wrapped in a dark-blue poncho and mounted on a jet-black charger, the lasso of the Pampas hanging from his saddle. Garibaldi had arrived, and Margaret did not wonder when she heard that the next day, after Mazzini had put the question to the troops, the ranks shouted their answer boldly, courageously, *"Guerra!"* On the morning of April twenty-ninth, Margaret watched while the Lombard Bersaglieri under their dauntless young leader, Manara, marched into Rome, their black-green plumes waving from their broad-brimmed hats, the Cross of Savoy on their belts. In the evening she heard the drums beat to arms and now all of Rome was a glitter of swords and helmets, guns and daggers, standards and cockades. The *Trasteverines,* fierce figures now, with spears in their hands and knives in their teeth, mounted the steep ascent to the Janiculum. No screaming, gesti-culating chestnut vendors now, but small regiments, bat-talions, Civica—Giovanni along with the others—flocked to the walls or guarded the barricades. On the Janiculum Garibaldi stood for the defense. All Rome waited, breath-less.

Margaret too, in her room overlooking the Pope's gardens, waited, and tried to clarify the confused reports that came to her during the last day of April. She could see the smoke; she could hear the firing of guns and the skirmishers' volleys beyond St. Peter's. The French, she was told, had been greeted with grapeshot, and cannon had been opened against the Vatican wall. Garibaldi's Legions had swarmed over the Corsini, breaking into the vineyards beyond, and the bearded, long-haired soldiers had met the French in their shakoes body to body with guns and bayonets and hands. Then came the cry of vic-tory, students screaming the news through the streets. The French had been driven from the field. At night, Margaret, looking below, saw the city illuminated; in every window a candle burned; on every street great crowds shouted the triumph.

Later in the evening, Giovanni brought word to Mar-garet that Mazzini had decided to free the French prison-ers, but the wounded remained to be nursed. When Princess Belgiojoso sent her a letter the same night to invite her to act as nurse at the Fate-bene Hospital, Mar-garet knew that her chance to partake in the struggle had come at last. She too would join Ossoli in the defense. If he mounted guard, she would help men who groaned from gunshot wounds and fever; she would carry books and flowers to them; she would make lint and bandages. In her way she would act and hope for better worlds where treason could not triumph, where tyranny would die.

There were friends in Rome to whom she told her hopes, who trusted like herself that good would triumph. Arthur Clough had arrived at the Hotel d'Angleterre and Margaret spoke to him about Mazzini. Clough told her that Mazzini had admitted to him the possibility that Rome might fall, but on the night of April thirtieth Clough and Margaret, the Storys and Giovanni stilled their doubts. The voice of doubt could not be heard that night, for the very air was filled with the sound of triumph.

To the Storys' home in the Piazza di Spagna Margaret had rushed with every bit of news that came to her. With her friends she had gone to the Piazza del Popolo to meet Princess Belgiojoso and hear the speeches after the French had landed at Civita Vecchia. Together they had looked at the enemy watchfires and seen the Guardia Civica hold up their hats on their bayonets as they screamed *"Si!"* in answer to Sterbini's question whether they were ready to defend the city.

Thrown together so in the last mad days of April, they had become more intimate than ever before, and Margaret, fearful now lest Giovanni fall at the hands of the enemy, decided to take Emelyn Story into her confidence. She told her that she was married, that her child was in Rieti, and she asked Emelyn to keep her secret. Then Margaret begged her friend to take little Nino home to her mother in America in case she or Giovanni should die. In addition, she gave Emelyn a letter and Angelo's birth certificate, asking her to keep a solemn pledge of secrecy. Margaret was grateful for the helping hand of a friend across her life's strange ways, and felt a little more consoled at the prospect of her uncertain future.

While Giovanni mounted guard, Margaret spent the May days with the Storys, speculating with them at breakfast over the French retreat. Frank Heath, a friend of William Story, charming and Hamlet-like, stout and mustachioed, was often with them and occasionally escorted Margaret to the hospital. The Storys also accompanied her to the Pellegrini Hospital to give Mme. Belgiojoso a donation and on the way home they all stopped at Spillman's to get ices for the Princess. Together they walked to the Vatican Gardens to see Ossoli engaged in the defense and, walking along the wall, saw the posts of the Guard who had fought so magnificently on April thirtieth, and who now brimmed over with stories of the plan of battle and the heroism of the men.

Early in May the Storys moved to the Casa Diez on the Via Gregoriana to join Frank Heath and the few Americans who still remained in Rome. Mazzini soon ordered a guard for the house and Margaret sat with her friends while they waited, knowing not for what, knowing only that another struggle lay before Rome. At the Casa Diez they gathered together, making salads, talking, hearing a little music, watching the moonlight over the balcony, listening to the distant sounds of the city. Shortly after, Margaret decided to leave her room on the Piazza Barberini and she too settled on the top floor of the Casa Diez under the protection of the American flag. There they spoke together, rejoicing at the news of Garibaldi's defeat of the Neapolitans, wondering what the arrival of Lesseps would mean, and how long the suspension of hostilities would continue. The galleries were closed; the gates of Rome were shut, the streets lined with barricades and the churches converted into hospitals. The Casa Diez was a tiny island of retreat in the expectant, waiting city. Margaret waited also, while the Storys continued their salad-making and speculation. Mazzini was in lodgings, they said, playing his guitar alone at night, and William Story reported that his black eyes were dim now, his beard grizzled, his face haggard and worn. Priests, they said, were walking arm in arm with soldiers in the cafés and *legnos*. The Romans had sent cigars and snuff to the French. What did it mean? Margaret and the Storys waited for the answer. Ossoli came in now and then, telling Margaret of the destruction of the lovely trees in the Villa Borghese, hewn down for defenses. He too sat with them, sombre in his dark-brown, red-corded military suit, silent, waiting. At last the Storys decided to wait no longer, and to leave the city for Germany as soon as they could find horses. For them the outcome was impersonal. They could travel on to pleasanter scenes. But Margaret's very life was bound up with the barricades outside. The gates of Rome could not open to set her free.

While she waited—alone now except for Giovanni— to learn the outcome of the struggle Margaret enjoyed the experience of sitting to Thomas Hicks for her portrait. In his studio, a little back from the street on the Via Margutta, she found the painter standing before his easel, and as she posed for him he took up his brushes to add a fold to the draperies of her dress or a touch to the columns in the background. He chatted lightly as he sketched, of his order for a cabinet picture or his system of coloring or of his childhood when he had learned coach painting. Now he spoke of his old friend John Kensett who used to climb the hill over the studio every evening to see St. Peter's in the sunset. Margaret forgot her cares as she listened to Hicks gayly reminiscing about the glees that the American painters had enjoyed in his rooms, or of Christopher Cranch, who had sung Moore's melodies so delightfully. It was pleasant to hear of the game of pool that Hicks had played in happier times, while a fat British troubadour strummed a guitar and rolled up his round blue eyes as he trolled a sentimental ditty. The painter went back even to earlier days, recalling to Margaret his portrait of St. John that had hung in the New York National Academy. As he spoke, she could almost forget the defenses that lined the streets outside, Gio-

vanni standing guard, the baby she had left in Rieti.
The painting itself was quite different from the daguerreotype she had sat for at Plumbe's Galleries; it seemed
to reflect another, more serene Margaret. Indeed, she was
grateful to Hicks for the serenity of the brief hours in
his studio, and was loath to leave when the church bells
ushered in the evening.

The bells had tolled away a whole month by the time
Margaret learned that Garibaldi had returned to Rome
on the last day of May and Lesseps had signed an agreement with the Triumvirs, assuring them that the French
would protect Rome against Austria and all the world.
The barricades were stronger than ever in the streets, but
Margaret saw that the soldiers were less preoccupied with
military affairs than with sitting next to the market-men
shelling peas. Rome was disturbed the next day to hear
that Oudinot had repudiated Lesseps' armistice, but the
General had, at least, made a gentlemanly agreement not
to attack the place until Monday, the fourth of June.
There would be a few more days of peace, Margaret
thought, while Garibaldi's men were stationed on the west
bank. Garibaldi himself was ill, but there was no great
need of vigilance since the city would have all of Sunday
to prepare for the attack. If the soldiers insisted on shelling a few more peas, there surely was no necessity of
denying them their enjoyment.

At four in the morning of Sunday, June third, Margaret was awakened from sleep in her room on the top
floor of the Casa Diez by the noise of sappers' picks and
guns, rolls of cannon and volleys of musket fire. She
quickly looked out of the window in the direction of the
Porta San Pancrazio and saw the smoke of the discharges, the flash of the bayonets. With her glass she
could see the men—orderlies dashing about to search, no
doubt, for their regiments, armed civilians pushing their
way across the bridges among cheering crowds, the bright

red tunics and round hats of Garibaldi's Legion filing toward the Porta San Pancrazio, and the infamous French, their gun barrels flashing in the early morning sunlight. Now Margaret walked out to the loggia to hear the bells clanging from every campanile, the drummers beating the alarm, the distant sound of the *Marseillaise* that the bands played to shame the French with the irony. On the hilltop she saw the balcony of the Corsini crowded with French soldiers while Garibaldi sat on his white horse, sending up division after division to dash at the garden gate. Through the narrow passageway Margaret watched Manara's men rushing up the slope under a storm of bullets, while the distant cries of *Avanti! Avanti!* echoed over the ringing bells and drumbeats.

The sun rose higher in the skies and the sultry noon settled over the city. Margaret stood silent on the loggia, holding her glass to see the wounded slung in scarfs or rolled back through the streets on handbarrows, to see the dead piled in the open loggias near the Villa. All day long the heavy cannonade boomed through the city, musket answering musket with fire and smoke. Then she saw the gunners, the infantry, mobs of citizens and artists flooding through the Porta San Pancrazio, sweeping along in a dense mass to the Villa. The Corsini was a ruin of charred debris, bodies and arms. Through the trees Oudinot's army flashed, regiment behind regiment, till the pines threw long shadows in the dusk. After the last gleam of light flickered over the city Margaret turned from the loggia, wondering what the outcome had been, wondering where Giovanni was in all the tumultuous city, dreading to think that perhaps he too might lie among the heaps of the dead.

Not until later did she learn that three hundred Italians lay dead or wounded, that Giovanni had escaped, but that the French had captured the Valentini and the Corsini, and were besieging Rome. The city was afire with bursting rockets. Day after day shells flew over the Janiculum, shattering the *Trastevere* below. Now Margaret learned the distinction between the two-handled bomb and the hollow grenade. She could not laugh when the Italians greeted the bursting shells with cries of *"Ecco un Pio Nono!"* For the Villa Borghese, the villa of Raphael, was laid waste, and the trees cut down at the Villa Albani. Burnt was the Villa Salvage, with all its fine frescoes, and the banks of the Tiber were shorn of their trees. Garibaldi still sat on his horse in his short white poncho, smoking his cigar through the day, but the French light cavalry in their little *kepis* were sweeping over the Campagna, cutting off the convoys from Rieti, and in the courtyard of the Fate-bene Hospital one of their rockets had burst.

The wounded men called to Margaret as she entered the hospital, saying that they did not want to die like mice in a trap. Now that the bombardment continued incessantly she spent seven or eight hours a day at the Fatebene or the Pellegrini, comforting the wounded students from Pisa and Pavia, Padua and Rome. She had learned much from Princess Belgiojoso, who had given up a distinguished Paris salon to serve the Republic, and who now sat long nights at the bedside of the dying poet Mameli, reading Dickens to him by the light of a little oil lamp. Every day Margaret watched the carts of the wounded, dreading to find in one of them the face she knew so well. As she moved about the wards where fair young men were bleeding to death, she felt herself a Mater Dolorosa. The woe of all the mothers who had borne these men was hers; in twenty years her own son might be thus cut down. The men themselves seemed even braver now than on the field. She saw one in his narrow bed kissing the pieces of bone that had been extracted from his arm, hanging them round his neck as relics and mementos. She wept sometimes when she could not relieve the pain of the suffering, and one crippled young man, seeing her in tears, clasped her hand whispering, *"Viva l'Italia."* *Cara bona donna,* they called her. God is good; God knows, they said. And one soldier remarked to her joyfully as she sat near his bed, "Think that I can always wear my uniform on *festas* just as it is now, with the holes where the balls went through, for a memory." The sturdy Garibaldians spoke to her of their chief and she in turn brought them books or told them the news of the day. In the Pope's Palace on the Quirinal she walked with the convalescents, one with his sling, another with his crutch, while the gardener played the waterworks for the soldiers and gathered flowers for her, their friend. As she walked through the wards before returning home the men raised themselves on their elbows to catch a last glimpse of her, calling out, "When will the Signora come again?"

She came as often as she could, for now she had few friends in Rome, save Giovanni, whom she could not see frequently. Sometimes she carried to him a concealed basket of provisions which he promptly shared with his comrades. Margaret sought him out at his post, finding him exhausted and faint for want of rest, but still resolute in his determination to follow Mazzini's ideals. The wall that he defended was stained with blood. Giovanni showed her pieces of a bomb that had burst at his side, and she saved a bit of it as a relic. Whenever he could, he came to her, to comfort her, to get the handle of her parasol mended, to speak of the hospitals and the wounded. But he could not leave his post for long, and she dared not stay with him, nor had she the heart to leave him. Their little hurried notes were all that remained now, and she left word for him at the Casa Diez, telling him when she would return, thanking God that he was still alive. He answered, dashing off a line to the Casa, begging her not to overwork, and to take care of herself for little Angelo's sake.

It was hard that she could not see the baby during the

siege. Every dreadful possibility now arose in her mind
as an actuality. He would be hurt by the Croats, the house
would be burned over his head, and if he escaped how
would they get the money to buy his bibs and primers?
Every day in the burning sun she waited among the
crowds at the post office for letters about him, letters that
demanded money for the care of the child. Amid the roar
of the bombardment she heard his voice, crying for her,
the helpless moan that musketry could not drown nor cannon stifle.

So from day to day she lived, wondering as the moon
rose that she had survived another sunset. The few letters
that drifted in from America filled her with nostalgia,
with a desire to escape to the peace of her home. Ellen
was living with her mother at Manchester and Richard
had married Sarah Batchelder. He sent money to Margaret and she longed to see him and her mother once
again. At first, before the French had arrived at Civita
Vecchia, Margaret had thought she would never find a
tranquil abode in her family. She was caught in such a
net of ties that she despaired of going back; America was
so far away that return seemed impossible. But now she
wanted to go home for the baby's sake, and in one of
her hurried notes to Giovanni she told him so, begging
that if ever he loved another he would think first of
Angelo.

Her hopes had been raised so high before that first
dreadful Sunday in June. Rome's future and her own were
linked together in an indissoluble tie. Rome's triumph
would have meant Giovanni's success, and his success, her
own. Now each day brought greater desolation to the city
she had loved and with every bursting meteor that shattered the pine trees her own hopes fell. She was weary
and faith soared and sang no more. She had played for a
new stake and was losing. Rome still was playing for a
high stake, but now the struggle seemed hopeless. On the

night of the twentieth outside the walls of the Casa Giaco-metti, the Italians had won a victory with their bayonets, but by the next day a fiery rain fell thick over the Piazza di Gesu, and a tremendous cannonade announced that the French had made the breach and entered the city.

After that Margaret waited despairingly while day followed day in a week of defeat. First Sterbini, hoping to regain his power, exploited Garibaldi's name in a plot that ended in a fiasco. Then Mazzini quarreled with Gari-baldi, who gave up his command, but later returned to his post on the Janiculum. The besieged city seethed with unrest. Each day Margaret heard of another familiar place that had been shelled. Holes had been torn in the Spada; the roof of the Church of San Pietro in Montorio collapsed; in the Piazza di Spagna, where Margaret had walked so often, and on Santo Spirito, bombs had fallen. Over the post office, where she had waited so often for letters from Rieti, the lightning of musketry made fire-works in the air. In her room in the Casa Diez she heard the sound of the storm alarm. At the news that came to her in whispers she grew sick at heart. The French were crushing the batteries with cannon they had stolen from Civita Vecchia. The water supply was cut off. Provisions were seized. As Margaret walked to the hospitals, balls and bombs whizzed and burst near her. While she waited alone in the Casa Diez, Rome fell, fell amid rain and ruin. Not Garibaldi's sabre, nor all the cries of *Viva l'Italia* could save the city. With butt and bayonet, lance and knife, the French closed in upon the Italians, raked their lines, stormed their defenses. The city she had loved was no more.

June slipped into July and Giovanni brought Margaret the melancholy news of a resolution passed by the As-sembly, a resolution that meant surrender. Mazzini, he said, had resigned, and was wondering what next to do as he sat in the home of his friend Gustavo Modena at 60

Piazza di Picena. He had grown old, Giovanni said; his dark eyes were bloodshot; his hair was turning white. Garibaldi was leaving Rome with his men, and as Margaret walked along the Corso, the lancers galloped by in full career. She followed them to the piazza of St. John Lateran, waving farewell to the bright red tunics and the plumed hats, seeing Garibaldi turn his spyglass upon Rome for a moment and then lead the way through the gate. In place of the Legion, of the Bersaglieri, the French entered, filling the courtyards of the Quirinal, sounding their drums and trumpets, swaggering into the cafés as the Italians walked out. The National Guard was dissolved and Giovanni wept aloud when he saw the French eagles flying over Rome. Now Margaret saw in the gay, free city of yesterday, martial law executed. At the point of the bayonet she with all of Rome was driven home at half-past nine. A boy crowed like a cock at the French soldiery and three families were carried to prison. She saw the insignia of the Republic taken down. She read the edict commanding all foreigners who had served the Republic to leave within twenty-four hours. Rome was taken, was hers no longer.

She would have sold her hair or given her blood could it have helped. Now there was nothing to do but leave a fallen city. Hurriedly she prepared for her departure, packing and sending letters. To Lewis Cass, the American Envoy, Margaret wrote, asking for aid. When he came to her room she told him her secret and obtained through him a passport for Mazzini. She wrote also to Carlyle, requesting his assistance with booksellers for the History of the Late Italian Revolution which she was engaged in writing. There was still time, as she sat in the upper story of the Casa Diez, for a letter to the *Tribune,* pleading for help from America, for money and good cheer so that the nations would wait no more to see how long Rome could bear defeat. As she looked out from the loggia over the ruined city Margaret knew that her heart would ever remain in Italy, that Rome was her country. Surely mankind still was one, and beat with one great heart. Yet she trembled as she thought of the past, of her own hopes, and Giovanni's, and Rome's. Not words, not thoughts, could alter the one irrevocable fact. The Roman castles she had built out of shells in Cherry Street had fallen. The warm and colorful city where she had walked and loved and lingered was warm and colorful no longer. She dared not remember the chestnut vendors, or the contadini whirling in the *Saltarello,* or the yellow Tiber, or St. Peter's dome glittering in the sunlight. Rome was a word, for all the genius of the dear land that she had loved was once again enslaved.

Margaret and Giovanni set out together for Rieti, arriving there only to find that Angelo was ill from a diet of bread and wine. Giovanni stayed long enough to see the baby slowly regain his health and joyous spirits, and to walk about with Margaret in what seemed to them another world of tranquil, red-brown roof tops. As they wandered about they saw the casinos and convents gleam pleasantly from the hillsides, while Madonna-veiled, bare-legged women twirled their distaffs at every door. From their window in a rustic *locanda* they watched the girls in their colored petticoats, with silver needles in their hair, gather at the fountain to fill their water vases. At half-past seven Margaret and Giovanni occasionally joined the parade of baronesses and countesses and Spanish soldiers who ambled along the Rietan Corso as the band played.

Soon Giovanni left for Rome to sell Margaret's effects and obtain money by renouncing his claims on a vineyard that he had inherited. Left alone Margaret nursed the baby and tried to think more of the future than of the past. The past could not be forgotten, however. A little note that Pickie sent to "Aunty Margaret that has gone to Europe" carried her back to the *Tribune* office and a

little boy who often lost his temper but could never lose
his charm. More ominously the past intruded when only
a little later she read in a letter from Greeley, "Ah, Margaret, the world grows dark with us. You grieve, for
Rome is fallen; I mourn, for Pickie is dead." Then the
past suddenly became the future and Margaret feared
that Angelo too—like Waldo and like Pickie, like all her
sweet children—would die.

But Angelo did not die. Gradually he regained his
strength and now Margaret decided to tell her mother
and the world her secret. There was no hope for Giovanni
and herself in Rome and she could not return to America
without disclosing the strange story she had lived. Sitting
on the loggia above the fountain she wrote to her mother,
saying that she had a little son and was married to a
Roman. She told her of Giovanni's sympathy with liberal
principles and his sweetness of temper. In him, she said,
she had found a home. Together they would go to Florence for the winter and then perhaps return to America.
She begged her mother to write Angelo's name in her
Bible, hoping that God would let him live to see her. No
longer now would she have to speak to her mother of her
secret in the quiet night; no longer harbor her love in
silence. The world might wag its tongue; she at last was
free.

Through Horatio Greenough Margaret and Giovanni
obtained permission to remain in Florence. They spent the
first days of the autumn with their baby undisturbed under
the pontifical authorities at Perugia, though at first the
police had talked of sending them out of Tuscany. Every
morning Margaret went with Giovanni to some church
rich in pictures and returned at noon for breakfast. Then
they went together to sit under the trees near San Pietro
while Margaret read Nicolo di' Lapi or talked with
Giovanni about the vague possibility of a new revolution in Rome.

At last, after the tumultuous days of June and the hurried flight to Rieti, Margaret settled for the winter at the Casa Libri on the corner of the Piazza Maria Novella and the Via della Misericordia. For the first time in her life she had her own home and could live in peace with her baby and her husband. The house itself was modern and well built, the small rooms on the sixth story quiet and comfortable, and Margaret had only to look out of her window for a sight of the lovely campanile of the Church of Santa Maria Novella. Every morning the baby was carried into his parents' little room, where he drew the curtain with his dimpled hand, kissed Margaret violently, patting her face, crowing, laughing, blowing "bravo," and revealing quite definitely that he had arrived at the knowing age of over one year. As a suitable reward for Angelo's accomplishments, Margaret tied him in his chair and gave him his playthings. Then came the baby's great hour when near the stove in the dining room his mother washed and dressed him, while he proceeded to wash and dress her at the same time, throwing the water about and laughing archly. At midday the nurse whom Margaret had engaged in Rieti took Angelo for his outing in the shady lanes of Florence where the bands played and children sat with their nurses.

With the nap that followed, this gave Margaret about three hours every day for her own work. While Nino slept she sat before her wood fire reading Louis Blanc's *Ten Years,* Lamartine's *Girondists* or Macaulay's *History* of the James II period. When she tired of this kind of book she dipped into Mrs. Jameson's *Italian Painters* to read the account of Correggio, a true servant of God in his art, and to scribble in the margin, "And yet all might be such!" Then, laying her journals and manuscripts on the table before her, Margaret took up her pencil to work on her book. She had completed two volumes of it by now, and looked forward to the day when it would be ready for the press. It had already been given more time and labor than anything else she had published. The raw material was there, the observations she had made on the most minute event of the revolution. Now the work must be polished and refined so that this story of the great movement for Italian liberty and unity would reach a wide public. The hours flew as she changed the rough notes of her journal into an account of the struggle in Rome, as she changed yesterday's living scenes into tomorrow's history. Soon the baby awakened and Giovanni wanted to go on a little excursion with Margaret. The journals and manuscripts were piled on the table, and Margaret put on her cloak for a walk with her husband.

Sometimes they wandered only to the near-by Church of Santa Maria Novella and the Via val Fonda. Occasionally they drove together to the Cascine and sat on a stone seat in the sunny walk to see the people pass, the Grand Duke and his children, the elegant Austrian officers who, Margaret murmured to Giovanni, would be driven out of Italy when Angelino was a man. There they sat and read while the birds sang, or nodded to Mrs. Greenough as she passed in her carriage. Often they went to the Duomo, contrasting it with St. Peter's which they thought so much more splendid, so poignant to them, with the memory of their first meeting.

In the evening they returned to the Casa Libri and their bright firelit room. The baby sat on a little stool between them and Margaret looked happily about the room, glancing at its polished floor and frescoed ceiling, and at the oval table with its brass lamp and cups for olive oil. This at last was home, hers and Giovanni's. She looked at him as he sat near her reading an Italian book, dressed in the red-corded suit of the Guardia Civica that he still wore indoors. Giovanni looked up from the pages to smile or to call her very cautiously and deliberately, "Mother." Margaret knew that his love of the baby had made him forget his brother Giuseppe, and some of the misery of the last hours in Rome. She too could almost forget the past in the comfort of their little room. As they sat close together, the baby would sometimes surprise them, looking up from his little stool, to ask for a "kiss" instead of a *"basia."* Usually he contented himself with an attempt to sing and drum in imitation of the bands that he had heard on the Piazza. Though he could not walk yet, he was full of pranks, especially by evening, and on Christmas night he quivered with excitement over his three new toys, loving the bird, shouting over the horse, holding the cat's face close to his. These were calm and happy hours before Giovanni turned out the oil lamp and Margaret lowered the curtains for the night.

On other evenings Margaret heard the hollow voice of the porter, calling to his child, *"Lita! e la cara Signora in casa?"* and then she knew that a guest had come. Usually it was Horace Sumner who appeared at the door, having announced his visit with a gift of wildflowers sent early in the morning. Margaret was glad to know that her young friend of Brook Farm days lived near to them in Florence, and though he seemed to her slow and old in his ways, it was pleasant to reminisce with him about brewis and pandowdy, Isaac Hecker and John Dwight, and Lloyd, whom he had known well at the Farm. Giovanni also was glad to meet Horace Sumner, for of late he had been forming a taste for books and was eager to exchange lessons with Margaret's friend. She sat quietly while Giovanni mouthed a few English phrases and Horace picked up a little Italian. It was strange to think of Roxbury while they sat together here, before a bright fire in the Piazza Maria Novella. Margaret had never thought, when she visited Brook Farm so many years before, that the young boy who had listened with such ad-

miration to her eloquent words in the Eyrie would now sit
before an oval table in a little Florentine house teaching
English to her husband.

There were other ways also to vary the quiet months.
Margaret had friends in Florence and often she was invited to visit them of an evening. Once it was a children's
party arranged by Mrs. Greenough, and Margaret drew
from the lottery a toy that Angelo liked better even than
his bird or horse or cat. It was a child sleeping on the
neck of a tiger, and the baby never stopped hugging it and
whispering to it. On other occasions Margaret left Nino
with his nurse, and Giovanni escorted her to her friends.
Whenever English was too fluently spoken he left for the
Caffè d'Italia or for vespers at a near-by church, since
despite Horace Sumner's lessons he still found the language very difficult. As for Margaret, she enjoyed spending an evening now and then with the Greenoughs. She
still found the sculptor a man of magnanimity with a deep
sense of democracy, and she took keen pleasure in attending the ballet at the Perzola where the Greenoughs
had a box. If they had been surprised at first at the news
of Margaret's marriage, they accepted it tactfully as a
fait accompli, often inviting the Ossolis for a walk or a
cup of tea. Mme. Arconati Visconti was wintering in
Florence also, and with her Margaret passed many a
pleasant hour in her villa or on the Cascine. Mme.
Arconati presented her with a small marble figure of a
child playing among vine leaves which Margaret treasured as a token of their friendship. Walter Savage
Landor was occasionally to be seen in his villa on the
Fiesolean slope, not far from Maiano, and Margaret
reverenced the whimsical fancies of his old age as much
as she admired his poems.

If such visits did not provide the long winter evenings
with sufficient variety, there were always the soirees given
twice a week by Messrs. Mozier and Chapman. Mar-

garet's intimacy with the Moziers had increased during the winter in Florence since she had undertaken to tutor their daughter, while the sculptor allowed Giovanni to try his hand at modeling in his studio. The Moziers lived in a very handsome house and Margaret enjoyed an occasional Saturday evening in their company. Joseph Mozier still seemed more the shopkeeper than the artist, but it was amusing to hear his rapid stream of talk about the lack of genius of his fellow sculptors. John Gadsby Chapman enlivened the evening with the story of his wanderings over Calabria in a goatskin and untanned shoes, or the account of the suit of armor he had bought in Florence. Margaret was interested in hearing the views of a man who had decided that designing book illustrations for Harper Brothers in New York did not satisfy him. A painter, he said, was like a fish out of water in America. Chapman was free with his advice on sketching, for he believed that any one who could learn to write could learn to draw. Indeed, he declared, he had proven his thesis by his own painting of Hagar and Ishmael Fainting in the Wilderness, and planned to write a book on the subject one day.

Had the overheated rooms not given Margaret a headache, she would have enjoyed hearing Mozier's remarks about William Page, the artist who had ideas on every subject from new methods of measuring the human body and experiments in color to Swedenborgianism and Shakespeare's death mask. Thomas Read, the lively young poet-painter who had just come to Florence, figured in the conversation also, and had the stoves not given off so much heat, she would have delighted in the talk about the gay, curly-haired artist who had found so many Murray Guide Books in Florence, trotting about with half a dozen beggars whining at their heels.

As it was, Margaret found the rooms too stuffy for comfort, and soon Mozier's talk became a ferment of unscrupulous gossip and malicious scandal. He was not beyond whispering a taunt at Giovanni's incompetence with the mallet, even when he was thinking of Germano's, for Margaret's Italian acquaintance had also drifted into Mozier's studio, and had been exposed as a dishonest imposter and an ignoramus. Accuracy did not seem to be Joseph Mozier's forte. Gossip was too tempting a morsel for him to resist. Finally Margaret decided that the air in the sculptor's handsome rooms was too close for enjoyment, and she put on her wraps to return to the Piazza Maria Novella.

At one home in Florence Margaret knew that malice would never degrade, nor gossip disturb the charm of conversation. Along the Via della Scala she walked, turning down the Via Maggio, until she came to the old palace of Casa Guidi. Up the spacious staircase she mounted, passing the vestibule and the hall that opened onto a balcony, until she arrived at the large drawing room. Margaret glanced toward the window from which she could see the ancient Church of San Felice, and looked about at the mirrors, the great green velvet sofa, and, drawn close to the open fire, the deep easy chair. Almost lost in it was Elizabeth Barrett Browning, who turned her dark eyes to Margaret, held forth her slender fingers, and beckoned her to a chair. How pale and small she looked, Margaret thought, with those black ringlets clustering under her cap, down her neck. Her eyes—how bright and dark they glowed, as she spoke to her guest in a voice that was at once shrill and sweet. Sitting together before the fireplace, they spoke of their babies, of Angelo's little ways and Pennini's newest cap pattern. Surely, Margaret said, it is better to give the world a living soul than part of one's life in a book, and yet she would soon know the worth of her own book, but she must wait long to see what Angelo's worth would be. Mrs. Browning smiled, asking Margaret about her book. It was still less surprising somehow to know that Miss Fuller had retired from the Roman field with a manuscript than that she had emerged from the struggle with a husband and a child. Everything else that she had written, Margaret said, was in the form of sketches, thrown out in haste for the means of subsistence. This book on the history of the Italian Revolution would, she thought, be the only work that would represent her at all. Certainly it was the only work that would express her own revolutionary spirit. Despite the fact that Mrs. Browning had different opinions about social reform, having, as she confessed, viewed the world from the windows of Casa Guidi rather than from the barricaded streets of Rome, she expressed her admiration for Margaret's truth and courage in coloring the book with socialistic views that might draw the wolves upon her.

As Margaret sat, glancing at the tapestried walls and the bright fire, turning now and then to Mrs. Browning's pale face and dark eyes, she heard a step on the stairs and Robert Browning entered the room, cheerful and glowing after his walk. With his blue eyes and healthy tanned skin, his beaked nose and dark hair he seemed the antithesis of his wife, whom he stooped to greet. Browning sat down opposite her, and Margaret, sitting between them, gazing down at the fireplace, felt suddenly as if a curtain had fallen between herself and them. She felt a great sadness, a cloud of gloom which she could not explain. Gravely she listened while Browning spoke of the changes that had taken place in Florence, changes that seemed strangely to correspond with those that she had just experienced. Even from his little walk, he said, he could see that hope and gaiety had left the city. Margaret reminded them that even the bands of men who had sung their chants of liberty when she had first visited Florence were gone, and in their place a sombre, desolate silence prevailed. The Brownings recalled that in those happier days they had ridden far into the country, eating strawberries and drinking milk out of the peasants' basins. With an emphatic gesture, Browning remarked that once he had been forced to escape from a festivity when the sound of Garibaldi's hymn brought the Austrian police knocking at the door. Margaret too remembered the Austrian officers, the French eagles, which had forced her to escape from something other than a festival. She had become an enthusiastic socialist, she admitted. Elsewhere was no comfort, no solution for the problems of the times. The way of peace, she said, was best, but she herself was still not sure whether she could keep her hands free from blood. Italy was bereft. "The great depart, and none rise up to fill their vacant seat." Browning looked at his visitor, wondering whether the white skin of the grape, the pomegranates, the fig trees, the cypress, the Casa Guidi itself were not enough for poetry. Mrs. Browning turned her dark eyes to Margaret, knowing in her heart that liberty was more than a song that had been sung beneath Casa Guidi windows. From the windows now they could see the Church of San Felice in the darkness, could hear the bells tolling the hour, reminding Margaret that it was time to return to Angelo and Giovanni, that for her, after all, Italy was not entirely bereft.

Yet even the polished floor and frescoed ceiling of Margaret's room, with the baby on his stool and Giovanni in the chair next to her, seemed lonely when she read the news from home. More than ever now the little details of her friends' lives—word that Newcomb had spent the summer in Newport, that Thoreau was studying the woodlands of Concord, that Alcott had given a conversation on *The Times*—filled her with the desire to return and be among kindred once again. With deep regret that she had not been more of a friend to Poe, Margaret learned that on October eighth he had been buried and that no one could ruffle the plumes of the Raven again. A more poignant nostalgia was hers when she received the

kind and generous note with which her mother answered
Margaret's letter about her marriage. "If he continues
to make you happy," she read, "he will be very dear to
me, for long have I felt sickness, great pain in the thought
of putting off the body that I should leave you peculiarly
lonely." How strange it was, she considered, glancing
down the page, to know that her mother had not been
able to make out Giovanni's name. "I can make out
Angelo, Eugene, Philip, but not your husband's name.
Is it Orsoli or Orsoni?" She would know soon, Margaret
thought, both his name, and himself. By this time Margaret realized that all Boston and New York had heard
the news, Longfellow and Emerson, Sarah Ripley and
Marcus Spring confirming for the benefit of Beacon Street
or Broadway word of Margaret's marriage to a revolutionary marquis. It would take no little courage, she was
convinced, to walk down Beacon Street arm in arm with
a revolutionary marquis, but Margaret knew that after
so many tests, her courage would not fail her then.

There seemed indeed no reason to tarry longer in
Florence. Margaret's headaches had returned and during
the damp, chilly winter she as well as Giovanni had suffered. There was a dangerous pressure on her brain, and
if she must be ill surely it would be better to be ill at
home. She had long since learned to be a willing adept in
economy, but now Margaret knew that there was no
career open to Giovanni in Italy, and she herself could
earn more money by publishing her book in America than
by waiting any longer in Florence. What was there, after
all, to wait for? After a number of years, perhaps, a new
revolution might favor a return; she could not leave this
beloved land without the hope of some day coming back.
But now she wanted to go home. Giovanni also was
willing, seeing in America, as did all *Giovine Italia,* the
land of liberty.

It was difficult to know what boat to select. Margaret

had read of the wreck of the "Argo" on its voyage to France; the "Royal Adelaide" and the "John Skiddy" had gone down. They must choose a seaworthy vessel, but on the other hand, they could not afford a passage in such an expensive steamboat as the "Cambria." It was with great delight, therefore, that during a stroll through one of the galleries Margaret met a young American couple who introduced themselves as Captain and Mrs. Seth Hasty. They had sailed for the Mediterranean, they said, in the five-year-old packet ship "Elizabeth" of which Captain Hasty was master. They chatted on for a while, the captain discussing the Hasty farm in Scarboro, Maine, and his wife reminiscing about her own home in Black Point. They seemed to Margaret a pleasant couple, and when Captain Hasty remarked that his ship was lying at anchor in the harbor at Leghorn, she determined to look at it and perhaps select a stateroom.

With Mrs. Mozier Margaret inspected the boat, finding it already laden with marble and silk for the two-months' voyage home. Though marble was a heavy bulk for the small sailing vessel to carry, Margaret was pleased to learn that it was Powers' statue of John Calhoun that added weight to the cargo. Besides, had not the name Elizabeth ever been a good omen? Margaret selected her room, arranging for a few changes, and engaged passage for the voyage with a bill for three hundred and thirty-six dollars that she drew on Marcus Spring through Fienzi and Hall.

It seemed ironical to her that as soon as she had definitely decided to sail, she should have received a packet from the Springs, which, had it arrived two weeks earlier, might have induced her to remain in Italy. It contained the first word of encouragement, the first glimpse of aid that had come to her, but it arrived too late for her to cancel her reservations. Now it was also decided that Horace Sumner would return on the "Elizabeth" with

Margaret and Giovanni. The sails were set. Soon the vessel would clear port. There was no turning back now.

Three days before her departure Margaret wrote to her mother, sending her love, hoping that they would be able to pass some time together yet in this world. But, she added, remembering the "Argo," the "John Skiddy," recalling the belated arrival of the packet from the Springs, if God decrees otherwise—here and *Hereafter*— she would be her dearest mother's loving child. For her friends she sent home a box of presents and souvenirs, lest, by some decree of the strange fate that had always pursued her, she should not again see her fatherland.

Nothing remained now but to pack and say farewell. She must, of course, buy an immense stock of baby linen for Angelo so that he would look his best for his grandmother. Then there were the supplies that would be needed for the long journey, a goat for the baby's milk, oranges and lemons, soda, hard bread, and a medicine chest. The "Elizabeth" did not carry its own farmyard, and whatever was to be cooked for Nino on the grates of the deck would have to be purchased in Florence. She must also engage an Italian girl to care for the baby during the voyage. To Draper in Paris Margaret forwarded a trunk of papers, and proceeded to pack the other bags that she would take with her.

In the lower compartment of her black leather trunk Margaret placed her clothing, her nightgowns and shifts, her silk fringed dress and her muslin, and Nino's pretty frocks and petticoats. There was an engraving that must be carefully packed, along with her Bible with the hymn of Novalis in the flyleaf. Now all the pamphlets and newspapers that she had collected in Italy, files of the democratic *Pacifique* and *Il Nazionale* of Florence must be tied up, the journal with its telling inscription, "Rome, 1849," placed in the small trunk, all the letters from Mme. Arconati and Mazzini laid in the upper compartment. Those other dearer letters that Giovanni had sent to Aquila and Rieti remained to be arranged separately and packed along with a lock of his dark hair. Margaret slipped her little desk into a cover, and proceeded to help Giovanni with his carpet bag. As she surveyed the trunks she could not help thinking how much of her life they represented, how many tokens there were of a life she had never dreamed she would live that far-off day when the "Cambria" cleared for Liverpool. The "Elizabeth" would carry a different burden home—a lock of dark hair, a baby's frock, a manuscript about a struggle for liberty and a city made desolate of hope.

A few days before Margaret left for Leghorn the Greenoughs and the Brownings visited the Casa Libri to bid their friends good-bye. The night before she left Florence Margaret saw the Brownings once again, and as they spoke of the "Elizabeth" she remarked that Giovanni had once been warned to shun the sea as it would be fatal to him. "That does not much discompose you?" Browning asked jestingly. Giovanni smiled, shaking his head. Margaret was silent, but then she too smiled, saying, "Our ship is called the 'Elizabeth,' and I accept the omen." Mrs. Browning pressed upon her a ring with a carbuncle in it as a parting gift, and Margaret wondered if her friend knew that the stone had always been peculiarly her own. In return she presented Mrs. Browning with a Bible, from Angelo to Pennini, inscribing in the flyleaf the words, "In memory of Angelo Eugene Ossoli." Farewells were said to the Brownings and to Italy, to everything that had been Margaret's life for almost three years.

With the white goat and the trunks, with Horace Sumner and Celesta Pardena, the Italian servant whom Margaret had engaged, the Ossolis left for Leghorn. As they went with the Hastys to board the boat Margaret told them with how much pleasure she anticipated her homecoming. She turned to bid a last farewell to Italy, saying that she hoped to see again its sunny shores. Mazzini, Margaret knew, had returned to London with his canaries, and in his place Pope Pius had arrived again in Rome. Perhaps the shores would be sunnier with a brighter hope when next she saw the Eternal City. In the year 1850 there seemed no room for hope in Italy. That year of the mid-century now appeared to Margaret the time when she would stand on a plateau in the ascent of life and take more clear and commanding views than before. From the deck of the barque "Elizabeth" on May seventeenth she watched the receding city, until she could see nothing but a pin point where towered some lofty campanile, until she saw nothing but waves about her, and the open sea stretching, it seemed, to all eternity.

BOOK THREE:
BETWEEN TWO WORLDS

CHAPTER XVII

THE BARQUE "ELIZABETH"

THOUGH THE stout barque "Elizabeth" made slow progress over the waters, Margaret and Giovanni both were seasick, and often wished they had little Angelo's "sea legs." Yet, despite headache and pains in her back Margaret soon accustomed herself to the violent motion of the vessel and even began to enjoy life on shipboard. Every morning she opened her little desk to add a line or polish a phrase of her manuscript, while the Hastys and Horace Sumner helped Giovanni with his English and received a few lessons in Italian themselves. Angelo played quietly with his alabaster dove or rolled his blue eyes at the goat which would give him milk for luncheon. The grates on the deck soon sizzled with food cooked under Joseph McGill's supervision and the Hastys joined the travelers at the long table for a snack of hard bread and oranges.

During the afternoons Margaret sat or walked on the deck, becoming gradually familiar with the boat and its crew. To Nino she pointed out the spars and rigging, the planks and timbers, while Charles Davis, the first mate, took time off to show the little boy the cargo—sacks of juniper berries and oil-flasks, casks of almonds, blocks of rough Carrara, boxes of paintings, Leghorn braid, and silk. Celesta Pardena often took little Nino on the rounds, watching him play with George Bates, the steward, who seemed to take quite a fancy to the child. Sometimes they looked on while the Swedish seamen painted a little during the quiet afternoons. It was pleasant to walk along the hard planks of the deck, seeing the sails swell in a light wind, feeling the sun, enjoying the careless delight of being in a world apart. In the evenings the Hastys played games with the Ossolis, celebrating Margaret's fortieth birthday on the sixth day out, and so the first happy week passed by.

On May twenty-fifth Captain Hasty decided not to join the evening games, for he said that he was suffering from violent pains in his head and back. He retired to the sofa in his stateroom and Margaret carried the baby in to visit him. Mr. Bates and John Helstroom, second mate, bobbed in and out, eager to serve their master. The next day Mrs. Hasty told Margaret that the captain was feverish and that a constant, convulsive cough was weakening him. In the few moments during the day that Mrs. Hasty left the sick room she confided to Margaret her fears for her husband, informing her that a red eruption was spreading over his body and that his throat was so swollen he could not swallow. Whenever he had strength to speak he begged his wife to read a chapter in the Bible. Once, Mrs. Hasty said, he asked her to sing one of their favorite hymns, but she had been too moved to utter a sound. Always he said that he hoped to find medical aid in Gibraltar, to recover and return to America.

On the night of June first the "Elizabeth" weighed anchor off Gibraltar, and the mates went down to Captain Hasty's room to take orders. Later, Margaret was stunned to learn that in the morning the captain had died. Boats came and went from the shore with much consultation among the authorities about quarantine regulations. Between comforting the forlorn Mrs. Hasty and seeing that Angelo was taken care of, Margaret walked about, listening to the reports of the officials. Finally it was decided that since Captain Hasty had probably died of smallpox, he could not be buried on shore. In the port the ships at anchor lowered their flags at half-mast, and at sunset, Captain Hasty, late commander of the "Elizabeth," wrapped in the flag of his nation, was carried to his rest. A calm, soft, glowing afternoon had succeeded a morning of bleak, cold wind. Margaret watched from the deck as the American consul's barge towed out a small boat from the "Elizabeth" which bore the captain's body. It was a sad moment for Mrs. Hasty and the crew as the sun set over the Strait of Gibraltar, and the "Elizabeth" was left, riding at anchor in the darkness, without a master.

For a week the barque was detained at Gibraltar because of adverse winds, and while the crew waited to hoist the sails Margaret comforted Mrs. Hasty, writing, at her request, to her parents of the tragedy that had overtaken her. There was nothing to do off Gibraltar Bay but write letters, and Margaret took out her portfolio to drop a line to Marcus Spring, telling him of the bill that she had drawn upon his account, and of Captain Hasty's death. Ossoli had had smallpox, she wrote, and so was safe. But in the earlier days, before she had suspected that disease, Margaret had carried the baby into the sick room and feared that he might be stricken. As she glanced through the letter, she felt that it breathed a melancholy tone. But so be it. The voyage had not been propitious so far, and she would not try to hide her own forebodings. To the Brownings, her "dear precious friends," Margaret also wrote, telling them of the ravages of the smallpox, saying that they were about to continue their voyage, uncertain if the fatal disease were not waiting to break out among them when once more they were out of reach of help. Playfully, she bade them write to her and guess what the first thing would be to meet her at home.

On the ninth of June, the "Elizabeth" took to the sea again, after it had been decided that the mate, Mr. Henry Bangs, would act as captain. Though he confessed that he was inexperienced, the crew must have a master, and Mrs. Hasty said that her husband had taught her enough navigation on the outward trip to help along now and then. Once again, Margaret watched from the deck until the last strip of land diminished to a point, and the sails of the "Elizabeth" billowed in the rising wind.

Two days later Margaret knew that her fears for Nino had not been groundless. He found no pleasure now in playing with Mr. Bates, nor in stroking the white goat, nor in fondling his alabaster dove. Margaret put him to bed and sat next to him, watching over him, placing wet applications on his skin. With Giovanni she sat day after day, despairing when Nino's eyes were closed and sightless, when his head and face became swollen, and his body was covered with pustules. Giovanni was almost resigned to disaster, telling Margaret that life had seemed so hard to him that he would be willing the baby should be spared the struggle. But Margaret would not give him up. To this she would not be resigned. And nine days after Nino had been stricken, she discovered with joy that the baby could see again, could see the alabaster dove, Celesta Pardena, and all his little world. Now his recovery was rapid, and Margaret sat by his bed, singing to him, while Giovanni arranged his toys around his coverlet. Finally, with great ceremony, they carried him to the sitting room and laid him on the sofa so that he could receive his friend, Mr. Bates, in state.

Surely after these two disasters, the "Elizabeth" would come to her final anchor in safety. The weeks rolled by, weeks of deck-walking and writing, of playing with Angelo and watching once again the spars and rigging. Joseph McGill did the cooking, Mr. Bates stopped now and then to join in a game with Nino, Mr. Bangs steered his ship toward port. With joy they all hailed the rising of the southeast wind which would carry them so speedily to shore. There was a moon now climbing the heavens, and Margaret enjoyed watching it glimmer on the waters, telling Mrs. Hasty it would be her last moonlight night at sea, since they were certain to reach port before another crescent shone in the skies. At length the trunks were brought to Margaret's cabin and she took all her clothing out, showing Mrs. Hasty Nino's little dresses, deciding on the frock he was to wear on shore. Soon the long voyage would be over, and Margaret would see once again her mother, be once again among friends.

Perhaps Greeley would come, his trousers tucked into the tops of his boots, his neckcloth awry, to greet again his friend of distant years. Alcott would raise his serene eyes to search in the azure heavens for signs of the golden age. Thoreau would still be trapping in the woodside the secrets of bird and hare and muskrat. Emerson would await her in his study, eager perhaps to speak of a far-off constellation that he had seen on a bright and starry night. To the New World Margaret would bring word of the Old, of Wordsworth and his hollyhocks, George Sand and her salon, Mazzini and his wasted hopes, as she sat once again in the plain white house in Concord. And Caroline Tappan and Sarah Clarke, Elizabeth Peabody and Anna Ward, all the ladies of West Street, would ask, perhaps, for another Conversation, about Rome to-day instead of yesterday. To them all, to Ellen and Ellery, to her mother and her brothers, Margaret would carry her treasures, her husband and her son. In the New World to which she returned, would she not find again her place, act out her being, live the life before her?

On Thursday evening, July eighteenth, home seemed so near to Margaret that she had only to sleep one night for the dream to turn into reality. They were between Cape May and Barnegat, Mr. Bangs reported.[1] When daylight showed the highlands of Navesink he would take a pilot and run before the wind past Sandy Hook. In the morning, he promised, he would anchor the "Elizabeth" in New York harbor. The trunks were in the cabin. Nino's prettiest frock had been laid out for him to wear

[1] In reality they were near Fire Island.

in the morning. He would dream the night away, and arise to find himself in the New World.

During the evening the southeast wind that had borne them along so steadily rose to a slight gale. Under close-reefed sails the ship ran northward, driven headlong through the night. In her cabin Margaret could hear the high surf, the sea breaking, the moan of the wind. She stirred restlessly, listening to the driving rain, the creaking timbers. Toward morning she heard Mr. Bangs leave his cabin, to take soundings no doubt. All must be safe, however, for shortly after she heard him retire again to his berth. Margaret turned in her bed to sleep the early hours away.

Before daylight she was awakened by a violent shock. The ship struck sidewise, canted, thrust head on. Waves poured down into the cabin through the skylight. Margaret heard the sound of the small boats being smashed and torn away. With Giovanni she fled from the cabin in her night clothes, meeting Horace Sumner and Mrs. Hasty in the narrow passageway. Now piercing screams filled the air, reports that the ship had struck on a sandbar, that a hole had been broken in her side, that the sea was pouring in. "Cut away!" Mr. Bangs cried out. Then Margaret heard the crash of falling timbers and the thunder of the sea. She saw the cabin skylight dashed to pieces, the cabin door wrenched away. With Celesta Pardena and Nino she and Giovanni reached the windward cabin walls, and sat against them, side by side, their feet braced against the long table. Angelo whimpered, shivering in his nightdress. Margaret tried to comfort him. Giovanni prayed.

At daybreak Mr. Davis, first mate, reached the cabin with some of his seamen, and, while the surf pounded and the hurricane roared, he helped the passengers to the forecastle. Margaret saw him grasp Mrs. Hasty's hand, but suddenly the sea swept her into the hatchway. Davis was quick. He seized her hair in his teeth, caught a support with both his hands, and set Mrs. Hasty on her feet. Nino's turn came soon. Carried in a canvas bag that was slung around the neck of a sailor, he was taken from the cabin. Margaret followed, across the gaping hatchway.

Now all hands on board made their way to the topgallant forecastle, while water poured into the ship. Margaret and Giovanni, Horace Sumner and Mrs. Hasty sat with Celesta Pardena and Nino, huddled together. One or two were wrapped in the loose overcoats of the seamen. Margaret waited, holding her breath as every wave lifted the forecastle roof and washed over the passengers. She watched, while the sea swept over the ship. Three times, as they sat close together, silent now in their fear, Margaret saw Mr. Davis return to the cabin. First he made the dangerous crossing to get Captain Hasty's watch for Mrs. Hasty. Later he went for the money-drafts and rings in Margaret's desk. A third time he ventured again for a bottle of wine and a drum of figs that the others might eat to gain some warmth. Margaret turned to Mrs. Hasty, saying, "There still remains what, if I live, will be of more value to me than anything." But she could not let Mr. Davis risk another passage over the hatchway to retrieve her manuscript.

At nine in the morning, while the ship careened on its side and the planks were dashed with the tremendous rush of water, one of the sailors took Margaret's life preserver to swim ashore and summon a lifeboat. As they waited in the forecastle, Margaret saw one seaman after another, George Sanford, Henry Westervelt, Hans Lauron, the Swedish sailors who had painted on deck during the first careless week of the crossing, plunge into the sea with a spar for support. Before they left, Margaret and Mrs. Hasty gave them messages for their friends if they ever reached the shore. Margaret dared not speak as she saw Horace Sumner turn from the forecastle and spring overboard.

At one o'clock, during the driving rain, word was passed round that a lifeboat had appeared. But as they waited, hearing the howling hurricane, they soon realized that no attempt was made to launch her. Now Mr. Bangs came into the forecastle, shouting, above the storming sea, that the tide would turn soon, that the wreck could not hold together through another flood, that the passengers must prepare to abandon ship. There were planks, he called, on which they could sit, grasping the handles of a rope while a sailor would swim behind. Margaret looked at Giovanni, at her baby. She would not leave them here and venture alone on those mountain waves.

At flood tide, the forecastle filled with water; the afterparts were shattered. The gale swelled; the cabin went by the board. The dragging, grinding ship was breaking up. Everyone now fled to the deck, clustering together round the foremast. Quickly, Margaret and Mrs. Hasty divided their money, tying it in handkerchiefs around them. Margaret watched, swept by the blinding rain, as Mrs. Hasty seized a plank and leaped overboard with Davis behind her. She saw the timbers smashed, her black leather trunk, Giovanni's carpet bag washed into the sea. Mr. Bangs pushed his way toward her, begging her to grasp a plank and leave. No, she said. She would not go alone. Instead she waited, holding Nino in her arms, seeing the spars chopped and broken by the sea, the casks and boxes washed away. The swells increased constantly. She turned to look at the shore, a lonely waste of sand hills, bleak and desolate in the spray and violent rain. She heard Celesta Pardena's shrieks above the howling surf. She saw the main and mizzenmasts cut away. In the confusion she heard a cry that the heavy marble in the hold had broken through the bottom, that the ship was bilging. The bow held fast, the stern swung round, the "Elizabeth" careened inland, her broadside bared to the shock of the sea.

Now Margaret heard the order, "Save yourselves!"
One after another the sailors jumped overboard. Mr.
Bates shouted to her, and Joseph McGill called out, urg-
ing her to try the planks that were ready in the lee of the
ship. She did not answer. Mr. Bates grabbed Nino from
her arms and plunged with him into the sea.

Margaret sat with her back to the foremast in her
white nightdress, her long, drenched hair falling over her
shoulders, her hands pressed over her knees. In the tearing rain Mr. McGill rushed by, and she cried out to him,
"I see nothing but death before me—I shall never reach
the shore." The mast was loosened from the hull, rising
and falling with every billow. Margaret saw death before
her, saw Giovanni and Celesta caught in the rigging, saw
the carpenter and the cook thrown far upon the bow.
Then with a grating jar, the foremast was wrenched
away, carrying the deck with it. A mountain wave lashed
the ship, washed Margaret away as the foremast fell.
Hurled from the depths of the sea rode death, the master,
over the broken spars and shattered planks, over the fallen masts of the barque "Elizabeth."

THE END

BIBLIOGRAPHY

Throughout the book the principal sources have been the Fuller Manuscripts at Harvard College Library, Vols. I through XVII, *Works of Margaret Fuller Ossoli,* Vols. I through V, Box A, Box B, Box of Extracts, and Box of Journals. Next in importance come the Fuller Papers at the Boston Public Library, consisting of Unmarked Folder, Folders 15, 33, B4-55, Folder of Fuller MSS checked, MS. F.1. 2, I and II, and the manuscript Love Letters to James Nathan.

Works to which the writer has referred for almost every chapter include Katherine Anthony, *Margaret Fuller, a Psychological Biography.* New York: Harcourt, Brace, 1921; Margaret Bell, *Margaret Fuller.* New York: Charles Boni, 1930; James F. Clarke, Ralph Waldo Emerson, and William Henry Channing, editors, *Memoirs of Margaret Fuller Ossoli.* London: Richard Bentley, 1852, Vols. I, II, and III; Edward Waldo Emerson and Waldo Emerson Forbes, editors, *Journals of Ralph Waldo Emerson with annotations.* Boston: Houghton Mifflin, 1910-1912, Vols. III-VIII; Thomas Wentworth Higginson, *Margaret Fuller Ossoli.* Boston: Houghton, Mifflin, 1884; Julia Ward Howe, *Margaret Fuller (Marchesa Ossoli).* Boston: Roberts, 1883; Ralph L. Rusk, editor, *The Letters of Ralph Waldo Emerson.* New York: Columbia University Press, 1939, Vols. I-VI.

Books frequently referred to include Seth Curtis Beach, *Daughters of the Puritans A Group of Brief Biographies.* Boston: American Unitarian Association, 1905; Frederick Augustus Braun, *Margaret Fuller and Goethe. The Development of a Remarkable Personality, Her Religion and Philosophy, and Her Relation to Emerson, J. F. Clarke and Transcendentalism.* New York: Henry Holt, 1910; James Elliot Cabot, *A Memoir of Ralph Waldo Emerson.* Cambridge: Riverside Press, 1887, Vols. I and II; Arthur W. Calhoun, *A Social History of the American Family from Colonial Times to the Present.* Cleveland: Arthur H. Clark, 1918, Vol. II; Ellery Channing, *Poems of Sixty-Five Years,* edited by Franklin B. Sanborn. Philadelphia: James H. Bentley, 1902; Ednah Dow Cheney, *Reminiscences.* Boston: Lee and Shepard, 1902; Henry Steele Commager, *Theodore Parker.* Boston: Little, Brown, 1936; Moncure Daniel Conway, *Emerson at Home and Abroad.* Boston: James R. Osgood, 1882; Moncure Daniel Conway, *Life of Nathaniel*

[493]

Hawthorne. London: Walter Scott, n.d.; George W. Curtis, *Early Letters to John S. Dwight,* edited by George Willis Cooke. New York: Harper, 1898; Ralph Waldo Emerson, *Lectures and Biographical Sketches.* Boston: Houghton Mifflin, 1883; Harold Clarke Goddard, *Studies in New England Transcendentalism.* New York: Columbia University Press, 1908; Horace Greeley, *Recollections of a Busy Life.* New York: J. B. Ford, 1868; Julian Hawthorne, *Nathaniel Hawthorne and His Wife, a Biography.* Boston: Ticknor, 1884, Vols. I and II; Thomas Wentworth Higginson, *Eminent Women of the Age.* Hartford: S. M. Betts, 1869; Marc Anthony de Wolfe Howe, *Holmes of the Breakfast-Table.* London: Oxford University Press, 1939; Andrew Macphail, *Essays in Puritanism.* Boston: Houghton, Mifflin, 1905; Harriet Martineau, *Retrospect of Western Travel.* London: Saunders and Otley, 1838, Vols. I and II; Charles Eliot Norton, editor, *The Correspondence of Thomas Carlyle and Ralph Waldo Emerson 1834-1872.* Boston: James R. Osgood, 1883, Vol. II, and *Supplementary Letters.* Boston: Ticknor, 1886; Vernon Louis Parrington, *The Romantic Revolution in America, 1800-1860.* New York: Harcourt, Brace, 1927; Edward L. Pierce, *Memoir and Letters of Charles Sumner.* Boston: Roberts, 1893, Vols. I and II; Edgar Allan Poe, *Works,* edited by Edmund Clarence Stedman and George Edward Woodberry. Chicago: Stone and Kimball, 1895, Vol. VIII; Franklin B. Sanborn and William T. Harris, *A. Bronson Alcott, His Life and Philosophy.* Boston: Roberts, 1893, Vols. I and II; Odell Shepard, editor, *The Journals of Bronson Alcott.* Boston: Little, Brown, 1938; Odell Shepard, *Pedlar's Progress: The Life of Bronson Alcott.* Boston: Little, Brown, 1937; Frank Preston Stearns, *The Life and Genius of Nathaniel Hawthorne.* Philadelphia: J. B. Lippincott, 1906; Justin Winsor, *Memorial History of Boston.* Boston: James R. Osgood, 1881, Vols. III and IV.

Specific references listed chapter by chapter follow:

CHAPTER I

Details concerning the Fuller genealogy and Margaret Fuller's early life appear in Elizabeth Abercrombie, *Fuller Genealogy, A Record of Joseph Fuller, Descendant of Thomas Fuller of Woburn and Middleton, Massachusetts.* Boston: David Clapp, 1897; Frederic Endicott, editor, *Record of Births, Marriages and Deaths and Intentions of Marriage in the Town of Canton, Massachusetts, from 1797 to 1845.* Canton: William Bense, 1896; Arthur Buckminster

Fuller, *Historical Notices of Thomas Fuller and His Descendants, with a Genealogy of the Fuller Family.* Boston: Henry W. Dutton, 1859; J. F. Fuller, *A Brief Sketch of Thomas Fuller and His Descendants.* Appleton, Wis.: Crescent Printing House, 1896; Richard Frederic Fuller, *Chaplain Fuller: Being a Life Sketch of a New England Clergyman and Army Chaplain.* Boston: Walker, Wise, 1863; Richard F. Fuller, "Memorials of Mrs. Margaret Fuller," *The Quarterly Journal of the American Unitarian Association,* VII, 1 (October 1859); Timothy Fuller, An Oration *Pronounced at Lexington, Massachusetts, on the fourth of July, A.D. 1814, by request of the Republican Citizens of Middlesex County, being the thirty-eighth anniversary of American Independence.* Boston: Rowe and Hooper, 1814; Rufus Wilmot Griswold, *The Prose Writers of America, with a survey of the intellectual history, condition, and prospects of the country.* Philadelphia: Parry and McMillan, 1859; Régis Michaud, *Autour d'Emerson.* Paris: Bossard, 1924; Harvey O'Higgins and Edward H. Reede, M.D., *The American Mind in Action.* New York: Harper, 1924.

Details of background, social and political, may be found in Charles Francis Adams, editor, *Memoirs of John Quincy Adams, comprising Portions of His Diary from 1795 to 1848.* Philadelphia: J. B. Lippincott, 1874-1877, Vols. V and VI; James Truslow Adams, *The Adams Family.* New York: Blue Ribbon, 1930; Edwin M. Bacon, *Literary Pilgrimages in New England to the Homes of Famous Makers of American Literature and among Their Haunts and the Scenes of Their Writings.* New York: Silver, Burdett, 1902; Samuel F. Batchelder, *Bits of Harvard History.* Cambridge: Harvard University Press, 1924; *Boston Mirror,* II, 28 (April 28, 1810); *Columbian Centinel,* May 23, 1810; Caroline H. Dall, "Transcendentalism in New England: A Lecture delivered before the Society for Philosophical Enquiry, Washington, D. C., May 7, 1895," reprinted from *The Journal of Speculative Philosophy,* XXIII, 1; Timothy Dwight, *Travels; in New England and New York.* New Haven: Timothy Dwight, 1821, Vol. I; Samuel A. Eliot, *A Sketch of the History of Harvard College and of its Present State.* Boston: Little and Brown, 1848; Edward Waldo Emerson, *Emerson in Concord, a Memoir written for the "Social Circle" in Concord, Massachusetts.* Boston: Houghton, Mifflin, 1889; Eliza Ware Farrar, *Recollections of Seventy Years.* Boston: Ticknor and Fields, 1866; John W. Freese, *Historic Houses and Spots in Cambridge, Massachusetts.* Boston: Ginn, 1897; Edward Everett Hale, *Memories of a Hundred Years.* New York: Macmillan, 1902, Vols. I and II; Edward Everett Hale, *A New England Boyhood*. Boston: Little, Brown, 1927; Albert Bushnell Hart, editor, *Commonwealth History of Massachusetts*. New York: States History Company, 1930, Vol. IV; Thomas Wentworth Higginson, *Old Cambridge*. New York: Macmillan, 1899; Abiel Holmes, *The History of Cambridge*. Boston: Samuel Hall, 1801; John Holmes, *Letters to James Russell Lowell and Others,* edited by William Roscoe Thayer. Boston: Houghton Mifflin, 1917; Daniel T. V. Hunton, *History of the Town of Canton, Norfolk County, Massachusetts.* Cambridge: John Wilson, 1893; *Independent Chronicle,* XLII, 3035 (May 21, 1810); Charles William Janson, *The Stranger in America.* London, 1807; *The Living Age,* 33:28-36 (April 3, 1852) and 33:289-300 (May 15, 1852); Elizabeth McClellan, *Historic Dress in America, 1800-1870.* Philadelphia: George W. Jacobs, 1910; Edgar G. Miller, Jr., *American Antique Furniture.* Baltimore: Lord Baltimore Press, 1937, Vol. I; Alfred Moe, *A History of Harvard.* Cambridge: Harvard University, 1896; N. Hudson Moore, *The Old Furniture Book, with a sketch of Past Days and Ways.* New York: Frederick A. Stokes, 1903; *North American Review,* 83: 261-264 (July 1856); Lucius R. Paige, *History of Cambridge, Massachusetts 1630-1877.* Boston: H. O. Houghton, 1877; Josiah Quincy, *History of Harvard University.* Cambridge: John Owen, 1840, Vol. II; *The Repertory,* VII, 41 (May 22, 1810); S. S. Simpson, *Two Hundred Years Ago; or, a Brief History of Cambridgeport and East Cambridge, with notices of some of the early settlers.* Boston: Otis Clapp, 1859; Marta K. Sironen, *A History of American Furniture,* edited by N. I. Bienenstock. New York: Towse, 1936; Elizabeth Cady Stanton, Susan B. Anthony, and Matilda Joslyn Gage, editors, *History of Woman Suffrage.* New York: Fowler and Wells, 1881, Vol. I; State Street Trust Company Monograph, *Boston, England and Boston, New England 1630-1930;* Caroline Ticknor, editor, *Dr. Holmes's Boston.* Boston: Houghton Mifflin, 1915; Frederick O. Vaille and Henry A. Clark, *The Harvard Book.* Cambridge: Welch, Bigelow, 1875, Vols. I and II.

CHAPTER II

Details of background appear in Samuel Abbott Green, *Facts relating to the History of Groton, Massachusetts.* Groton: University Press, 1912, Vol. I; Green, *Groton Historical Series, a Collection of Papers relating to the History of the Town of Groton,*

Massachusetts. Groton: University Press, 1887, Vols. I-IV; Green, *A Historical Sketch of Groton, Massachusetts, 1655-1890.* Groton, 1894; Hale, *Memories of a Hundred Years.*

CHAPTER III

Manuscript sources for this chapter include a letter from Margaret Fuller to the Rev. Mr. James F. Clarke, owned by Mr. James F. Clarke of Boston.

Details concerning Margaret Fuller's life between 1825 and 1833 appear in Thomas Wentworth Higginson, editor, *Harvard Memorial Biographies.* Cambridge: Sever and Francis, 1867, Vol. I; Oliver Wendell Holmes, "Cinders from the Ashes," *Atlantic Monthly,* XXIII, 115-123 (January 1869); Helen Neill McMaster, "Margaret Fuller as a Literary Critic," *The University of Buffalo Studies,* VII, 3 (December 1928); Margaret Fuller Ossoli, *Life Without and Life Within; or, Reviews, Narratives, Essays, and Poems,* edited by Arthur B. Fuller. Boston: Brown, Taggard and Chase, 1859; Samuel Smiles, *Brief Biographies.* Boston: Ticknor and Fields, 1861.

Details of background, social and political, may be found in Charles Francis Adams, *Richard Henry Dana, A Biography.* Boston: Houghton, Mifflin, 1890, Vol. I; James Truslow Adams, *The Adams Family; The Athenaeum Centenary—The Influence and History of the Boston Athenaeum from 1807 to 1907.* Boston: The Boston Athenaeum, 1907; Bacon, *Literary Pilgrimages in New England to the Homes of Famous Makers of American Literature;* Frances Bradshaw Blanshard, editor, *Letters of Ann Storrow to Jared Sparks.* Northampton: Smith College Studies in History, VI, 3 (April 1921); John White Chadwick, *Frederic Henry Hedge, A Sermon.* Boston: George H. Ellis, 1890-1; Alexander Corbett, "Papanti's Is No More," *Boston Globe,* 1899, in Scrapbook of Bostonian Society; Thomas Dowse, *Catalogue of the Private Library of Thomas Dowse, of Cambridge, Massachusetts, presented to the Massachusetts Historical Society, July 30, 1856.* Boston: John Wilson, 1856; Rev. George E. Ellis, "Parker at Cambridge," *The Christian Register,* January 7, 1892; Ruth E. Finley, *The Lady of Godey's, Sarah Josepha Hale.* Philadelphia: J. B. Lippincott, 1931; *Godey's Lady's Book,* Vol. I (1830), and Vol. VII (1833); Henry David Gray, *Emerson, A Statement of New England Transcendentalism as Expressed in the Philosophy of Its Chief Exponent.* Leland Stanford Junior University Publications, University Series, 1917; Harvard Class of 1829, *The Latest Poems of the Class of 1829,* 1882-9; Frederic Henry Hedge, *Hours with German Classics.* Boston: Roberts, 1886; Frederic Henry Hedge, *Prose Writers of Germany.* Philadelphia: A. Hart, 1852; Mary Thacher Higginson, *Thomas Wentworth Higginson, The Story of His Life.* Boston: Houghton Mifflin, 1914; Thomas Wentworth Higginson, *Cheerful Yesterdays.* Boston: Houghton, Mifflin, 1901; Higginson, "His Brother's Brother," *Atlantic Monthly,* 84:175-182 (1899); Higginson, *Old Cambridge;* William H. Lyon, *Frederic Henry Hedge, A Sermon.* Brookline, 1906; *North American Review,* October 1830; "Old Dancing Days in Boston," 1886, in Scrapbook of Bostonian Society; Rev. John Pierce, *Diary.* Boston: Massachusetts Historical Society, January 1890; Josiah Quincy, *The History of the Boston Athenaeum.* Cambridge: Metcalf, 1851; Charles F. Read, "Lorenzo Papanti, Teacher of Dancing born 1799, Died 1872—a Paper read before the Society," *Proceedings of the Bostonian Society,* January 17, 1928; Sampson Reed, *Observations on the Growth of the Mind.* Chicago: E. B. Myers and Chandler, 1867; William S. Rossiter, editor, *Days and Ways in Old Boston.* Boston: R. H. Stearns, 1915; Ticknor, *Dr. Holmes's Boston;* Justin Winsor, editor, *Library of Harvard University, Bibliographical Contributions,* No. 46: The Class of 1828; Theodore F. Wolfe, *Literary Shrines—The Haunts of Some Famous American Authors.* Philadelphia: J. B. Lippincott, 1897.

CHAPTER IV

Manuscript sources include a letter from Margaret Fuller to the Rev. Mr. James F. Clarke, Groton, February 12, 1833, now owned by Mr. James F. Clarke of Boston.

Direct sources for Margaret Fuller's life between 1833 and 1836 include Ladbroke Black, *Some Queer People.* London: Sampson, Low Marston, 1931; *Boston Daily Advertiser,* XLII, 13 (November 27, 1834); Frederick A. Braun, "Margaret Fuller's Translation and Criticism of Goethe's *Tasso,*" *Journal of English and Germanic Philology.* Urbana: XIII, 202-213 (April 1914); Frederick T. Fuller, "Hawthorne and Margaret Fuller Ossoli," *The Literary World,* XVI, 11-15 (January 10, 1885); Richard Fuller, *Chaplain Fuller;* Richard Fuller, *Memorials of Mrs. Margaret Fuller;* Johann Wolfgang von Goethe, *Werke.* Stuttgart and Tübingen, 1833 (Margaret Fuller's copy, now owned by Mrs. John Dole of New York); McMaster, *Margaret Fuller as a*

Literary Critic; National Magazine, I, 314-320, 409-418, and 529-536 (October, November, and December 1852) ; Evelyn Winslow Orr, "Two Margaret Fuller Manuscripts," *The New England Quarterly,* XI, 4 (December 1938) ; Margaret Fuller Ossoli, *Art, Literature and the Drama,* edited by Arthur B. Fuller. Boston: Brown, Taggard and Chase, 1860; Ossoli, *Life Without and Life Within;* William Russell, *Eccentric Personages.* New York: The American News Company, 1866; Ida Tarbell, "The American Woman," *American Magazine,* 69:656-669 (March 1910) ; *The Western Messenger,* I, 101-108 (August 1835).

Details of background appear in Adams, *The Adams Family;* A. Bronson Alcott, *Concord Days.* Boston: Roberts, 1888; A. Bronson Alcott, *Ralph Waldo Emerson, an Estimate of His Character and Genius in Prose and Verse.* Boston: A. Williams, 1882; Queenie M. Bilbo, *Elizabeth Palmer Peabody, Transcendentalist.* MS. Doctoral Dissertation. New York University, 1932; Boston Athenaeum MS. Books Taken from the Athenaeum by Emerson; Van Wyck Brooks, *The Life of Emerson.* New York: E. P. Dutton, 1932; Mary Hosmer Brown, *Memories of Concord.* Boston: Four Seas, 1926. Orestes Augustus Brownson, *The Convert: or, Leaves from My Experience.* New York: Edward Dunigan, 1857; Katherine Kurz Burton, *Paradise Planters, The Story of Brook Farm.* New York: Longmans, Green, 1939; Caleb Butler, *History of the Town of Groton, including Pepperell and Shirley.* Boston: T. R. Marvin, 1848; John Jay Chapman, *William Lloyd Garrison.* Boston: Atlantic Monthly Press, 1913; Dr. John Thomas Codman, "The Men and Thought That Made the Boston of the Forties Famous," *The Coming Age,* II, 239-247 (September 1899) ; George Willis Cooke, *The Poets of Transcendentalism.* Boston: Houghton Mifflin, 1903; George Willis Cooke, *Ralph Waldo Emerson: His Life, Writings, and Philosophy.* Boston: James R. Osgood, 1882; Cooke, *Unitarianism in America, A History of Its Origin and Development.* Boston: American Unitarian Association, 1902; George W. Curtis, *Little Journeys to the Homes of American Authors.* New York: G. P. Putnam, 1896; Dall, *Transcendentalism in New England;* Eugene L. Didier, "A Group of Eminent American Women," *The Chautauquan,* 23:387-394 (July 1896) ; E. W. Emerson, *Emerson in Concord;* Ralph Waldo Emerson, *Essays.* New York: Thomas Nelson, n. d.; Octavius Brooks Frothingham, *Transcendentalism in New England, a History.* New York: G. P. Putnam, 1897; Arthur Gilman and Others, *Poets' Homes. Pen and Pencil Sketches of American Poets and Their Homes.* Boston: D. Lothrop, 1879; *Godey's Lady's Book,* Vol. XIII (July 1836) ; Samuel Abbott Green, *An Account of the Lawyers of Groton, Massachusetts.* Groton: University Press, 1892; Green, *Facts Relating to the History of Groton;* Green, *Groton Historical Series,* II, 2; Green, *A Historical Sketch of Groton;* Oliver Wendell Holmes, *Ralph Waldo Emerson.* Boston: Houghton, Mifflin, 1878; Harriet Martineau, *Autobiography,* edited by Maria Weston Chapman. Boston: James R. Osgood, 1877, Vols. I and II; Harriet Martineau, *Society in America.* New York: Saunders and Otley, 1837, Vol. I; *New York Tribune.* Extra. No. 63 (July 1880) ; *North American Review,* XXXIX, 85 (October 1834) ; Clara Endicott Sears, *Days of Delusion, A Strange Bit of History.* Boston: Houghton Mifflin, 1924; Gilbert Seldes, *The Stammering Century.* New York: John Day, 1927; *Select Journal of Foreign Periodical Literature.* Vols. I, II, III, and IV (January 1833—October 1834) ; Lemuel Shattuck, *A History of the Town of Concord, Middlesex County, Massachusetts, from its earliest settlement to 1832.* Boston: Russell, Odiorne, 1835; Margaret Sidney, *Old Concord, Her Highways and Byways.* Boston: D. Lothrop, 1888 and 1892; Stanton, Anthony, and Gage, *History of Woman Suffrage;* Caroline Ticknor, editor, *Classic Concord as portrayed by Emerson, Hawthorne, Thoreau and the Alcotts.* Boston: Houghton Mifflin, 1926; Annie Wall, "Early Transcendentalism in New England," *New England Magazine,* V, 162-170 (December 1886) ; Harry R. Warfel, "Margaret Fuller and Ralph Waldo Emerson," *PMLA,* L, 576-594 (1935) ; Lilian Whiting, *Boston Days.* Boston: Little, Brown, 1903.

CHAPTER V

Details giving direct information about Margaret Fuller's life at this period appear in Elsie Rhodes, "The Personality of Margaret Fuller," *Temple Bar,* 108:226-232 (June 1896) ; Franklin B. Sanborn, "A Concord Notebook: The Women of Concord— Margaret Fuller and Her Friends II," *The Critic,* 48:251-257 (March 1906).

Details of background appear in A. Bronson Alcott, *Sonnets and Canzonets.* Boston: Roberts, 1882; Boston Athenaeum Gallery, *Catalogues of Fine Arts Exhibitions* 1829-1839; Boston Athenaeum MS. Names of Strangers in Visitors' Book; *Boston Courier,* March 29, April 4, and April 5, 1837; *Catalogue of Books added to the Boston Athenaeum since the publication of the Catalogue in*

January 1827. Boston: Eastburn, 1840; John W. Chadwick, *Channing's Life and Work. A Discourse.* New York: James Miller, 1880; Grace Ellery Channing, *Dr. Channing's Note-Book —Passages from the unpublished manuscripts of William Ellery Channing.* Boston: Houghton, Mifflin, 1887; Ednah D. Cheney, editor, *Louisa May Alcott—Her Life, Letters, and Journals.* Boston: Roberts, 1889; James Freeman Clarke, *Memorial and Biographical Sketches.* Boston: Houghton, Osgood, 1878; Dr. John T. Codman, "The Brook Farm Association," *The Coming Age,* II, 33-38 (July 1899); *Daily Advertiser and Patriot,* March 21, 1837; Caroline H. Dall, *"Alongside" Being notes suggested by "A New England Boyhood" of Dr. Edward Everett Hale.* Boston: Thomas Todd, 1900; Paulina Wright Davis, *History of the National Women's Rights Movement,* n.p., 1871; Charles Dickens, *American Notes for General Circulation.* Philadelphia: Porter and Coates, 1867; Samuel Adams Drake, *Old Landmarks and Historic Personages of Boston.* Boston: Little, Brown, 1900; Octavius Brooks Frothingham, *Boston Unitarianism 1820-1850, A Study of the Life and Work of Nathaniel Langdon Frothingham.* New York: G. P. Putnam, 1890; Octavius Brooks Frothingham, *Recollections and Impressions, 1882-1890.* New York: G. P. Putnam, 1891; Phebe A. Hanaford, *Daughters of America; or, Women of the Century.* Augusta: True, 1882; Julia Ward Howe, *Reminiscences 1819-1899.* Boston: Houghton, Mifflin, n.d.; Harriet Martineau, *The Martyr Age in the United States of America: an Article from the London and Westminster Review for December, 1838.* New York: S. W. Benedict, 1839; Martineau, *Society in America;* Elizabeth Palmer Peabody, *Record of Mr. Alcott's School, exemplifying the Principles and Methods of Moral Culture.* Boston: Roberts, 1888; Elizabeth Palmer Peabody, *Reminiscences of Rev. William Ellery Channing.* Boston: Roberts, 1880; Rossiter, *Days and Ways in Old Boston;* Seldes, *The Stammering Century; Stimpson's Boston Directory* 1839-1845; *The Western Messenger,* No. 3 (September 1835); Enoch Cobb Wines, *Trip to Boston, in a series of letters to the editor of the United States Gazette.* Boston: Little and Brown, 1838.

CHAPTER VI

Manuscript sources for this chapter include a letter from Margaret Fuller to the Rev. Mr. J. S. Dwight, Groton, May 31, 1837, in the Dwight Papers 1832-1889—Brook Farm, in the Boston Public Library.

Details regarding Margaret Fuller's life in Providence may be found in *Book Notes, Historical, Literary and Critical, conducted by Sidney S. Rider,* X, 19 (September 23, 1893) ; Gamaliel Bradford, *Portraits of American Women.* Boston: Houghton Mifflin, 1919; S. [arah] M. [argaret] F. [uller], "Karl Theodor Körner," *The Western Messenger,* IV, 5 and 6 (February 1838) ; Hon. Henry L. Greene, "The Greene-Street School and Its Teachers, A Paper read before the Rhode Island Historical Society October 18, 1898," *Publications of the Rhode Island Historical Society,* New Series 6 (1898) ; Granville Hicks, "Margaret Fuller to Sarah Helen Whitman; an Unpublished Letter," *American Literature,* I, 419-421 (January 1930) ; Harriet Hall Johnson, "Margaret Fuller as Known by her Scholars," *The Christian Register,* April 21, 1910; Annie Russell Marble, "Margaret Fuller as Teacher," *The Critic,* 43:334-345 (October 1903) ; *The Radical,* VII (February 1870).

Details of background appear in Alcott, *Concord Days;* Samuel G. Arnold, *An Address delivered before the Rhode Island Historical Society, June 1, 1869.* Providence: Hammond, Angell, 1869; Albert Bielschowsky, *The Life of Goethe,* translated by William A. Cooper. New York: G. P. Putnam, 1909, Vols. I, II, and III ; James Freeman Clarke, *Autobiography, Diary and Correspondence,* edited by Edward Everett Hale. Boston and New York: Houghton, Mifflin, 1891; George Willis Cooke, *Historical and Biographical Introduction to The Dial.* Cleveland: Rowfant Club, 1902; Ralph Waldo Emerson, "The American Scholar, An Oration delivered before the Phi Beta Kappa Society at Cambridge, August 31, 1837," *Essays,* edited by Arthur Hobson Quinn. New York: Charles Scribner, 1920; Ralph Waldo Emerson, *Natural History of Intellect and Other Papers.* Boston: Houghton, Mifflin, 1893; *Evening Mercantile Journal,* Boston, September 1, 1837; Rufus Wilmot Griswold, *The Female Poets of America.* Philadelphia: Parry and McMillan, 1854; Julian Hawthorne, *Memoirs,* edited by his wife, Edith Garrigues Hawthorne. New York: Macmillan, 1938; Thomas Wentworth Higginson, "Part of Man's Life: The Sunny Side of the Transcendental Period," *Atlantic Monthly,* 93: 6-14; Elizabeth Hoar, "Mrs. Samuel Ripley," *Worthy Women of our First Century,* edited by Mrs. Owen Wister and Agnes Irwin. Philadelphia: J. B. Lippincott, 1877; Sarah S. Jacobs, *Nonantum and Natick.* Boston: Massachusetts Sabbath School Society, 1853; *The Liberator,* No. 42 (October 13, 1837) ; *Memoirs of Members of the Social Circle in Concord,* Third Series, 1840 to 1895. Cambridge: Riverside Press, 1907; John Neal, *Man. A Discourse be-*

fore the *United Brothers' Society of Brown University,* September 4, 1839. Providence: Knowles Vose, 1838; John Neal, *Wandering Recollections of a Somewhat Busy Life. An Autobiography.* Boston: Roberts, 1869; Henry Stedman Nourse, *The Hoar Family in America and Its English Ancestry.* Boston: David Clapp, 1899; Bliss Perry, editor, *The Heart of Emerson's Journals.* Boston: Houghton Mifflin, 1909; *Providence Journal,* July 17, 1837 and July 24, 1876; Franklin B. Sanborn, *Hawthorne and His Friends: Reminiscences and Tribute.* Cedar Rapids, Iowa: Torch Press, 1908; Seldes, *The Stammering Century;* Roger Faxton Sturgis, *Edward Sturgis of Yarmouth, Massachusetts 1613-1695 and His Descendants.* Boston: Stanhope, 1914; Caroline Ticknor, *Poe's Helen.* New York: Charles Scribner, 1916; Francis Tiffany, "Transcendentalism: The New England Renaissance," *Unitarian Review,* XXXI, 2 (February 1889).

CHAPTER VII

Direct source material for Margaret Fuller's life at Jamaica Plain includes R. F. Fuller, *Memorials of Mrs. Margaret Fuller;* S. M. Fuller, translator, "Conversations with Goethe in the Last Years of his Life, from the German of Eckermann," *Specimens of Foreign Standard Literature,* edited by George Ripley. Boston: Hilliard, Gray, 1839, Vol. IV; S. [arah] M. [argaret] F. [uller], "Letters from Palmyra," *The Western Messenger,* V, 24-29; Sarah Helen Whitman, "Review of Eckermann's Conversations with Goethe, translated by S. M. Fuller," *Boston Quarterly Review,* III, 9 (January 1840).

Details of background appear in Mary Caroline Crawford, *Romantic Days in Old Boston.* Boston: Little, Brown, 1910; Clarence L. F. Gohdes, *The Periodicals of American Transcendentalism.* Durham, North Carolina: Duke University Press, 1931; Caroline Matilda Stansbury Kirkland (pseud. Mrs. Mary Clavers), *A New Home—Who'll Follow? or, Glimpses of Western Life by an Actual Settler.* New York: C. S. Francis, 1839; *North American Review,* April 1840; Theodore Parker Manuscript Journals in the American Unitarian Association, Vol. II; Charles F. Read, *Lorenzo Papanti, Teacher of Dancing;* Franklin B. Sanborn, editor, "The Emerson-Thoreau Correspondence," *Atlantic Monthly,* LXIX, 415 and 416 (May and June 1892); Samuel G. Ward, translator, *Essays on Art by Goethe.* Boston: James Munroe, 1845.

CHAPTER VIII

Direct sources for Margaret Fuller's Conversations in West Street include *The Athenaeum,* No. 1267 (February 7, 1852); L. H. Boutell, "Margaret Fuller Ossoli," *The Chautauquan,* 11:699-705 (September 1890); Clarke, *Autobiography, Diary and Correspondence;* Caroline W. Healey Dall, *Margaret and Her Friends or Ten Conversations with Margaret Fuller upon the Mythology of the Greeks and Its Expression in Art held at the House of the Rev. George Ripley, Bedford Place, Boston, beginning March 1, 1841.* Boston: Roberts, 1895; George M. Gould, *Biographic Clinics.* Philadelphia: P. Blakiston, 1904, Vol. II; Granville Hicks, "A Conversation in Boston," *Sewanee Review,* 39:129-143 (April 1931); Hicks, *Margaret Fuller to Sarah Helen Whitman; University Magazine,* 2:542-551 and 686-704 (November and December 1878); Amy Wellington, *Women Have Told, Studies in the Feminist Tradition.* Boston: Little, Brown, 1930.

Details of background appear in Henry Barnard, *Biographical Sketch of Horace Mann, LL.D., reprinted from Barnard's American Journal of Education for December 1858; Boston Almanac,* 1839; Burton, *Paradise Planters;* George Catlin, *A Descriptive Catalogue of Catlin's Indian Gallery, exhibiting at the Egyptian Hall, Piccadilly, London, 1840; Ednah Dow Cheney 1824-1904, Memorial Meeting, New England Women's Club, Boston, February 20, 1905.* Boston: George H. Ellis, 1905; Ednah Proctor Clarke, *An Opal—Verses.* n.p., 1896; George Willis Cooke, "The Dial: An Historical and Biographical Introduction, with a List of the Contributors," *Journal of Speculative Philosophy,* XIX, 225-265 (July 1885); Cooke, *Historical and Biographical Introduction to The Dial;* Julia C. Dorr, *Bride and Bridegroom, A Series of Letters to a Young Married Couple.* Cincinnati: Hitchcock and Walden, 1873; D. [J. S. Dwight], "The Concerts of the Past Winter," *The Dial,* I, 1 (July 1840); R. Buckminster Fuller, *Nine Chains to the Moon.* Philadelphia: J. B. Lippincott, 1938; Nathaniel Hawthorne, *The American Notebooks, based upon the original manuscripts in the Pierpont Morgan Library and edited by Randall Stewart.* New Haven: Yale University Press, 1932; Arnold Hermann Ludwig Heeren, *Ancient Greece,* translated by George Bancroft. London: Henry G. Bohn, 1847; James Russell Lowell, "Studies for Two Heads," *Complete Poetical Works.* Boston: Houghton Mifflin, 1923; Maria White Lowell, *Poems, with Unpublished Letters and A Biography by Hope Jillson Vernon.*

BIBLIOGRAPHY 505

Providence: Brown University, 1936; *Ann Phillips, Wife of Wendell Phillips, a Memorial Sketch*. Boston: Riverside Press, 1886; Sironen, *A History of American Furniture;* Whiting, *Boston Days*.

CHAPTER IX

Direct sources concerning Margaret Fuller and *The Dial* include Anna C. Brackett, "Margaret Fuller Ossoli," *The Radical*, IX, 354-370 (December 1871); Cooke, *The Dial: An Historical and Biographical Introduction;* Cooke, *Historical and Biographical Introduction to The Dial; The Dial: A Magazine for Literature, Philosophy, and Religion*. Boston: Weeks, Jordan, 1841-1844; Eugene L. Didier, *A Group of Eminent American Women;* [Margaret Fuller], "Chat in Boston Bookstores," *Boston Quarterly Review*, III, 9 and 10 (January and February 1840); S. M. Fuller, *Günderode*. Boston: E. P. Peabody, 1842; S. Margaret Fuller, *Literature and Art*. New York: Fowler and Wells, 1852; S. Margaret Fuller, *Papers on Literature and Art*. London: Wiley and Putnam, 1846; Gohdes, *The Periodicals of American Transcendentalism;* George Keats, Four Manuscript Letters to the Rev. Mr. James Freeman Clarke, owned by Mr. James F. Clarke of Boston, edited by Madeleine B. Stern for *PMLA,* March 1941; Franklin B. Sanborn, *A Concord Note-Book;* Franklin B. Sanborn, Manuscript concerning Margaret Fuller and *The Dial,* in Thoreau, *The Service* 1840, MS. in Pierpont Morgan Library; Algernon Tassin, *The Magazine in America*. New York: Dodd, Mead, 1916.

Details of background appear in Newton Arvin, editor, *The Heart of Hawthorne's Journals*. Boston: Houghton Mifflin, 1929; Bilbo, *Elizabeth Palmer Peabody, Transcendentalist;* Willard Grosvenor Bleyer, *Main Currents in the History of American Journalism*. Boston: Houghton Mifflin, 1927; Boston Athenaeum, *Catalogues of the Fourteenth and Fifteenth Exhibitions of Paintings in the Athenaeum Gallery,* 1840 and 1841; Horatio Bridge, *Personal Recollections of Nathaniel Hawthorne*. New York: Harper, 1893; Brooks, *The Life of Emerson;* Brown, *Memories of Concord;* Burton, *Paradise Planters;* William Ellery Channing, *Thoreau the Poet-Naturalist, with Memorial Verses,* edited by Franklin B. Sanborn. Boston: Charles E. Goodspeed, 1902; Maria Weston Chapman, *Right and Wrong in Massachusetts*. Boston: Henry L. Devereux, 1840; George Willis Cooke, "Emerson and Transcendentalism," *New England Magazine,* 28:264-280 (May 1903); John T. Flanagan, "Emerson and Communism," *The New*

England Quarterly, X, 2 (June 1937); *Godey's Lady's Book,* Vol. XX (1840); Zoltán Haraszti, *The Idyll of Brook Farm as Revealed by Unpublished Letters in the Boston Public Library.* Boston: Boston Public Library, 1937; Hawthorne, *The American Notebooks;* Nathaniel Hawthorne, *Mosses from an Old Manse.* New York: A. L. Burt, n.d.; M. T. Higginson, *Thomas Wentworth Higginson;* T. [homas] W. [entworth] H. [igginson], "Walks with Ellery Channing," *Atlantic Monthly,* 90:537 (July 1902); George Frisbie Hoar, *Autobiography of Seventy Years.* New York: Scribner, 1903, Vol. I; J. W. Howe, *Reminiscences;* Rose Hawthorne Lathrop, *Memories of Hawthorne.* Boston: Houghton Mifflin, 1923; *Memoirs of Members of the Social Circle in Concord,* Second Series, 1795 to 1840. Cambridge: Riverside Press, 1888; Theodore Parker Manuscript Journals in the American Unitarian Association, Vols. I and II; Franklin B. Sanborn, *Henry D. Thoreau.* Boston: Houghton Mifflin, 1896; Franklin B. Sanborn, *The Personality of Thoreau.* Boston: Charles E. Goodspeed, 1901; Franklin B. Sanborn, *Recollections of Seventy Years.* Boston: Richard G. Badger, 1909, Vol. II; Leonora Cranch Scott, *The Life and Letters of Christopher Pearse Cranch.* Boston: Houghton Mifflin, 1917; Sears, *Days of Delusion;* Stanton, Anthony, and Gage, *History of Woman Suffrage;* Josephine Latham Swayne, *The Story of Concord told by Concord Writers.* Boston: E. F. Worcester, 1906; Henry David Thoreau, *Familiar Letters,* edited by Franklin B. Sanborn. Boston and New York: Houghton Mifflin, 1906; Henry D. Thoreau, *Letters to Various Persons,* edited by Ralph Waldo Emerson. Boston: Ticknor and Fields, 1865; Henry D. Thoreau, *A Week on the Concord and Merrimack Rivers.* New York: Walter Scott, n.d.; Ticknor, *Classic Concord;* Annie Wall, *Early Transcendentalism in New England;* Whiting, *Boston Days.*

CHAPTER X

Details of background appear in Arvin, *The Heart of Hawthorne's Journals;* Bilbo, *Elizabeth Palmer Peabody, Transcendentalist;* George P. Bradford, "Reminiscences of Brook Farm by a Member of the Community," *Century Magazine,* 45 (N.S. 23): 141-148 (November 1892); Albert Brisbane, *Social Destiny of Man: or, Association and Reorganization of Industry.* Philadelphia: C. F. Stollmeyer, 1840; Henry F. Brownson, *Orestes A. Brownson's Early Life: from 1803 to 1844.* Detroit: H. F.

Brownson, 1898, Vol. I; Orestes A. Brownson, "Brook Farm," *The United States Magazine and Democratic Review,* N.S. XI, 481-496 (November 1842) ; Orestes A. Brownson, *New Views of Christianity, Society, and the Church.* Boston: James Munroe, 1836; Burton, *Paradise Planters; The Cambridge History of American Literature.* New York: G. P. Putnam, 1918, Vol. II; Edward Cary, *George William Curtis.* Boston: Houghton Mifflin, 1895; John Thomas Codman, *Brook Farm Historic and Personal Memoirs.* Boston: Arena, 1894; George Willis Cooke, "Brook Farm," *The New England Magazine,* XVII, 391-407 (December 1897) ; George Willis Cooke, *John Sullivan Dwight, Brook-Farmer, Editor, and Critic of Music.* Boston: Small, Maynard, 1898; Crawford, *Romantic Days in Old Boston;* Dall, *Transcendentalism in New England;* John Dunlop, *The Universal Tendency to Association in Mankind.* London: Houlston and Stoneman, 1840; Ralph Waldo Emerson, "Notes of Life and Letters in Massachusetts," *Atlantic Monthly,* 52:529-543 (October 1883) ; Charles Fourier, *Le Nouveau monde industriel.* Brussels: Hauman, 1841, Vols. I and II; Octavius Brooks Frothingham, *George Ripley.* Boston: Houghton, Mifflin, 1882; Frothingham, *Recollections and Impressions;* Parke Godwin, *A Popular View of the Doctrines of Charles Fourier.* New York: J. S. Redfield, 1844; Gohdes, *The Periodicals of American Transcendentalism;* Haraszti, *The Idyll of Brook Farm;* Hawthorne, *American Notebooks;* Nathaniel Hawthorne, *The Blithedale Romance.* New York: A. L. Burt, n.d.; Higginson, *Cheerful Yesterdays;* Morris Hillquit, *History of Socialism in the United States.* New York: Funk and Wagnalls, 1910; Georgiana Bruce Kirby, "My First Visit to Brook Farm," *The Overland Monthly,* V, 9-19 (July 1870) ; Georgiana Bruce Kirby, "Reminiscences of Brook Farm," *Old and New,* III, 425-438, IV, 347-358, and V, 517-530 (1871-1872) ; Georgiana Bruce Kirby, *Years of Experience: An Autobiographical Narrative.* New York: G. P. Putnam, 1887; Charles G. Mackintosh, *Some Recollections of the Pastors and People of the Second Church of Old Roxbury afterwards First Church, West Roxbury.* Salem: Newcomb and Gauss, 1901; John Humphrey Noyes, *History of American Socialisms.* Philadelphia: J. B. Lippincott, 1870; Marianne Dwight Orvis, *Letters from Brook Farm 1844-1847,* edited by Amy L. Reed. Poughkeepsie: Vassar College, 1928; Theodore Parker, *West Roxbury Sermons 1837-1848.* Boston: American Unitarian Association, 1902; [Amelia?] Russell, "Home Life of the Brook Farm Association," *Atlantic Monthly,* 42:458-466 and

556-563 (October and November 1878); Annie M. Salisbury, *Brook Farm.* Marlborough, Massachusetts: W. B. Smith, 1898; Scott, *The Life and Letters of Christopher Pearse Cranch;* John Van Der Zee Sears, *My Friends at Brook Farm.* New York: Desmond Fitz Gerald, 1912; Ora Gannett Sedgwick, "A Girl of Sixteen at Brook Farm," *Atlantic Monthly,* LXXXV, 394-404 (March 1900); Lindsay Swift, *Brook Farm, Its Members, Scholars, and Visitors.* New York: Macmillan, 1900; Arthur W. Tarbell, "The Brook Farm Experiment," *The National Magazine and Illustrated American Monthly,* VII, 195-203 (December 1897); Wolfe, *Literary Shrines.*

CHAPTER XI

Manuscript sources include Margaret Fuller to Sarah [Freeman Clarke], Cambridge, May 8, 1843.

Direct details regarding Margaret Fuller's journey to the West appear in Richard V. Carpenter, "Margaret Fuller in Northern Illinois," *Journal of the Illinois State Historical Society,* II, 4 (January 1910); S. M. Fuller, *Summer on the Lakes in 1843.* Boston: Little and Brown, 1844; Griswold, *The Female Poets of America;* Margaret Fuller Ossoli, "Summer on the Lakes," *At Home and Abroad, or Things and Thoughts in America and Europe,* edited by Arthur B. Fuller. Boston: Crosby, Nichols, 1856.

Details of background may be found in Clarke Family Records owned by Mr. James F. Clarke of Boston; Dickens, *American Notes for General Circulation;* Howe, *Reminiscences;* Mrs. Anna Jameson, *Winter Studies and Summer Rambles in Canada.* New York: Wiley and Putnam, 1839, Vols. I and II; Justinus Kerner, *The Seeress of Prevorst, being Revelations concerning the inner life of man and the inter-diffusion of a world of spirits in the one we inhabit,* translated by Mrs. Crowe. New York: Harper, 1845; Lathrop, *Memories of Hawthorne;* Martineau, *Society in America;* Sanborn, *The Emerson-Thoreau Correspondence;* Sanborn, *Henry D. Thoreau;* Sears, *Days of Delusion;* Seldes, *The Stammering Century;* Thoreau, *Letters to Various Persons;* Whiting, *Boston Days.*

CHAPTER XII

Direct details appear in Fuller, *Hawthorne and Margaret Fuller Ossoli;* S. M. Fuller, *Papers on Literature and Art;* Ossoli, *Life*

Without and Life Within; S. M. F. Ossoli, *Summer on the Lakes; with autobiography.* London: Ward and Lock, 1861.

Details of background may be found in Albert Brisbane, *Concise Exposition of the Doctrine of Association.* New York: Redfield, 1844; Burton, *Paradise Planters;* Robert Carter, "The Newness," *The Century,* 39:124-131 (November 1889); Lydia Maria Child, *Isaac T. Hopper: A True Life.* Boston: John P. Jearett, 1853; Moncure Daniel Conway, *Autobiography, Memories and Experiences.* London: Cassell, 1904, Vols. I and II; Cooke, *John Sullivan Dwight;* Davis, *History of the National Women's Rights Movement; The Dial,* III, 1 (July 1842), III, 4 (April 1843), IV, 2, 3, and 4 (October 1843, January 1844 and April 1844); Ralph Waldo Emerson, *Letters to a Friend* [Samuel G. Ward] *1838-1853,* edited by Charles Eliot Norton. Boston: Houghton, Mifflin, 1899; Ralph Waldo Emerson, "New England Reformers," *Essays,* Second Series; *Godey's Lady's Book,* Vols. 24, 25, and 28 (1842 and 1844); Parke Godwin, *Democracy, Constructive and Pacific.* New York: J. Winchester, 1844; Parke Godwin, *George William Curtis, A Commemorative Address delivered before the Century Association, New York, December 17, 1892.* New York: Harper, 1893; Howe, *Reminiscences;* Sylvester Judd, *Margaret: A Tale of the Real and the Ideal, Blight and Bloom.* Boston: Roberts, 1871; Kirby, *Years of Experience;* Lathrop, *Memories of Hawthorne;* Horace Mann, *Thoughts Selected from the Writings.* Boston: H. B. Fuller, 1867; *Memoirs of Members of the Social Circle in Concord,* Third Series; Noyes, *History of American Socialisms;* Orr, *Two Margaret Fuller Manuscripts;* Orvis, *Letters from Brook Farm 1844-1847;* Sanborn, *Hawthorne and His Friends;* Stanton, Anthony, and Gage, *History of Woman Suffrage;* State Street Trust Company Monograph, *Boston, England and Boston, New England.*

CHAPTER XIII

Direct details may be found in S. Margaret Fuller, "The Great Lawsuit: Man versus Men: Woman versus Women," *The Dial,* IV, 1 (July 1843); S. Margaret Fuller, *Woman in the Nineteenth Century.* London: H. G. Clarke, n.d.; Margaret Wallace, "Margaret Fuller: Critic," *The Bookman,* 69:60-67 (March 1929).

Details of background appear in Justin Harvey Smith, *The Annexation of Texas.* New York: Baker and Taylor, 1911.

CHAPTER XIV

Manuscript sources include Margaret Fuller to Wiley and Putnam, and Margaret Fuller's letters to Evert A. Duyckinck in Folder Duyckinck Coll. Fuller at the New York Public Library.

Direct details appear in *Brownson's Quarterly Review*, II, 249-257 (April 1845) ; *The Christian Examiner*, XXXVIII, 416-417 (May 1845) ; Charles Tabor Congdon, *Reminiscences of a Journalist*. Boston: James R. Osgood, 1880; S. Margaret Fuller, "The Liberty Bell," *The Liberty Bell by Friends of Freedom*. Boston: Massachusetts Anti-Slavery Fair, 1846; Margaret Fuller, *Love-Letters 1845-1846, with an introduction by Julia Ward Howe, and Reminiscences of Ralph Waldo Emerson, Horace Greeley, and Charles T. Congdon*. New York: D. Appleton, 1903; S. M. Fuller, *Papers on Literature and Art*, Parts I and II ; Chandler Robbins Gilman, *Life on the Lakes: being tales and sketches collected during a trip to the pictured rocks of Lake Superior*. New York: G. Dearborn, 1836; Sara Josepha Hale (Buell), *Women's Record; or Sketches of all Distinguished Women, from the Creation to A. D. 1854 arranged in Four Eras, with selections from female writers of every age*. New York: Harper, 1860; Kirby, *Years of Experience;* Carolyn B. La Monte, "The Critical Work of Margaret Fuller," *Poet-Lore*, VII, 10 (1895) ; A.G.M., "The Condition of Woman," *Southern Quarterly Review*, X, 148-173 (July 1846) ; *National Magazine*, I, 314-320, 409-418, and 529-536 (October, November, and December 1852) ; *The New York Tribune*, IV, 209 (December 7, 1844)—VI, 98 (August 1, 1846) ; *The New York Tribune*, Weekly Edition, December 14, 1844— December 13, 1845; O'Higgins and Reede, *The American Mind in Action;* Ossoli, *Life Without and Life Within;* Wallace, *Margaret Fuller: Critic*.

Details of background are to be found in Hervey Allen, *Israfel— The Life and Times of Edgar Allan Poe*. New York: Farrar and Rinehart, 1934; *Alphabetical and Analytical Catalogue of the New-York Society Library with a Brief Historical Notice of the Institution*. New York: James Van Norden, 1838; *Supplementary Catalogue*, 1841; Herbert Asbury, *Ye Olde Fire Laddies*. New York and London: Alfred A. Knopf, 1930; Walter Barrett, Clerk, *The Old Merchants of New York City*. New York: Carleton, 1863; W. Harrison Bayles, *Old Taverns of New York*. New York: Frank Allaben Genealogical Company, 1915; John Preston Beecher, "About New York with Poe," *The Curio*, I, 5 and 6

(January and February 1888); Henry Augustin Beers, *Nathaniel Parker Willis*. Boston: Houghton, Mifflin, 1885; Bleyer, *Main Currents in the History of American Journalism;* William Thompson Bonner, *New York The World's Metropolis 1623-4—1923-4.* New York: R. L. Polk, 1924; *The Book Buyer,* XXII (February-July 1901); Mary L. Booth, *History of the City of New York.* New York: W. R. C. Clark, 1867, Vol. II; Anne Charlotte Lynch Botta, *Memoirs written by her Friends, with selections from her correspondence and from her writings in prose and poetry,* edited by Vincenzo Botta. New York: J. Selwin Tate, 1894; Fredrika Bremer, *America of the Fifties,* selected and edited by Adolph B. Benson. New York: American-Scandinavian Foundation, 1924; Fredrika Bremer, *The Homes of the New World,* translated by Mary Howitt. New York: Harper, 1853, Vols. I and II; *Broadway Journal,* I, 1 (January 4, 1845)—I, 26 (June 28, 1845) and II, 1 (July 12, 1845)—II, 22 (December 6, 1845); *Brooklyn Directory,* 1844 and 1845; Brooks Brothers, *Chronicles 1818-1909, being a record of sundry happenings which have had place since A. D. 1818 in that part of Greater New York which at present is distinguished as the Borough of Manhattan.* New York: Cheltenham Press, 1909; Henry Collins Brown, *Book of Old New York.* New York: privately printed, 1913; Henry Collins Brown, *Brownstone Fronts and Saratoga Trunks.* New York: E. P. Dutton, 1935; Henry Collins Brown, *Fifth Avenue Old and New 1824-1924.* New York: The Fifth Avenue Association, 1924; Henry Collins Brown, *Glimpses of Old New York.* New York: privately printed, 1917; Henry Collins Brown, *Old New York.* New York: Valentine Manual Press, 1922; Brown, *Valentine's Manual of Old New York,* Nos. 5, 6, and 7, New Series. New York: Valentine's Manual, 1920, 1921, and 1922; T. Allston Brown, *A History of the New York Stage from the First Performance in 1732 to 1901.* New York: Dodd, Mead, 1903, Vol. I; *Bulletin of the New York Public Library,* V, 3 (March 1901) and V, 6 (June 1901); Alfred Bunn, *Old England and New England.* London: Richard Bentley, 1853; William Allen Butler, *Evert Augustus Duyckinck A Memorial Sketch Read before the New York Historical Society, January 7, 1879.* New York: Trow, 1879; Killis Campbell, *The Mind of Poe and Other Studies.* Cambridge, Massachusetts: Harvard University Press, 1933; Robert J. Carlisle, *An Account of Bellevue Hospital with a Catalogue of the Medical and Surgical Staff from 1736 to 1894.* New York: Society of the Alumni of Bellevue Hospital, 1893; *Catalogue of the Exhibition of the New York Gallery of the Fine Arts.* New York: James Van Norden, 1844; *Catalogue of the Exhibition of the New-York Gallery of Fine Arts, Now Open, in the Rotunda in the Park.* New York: E. B. Clayton, n.d.; *Catalogue of Statues, Busts, Studies, etc., forming the collection of the Antique School of the National Academy of Design.* New York: Israel Sackett, 1846; *Catalogue of the Twentieth Annual Exhibition of the National Academy of Design.* New York: Israel Sackett, 1845; David Lee Child, *The Taking of Naboth's Vineyard, or History of the Texas Conspiracy, and an examination of the Reasons given by the Hon. J. C. Calhoun, Hon. R. J. Walker, and others, for the Dismemberment and Robbery of the Republic of Mexico.* New York: S. W. Benedict, 1845; Child, *Isaac T. Hopper;* Lydia Maria Child, *Letters from New York.* New York: C. S. Francis, 1845; Cassius M. Clay, *Letters to the Editor of the Tribune: Slavery: The Evil—The Remedy.* Lexington, Kentucky: November 1843; Cassius M. Clay, *Life, Memoirs, Writings and Speeches.* Cincinnati: J. Fletcher Brennan, 1886, Vol. I; Cassius M. Clay, *Writings, including Speeches and Addresses, edited by Horace Greeley.* New York: Harper, 1848; John R. Commons, and others, editors, *A Documentary History of American Industrial Society.* Cleveland: Arthur H. Clark, 1910, Vol. VII; John R. Commons, "Horace Greeley and the Working Class Origins of the Republican Party," *Political Science Quarterly,* XXIV, 3 (September 1909) ; Cooke, *John Sullivan Dwight;* Henry B. Dawson, *Old New York Revived,* n.p., n.d.; J. C. Derby, *Fifty Years among Authors, Books and Publishers.* New York: G. W. Carleton, 1884; Dickens, *American Notes for General Circulation;* Fred Dietz, *1913, A Leaf from the Past—Then and Now.* New York: R. E. Dietz, 1914; *Doggett's New York Business Directory* for 1844 and 1845; *John Doggett's New York City Directory* for 1844 and 1845, 1845 and 1846, 1846 and 1847; *Doggett's New York City Street Directory for 1851.* New York: John Doggett, 1851; Evert A. Duyckinck, *New York, Past and Present.* New York: Frank Leslie, 1870; Pliny Earle, M.D., *Memoirs with Extracts from his diary and letters (1830-1892) and selections from his professional writings (1839-1891),* edited by F. B. Sanborn. Boston: Damrell and Upham, 1898; Dr. Pliny Earle, *The Psychopathic Branch of the New York Hospital at Bloomingdale, White Plains, New York.* Revised by Samuel B. Lyon. New York, 1904; Pliny Earle, *Twenty-fourth, Twenty-fifth, and Twenty-sixth Annual Reports of the Bloomingdale Asylum for the Insane.* New York: Egbert, Hovey and King, 1845, 1846, and 1847; *John W.*

Edmonds, Justice of the Supreme Court of the State of New York. n.p., n.d.; Hon. Thomas Dunn English, "Reminiscences of Poe III," *The Independent,* 48:2500 (October 29, 1896); Alexander H. Everett, "Harro Harring: A Biographical Sketch," *The United States Magazine and Democratic Review.* N. S. XII (October, November, and December 1844); Emily Johnston de Forest, *James Colles 1788-1883 Life, and Letters.* New York: privately printed, 1926; Dixon Ryan Fox, *The Decline of Aristocracy in the Politics of New York.* New York: Columbia University, 1918; Rodman Gilder, *The Battery.* Boston: Houghton Mifflin, 1936; William F. Gill, *The Life of Poe.* London: Chatto and Windus, 1878; *The Great Metropolis or New York in 1845.* New York: John Doggett, n.d.; Eliza Greatorex, *Old New York from the Battery to Bloomingdale, Etchings by Eliza Greatorex, text by M. Despard.* New York: G. P. Putnam, 1875, Vols. I and II; Horace Greeley, Manuscript Letters owned by the Library of the New York Historical Society; Greeley Papers 1836 - 1850 and 1845 - 1847 at the New York Public Library; Green, *An Account of the Lawyers of Groton;* Rufus Griswold, *Passages from the Correspondence and Other Papers.* Cambridge, Massachusetts: W. M. Griswold, 1898; Hale, *Memories of a Hundred Years,* Vol. II; *The Harbinger, devoted to Social and Political Progress,* Vol. I (1845); Harro Harring, *Dolores: A Novel of Humanity.* New York: Dolores Office, 1853; Charles H. Haswell, *Reminiscences of New York by an Octogenarian (1816 to 1860).* New York: Harper, 1896; Philip Hone, *Diary 1828-1851,* edited by Allan Nevins. New York: Dodd, Mead, 1927, Vol. II; N. T. Hubbard, *Autobiography with Personal Reminiscences of New York City from 1798 to 1875.* New York: John F. Trow, 1875; Frederic Hudson, *Journalism in the United States from 1690 to 1872.* New York: Harper, 1873; James Gibbons Huneker, *The Philharmonic Society of New York and Its Seventy-fifth Anniversary. A Retrospect.* n.p., n.d.; John H. Ingram, *Edgar Allan Poe.* n.p., 1880, Vol. II; *Jones and Newman's Pictorial Directory of New York.* New York: Jones and Newman, 1848; Charles King, *Progress of the City of New York during the last fifty years; with notices of the principal changes and important events. A lecture delivered before the Mechanics' Society at Mechanics' Hall, Broadway, on December twenty-ninth, 1851.* New York: D. Appleton, 1852; *The Knickerbocker or New-York Monthly Magazine,* XVI, 2 (August 1840) and XVI, 5 (November 1840); Henry Edward Krehbiel, *The Philharmonic Society of New York.* New York: Novello, Ewer,

1892; Martha J. Lamb, *History of the City of New York: Its Origin, Rise, and Progress.* New York and Chicago: A. S. Barnes, 1880, Vol. II; Lathrop, *Memories of Hawthorne;* Emile Lauvriere, *The Strange Life and Strange Loves of Edgar Allan Poe,* English version by Edwin Gile Rich. Philadelphia: J. B. Lippincott, 1935; Theodore Leger, *Animal Magnetism or Psycodunamy.* New York: D. Appleton, 1846; John William Leonard, *History of the City of New York 1609-1909.* New York: Journal of Commerce and Commercial Bulletin, 1910; Samuel Longfellow, editor, *Final Memorials of Henry Wadsworth Longfellow.* Boston: Ticknor, 1887, Vol. II; Benson J. Lossing, *History of New York City, embracing . . . a full account of its development from 1830 to 1884.* New York: George E. Perine, 1884; Anne C. Lynch, *Poems.* New York: George P. Putnam, 1849; Anne C. Lynch, *The Rhode-Island Book: Selections in Prose and Verse, from the Writings of Rhode-Island Citizens.* Providence: Charles Burnett, 1846; Dr. R. Osgood Mason, "History of the Philharmonic Society of New York," *American Art Journal,* 42:4, 5, and 6 (1884); R. Osgood Mason, *Sketches and Impressions Musical, Theatrical, and Social (1799-1885) including a sketch of the Philharmonic Society of New York.* New York: G. P. Putnam, 1887; John Flavel Mines, *A Tour around New York and My Summer Acre being the recreations of Mr. Felix Oldboy.* New York: Harper, 1893; Meade Minnigerode, *The Fabulous Forties 1840-1850.* New York: Garden City, 1924; Frank Moss, *The American Metropolis from Knickerbocker Days to the Present Time New York City in all its various phases.* New York: Peter Fenelon Collier, 1897, Vols. I, II, and III; Hopper Striker Mott, *The New York of Yesterday, a Descriptive Narrative of Old Bloomingdale.* New York and London: G. P. Putnam, 1908; Mount-Pleasant State Prison, *Annual Report of the Inspectors,* No. 16, January 19, 1846; *The National Cyclopedia of American Biography.* New York: James T. White, 1904, Vol. XII; *New York Mirror,* IV, 12 (June 27, 1846); Mary Gove Nichols, *Reminiscences of Edgar Allan Poe.* New York: Union Square Book Shop, 1931; Charles Eliot Norton, editor, *Letters of James Russell Lowell.* New York: Harper, n.d., Vols. I and II; Rev. Samuel Osgood, *New York in the Nineteenth Century. A Discourse delivered before the New York Historical Society, November 20, 1866.* New York: John F. Trow, 1868; James Parton, *The Life of Horace Greeley, Editor of "The New-York Tribune," from his birth to the present time.* Boston: Houghton, Mifflin, 1893; *A Peep into Catharine Street, or the Mysteries*

of Shopping, by a Late Retailer. New York: John Slater, 1846;
William S. Pelletreau, *Early New York Houses with Historical
and Genealogical Notes.* New York: Francis P. Harper, 1900;
Philharmonic Society of New York, *Fourth Annual Report.* New
York: William C. Martin, 1846; Mary E. Phillips, *Edgar Allan
Poe the Man.* Chicago: John C. Winston, 1926, Vol. II; Edgar
Allan Poe, "The Facts in the Case of M. Valdemar," *Works.*
New York: Redfield, 1856, Vol. I; "Edgar Allan Poe's New York
Then and Now," *New York Sun,* March 18, 1906; Prison Asso-
ciation of New York, *Annual Report,* December 1844. New York:
Jared Bell, n.d., *Second Report,* 1846, and *Third Report,* 1847,
Part I; Prison Association of New York, *First Report of the Fe-
male Department.* New York: W. E. Dean, 1845, and *Fourth
Annual Report,* 1849; *Reports of the Joint Special Committee in
relation to the Public Prisons on Blackwells Island.* Board of
Aldermen. Documents 27 and 28. New York: McSpedon and
Baker, 1849; Constance Mayfield Rourke, *The Trumpets of Jubi-
lee.* New York: Harcourt, Brace, 1927; Sanborn, *Henry D.
Thoreau; Scrapbook containing obituary notices of Mrs. Ann S.
Stephens* in New York Public Library; *Scrapbook of Newspaper
Clippings on Old New York* in New York Public Library; Catha-
rine Maria Sedgwick, *Life and Letters,* edited by Mary E. Dewey.
New York: Harper, 1871; John Augustus Shea, *Poems—collected
by his son.* New York, 1846; Elizabeth Oakes Smith, "Reminis-
cences," *Baldwin's Monthly,* IX, 3 (September 1874); Albert H.
Smyth, *Bayard Taylor.* Boston: Houghton, Mifflin, 1896; Charles
Sotheran, *Horace Greeley and Other Pioneers of American Social-
ism.* New York: Humboldt, 1892; Richard Henry Stoddard,
"Mrs. Botta and Her Friends," *The Independent,* XLVI, 2357
(February 1, 1894); I. N. Phelps Stokes, *Iconography of New
York,* Microfilm at New York Public Library; William L. Stone,
History of New York City from the Discovery to the Present Day.
New York: Virtue and Yorston, 1872; Algernon Tassin, *The
Magazine in America;* Bayard Taylor, *John Godfrey's Fortunes;
related by himself. A Story of American Life.* New York: G. P.
Putnam, 1865; Henry David Thoreau, *Walden or Life in the
Woods.* New York: Book League of America, 1929; Ticknor,
Poe's Helen; Mrs. Trollope, *Domestic Manners of the Americans.*
New York: Dodd, Mead, 1901, Vol. II; D. T. Valentine, *Man-
ual of the Corporation of the City of New York* for 1844-5 and
1845-6. New York: Levi D. Slamm and C. C. Childs, 1846; Nor-
man Ware, *The Industrial Worker 1840-1860.* Boston and New

York: Houghton Mifflin, 1924; Dixon Wecter, *The Saga of American Society—A Record of Social Aspiration 1607-1937.* New York: Scribner, 1937; Susan Archer Weiss, *The Home Life of Poe.* New York: Broadway Publishing Company, 1907; Sister Mary Michael Welsh, *Catharine Maria Sedgwick—Her Position in the Literature and Thought of Her Time up to 1860.* Washington, D. C.: Catholic University of America, 1937; Ludwig Wielich, "Philharmonic Society's Early Days An Interview with One of Its First Members," *The Opera Magazine,* I, 2 (February 1914); Nathaniel Parker Willis, *People I Have Met; or Pictures of Society and People of Mark, Drawn under a Thin Veil of Fiction.* New York: Baker and Scribner, 1850; James Grant Wilson, editor, *The Memorial History of the City of New-York from its first settlement to the year 1892.* New York: New York History Company, 1893, Vols. III and IV; Rufus Rockwell Wilson, *New York: Old and New, Its Story, Streets, and Landmarks.* Philadelphia and London: J. B. Lippincott, 1903, Vol. II; Theodore F. Wolfe, *Literary Haunts and Homes.* Philadelphia: J. B. Lippincott, 1901; Wolfe, *Literary Shrines;* Mary Alice Wyman, *Selections from the Autobiography of Elizabeth Oakes Smith.* Lewiston, Maine: Lewiston Journal Company, 1924; Mary Alice Wyman, *Two American Pioneers—Seba Smith and Elizabeth Oakes Smith.* New York: Columbia University, 1927.

CHAPTER XV

Manuscript sources include Margaret Fuller to Thomas Delf, Edinburgh, September 1, 1846; Margaret Fuller to Thomas Delf, undated letter; Margaret Fuller to Evert A. Duyckinck, MS. Letters in the New York Public Library; Margaret Fuller to J. S. Dwight, London, November 10, 1846, letter in the Massachusetts Historical Society; Margaret Fuller to Mrs. Howitt, Rome, April 18, 1847, letter in the Maine Historical Society; Margaret Fuller to Major Benjamin Perley Poore, Paris, February 3, letter in the Charles Roberts Autograph Collection; Margaret Fuller MS. in French, February 1847, owned by Mr. James F. Clarke of Boston.

Direct details appear in *The Athenaeum,* No. 999 (December 19, 1846); *Canadian Monthly,* XIII, 289-296 (March 1878); Mrs. Newton Crosland, *Memorable Women; The Story of Their Lives.* London: Griffin, Bohn, 1862; *Democratic Review,* XIX, 198-202 (September 1846); J. S. Dwight, "Review of *Papers on Literature and Art,*" *The Harbinger,* III, 16 (September 26, 1846); *Eclectic*

Magazine, XXVI, 171-178 (June 1852); *Eclectic Review*, III, 678-689 (June 1852); Margaret Fuller to Evert Duyckinck, London, October 30, 1846, *Bulletin of the New York Public Library*, V, 455-456 (January-December 1901); Margaret Fuller, *Love-Letters 1845-1846; The Harbinger*, III, 11 (August 22, 1846); Josephine Lazarus, "Margaret Fuller," *The Century*, XLV, 923-932 (April 1893); *National Anti-slavery Standard*, No. 322 (August 6, 1846); *The New York Tribune*, VI, 60 (June 18, 1846)— VI, 77 (July 8, 1846); Ossoli, *At Home and Abroad;* Leona Rostenberg, "Margaret Fuller's Roman Diary," *The Journal of Modern History*, XII, 2 (June 1940); Leona Rostenberg, "Mazzini to Margaret Fuller," *The American Historical Review*, October 1941; *Southern Literary Messenger*, XX, 129-140 (March 1854).

Details of background may be found in Hans Christian Andersen, *The Improvisatore*, translated by Mary Howitt. Boston: Houghton, Mifflin, n.d.; Arvin, *The Heart of Hawthorne's Journals; P. T. Barnum, Life written by himself*. New York: Redfield, 1855; Horace Bender [pseud. of Horatio Greenough], *The Travels, Observations, and Experience of a Yankee Stonecutter*. New York: G. P. Putnam, 1852; Henry Boynton, "Hiram Powers," *The New England Magazine*, XX, 5 (July 1899); Elizabeth Barrett Browning, *Letters*, edited by Frederic G. Kenyon. London: Smith, Elder, 1897, Vol. I; Elizabeth Barrett Browning, *Letters to Her Sister 1846-1859*, edited by Leonard Huxley. New York: E. P. Dutton, 1930; Robert Browning, *Letters* collected by Thomas J. Wise, edited by Thurman L. Hood. New Haven: Yale University Press, 1933; Jane Welsh Carlyle, *New Letters and Memorials*, annotated by Thomas Carlyle, and edited by Alexander Carlyle. London: John Lane, 1903, Vol. I; Cary, *George William Curtis;* John White Chadwick, *George William Curtis. An Address.* New York: Harper, 1893; William Ellery Channing, *Conversations in Rome: between an Artist, a Catholic, and a Critic.* Boston: Crosby and Nichols, 1847; Lydia Maria Child, *Memoirs of Mme. de Staël and Mme. Roland.* New York: C. S. Francis, 1847; Arthur Hugh Clough, *Prose Remains.* London: Macmillan, 1888; Conway, *Autobiography, Memories and Experiences*, Vol. II; Mantle Fielding, *Dictionary of American Painters, Sculptors, and Engravers.* Philadelphia: privately printed, 1926, Part II; James E. Freeman, *Gatherings from an Artist's Portfolio.* New York: D. Appleton, 1877; Monica M. Gardner, *Adam Mickiewicz the National Poet of Poland.* London: J. M.

Dent, 1911; W. M. Gillespie, *Rome As Seen by a New-Yorker in 1843-4.* New York: Wiley and Putnam, 1845; H. Greeley and H. J. Raymond, *Association Discussed; or, The Socialism of the Tribune Examined, being a controversy between the New York Tribune and the Courier and Enquirer.* New York: Harper, 1847; Kent Roberts Greenfield, *Economics and Liberalism in the Risorgimento—A Study of Nationalism in Lombardy.* Baltimore: Johns Hopkins Press, 1934; Frances Boott Greenough, editor, *Letters of Horatio Greenough to his Brother, Henry Greenough. With Biographical Sketches and Some Contemporary Correspondence.* Boston: Ticknor, 1887; Henry Greenough, *Ernest Carroll, or Artist-life in Italy. A Novel.* Boston: Ticknor and Fields, 1858; "Greenough, the Sculptor," *Putnam's Monthly,* I, 3 (March 1853); Lucy Gregory, *The Influence of George Sand on Margaret Fuller.* Columbia University Master's Essay, 1918; Gwilym Oswald Griffith, *Mazzini: Prophet of Modern Europe.* London: Hodder and Stoughton, 1932; Griswold, *Passages from the Correspondence and Other Papers;* Frank Harris, *Contemporary Portraits.* New York: Mitchell Kennerley, 1915; Nathaniel Hawthorne, *The Marble Faun or The Romance of Monte Beni.* Boston and New York: Houghton, Mifflin, 1895, Vol. I; Nathaniel Hawthorne, *Passages from the French and Italian Note-Books.* Boston: James R. Osgood, 1872, Vols. I and II; George A. Hicks, "Thomas Hicks, Artist, a Native of Newton," *Bucks County Historical Society Collections,* IV (1917); Thomas Hicks, *Eulogy on Thomas Crawford.* New York: privately printed, 1865; Thomas Wentworth Higginson, *Letters and Journals 1846-1906,* edited by Mary Thacher Higginson. Boston: Houghton Mifflin, 1921; George Stillman Hillard, *Six Months in Italy.* Boston: Ticknor and Fields, 1857; George Stillman Hillard, "Thomas Crawford: A Eulogy," *Atlantic Monthly,* XXIV, 141 (July 1869); Henry James, *William Wetmore Story and His Friends, from letters, diaries, and recollections.* Boston: Houghton, Mifflin, 1903, Vol. I; Miner K. Kellogg, *Justice to Hiram Powers. Addressed to the Citizens of New Orleans, 1848;* Bolton King, *A History of Italian Unity being a Political History of Italy from 1814 to 1871.* London: James Nisbet, 1899, Vol. I; Bolton King, *The Life of Mazzini.* London: J. M. Dent, 1911; C. Edwards Lester, *The Artist, The Merchant, and The Statesman, of the Age of the Medici, and of our Own Times.* New York: Paine and Burgess, 1845, Vols. I and II; C. Edwards Lester, *The Artists of America: A Series of Biographical Sketches of American Artists.* New York: Baker and

Scribner, 1846; John Francis Maguire, *Pontificate of Pius the Ninth*. London: Longmans, Green, 1870; Jesse White Mario, *The Birth of Modern Italy*. New York: Charles Scribner, 1909; Martineau, *Autobiography;* Countess Evelyn Martinengo-Cesaresco, *The Liberation of Italy 1815-1870*. New York: Charles Scribner, 1894; David Masson, *Memories of London in the 'Forties*. Edinburgh: William Blackwood, 1908; Giuseppe Mazzini, *Epistolario*. Imola: Paolo Galeati, 1918, Vols. XVI, XVII, and XVIII; Joseph Mazzini, *Letters,* translated by Alice de Rosen Jervis, introduction and notes by Bolton King. London: J. M. Dent, 1930; *Mazzini's Letters to an English Family 1844-1854,* edited and with an introduction by E. F. Richards. London: John Lane, n.d.; Joseph Mazzini, *Life and Writings*. London: Smith, Elder, 1891, Vol. V; Edward B. Merrill, *A Tribute to the Life and Public Service of George William Curtis, read before the American Social Science Association, at Saratoga, New York, September 8, 1893;* Samuel Osgood, *Thomas Crawford and Art in America. Address before the New York Historical Society, upon the Reception of Crawford's Statue of the Indian, Presented by Frederic de Peyster*. New York: John F. Trow, 1875; Parton, *The Life of Horace Greeley;* Mary E. Phillips, *Reminiscences of William Wetmore Story*. Chicago: Rand, McNally, 1897; Hiram Powers, "Letters to Nicholas Longworth, Esq., 1856-1858," *The Quarterly Publication of the Historical and Philosophical Society of Ohio,* I, 2 (April-June 1906); Hiram Powers, *Vindication of Hiram Powers in the "Greek Slave" Controversy*. Cincinnati: Office of the Great West, 1849; *Proceedings at a Meeting of the Century Association held in memory of John F. Kensett, December, 1872;* T. Buchanan Read, *A Memoir*. Philadelphia: privately printed, 1889; Marie-Thérèse Rouget, *George Sand "Socialiste."* Lyon: Bosc and Riou, 1931; George Sand, *Correspondance 1812-1876*. Paris: Calmann Levy, 1882, Vol. II; Scott, *The Life and Letters of Christopher Pearse Cranch;* Elizabeth Oakes Smith, editor, *The Mayflower for 1848*. Boston: Saxton and Kelt, 1848; Madeleine B. Stern, "New England Artists in Italy 1835-1855," *The New England Quarterly,* XIV, 2 (June 1941); William Wetmore Story, "The King of the Beggars" from *Roba di Roma*. In *A Library of the World's Best Literature,* edited by Charles Dudley Warner. New York: International Society, 1897, Vol. XXXV; John R. Tait, "Reminiscences of a Poet-Painter," *Lippincott's Magazine of Popular Literature and Science,* XIX, 17 (March 1877); George Macaulay Trevelyan, *Garibaldi's Defence of the Roman Republic 1848-9*. New

York: Longmans, Green, 1928; Henry T. Tuckerman, *Book of the Artists. American Artist Life, comprising biographical and critical sketches of American Artists: preceded by an historical account of the rise and progress of art in America.* New York: G. P. Putnam, 1867; Henry T. Tuckerman, *The Italian Sketch Book.* New York: J. C. Riker, 1848; Henry T. Tuckerman, *A Memorial of Horatio Greenough consisting of a Memoir, selections from his writings, and tributes to his genius.* New York: G. P. Putnam, 1853; Luigi Villari, *Italy.* New York: Charles Scribner, 1929; Lilian Whiting, *The Brownings.* Boston: Little, 1911; G. M. Young, *Early Victorian England 1830-1865.* London: Oxford University Press, 1934, Vols. I and II.

CHAPTER XVI

Manuscript sources include Margaret Fuller to Mrs. William Story, Rome, November 28, 1838 [sic], letter at Columbia University; Marcus Spring to Ralph Waldo Emerson, April 7, 1850, letter in the Ralph Waldo Emerson Memorial Association; Henry D. Thoreau, Portion of leaf concerning efforts to reconstruct the shipwreck on Fire Island, June 16th, [sic] 1850 in Henry D. Thoreau, *Poems, Essays and Autograph Letters* in the Pierpont Morgan Library.

Direct details appear in Willis J. Abbot, *Notable Women in History.* Philadelphia: John C. Winston, 1913; *Boston Journal,* August 15, 1857; *Classic Memoirs,* edited by Justin McCarthy, Richard Henry Stoddard, and others. New York: Colonial Press, 1901, Vol. II; Crosland, *Memorable Women;* Caroline Wells Healey Dall, *Historical Pictures Retouched.* Boston: Walker, Wise, 1860; *Democratic Review,* XXX, 513-529 (June 1852); F. Fuller, *Hawthorne and Margaret Fuller Ossoli;* Margaret Fuller, *Love-Letters;* S. Margaret Fuller, "Italy," *The People's Journal.* London: People's Journal Office, n.d., Vol. IV; Louis C. Jones, "A Margaret Fuller Letter to Elizabeth Barrett Browning," *American Literature,* IX, 1 (March 1937), original in Abernethy Library of American Literature; Lazarus, *Margaret Fuller;* O'Higgins and Reede, *The American Mind in Action;* Ossoli, *At Home and Abroad; Portland Evening Express and Advertiser,* May 23, 1910; *Prospective Review,* VIII, 199-218 (April 1852); Leona Rostenberg, "Elizabeth Barrett Browning to Margaret Fuller," unpublished; Rostenberg, *Margaret Fuller's Roman Diary;* Rostenberg, *Mazzini to Margaret Fuller;* Sanborn, *A Con-*

cord Note-Book; Southern Literary Messenger, XX, 129-140
(March 1854); Thoreau, *Familiar Letters.*

Details of background may be found in Robert Greenhalgh
Albion, *The Rise of New York Port (1815-1860).* New York:
Charles Scribner, 1939; Andersen, *The Improvisatore;* Arvin, *The
Heart of Hawthorne's Journals;* Bremer, *The Homes of the New
World;* E. B. Browning, *Letters,* Vols. I and II; E. B. Browning,
Letters to Her Sister; R. Browning, *Letters;* John Gadsby Chap-
man, *The American Drawing Book: A Manual for the Amateur,
and Basis of Study for the Professional Artist.* New York: J. S.
Redfield, 1858; G. K. Chesterton, *Robert Browning.* London:
Macmillan, 1926; Arthur Hugh Clough, "Amours de Voyage,"
Poems. London: Macmillan, 1903; Clough, *Prose Remains;* Man-
fred Eimer, "Drei Briefe von Elizabeth P. Peabody über Nathaniel
Hawthorne," *Archiv für das Studium der Neueren Sprachen und
Literaturen,* N. S. 33 (1915); Fielding, *Dictionary of American
Painters, Sculptors, and Engravers;* Gillespie, *Rome As Seen by a
New-Yorker;* William Godwin, *Memoirs of Mary Wollstonecraft
Godwin, author of "A Vindication of the Rights of Woman."*
Philadelphia: James Carey, 1799; Green, *An Account of the Law-
yers of Groton;* Greenfield, *Economics and Liberalism in the Risor-
gimento;* Henry Greenough, *Ernest Carroll;* Horatio Greenough,
Letters to his Brother Henry Greenough; Griffith, *Mazzini: Pro-
phet of Modern Europe;* Hanaford, *Daughters of America;* Marie
Hansen-Taylor and Horace E. Scudder, *Life and Letters of Bayard
Taylor.* Boston: Houghton, Mifflin, 1885, Vol. I; Lewis R. Har-
ley, *Confessions of a Schoolmaster and Other Essays.* Philadelphia
and London: J. B. Lippincott, 1914; Harris, *Contemporary Portraits;* Hawthorne, *Passages from the French and Italian Note-
Books,* Vols. I and II; Hicks, *Eulogy on Thomas Crawford;* Higginson, *Letters and Journals;* Hillard, *Six Months in Italy;* M. A.
de Wolfe Howe, *Memories of a Hostess A Chronicle of Eminent
Friendships drawn from the diaries of Mrs. James T. Fields.* Boston: Atlantic Monthly Press, 1922; James, *William Wetmore
Story and His Friends;* Robert M. Johnston, *The Roman Theocracy and the Republic.* London: Macmillan, 1901; King, *A History of Italian Unity;* King, *The Life of Mazzini;* S. Longfellow,
editor, *Final Memorials of Henry Wadsworth Longfellow,* Vol.
II; James Russell Lowell, "A Fable for Critics," *Complete Poetical
Works;* Maguire, *Pontificate of Pius the Ninth;* Aldobrandino
Malvezzi, *La Principessa Cristina di Belgiojoso.* Milano: Treves,
1937, Vol. III; Martinengo-Cesaresco, *The Liberation of Italy;*

Mazzini, *Letters,* translated by Alice de Rosen Jervis; *Mazzini's Letters to an English Family;* John Lothrop Motley, *Correspondence,* edited by George William Curtis. New York: Harper, 1889, Vol. I; Joseph Mozier, *A Collection of Photographic Reproductions of Joseph Mozier's Sculptures* (photographs in New York Public Library); Parton, *The Life of Horace Greeley;* Phillips, *Edgar Allan Poe the Man,* Vol. II; Phillips, *Reminiscences of William Wetmore Story; Proceedings of the Public Demonstration of Sympathy with Pope Pius IX, and with Italy, in the City of New York, on Monday, November 29, 1847.* New York: William Van Norden, 1847; Thomas Buchanan Read, "Letters," edited by Alice E. Smith, *The Ohio State Archaeological and Historical Quarterly,* XLVI, 1 (January 1937); T. Buchanan Read, *A Memoir;* Thomas Buchanan Read, *Poetical Works.* Philadelphia: J. B. Lippincott, 1883; Scott, *Life and Letters of Christopher Pearse Cranch;* Rodman J. Sheirr, "Joseph Mozier and His Handiwork," *Potter's American Monthly,* VI, 49 (January 1876); William Wetmore Story, *Conversations in a Studio.* Boston and New York: Houghton, Mifflin, 1890, Vol. I; William Wetmore Story, *Excursions in Art and Letters.* Boston and New York: Houghton, Mifflin, 1891; William Wetmore Story, *Roba di Roma.* Philadelphia: J. B. Lippincott, 1870; Tait, *Reminiscences of a Poet-Painter;* G. R. Stirling Taylor, *Mary Wollstonecraft, a Study in Economics and Romance.* London: Martin Secker, 1911; William Roscoe Thayer, *The Dawn of Italian Independence.* Boston: Houghton Mifflin, 1893, Vol. II; Trevelyan, *Garibaldi's Defence of the Roman Republic;* Henry T. Tuckerman, *Artist-Life: or Sketches of American Painters.* New York: D. Appleton, 1847; Tuckerman, *Book of the Artists;* Villari, *Italy;* H. Remsen Whitehouse, *A Revolutionary Princess Christina Belgiojoso-Trivulzio Her Life and Times 1808-1871.* New York: E. P. Dutton, 1906; Whiting, *The Brownings.*

CHAPTER XVII

Manuscript sources include Thoreau, Portion of leaf concerning efforts to reconstruct the shipwreck on Fire Island.

Direct details may be found in Black, *Some Queer People;* E. B. Browning, *Letters;* R. Browning, *Letters;* Fuller, *Love-Letters;* Willard E. Martin, "A Last Letter of Margaret Fuller Ossoli," *American Literature,* V, 66-69 (March 1933); Ossoli, *At Home and Abroad;* Perry, *The Heart of Emerson's Journals;* Portland

Evening Express and Advertiser, May 23, 1910; Sanborn, *A Concord Note-Book;* Thoreau, *Familiar Letters.*

Details of background appear in Albion, *The Rise of New York Port;* Bremer, *The Homes of the New World;* Charles T. Libby, *The Libby Family in America, 1602-1881.* Portland: B. Thurston, 1882.

INDEX